VLAD THE IMPALER

SON OF THE DEVIL,
HERO OF THE PEOPLE

GAVIN BADDELEY
& PAUL WOODS

Ian Allan
PUBLISHING

VLAD THE IMPALER:
Son of the Devil, Hero of the People
Gavin Baddeley and Paul Woods

First published 2010

ISBN 978 0 7110 3442 6

Published by Ian Allan Publishing

an imprint of Ian Allan Publishing Ltd, Hersham, Surrey KT12 4RG.
Printed in England by CPI Mackays, Chatham, Kent ME5 8TD.

Visit the Ian Allan Publishing website at www.ianallanpublishing.com
Distributed in the Unites States of America and Canada by BookMasters
Distribution Services.

Contents

Acknowledgements

Above all, thanks to Keri O'Shea for her skilled editorial work throughout the project.

Thanks are also due to Boyd Rice for his insightful observations on Vlad, and Lawrence Burton for committing Dracula's crimes to canvas. A respectful salute is also due to Jay Slater and Nick Grant at IAP who have endured temporal tortures during the completion of this book that would have made Vlad himself wince!

Introduction

Behold an Empire of Blood ...
The once verdant fields around the besieged city are burning to black ash.
The foliage is scraped from the naked earth, robbed of its dignity like the
flesh and hair scraped from a flayed prisoner's scalp. As seen through the
dying soldier's eyes it is a vision of the infernal, yet it is arranged like the
bloodstained icons of the accursed Christian infidel.

For our staked and crucified young man – imploring the mercy of
death, if not the promise of Paradise, to visit him soon – is of the army of
Mahomet. He has fought in the name of his Sultan, near-namesake of
the blessed Prophet himself, and now he will spend out his last agonised
moments here, outside the distant infidel city of Tîrgovişte.

The nightmare landscape that fills his field of vision is borne witness by
his terminating senses, and supplemented by his fevered mind. As the
maimed and the mutilated howl and whinny, he perceives one who moves
impervious, untouched, through the carnage. It is the creature whose name
his people have damned with their verbal curses and sprayed sputum. It
grows closer, moving with stealth and confidence through the bodies of those
broken and torn asunder. Swatting away arrows with the distracted air
of one who brushes away a dungfly.

This demon, its thin downturned mouth gorged on sticky dark lifeblood,
is the hated Prince of legend. The defender of a decadent Christendom,
said to feast on the dying of the battlefield – whether they be his own men
or his noble Ottoman foe.

The hair of the monster is lustrous and black, as if he were one of the
soldier's fellow countrymen, yet his whey-like skin betrays the pallor of one
too suffused with death. This is the face of the unbeliever. The obscene.
The unholy. Its fetid breath pollutes the air, choking the Turkish warrior
as his own respiration becomes more laboured.

Pain and terror narrow the young man's eyes until they are no wider
than slits. But he can feel the hand of the Impaler upon him, and cannot
retreat from the tormented tableau of which he forms a part. Cannot resist
the probing talon that seeks to draw bloody sustenance from the gushing

wound of his lower abdomen …

… The apparition fades suddenly like a transient fever nightmare. In his agony, the young Turk finds his delirium ebbs and flows with every perspiration-drenched, arrhythmic beat of his agitated heart.

For he has been placed on this war-weary hillside that Allah has surely forsaken, assembled among rows of dying bodies as part of a crazed recreation of the suffering of the Christian prophet. He that would defend the culture of the Christ has crucified his prisoners of war, but with no such finesse as once displayed by the executioners of Ancient Rome.

Held down screaming as the Prince's lackeys drove the sharpened end of a wooden shaft into his bloodied rump, the Ottoman warrior has now become one with the stake from which he is suspended. Held limply aloft by the very thing that leaks the lifeblood and viscera from his punctured body, he is flooded by the mysterious chemical elements from which his god created him.

In such extremes of agony, madness is perhaps the only mercy. He cannot think rationally, for pain touches every fibre of his being. He cannot breathe, for in this parody of the crucifixion he is not the crucified but the broken cross, his arms and shoulders drawn gravitationally downwards, his dangling legs unable to support the pierced chest that harshly and rapidly gulps in air but is unable to exhale. The stake that passes through his upper chest and exits his back has ruptured his very humanity, leaving him a twitching, gasping mockery of that which the imams once told him was created in the form of the divine.

Yet it still leaves him mercilessly alive, trapped in a consciousness for which the only reality is pain.

If Allah's mercy were visited upon him now then all human sentience might end. Instead, that which he formerly beheld as the infernal aftermath of war becomes less grandiose in his dying moments. Burnt shrub. Splintered trunks of pine and beech. The moans of the wounded and the tortured are less real to him as his own suffering blocks out all else and his senses start to dim.

But the figure of the accursed infidel still remains, aloof and dispassionate among the rows of transfixed and impaled bodies. Immune to the piteous cries of the wounded and maimed who will never set foot within the modest little city over which he stands guard.

Behold, the Voivode of Wallachia; defender of a piss-pot kingdom of dirt. Lean and Latin of face, this is no monster but a very singular kind of man.

The Ottoman soldier tries to cry out, to implore his god to release him from his suffering with the gift of sudden death, whether by sword, fire or strangulation. But a voice needs the support of an upper body, and his is torn and twisted ...

Vlad Tepeş strides forward, eyeing his dying captives with a curiosity that still seeks the spiritual reality of death, no matter how many times he has witnessed its bodily contortions. And yet he remains unmoved by the agonies of the dying.

The young man feels a sickness at the root of the pain which tears apart his soul. To be gawped at in this moment of utter desolation by such a man is to deprive him of the dignity of a dog ...

Vlad III, 'son of the dragon', is no demon when seen at close quarters. No blood-gorging vurdalak but the well-weathered face of provincial power, his alert carrion eyes perched above a nest of angular bone and brush whiskers. The despotic ruler of a European backwater who would slaughter everyone in it – indeed, would lay waste to everyone and everything in the world – rather than relinquish one remote acre.

As Vlad's inscrutable gaze meets the dying agony of the Turkish soldier, the young man begins to choke and rattle as if coughing up his pierced guts.

It is just one more death and it matters not a jot in an uncertain world where the maintenance of power is a full-time occupation, and must be attended by any means possible. Wordlessly, instinctively, our young soldier of the Sultan's army expires with the knowledge that he has been destroyed not by some monstrous folk demon but by something worse.

Something human.

All too human ...

Chapter I

The Land Beyond the Forest

*'The belief in a supernatural source of evil is not necessary;
men alone are quite capable of every wickedness.' (Joseph
Conrad)*

In common with most Westerners, these authors first discovered
Transylvania through the pages of Bram Stoker's 1897 novel *Dracula*,
and the midnight tidal wave of Gothic film, literature, and suchlike
which have followed in its wake. Indeed, many in the West still suppose
it to be a legendary realm, a creepy equivalent of such fictional
kingdoms as Narnia or Oz. There's less excuse for such ignorance of
Eastern European geography in recent decades, largely due to the
publication in 1972 of *In Search of Dracula*, a landmark American study
by the history professors Radu Florescu and Raymond T. McNally.
The book first popularised the idea that, not only was Transylvania a
real place, a region to be found in Florescu's native Romania, but also
that Dracula was a real person, otherwise known as Vlad III, Vlad the
Impaler, or Vlad Țepeș (pronounced 'Tsepesh' – 'Impaler' in his native
tongue).

Vlad was a Wallachian Voivode, born in the region of Transylvania
around 1431. But just what is a Voivode, or indeed a Wallachian?
Wallachia is a region which, along with the neighbouring principalities
of Transylvania and Moldavia, forms the modern nation of Romania.
Voivode is an Eastern European term that translates roughly as
'warlord', though the exact meaning varies by nation and era. In our
case, the position also involved leadership during peacetime
(admittedly comparatively rare in Vlad's day) making it somewhat akin
to the post of the governor of a province (the term survives in this
context in modern Poland, where regions are still administered by
Voivodes, centrally appointed by the Polish Prime Minister). Yet in

Transylvania and Wallachia voivodeship had a hereditary component, and is thus also sometimes translated as 'prince' or 'duke' (though, sadly, seldom as 'count'). Vlad the Impaler inherited both the voivodeship of Wallachia and his infamous epithet from his father, Vlad II, otherwise known as Vlad Dracul – 'Dracula' meaning 'son of Dracul'.

The appropriate translation of 'Dracul' in this context is the subject of some debate. In Romanian it means both 'dragon' and 'devil' – mythical entities not unconnected in Biblical lore. Vlad II derived his epithet from his membership of the Order of the Dragon (a chivalric organisation we'll examine in greater detail later). Yet in Vlad III's case, as a ruler who actively used terror as a psychological weapon, it seems highly likely that the word's double meaning took on greater significance. Though the Impaler's modern apologists are keen to stress that his name was purely draconic rather than demonic in origin, a number of contemporary sources clearly disagree. His rival, Wallachian Voivode Dan III, describes Vlad as a devil on a number of occasions, while the Papal envoy to the Hungarian court during Vlad's imprisonment at Buda describes the Impaler as the 'Vlach [Romanian] tyrant Dracul, a name which they [Romanians] use for the Devil'. More recently, according to the Romanian historian Vasile Pârvan writing in 1992, 'out of all the Romance languages, the Romanian language was the only one in which "draco" has the meaning of an evil spirit, demon or devil, whereas in others, the word only has the meaning of snake or dragon'.

So, Dracula – son of the dragon, or son of the devil? Sometimes it's all a matter of perspective. The 11th-century Duke of Normandy, whose son William would conquer England in 1066, was known as Robert the Magnificent by his admirers, and Robert the Devil by those less impressed by his character. There are certainly examples of medieval monarchs who embraced sinister reputations to inspire dread in their enemies. While popular history remembers Richard I of England as a heroic figure, dubbed the Lionheart, he was guilty of a number of brutal war crimes. Chroniclers record that Richard was fond of making reference to a popular story that his dynasty originally sprang from the union between a French Count and a she-devil named Melusine. According to the legend, the demonic damsel flew out of a window upon being unmasked, leaving two of her offspring behind to father the Angevin dynasty. 'From the Devil we sprang and to the Devil we shall go,' grinned England's formidable 12th-century warrior king.

Like the Impaler 250 years later, the Lionheart was lauded as a

Crusader, and like Vlad, most of Richard's worst atrocities were perpetrated against his Islamic opponents. Most notoriously, in 1191, having successfully captured the Saracen port of Acre, Richard put all of his prisoners to death despite previously guaranteeing their safety if they surrendered. Some 2,700 defenceless Muslim soldiers were butchered on the plains outside Acre, in full view of the advance guard of Saladin's Saracen army that had arrived to relieve the city. As an example of medieval psychological warfare, it worked, and Saladin had trouble convincing his troops to garrison the forts that lay in Richard's path, intimidated as they were by the Lionheart's ruthlessness. Despite such incidents of bad faith and savagery, Richard's chivalric reputation remained untarnished. 'He did right to all and would not allow justice to be perverted,' praised one contemporary chronicler, while even a Muslim source of the day conceded that Richard's 'courage, shrewdness, energy and patience made him the most remarkable ruler of his times.'

Sympathetic contemporary and posthumous accounts of Vlad echo such sentiments, seemingly blind to, or at least willing to overlook, the bloodthirsty brutality that earned him the nickname 'Impaler'. At this early stage this gives us a vital clue as to how such an incredibly cruel leader like the original Dracula could enjoy heroic status as well as infamy. 'There can be no doubt that one of the king's primary functions – arguably *the* primary function – remained as warleader, and that his *virtus* [manly valour] continued to be a vital ingredient in his military and political success,' as it was still felt to be when Machiavelli wrote *The Prince*, according to medieval historian Matthew Strickland. Success in battle could cover a multitude of sins for a poor monarch, while the reputation and authority of an otherwise able ruler would invariably suffer if they failed to cut a convincing figure on the battlefield. In *By Sword and Fire*, his book on 'cruelty and atrocity in medieval warfare,' Sean McGlynn writes that royal mercy 'had its uses, but if too readily resorted to it was a fatal sign of weakness and lack of resolve. The warrior king, as *rex irae* [enraged lord], was to be more feared than a merciful one. The implications for warfare were frightening.'

***

During their research for *In Search of Dracula*, Florescu and McNally chanced upon the extensive research notes Bram Stoker made while writing *Dracula*. They had been acquired by Philadelphia's Rosenbach

Museum after lying largely unnoticed since being auctioned at Sotheby's in 1913, and have since formed the basis of all subsequent serious studies of Stoker's masterpiece. The notes establish the works of history and geography consulted by the author. Whether they list all of the research Stoker undertook during the six years he spent writing *Dracula*, however, remains controversial. If they do detail the extent of his research, then a book that Stoker borrowed from the local library while on holiday in the picturesque English fishing port of Whitby in 1890 is of particular interest. It's an 1820 volume by the English writer William Wilkinson, entitled *An Account of the Principalities of Wallachia and Moldavia*.

Significantly, it is the only book that we can be certain that Stoker consulted which actually mentions the historical Dracula. It contains a brief, broadly accurate synopsis of the military careers of Vlad the Impaler and his father, appended with a footnote which reads: 'Dracula in the Wallachian language means Devil. The Wallachians were, at that time, as they are at present, used to give this as a surname to any person who rendered himself conspicuous, either by courage, cruel actions, or cunning.' It was probably these two sentences that inspired Stoker to call his vampire Dracula, making it one of the most influential footnotes in literary history. Some experts, such as Florescu and McNally, contend that Stoker further explored the subject in research carried out in places such as the British Museum, but that this is not recorded in the notes surviving at the Rosenbach Museum. Others insist that these few paragraphs in Wilkinson's book represent the entire extent of Stoker's research into Vlad the Impaler.

Since the publication of *In Search of Dracula*, as we shall see, numerous writers and filmmakers have exploited the supposed connection between the medieval Dracula and his fictional undead namesake for background or even for the principal plot device of their work. Yet there remains a yawning gap between the bristling, longhaired warlord glowering aggressively out of 500-year-old woodcuts, and the urbane cloaked, supernatural lady-killer of modern pop culture with his slicked-back hair and incongruous evening dress. The evolution of Dracula from a fearsome 15th-century monarch to a 20th-century Hollywood horror cliché – from voivode to vampire via a Victorian Gothic novel – is, to put it mildly, tortuous. Recent film and fiction which has attempted to marry Vlad III with his vampiric namesake has done at least as much to cloud these bloody waters as to clarify the issue. Yet as fascination with the fictional Dracula remains undimmed, it has also cast some revealing shadows on the historical

Dracula who is the focus of our study.

Some have endeavoured to sever this cultural bloodline completely. In Vlad's Romanian homeland, the 500th anniversary of the Impaler's death in 1976 galvanised a movement to restore the ruler's reputation, reclaiming it from what some patriots saw as a deliberate racist libel against a local hero. It enjoyed official support, not least from Romania's leader, Nicolae Ceaușescu, the Communist dictator who would in time attain a reputation as black in its fashion as that of his medieval predecessor. (Though, as we shall see, the extent of Ceaușescu's endorsement of the Impaler remains controversial.) In the West, beginning in 1990, Canadian academic Elizabeth Miller has become the leading scholar contesting a connection between the fictional Dracula and Vlad the Impaler. The Professor of English literature has mounted a formidable campaign, fought with an impressive array of scholarly and popular publications asserting that any resemblance, if not wholly coincidental, is largely nominal. Her work has made it fashionable to emphasise the differences between the real Voivode and the fictional vampire, in contradiction to the connections which Florescu and McNally's scholarship identifies.

We'll revisit the debate in the pages that follow, though it's a controversy that has arguably been exhausted of fresh blood. Elizabeth Miller ably summarised her case in 'Filing for Divorce: Count Dracula vs. Vlad Tepeș', a paper delivered at an American conference on Dracula in 1997, while Raymond McNally offered a powerful rebuttal in his essay 'Separation Granted; Divorce Denied; Annulment Unlikely' two years later. Miller's work has helped open up the debate among scholars in liberal arts faculties over the reliability of Bram Stoker's research for *Dracula*. Stoker's novel has long excited academic attention, much of it unsympathetic. The book – like its Anglo-Irish author – is very much a product of its age, providing ripe fodder for those left-leaning scholars critical of the clichéd 'Victorian values' of Imperialism and sexual conservatism. *Dracula* has been dismissively interpreted as a work of paranoid patriotism or erotic dysfunction, of sexist repression or even anti-Semitism, by a legion of literary academics keen to use poor old Stoker's Gothic spinechiller as an excuse to parade their own faddish preoccupations with Freud, feminism or Foucault.

In October of 2009, a blogger by the name of Infinite Detox was quite taken with a selection of academic essays that appended the Norton edition of *Dracula* which they'd just read. So taken, that they compiled the most extraordinary theories into a post sarcastically entitled 'A Children's Treasury of Hilarious Dracula Fan Fiction'. The passages of pompous theorising quoted are unintentionally comical gems from the worst excesses of 'lit-crit' – such as critic Ellis Hanson's assertion that 'The chapel has become the anal orifice of castration and death, littered as it is with Dracula's fecal/phallic coffins' or, Talia Schaffer's bemusement that 'Dracula undresses Harker and folds his clothes yet somehow overlooks the prize in Harker's trousers. (Similarly, Harker magically feels all over Dracula's body without finding Dracula's key.)'

Professor Elizabeth Miller's work offered a new string to the bows of scholars eager to extract ammunition from the Dracula myth with which to press a liberal agenda. Her exposure of the disparity between the Gothic monster created by Bram Stoker in 1897, and the historical leader who fought for his country in the 1400s, offered opportunities to castigate the Count as an exemplar of cultural insensitivity. By turning an Eastern European hero into a bloodsucking fiend, Stoker and those Westerners who employed his character were guilty of ignorant bigotry, even racism. Ironically, in taking such a stance, some politically-correct commentators find themselves in some curious company. Over the past couple of centuries, a broad variety of voices have found themselves singing from a similar hymn-sheet – from rightwing radicals to reactionary communists. The story of Dracula – both the Count and the Impaler – is very much about strange bedfellows, where extreme situations inspire some improbable relationships and alliances.

In all fairness, Miller's scholarship on the subject is far more insightful, sober and sensible than the nonsense cited by Infinite Detox. In her capacity as curator of the Dracula Research Centre and editor of *The Journal of Dracula Studies* she has inspired invaluable contributions to the study of both Bram Stoker's most famous creation and his historical namesake (a number of them cited in this book). Yet it was Florescu and McNally who first stimulated international interest in the historical Dracula among the world's historians, triggering a broader interest in Romanian history in the global media and hence the general public. There can be little doubt that the building body of scholarship on the career of the historical Dracula owes much of its impetus to popular interest in his fictional namesake. If Vlad Dracula, Voivode of Wallachia, has enjoyed immortality, it is largely courtesy of Bram Stoker and Hollywood. 'As a historian, I separate fact from fiction, reality from myth; but this in no way diminishes the power of myth,' writes McNally. 'On the contrary, I accept that myth can have an even greater impact than facts.'

More interesting, perhaps, than nit-picking differences between Stoker's novel and documented history (though we ourselves may indulge in a little of this) is tracing the troubled relationship between myth and fact exposed by the brutal and colourful career of Vlad Dracula. For the Impaler exemplifies the way in which myth dominates our view of history's heroes and villains, his life and afterlife laying bare many intriguing, illuminating issues. This is of interest not just to horror fans and students of Victorian literature, but to those with an interest in politics, or indeed, morality. For the mythology surrounding Dracula is far older than Bram Stoker's novel. You might argue that the Impaler himself exploited it. It was certainly exploited by his enemies long before Ceaușescu sought to harness it for patriotic purposes. The story of the original Dracula, played out on the turbulent fringes of Western civilisation 500 years ago, touches upon religious conflicts and ethical dilemmas still vital today. There are echoes beyond the speakers at cinemas playing monster matinees, to the conflicts that wrecked the Balkans in the 1990s, even to the infamous cells of Abu Ghraib.

A good place to start our story is in Vlad's Transylvanian birthplace. You can learn a lot from a place name. The history of a region can be mapped out with place names – names which can hint at long forgotten inhabitants, suggest the significance which a place had in the distant past, act as *memento mori* for lost cultures and as statements of ownership for those who supplanted them. They can also lend a poetic ambience to a locale, contributing to the romantic pride that inspires revolutions and justifies atrocities. The backdrop to our story includes locales that translate evocatively as the Iron Gates and the Field of Crows – sites of great battles seemingly tailored to feature in the lyrics of stirring epics. There are few better examples of the power of place names than the name 'Transylvania'. Transylvania translates as 'beyond the forest' – a suggestive moniker entirely in keeping with a wild region on the borders of the imagination. The original derivation of the name is hotly contested today – concrete evidence of the enduring significance of simple place names.

Hungarian historians usually argue that 'Transylvania' derives from a medieval Latin translation of the Hungarian name for the district, Erdély. Romanian historians contend, however, that the name stretches further back, a hangover of the region's days as an Eastern outpost of the Roman Empire. Transylvania's very name has become a semantic battlefield in the centuries-old struggle between the Romanian-speaking Orthodox Christian Vlach and the Hungarian-speaking Catholic Magyar peoples for dominance of the region, where debates over rights of precedence have descended from wars of words to bloody physical conflict with depressing regularity. To further suggest the complexity of the region's legacy of troubled national and racial politics, Transylvania was also known as Siebenbürgen. Siebenbürgen – meaning 'seven citadels' – is a reference to the fortified towns of the district, from which the German-speaking Saxon population dominated trade, playing a pivotal part in the region's history during the medieval era.

In the second chapter of *Dracula*, Bram Stoker describes his setting's complex ethnic makeup as follows. 'In the population of Transylvania there are four distinct nationalities: Saxons in the South, and mixed with them the Wallachs, who are the descendants of the Dacians; Magyars in the West, and Szekelys in the East and North.' Duncan Light, associate professor of Geography at Liverpool Hope University, takes issue with this synopsis in 'The People of Bram Stoker's Transylvania', published in *The Journal of Dracula Studies* in 2005. In his article, Light argues that 'while Stoker clearly appreciated the multi-ethnic nature of Transylvania, his more detailed understanding of its population geography was patchy at best. Moreover, Stoker was selective in his representation of the various nationalities in Transylvania: some were highlighted for dramatic effect, whereas others were excluded altogether.'

In another article for *The Journal of Dracula Studies*, the Romanian scholar Carmen Maria Andras writes upon 'The Image of Transylvania in English Literature' (1999). She argues that, 'literary images of Transylvania as the home of the monster may offend the sensibility of many Romanian readers for whom Transylvania's image is an ideal and even sacred one: it represents the quintessence of the national history, a land blessed by God with all the possible beauty and richness, fertilised by the people's tears and the heroes' blood, the cradle of their Latin roots, source of the Romanian Enlightenment embodied in the Transylvanian School, and a province of a united Romania. Even though the positive representations surpass in number and quality the negative images, the latter have had a larger echo in the West, owing to their shocking character, and have developed into a literary sub-genre.'

Clearly Bram Stoker's depiction of Vlad the Impaler's Transylvanian homeland didn't impress everyone. Someone who is a fan of Stoker's novel is Christopher Lee, the distinguished and prolific British actor who made his name playing the fictional Count in a series of lurid Technicolor Gothic thrillers for the legendary horror movie studio Hammer Films. Lee's imperious, lupine portrayal remains the iconic image of Dracula in many eyes, over 50 years after he first donned the distinctive black cloak. It's something the actor has regarded with ambivalence since he first played the role in 1958. In part this is because Lee resented the typecasting that followed in the wake of his success, but also because he feels the scripts were often weak. In 1963, when he visited the character for the second time in *Dracula Prince of Darkness*, Lee simply refused to speak his lines in protest, replacing his dialogue with glares and hisses.

'I was always fighting, during all of the Hammer Dracula films over the years, to retain Stoker's original character and above all, to use his lines,' the actor said, when your author Gavin Baddeley spoke to him about the role. 'I kept on saying "Why do you write these stories and try and fit the character in; why not take Stoker's original, use the lines he wrote, and build a story around that? If you want to make a different story – by all means – but use his lines where appropriate." They almost never did.' Perhaps partially as a response to what he regarded as the inauthenticity of Hammer's adaptations, the actor agreed to take part in a documentary based upon Florescu and McNally's landmark text on the roots of Stoker's creation.

In Search of Dracula (not to be confused with the 1996 British documentary in which Lee also appears) was originally screened as a Swedish TV documentary entitled *Pa jakt efter Dracula*, before it was picked up and extended with further footage for international theatrical distribution in 1974. The film evidently enjoyed the co-operation of Florescu and McNally (it credits them as co-writers, and was largely filmed the year before their book came out, so must have enjoyed a preview of its contents) though they themselves confess in a 1994 revised edition of their book *In Search of Dracula* that the film was 'too talky and intellectual to be commercially successful'. Christopher Lee not only narrates the film, but also takes on the 'moustache, fur hat and flowing robes' of the historical Dracula, playing Vlad the Impaler in re-enactments filmed on location during the winter of 1971 in some of the Voivode's old haunts.

'I was so fascinated by the place that I brought back some soil as a souvenir,' the actor recalled in Peter Haining's *The Dracula Scrapbook*. 'And then in the next Dracula picture I made, *Dracula AD 1972*, I threw it onto a grave as my tribute to Bram Stoker's memory. But without doubt the biggest surprise I got came when I was shown a wood engraving of Vlad Dracula's face. You'll never believe it... but he looked exactly like *me*! It was really quite uncanny. And when someone suggested that maybe it was predetermined I should play *Dracula* I could hardly disagree.' While internationally famous as the vampire Count by the time he visited Romania, it is unlikely Lee would have been recognised by the locals, even if some of them apparently thought he looked a dead ringer for the Impaler whilst in costume.

The country had been under a Communist dictatorship since 1947, with the authorities vigorously suppressing the influence of 'decadent' Western media such as films. While most Warsaw Pact regimes also condemned most traditional historical heroes as parasitic members of the hated upper classes, the Romanian government was unusual in tolerating or even actively encouraging the patriotic veneration of the nation's past rulers. So any suggestion of the 15th-century Voivode Vlad as an unholy bloodsucker was particularly unwelcome in Bucharest. Stoker's novel was banned by Romania's Communist authorities, as were its numerous cinematic and literary offspring. Many ordinary Romanians were somewhat surprised when they eventually discovered that one of their homeland's medieval war heroes had apparently been moonlighting as a movie monster.

'The locals weren't at all pleased by our approach,' Christopher Lee admitted to Baddeley of his experiences filming on location for *In Search of Dracula*. 'They said, "this man's a national hero, he fought for Christendom, he repelled the Turks. He may have been bloodthirsty, but he's still a national hero." They didn't like the idea at all of him as a vampire in those days.' Since then, matters have changed somewhat perhaps, as capitalist hunger for foreign currency overcame at least some reservations, and as films and publications like *In Search of Dracula* triggered a budding niche tourist industry. While Stoker's *Dracula* and the films inspired by it remained banned, Communist authorities began to set up themed hotels and tours to cater for vacationing vampire enthusiasts. The policy remained to try and emphasise the distinction between the fictional Dracula, represented in Halloween-style attractions, and the medieval sites associated with the authentic Dracula, which were approached in a more respectful way.

Changing attitudes are reflected in such unlikely arenas as philately. Vlad the Impaler was the subject of a Romanian postage stamp issued in 1959, to commemorate the 500th anniversary of the ruler's foundation of the capital Bucharest. (It's open to speculation as to whether it is coincidence that the stamp was issued so soon after Christopher Lee first brought the fictional Dracula to international prominence with his iconic screen performance. Was the Communist regime deliberately casting the historical Dracula in a positive light to contrast with his latest on-screen demonisation?) Another Vlad the Impaler stamp was issued in 1976, this time as part of a concerted effort in Romania to commemorate the 500th anniversary of the death of the Voivode. Like its predecessor, it featured a statesmanlike, even benevolent portrait of the Impaler, with no suggestion of the cruelty that earned him his macabre soubriquet.

The third set of Romanian Vlad stamps appeared in 1997, eight years after the fall of the Communist regime. One stamp depicts the Impaler in a familiarly sympathetic light, but the other sees Vlad with his cloak drawn across his face, bats in the background, his eyes glowing red. It's almost as if, as a concession to its entry into modern Capitalist Europe, Romania finally officially recognises that Dracula has a dark side. Romania was just one of a number of nations issuing Dracula stamps in 1997. Britain, Ireland and Canada also issued their own versions, though all unambivalently depicting the fanged count of film and fiction, rather than his Wallachian namesake. This international wave of Dracula stamps was inspired by the centenary of the publication of Bram Stoker's *Dracula*. The same anniversary also offered an opportunity for one of your authors, Gavin Baddeley, to make a pilgrimage to Transylvania, as a number of his editors expressed an interest in publishing an article to mark the *Dracula* centenary.

Before he departed, Baddeley spoke to Christopher Lee, who'd made the same trip 26 years earlier. 'You go to that part of the world and it's exactly as Stoker describes it, though there's no evidence he ever went there,' the actor said. 'There are these great towering black crags wreathed in mist, with what looks like castles on the top, though they're not – they're rock formations. Of course, you're conscious of history when you go there, the very earth is soaked in blood and you know that.' So your author packed a copy of Stoker's *Dracula*, alongside the copy of *In Search of Dracula* his father had brought back from America for him when he was a child, and *Dracula: Prince of Many Faces*, Florescu and McNally's most recent study of Vlad the Impaler. There wasn't much other relevant literature easily available. While a number of modern scholars have taken Bram Stoker to task over the accuracy of aspects of his portrayal of Transylvania, in many respects he did a remarkably good job, considering the paucity of material published on the region.

Stoker chose Transylvania – 'one of the wildest and least known portions of Europe' – as the setting for the opening and climax of

Dracula because of that obscurity. As the furthest eastern fringe of European civilisation, it was sufficiently strange and remote to his Victorian English readership to seem a plausible locale for the bizarre manifestations of his plot. While the advances of modern transport and communications technology have brought Romania far closer to us today, it still exists under a certain cloak of mystery, one only tentatively lifted by the fall of Communism in 1989, joining NATO in 2004, and its controversial entry into the European Union in 2007. Even the best British bookshops seem to suffer something of a blind spot when it comes to much of Eastern Europe. Most English-speaking medieval historians of the era are far more interested in the local dynastic struggles of Western Europe than they are in the mighty clash of civilisations occurring on the continent's eastern borders between the 14th and 16th centuries, although these could have determined the fate of Christendom itself.

The history section of most good bookshops offers plentiful texts on the nations whose empires dominated Eastern Europe over the centuries – Turkey, Germany, and Russia – though their affairs in our field of focus seldom warrant much mention. The lure of Byzantium's lost glory has also attracted its share of attention, while the recent Bosnian War has encouraged a number of historians to delve into the troubled history of the Balkans. Yet, search for historical accounts of Europe's eastern borders and there is a curious vacuum – almost a blank space on the map – as if Transylvania and its neighbouring provinces are as mythical as many filmgoers imagine. On the odd occasion that books on the history of Romania, Hungary or Bulgaria are published, bookshops are often at a loss where to shelve them, and they usually end up haphazardly filed next to Russian history.

The Battle for Christendom (2008), by Frank Welsh, is one of the few popular history books to address medieval Eastern Europe. His central figure is the Hungarian king and Holy Roman Emperor, Sigismund (1368-1437), also the ruler ultimately responsible for bestowing the title 'Dracul' on Vlad the Impaler's father, and therefore in a sense indirectly responsible for creating Dracula. He was also the figure, according to Welsh, whose political talents 'rescued Christian Europe from the danger of imminent disintegration; and when crisis threatened, deployed the military force to avert it. Yet Sigismund, it seemed, had been entirely neglected by British and American historians.' Welsh also notes that, amongst those historians who do address this pivotal period, several misidentify many of the principal Eastern European protagonists.

VLAD THE IMPALER

The same often happens with those more general medieval studies that can't resist the temptation to reference Vlad because of the Dracula connection, such as Sean McGlynn whose mention of the Impaler is practically his only reference to Eastern Europe in *By Sword and Fire*. McGlynn's otherwise exemplary study confuses Vlad the Impaler with his father Vlad Dracul (a common error, which also occurs in the 1820 William Wilkinson book that first inspired Bram Stoker to call his immortal character 'Dracula'.) Osprey, the prolific British military history publisher responsible for literally hundreds of books on every aspect of warfare have produced only a handful of titles on this pivotal period, but amongst those few we have David Nicolle's *Hungary and the Fall of Eastern Europe 1000-1568* (1988) and his account of the Battle of Nicopolis in 1396.

Oddly enough, one of the most reliable and well-written books on the military and political history of late medieval Eastern Europe in English is a 2006 volume, written as a sourcebook for the *Warhammer* tabletop wargaming rules. Whilst entitled *Vlad the Impaler*, it actually presents an overview of the entire region, encompassing Hungary, the Balkans, Greece and the Ottoman Empire as well as the Romanian principalities between 1280 and 1520. Just as historians tend to concentrate on Western Europe in the Middle Ages at the expense of more significant events to the east, so John Bianchi, principal author of *Vlad the Impaler*, is unusual as a medieval wargamer who focuses on Eastern European conflict. 'Colloquially, I think that this region was the front door to Europe, and that the conflicts of the 14th through 16th centuries were "the main event" in European warfare, where more innovation, creativity, and on the other side, cruelty and destruction were evident,' John told us. 'That's why I continue to find this region fascinating, and I think this offers the best explanation for why this region, so rich in resources, continues to be among the poorest parts of Europe to this day.'

Baddeley didn't have access to Bianchi's excellent study when he went to Romania in 1997, but one of the most valuable guides he discovered upon arrival was *History of Romanians*, a book published in Bucharest the previous year. Written by two native academics, Dr Mircea Dogaru and Dr Mihail Zahariade, the print quality is poor and the English pretty awkward, but such limitations are wholly eclipsed by the value of a passionate text suffused with wounded patriotic pride, offering an invaluable insight not just into Romanian history, but also the Romanian psyche. Dogaru expresses part of the motivation for writing the book as his despair at the international media's ignorance of Eastern Europe: 'Is it really necessary to be a catastrophe, an earthquake, a war so that Budapest, Bucharest should not be confused with each other?' Dracula tourism also comes in for a sideswipe from Dr Dogaru. He accuses 'Western man' of falling for spin originating from Romania's enemies 'with the purpose of extending the vices of the vampire "Dracula" over all the Romanian people. He knows today that those strange Latins at the Danube are drinkers of innocent blood, racists and incapable of governing themselves!'

History of Romanians is a book bursting with patriotic pique and fervour, which tells the story of the 'Romanian miracle' – that miracle being that the nation has survived at all. It is a realm under 'everlasting siege', constantly beset by powerful forces on every side, determined to prevent its unification or to pull the country apart. Time and again, world powers have bartered over Romanian territory behind closed doors, while Romania's impotent diplomats were left out in the cold, presented with the latest redrawing of the Eastern European map as a *fait accompli*. Perhaps the most notorious example was the Molotov-Ribbentrop Pact of 1940 between Nazi Germany and Soviet Russia, by which the Romanians lost around a third of their population and territory to the USSR and Hitler's Hungarian and Bulgarian allies. It wasn't an isolated case. Dogaru lists numerous other conferences and treaties which compromised Romania's integrity – at Tilsit in 1807, Tehran in 1943, Yalta in 1945 and Malta in 1989 – where he believes foreign governments have dictated the future of his long-suffering nation.

For much of the country's history, the Romanian-speaking Vlach majority have existed as second-class citizens, subordinate to Hungarian-speaking Magyars, the German-speakers locally known as Saxons, and Ottoman Turks. The geographical advantages the Romanian principalities enjoy have also proven a curse. A wealth of natural resources, rich mineral deposits and fertile soil made the principalities tempting targets for ambitious neighbours. More importantly, Romania's status as an effective crossroads on Europe's south-eastern border put her in a potentially lucrative position on many important trade routes, but also in the path of numerous invading armies. 'When the North wanted to go to the South, or the West wanted to touch the East, they have met here,' wrote the Romanian man-of-letters Nicolae Iorga in 1913. The natural defences offered by the region's impenetrable forests and the daunting peaks of the Carpathian Mountains often only seemed to aggravate the problem, making it a natural buffer state for a succession of empires.

VLAD THE IMPALER

One of the brochures Baddeley picked up when he touched down in Bucharest synopsised the situation in a similar spirited – and somewhat aggrieved – patriotic tone to that adopted by Dogaru and Zahariade. 'Once upon a time the frontier of the Ottoman Empire stopped by the Danube. Not willingly, as the Romanians – for 450 years – had to alternate the sword and the diplomacy to stop it there. Behind the shield of the Romanians, the countries of Central Europe could develop their manufactures, trade, cities and culture. Is there anything like a faint feeling of gratitude on their part? Not that we could detect so far?' The brochure was one issued by Romantic Travel, a Romanian company that offered a number of themed tours in collaboration with the Transylvanian Society of Dracula, an organisation dedicated to the study of both the factual and fictional Dracula. (Elizabeth Miller is president of the English-speaking Chapter of the international Society.) Your correspondent resolved to make his own way in his exploration of Vlad's realm. The following chapter is adapted from the notes Gavin Baddeley made on his Transylvanian trek of 1997.

CHAPTER II

Stranger in a Strange Land

*'I read that every known superstition in the world is
gathered into the horseshoe of the Carpathians, as if it were
the centre
of some sort of imaginative whirlpool; if so my stay may be
very interesting.' (Dracula, Bram Stoker)*

The first trace of Vlad's presence I encountered was a billboard I passed on the taxi ride from Bucharest airport, advertising a Dracula-themed strip club. Some might take this as emblematic of the prostitution of Romania's heritage to capitalist exploitation. Perhaps. I had already resolved, however, to focus upon the historical Dracula rather than his fictional alter-ego during the short time my schedule and budget allowed, and so chose to forgo any offbeat insights such an establishment might offer. Bucharest didn't become Romania's capital until 1862. In Vlad's day, the Royal Court was established in Tîrgovişte, some 80 kilometres to the northwest. Vlad Dracula left his mark on Bucharest by building a palace there, now known as the Curate Veche ('the Old Princely Court'). It's recently become the focus of attempts to restore Bucharest's historic centre, and as I understand now hosts a museum.

When I went in 1997, however, it was in a somewhat sorry state – an unimpressive jumble of ruined walls, precarious arches and lonely pillars that could only be viewed through some railings. The building had scarcely survived the final, turbulent weeks of the Impaler's reign in 1476, with a succession of fires and earthquakes largely finishing the job, and the remainder had apparently been lucky to escape demolition. Its survival in the face of the communist modernisers and capitalist developers is perhaps a modest indication of the residual respect the old Voivode still commanded after over five centuries. My next stop in

23

VLAD THE IMPALER

Bucharest was the Romanian National History Museum. Vlad could be found among an array of busts standing mute sentry in the foyer commemorating the nation's notable leaders, whilst upstairs in the medieval gallery were a number of displays dedicated to the era, including a case focusing on the Impaler himself. There was a portrait, and a number of documents bearing his signature (including the one where the name of Bucharest was first recorded, depicted on the 1959 Dracula stamps).

This was as close as I was likely to get to the original Dracula in Bucharest, a city then struggling to shrug off the weight of more recent history, so I bought a ticket to my next destination, the Transylvanian town of Braşov. Braşov, long regarded as the heart of Transylvania, was a trade hub during Dracula's lifetime and was known to its dominant Saxon population as Kronstadt. In 1950, the Communists who'd taken power three years earlier renamed it Stalin City, though happily the name didn't stick. The Communist dictator Nicolae Ceauşescu endeavoured to convert Braşov into an industrial centre in the 60s, and the spectre of his rule still hung heavy over Romania when I visited. Sat on the train heading north from Bucharest into Transylvania, I alternated between staring out of the window and leafing through my copy of *Dracula*, keen to test Christopher Lee's assertion to me that Stoker had captured the essence of its landscape.

'All day long we seemed to dawdle through a country which was full of beauty of every kind,' records Stoker's character Jonathan Harker while making his own train journey through Transylvania. 'Sometimes we saw little towns or castles on the top of steep hills such as we see in old missals; sometimes we ran by rivers and streams which seemed from the wide stony margin on each side of them to be subject to great floods. It takes a lot of water, and running strong, to sweep the outside edge of a river clear.'

Later on, Harker describes the Carpathians: 'Right and left of us they towered, with the afternoon sun falling full upon them and bringing out all the glorious colours of this beautiful range, deep blue and purple in the shadows of the peaks, green and brown where grass and rock mingled, and an endless perspective of jagged rock and pointed crags, till these were themselves lost in the distance, where the snowy peaks rose grandly. Here and there seemed mighty rifts in the mountains, through which, as the sun began to sink, we saw now and again the white gleam of falling water.' There are several such picturesque passages on the local countryside in the earlier chapters of *Dracula* which wouldn't look out of place in a Romanian tourist board publication, and in some respects it is hard to see why some have found Stoker's depiction of Transylvania so offensive. Obviously, Gothic horror aside, he paints a very attractive and – as Christopher Lee says – accurate picture of the region's stunning, frequently dramatic landscape.

Putting 'Gothic horror aside' might seem a tall order to those who feel that choosing to set a tale of terror in any locale represents an implicit insult to the setting. Transylvania seems strange and somewhat backward to Jonathan Harker – as it had to many of the British travel writers Stoker consulted while researching *Dracula*. While modern liberal sensibilities may frown upon such judgemental observations, when Stoker was writing, rural Transylvania was largely a backwater of the Austro-Hungarian Empire, its Romanian peasant population oppressed by Hungarian overlords, determined to impose Magyar culture upon the principality's Vlach majority. It would have seemed like stepping back in time for a Londoner like Harker, hailing from the capital of the industrial heartland of the Victorian age. When I visited, a century later, part of the region's charms lay in curious anachronisms, like getting stuck in a traffic jam headed by a horse and cart, causing a tailback of motorised traffic on one of the badly-laid motorways of the Communist era.

There is no question that Stoker was trying to evoke a deep sense of the foreign in his exploration of Transylvania in *Dracula*, though whether this reflects racism or an attempt to tap into something basic to human nature is another matter. Much of the appeal of travel derives from the ambivalent pleasure of culture shock, that simultaneous allure of the exotic that inevitably comes with the uneasy sense of alienation. It is born of the unnerving experience of encountering curious customs and beliefs that seem like superstitions to outsiders, of the constant background of foreign tongues and the absence of the comforting safety net of familiarity which we take for granted at home. As the Count himself puts it in Stoker's novel: 'a stranger in a strange land, he is no one. Men know him not, and to know not is to care not for.' (The phrase 'stranger in a strange land' is a reference to the Biblical Book of Exodus – it was used as the title for a famous novel by the science fiction author Robert A. Heinlein.)

Despite the hospitality of the natives – the Romanians are a warm and friendly people – culture shock was something I experienced on my visit to Transylvania, as I have in most of the far-flung places that I have visited, where English meant little, and the everyday realities of life became forays into the unfamiliar. That unnerving sense of strangeness is surely a necessary companion to the stimulating delights of discovery, whatever your destination. In a chiller like *Dracula*, it is unsurprising that Stoker offset his admiring descriptions of the local landscape with intimations that his initial protagonist is feeling increasingly out of his depth in an ancient realm where he doesn't understand the ground rules. A recent horror film that plays with similar fears is Eli Roth's 2008 horror movie *Hostel*. While most notorious for belonging to the harrowing 'torture porn' subgenre, *Hostel* is rather subtler than most of its grisly imitators.

Like Jonathan Harker, Roth's protagonists – cocksure American tourists rather than a stoic English solicitor – find themselves heading into the heart of Eastern Europe. While *Hostel*'s critics focused upon the sadistic scenes of torture that characterise the second half of the film, Roth's earlier scenes create an effective sense of building paranoia as the confidence of his arrogant heroes dwindles as they find themselves fish out of water, just waiting to be reeled in. On the coach from Bistritz, Stoker's hero Harker lets the beautiful landscape overwhelm his misgivings, though reflects 'had I known the language, or rather languages, which my fellow-passengers were speaking, I might not have been able to throw them off so easily'. The American backpackers in *Hostel* are similarly blissfully unaware that the beautiful Eastern Europeans are actually discussing their imminent brutal demise while smiling sweetly. The film's gruesome climax is set in Slovakia, and some natives were unimpressed. 'I am offended by this film,' blustered a local politician. 'I think that all Slovaks should feel offended.'

Roth countered that his film's main target was American ignorance. 'In talking to Americans, I realised they have absolutely no idea that Slovakia exists,' he told a press conference in the Czech capital of Prague. 'The latest statistics I found was that 12 percent of Americans own a passport. Twelve percent. They do not travel, but they think they own the world, and their dollar will buy everything. When I told people I was going to film in Prague, they said "Oh, Czechoslovakia – bring toilet paper." They still think it's some communist country from the 1950s. So when I said Slovakia I knew that Americans do not know the difference between the Czech Republic, Slovakia, Czechoslovakia, it's just one big Eastern bloc where there's always a war going on. So Slovakia in the movie, it's not really Slovakia, it's movie Slovakia, and it's based on American stereotypes and these stereotypes, that the cars are old, the people are old, the telephones are old, these are the stereotypes that lure these guys into going there, they believe it and they pay for it. These people get punished for these beliefs.'

Roth observes that the popularity of *The Texas Chain Saw Massacre* and the consequent sequels and remake hadn't damaged Texan tourism. He's right. While the success of Stoker's novel has helped to emphasise Transylvania's Gothic side to an unprecedented degree, most visitors who come hoping to experience the thrills found in the fictional *Dracula* will leave with fond memories of the natural beauty of the land the author describes. Everywhere has its share of darkness. Just a couple of years before Bram Stoker began writing his masterpiece, London was shocked by a series of horrific murders by a killer who became known as 'Jack the Ripper', courtesy of a series of dubious, gloating confessional letters to the press. The unsolved case caught the imagination of the international media, Jack subsequently becoming a dark mythic figure almost akin to Stoker's fictional Count. Stoker made brief reference to the Ripper in the preface to an Icelandic 1901 edition to *Dracula*, leading some commentators to suggest that the inspiration for his novel had more to do with the horrors of London's East End than the far reaches of Eastern Europe.

'Whether we like it or not, we are the "country of Dracula",' sighed the Romanian columnist Octavian Paler, in petulant mood, commenting upon the World Dracula Congress being held in Bucharest in 1995. 'So we will nurse our own dignity which is hurt by the ignorance and indifference of foreigners, by showing the world that at least in one domain we have no rivals!' While Transylvania may be a reluctant world leader in the specific field of vampire tourism, in the broader realm of macabre sightseeing, it certainly enjoys some competition. 'All good English tourism and even the most casual Anglophilia are rooted in a love of bloodshed; almost every major tourist attraction is famous because someone died there in a spectacularly unpleasant fashion,' according to the American humorist Joe Queenan in *Queenan Country*, his 2004 travelogue detailing a trip to 'the Mother Country'.

Perhaps the most pertinent point is that both Transylvania in Romania and London's East End have proven magnets of morbid fascination for tourists. Whitechapel in London offers regular Ripper walks, just as the Romantic Travel agency offers Dracula tours in modern Romania. The London Dungeon is a popular tourist attraction which combines horrific historical tableaux with haunted house style thrills, focusing on the bloodiest episodes from the British capital's past. Inevitably, Jack the Ripper takes centre stage. (In years gone by, the attraction also boasted a Vlad the Impaler tableau.) First opening its doors in 1976, the London Dungeon was sufficiently successful to spawn branches in York, Edinburgh, Hamburg and Amsterdam, all trading on the darkest episodes from their local history to the delight of streams of horrified tourists.

Just as some Romanians object to visitors drawn to their homeland in the hope of seeing a vampire, there have been objections to those who treat Jack the Ripper's old stalking grounds in London's East End as a tourist attraction. In 1976, the Ten Bells Pub in Whitechapel – widely reputed to have been patronised by a number of Jack's victims – changed its name to the Jack the Ripper in the hope of attracting tourist trade. Twelve years later, on the centenary of the murders, popular protest convinced the owners to return the pub to its original name. Objections, however, came primarily not from locals, but radical feminists who regarded the Ripper as a sort of patron saint of violence against women, and any interest in the case as an effective celebration of misogyny. Yet the Jack the Ripper pub was launched by an East End local, Bobby Wayman, and he was disdainful when his successor as landlord bowed to pressure from campaign groups like Women Against Violence Against Women, to return it to the Ten Bells. (For the full story, see *Saucy Jack*, the second volume in the Devil's Histories series.)

It's a fair guess that the majority of those who picketed the pub came from outside the borough, perhaps those with their own axes to grind or stories to sell. Whether they are actually representative of the opinions of those around them is of course another matter. For most East Enders, the story of Jack the Ripper is just spooky local lore. If it brings in a few curious tourists, unlikely otherwise to visit one of London's less scenic districts, then local businesses won't complain. As far as I could determine when I visited Transylvania, local feeling was much the same on the subject of Dracula. It might be tiresome to be stereotyped by ignorant tourists and lazy foreign journalists, but the foreign currency was welcome and the arrival of curious travellers was unlikely to destroy the legacy of a time-tested figure like Vlad.

Overall, most Romanians had more important things on their minds than whether some movies may have misrepresented a medieval monarch. The scars were still fresh from decades under the repressive regime of Nicolae Ceaușescu. Significantly, of the six Eastern European Communist regimes that fell in 1989, only Romania's revolution was violent, a week of trauma that claimed over 1000 lives before the execution of Ceaușescu and his hated wife Elena on Christmas Day brought the curtain down on the brutal drama. Understandably, for most Romanians, the recent bullet-holes that pocked many public buildings were a greater concern than the true identity of Dracula's Castle, the living legacy of a Communist dictator executed just eight years earlier more relevant than the significance of a medieval tyrant dead for over five centuries. But, with the benefit of distance enjoyed by an outsider, are there connections? As we shall see, this question itself raises some interesting controversy.

When Christopher Lee visited Transylvania in 1971, the worst of Ceauşescu's modernising initiatives had yet to hit the country. The same year that the British actor was visiting Romania, the Romanian dictator was touring China, North Korea and North Vietnam. Sadly for his citizens, Ceauşescu was much impressed, instituting a series of increasingly repressive policies on his long-suffering people, while his regime stepped up a programme of fostering heavy industry and urbanisation. The chief aspect of the Transylvanian countryside that jarred with Stoker's descriptions when I visited were the vistas of cancerous concrete, rusting twisted iron and dirty broken glass that blighted so much of the landscape. Such ugly monuments to the failure of forced progress ringed Braşov, a city that witnessed the first violent rumbles of revolt against the Communist despot in 1987. But once you penetrated the city's suburban sprawl to Braşov's ancient heart, it was a different story.

Vlad Dracula's era was something of a golden age for Braşov. Despite its precarious position near the frontline of almost constant conflict between Christian Europe and the advancing Ottoman Empire, the city thrived in the 15th century. The formidable stone fortifications built in the period – many of them still standing – are a monument, not just to the turbulent times, but also to the commercial power the city enjoyed. While war may have impacted upon trade, it proved a bonanza for Braşov's busy arms manufacturers, who fashioned bows, swords, shields – and increasingly state-of-the-art gunpowder weapons – in volumes that qualified as medieval mass production, five centuries before Ceauşescu attempted to turn the city into a hub of heavy industry. During the 1400s, Braşov armed the forces of most of the Christian warlords we shall be encountering in the following pages, including Vlad Dracula. The city played a pivotal part in the life of the Impaler, who interacted with its citizens both as professed friend and ruthless foe.

The first thing that struck me upon arrival in Old Braşov was how Teutonic the architecture looked. In some of its more salubrious streets, you could have been in Bremen or Salzburg. Braşov was one of the 'seven citadels' dominated by Transylvania's German-speaking

Saxon population, who in turn dominated commerce and crafts throughout the region. Somehow Braşov, known as Kronstadt by the Saxons, has more of a fairytale than Gothic feel – an ambience more suggestive of the Brothers Grimm than Hammer horror. There is a quaint local legend (included in the Grimms' *Deutsche Sagen* of 1816) that explains the seemingly incongruous presence of so many Germans so far from home. As the fairy story goes, when the Pied Piper charmed all of the children of Hamelin away from their parents in revenge for being cheated of his rat-catcher's fee, he led them into a cave, then through a series of tunnels, never to be seen again.

They finally emerged, so it is said, somewhere near Braşov's main square. (Our friends at Romantic Travel offered an excursion to the very grotto from which they emerged, claiming to be 'the only tour-operator who can offer you this tour, as it is the only one, knowing the location of the cave'.) Even here there are sinister undertones of our broader subject. The emotive idea of children being stolen which provides the macabre climax to 'The Pied Piper of Hamelin' has grim resonance in the medieval and renaissance history of Eastern Europe. The Ottoman Empire demanded not just gold and material goods from its vassal states, but a tribute of boys, who would be conscripted into the Turkish Sultanate's army and administration as slaves. It was this cruel but effective practice which, by some accounts, finally committed Vlad the Impaler to a collision course with the Ottomans, when he refused to countenance Wallachian youth being exported to the Orient.

In reality, German colonists arrived willingly in Transylvania in the 12th century. They were invited to establish strongholds in the region by its Hungarian overlords in order to exploit local resources and trade. These miniature city-states, governed by quasi-independent councils, became a vital buffer for Hungary against threats from the south. In effect, the Saxons became the region's middle class, with Hungarian knights above them, and the Romanian-speaking Vlach majority at the bottom of the heap. The situation was formalised in 1438 as the Unio Trium Nationum (union of three nations), an oppressive pact of mutual support against domestic peasant uprisings and Ottoman invasion, from which the Vlachs were pointedly excluded. In *Balkan Ghosts: A Journey through History* (1993) Robert D. Kaplan describes it as 'a medieval apartheid system, in which the Hungarians and the Saxon Germans, whether Protestant or Catholic, enjoyed all the rights.'

Such racial and political tensions helped provide the background for the tragedy that inspired my visit, for Braşov was the site of one of Vlad Dracula's most notorious atrocities in 1459, when the Vlach Voivode visited terrible vengeance on the Saxon population. It was Vlad's Srebrenica – the war crime that helped establish Vlad as the Impaler, in European eyes at least. 'And he set off with all his army and went to Wuetzerland,' reads one significant account (Wuetzerland being a German name for the region surrounding Braşov). 'Early one morning he came to the villages, castles and towns. All those he overcame, he also destroyed and had all the grain and wheat burned. And he led away all those whom he had captured outside the city called Kronstadt near the chapel called St Jacob. And at that time Dracula rested there and had the entire suburb burned. Also as the day came, early in the morning, all those whom he had taken captive, men and women, young and old, he had impaled on the hill by the chapel and all around the hill, and under them he proceeded to eat at table and get his joy that way.'

It was strange being in the same city in which this had happened – a scene depicted in a number of German woodcuts that I had pored over as a teenager. This massacre was particularly infamous because of the reputed episode whereby, while eating his dinner among the impaled corpses, the Impaler was reputed to have dipped his bread in the blood of one of his victims and eaten it. It's a significant detail, as it's one of the only episodes that plausibly show the original Dracula as literally bloodthirsty. It's also a controversial one, as some historians insist that it is a modern fabrication. The two most famous woodcuts depicting the notorious meal are stylised in the fashion of the day (one is from Nuremberg in 1499, the other from Strasbourg, 1500) and are evidently not drawn from life, but I still felt the hairs on my neck rise as I visited the setting of these grim medieval cartoons. A number of modern sources site the grisly feast as taking place on Mount Timpa, an imposing forested peak that overlooks the old city walls, now surrounded by urban sprawl. Today a crass Hollywood-style sign advertising the city's name looks over Braşov. In 1459, Dracula used the slopes of Mount Timpa to promote an altogether grimmer message.

Braşov offers the perfect base for a visit to the highlight of many Dracula tours: Castle Bran. This imposing structure guards one of the strategic mountain passes between Transylvania and Wallachia that made Braşov such an important trade centre. Today, it is emblematic of Romania's ambivalent relationship with Dracula tourism. Castle Bran certainly looks the part of a Gothic lair and when tourists began to take an interest in Vlad, the communist authorities actively promoted it as an easily-accessible attraction that might keep vulgar sensation-seekers away from authentic sites associated with a national hero. Christopher Lee was filmed there in full Impaler regalia for *In Search of Dracula*, yet there is no sound evidence to connect it with the historical Dracula, and it is in the wrong location for the Count's lair in Stoker's novel. Our Romantic Travel brochure dismisses it as 'the trial and trap of Castle Bran, a fake Castle Dracula, set in the way to the genuine Castle, in order to stop the mobs from pestering the solitude of the Count'.

The castle is well worth a visit regardless of the authenticity of its connections with Vlad the Impaler. It is perfectly plausible that the Voivode stayed there at some point in his career. His grandfather Mircea the Elder certainly owned the castle, and some believe Vlad used it as a base for his notorious raid on Braşov, yet conclusive documentary evidence of any firm connection between Castle Bran and the Impaler remains elusive. If nothing else, the tourist in search of Dracula souvenirs will find rich, if tacky, pickings in the car park beneath. As an intriguing afterward, Dr Marius Mircea Crişan made some interesting observations in an article entitled 'The Models for Castle Dracula in Stoker's Sources on Transylvania' in a 2008 article for *The Journal of Dracula Studies*. The Romanian academic pays particular attention to the illustrations in two of the books we know that Stoker consulted while researching his novel – Charles Boner's *Transylvania: Its Product and Its People* (1865) and *Magyarland: Being the Narrative of Our Travels Through the Highlands and Lowlands of Hungary* (1881) by Nina Elizabeth Mazuchelli.

Dr Crişan notes that both books not only feature pictures of Castle Bran, but descriptions of the fortress likely to have stirred the imagination of a Gothic novelist looking for a suitable Transylvanian den for his villain. 'Nothing can be more romantic than the fortress; its position among the solitary rocks, its construction and seeming inaccessibility, make it the very ideal of such sort of dwelling...' notes Boner. 'Within are narrow passages and galleries, strange nooks and zigzag stairs, and dark corners irresistibly attractive, and in the thick wall was a low prison where no ray could ever enter.' 'Anything more wild and romantic than the position of the castle cannot be conceived,' concurs Mazuchelli. 'Its accessories [remind] the spectator of the nursery tales of his childhood – of Blue-beard and Giant Despair. Inside there are grim passages, trap-doors, and yawning depths, all bearing silent witness to the troublous times when these borders were invaded by the Tartar and the Turk.' So, the possibility remains that, when the Romanian tourist authorities identified Bran as Castle Dracula, they may inadvertently have been right.

The next destination on my whistle-stop tour of Transylvania, on the surface, has an even more tenuous link with Dracula. Cluj figures briefly in Bram Stoker's novel under its Germanic name of Klausenburg, though he chiefly uses it to literally add a little local flavour to the text, detailing some of the Transylvanian delicacies Jonathan Harker enjoys whilst staying there overnight. Christopher Lee might have recognised the name Klausenburg from the script for *Dracula*, as, in their condensed version of Stoker's novel, Hammer chose to locate Castle Dracula nearby. Though he perhaps wouldn't have recognised the place, for in contrast to the frightened village Hammer Films built on the sets at Bray Studios in Berkshire, Cluj is a thriving city, the third largest in Romania. It enjoyed particular prosperity in the late 19th century, when it became the capital of Transylvania during Austro-Hungarian rule of the principality, the Hungarians referring to the city as Kolozsvár. If Braşov has a Teutonic flavour, then Cluj retains strong traces of Hungarian influence in its architecture and atmosphere. (The dishes Harker describes are more like spicy Magyar cuisine than hearty Romanian – he blames the hot paprika for the nightmare he experiences during his stay.)

In 1974, the Communist authorities added the suffix Napoca – the settlement's Roman name – to Cluj as part of a programme by Ceauşescu's government to underline Romania's links to the Ancient Roman Empire. Emphasising the theory that the Vlachs were the direct descendants of Rome's Dacian colony was a nationalistic statement, a reaffirmation that the nation's Romanian population pre-dated the Hungarian Magyar invasion. Empires are curious things. The Romanians are happy, even eager, to acknowledge that their Dacian forebears were conquered and absorbed into the Roman Empire (hence the very name 'Romania'). A reproduction of Trajan's Column, erected in AD113 to celebrate the Roman emperor's victories in the Dacian Wars, takes pride of place in the Museum of Romanian History in Bucharest. Subsequent conquests have not sat so easy with national pride. In particular, Hungarian claims on Transylvania remain a sensitive topic.

The reasons for my visit to Cluj-Napoca were not unrelated to such fierce regional rivalry: one of the city's historical claims to fame is as the birthplace of the Hungarian king Matthias Corvinus. He plays a central role in the career of Vlad Dracula, arresting the Impaler in 1462 after a meeting at Braşov, and keeping him as his reluctant guest in Hungary for 12 years. Looking out from the hotel balcony I could see the large statue of Matthias Corvinus, an impressive edifice portraying the king as a triumphant warlord, dominating Piata Unirii in suitably regal style. Piata Unirii translates as 'Union Square'. It was renamed from Piata Libertatii, or Liberty Square, four years previously by the city's mayor, Gheorghe Funar. Funar had an ideological axe to grind – renaming the square was another deliberate nationalistic statement – this time celebrating Transylvania's reunification with Romania. As a further statement, the Mayor removed the lettering from the statue of Matthias Corvinus that identified him as a Hungarian monarch, then surrounding the figure with a spread of Romanian flags.

Gheorghe Funar remains one of Romania's most colourful and controversial political figures, establishing himself on the national stage with his twelve years as municipal head of Cluj-Napoca. Many regard him as a dangerous opportunist, a racist demagogue, the 'Mad Mayor' who fanned the flames of ancient ethnic strife between Hungary and Romania in the pursuit of personal power, draping every available surface in the Romanian tricolour flag and missing no opportunity to provoke the city's substantial – though fast diminishing – Magyar population. While I was there, local gossip maintained that Mayor Funar was engaged in a peculiar form of archaeological warfare. Apparently, he supported claims that there were important Roman remains beneath Piata Unirii, whose excavation would require the removal of the statue of Matthias Corvinus entirely. Happily, this never happened, and Funar's career was already in decline, as Romania strengthened her ties of friendship with her Hungarian neighbour in defiance of the fulminating Funar.

Yet he clearly tapped into powerful popular opinion with his crass appeal to Romanian nationalist sentiment, something expressed by reference to the career of the nation's most controversial hero, Vlad Dracula. In Bram Stoker's *Dracula*, in words that might warm Gheorghe Funar's heart, the Count describes his Transylvanian homeland as 'ground fought over for centuries by the Wallachian, the Saxon, and the Turk. Why, there is hardly a foot of soil in all this region that has not been enriched by the blood of men, patriots or invaders. In the old days there were stirring times, when the Austrian and the Hungarian came up in hordes, and the patriots went out to meet them, men and women, the aged and the children too, and waited their coming on the rocks above the passes, that they might sweep destruction on them with their artificial avalanches.'

Having made pilgrimage to the house in which one of Vlad Dracula's most effective opponents was born, it was clearly time to pay tribute to the birthplace of the Impaler himself. The final destination on my brief

Transylvanian sojourn was also the highlight of my expedition. Sighisoara is tiny compared to the other Transylvanian cities I had visited, though during the Middle Ages, like Braşov it had been a significant centre for trade and industry. Unlike Braşov, it had largely escaped the attentions of Communist modernisers and capitalist developers, and Sighisoara is perhaps the best-preserved, inhabited example of a medieval citadel in Eastern Europe. Just as Bucharest is first mentioned in a document signed by Vlad the Impaler, Sighisoara's name was first recorded in one relating to his father. Vlad Dracul was stationed in Sighisoara under the command of the Holy Roman Emperor Sigismund in 1431, guarding the Transylvanian border, awaiting the opportunity to ride into Wallachia and claim his birthright as Voivode. The same year he arrived, his second son and namesake was born, the man who would enter immortality as Dracula.

The house where Dracula was born still stands, though opinion differs as to how much of the building dates back to the 15th century. Upon arrival at Sighisoara, a woman at the station approached me, offering accommodation – I initially refused, but when she promised that my room would be mere yards from Dracula's birthplace, I couldn't resist. By this point in my journey, though tired and dirty, (the bathroom contained archaic plumbing beyond my pampered comprehension) I still felt a sense of curious elation at coming so close to the very source of my expedition. True to the lady's word, our house was only a couple of doors away from the house identified by a plaque as the one in which Vlad was born in 1431. It's an unassuming building in many respects:, a squat, mustard-coloured three-storey house – far from palatial, and certainly a modest residence for a regional governor like Dracula's father. Far more functional than luxurious, in common with many of the medieval merchants' houses in Sighisoara, it gave the impression of a miniature fortress – the sort of house where a cautious man might live in turbulent times – with thick walls sparsely punctuated by small windows.

This house appeared to be just a bar when I visited, and the locals seemed friendly, though my feeble Romanian precluded any meaningful conversation. The only foreigner in the room, I was served a bottle of local beer with Vlad on the label, but quickly gave up my efforts to secure an invitation upstairs, where my information indicated that there was a mural relevant to my visit. It depicts three men and a woman sat at a table feasting. Only the central figure has survived the ravages of time well. 'The portrait is that of a rotund man with a double chin, a long well-waxed moustache, arched eyebrows, and a finely-chiselled nose,' according to Florescu and McNally in *In Search of Dracula*. 'The similarity of the brown, almond-shaped eyes to those of the famous portrait of Dracula preserved at Ambras Castle suggests that this may be the only surviving portrait of Dracula's father, Vlad Dracul.' The mural post-dates Vlad by some years, so their supposition may be somewhat wishful. The figure looks strikingly Turkish, which is perhaps evidence that it depicts a later resident, though you might also ponder on what it might suggest if it does depict Vlad Dracul. Dracul spent his reign oscillating between the Ottoman east and Hungarian west – is this the portrait of a ruler divided between the lure of Turkish luxury and his military vows to his Christian sovereign? If so, this is a point of clear distinction between Vlad Dracula and his father. For, unlike Dracul, Dracula would prove an implacable foe to the Ottomans.

While Brașov struck me with its Germanic overtones, and Cluj had a distinctly Hungarian influence, somehow Sighisoara felt profoundly Romanian, however ahistorical such a statement might be. At the citadel's centre is the Church on the Hill, a solid 14th-century Saxon building reached by a picturesque covered wooden stairway, the 175-step ascent rewarded by a wonderful view over the town. The town's well-preserved medieval defences still feature nine of the original fourteen towers. In common with Transylvanian custom, their construction was financed by the town's prosperous guilds, their names indicating those responsible – there is a Furrier's Tower, a Smith's Tower, a Shoemaker's Tower, a Locksmith's Tower – giving a vivid surviving indication of the businesses once important to the town's economy.

Local lore has it that young Vlad took a particular interest in the Tailor's Tower, the stout stone gatehouse that bestrides old Sighisoara's main gate. This was the location where prisoners were taken for execution, and according to popular tradition, the infant Impaler liked to peer out of the window of his second storey bedroom with avid interest at the condemned being led to their deaths. Whether his older brother Mircea, Vlad's senior by four years, shared his morbid fascination isn't recorded. Vlad certainly wouldn't be the first schoolboy with an unhealthy interest in the macabre, and such proclivities had plentiful opportunities for satisfaction during the brutal era of the Middle Ages, as the deterrence of punishment was a priority in the penal policy of the era, and savage executions were deliberately held as public ceremonies. How effective that deterrence was is perhaps open to question. To briefly revisit our theme of comparing English brutality with that of Transylvania, a grisly case from 13th-century England serves as a good reminder that judicial savagery was most certainly not an Eastern European monopoly in the Middle Ages, any more than Vlad was unique in his youthful fascination with it.

In 1221, a man named Thomas of Eldersfield (a village near Tewkesbury in Gloucestershire) was found guilty of assaulting a rival named George with an axe after a drunken argument. Technically, this was a hanging offence, but the court showed Thomas leniency, though how merciful this looks to modern eyes is another matter. Dr Richard Holt gave a lecture on the case in 1991, saying that the judges 'sentenced Thomas to be mutilated – to be blinded and castrated. This was to be carried out on the spot, and not by court officials but by the accusers – George and his friends, who set to enthusiastically. The damaged eye came out easily enough, but the other was more intractable: blinding meant the physical tearing out of the eyeball, and they had to re-sharpen the blinding tools several times before they could get the job done. After that the castration was easy, which they did roughly – and then tossed the testicles into the watching crowd. At the front was a gang of youths, who began to kick them backwards and forwards between the girls who had come with them.'

As a bizarre postscript to the story, the case attracted particular attention because of a supposed miraculous recovery by Thomas, who claimed that his eyes and testicles began to grow back after a vision brought on by diligent prayer. Such holy happy endings aside, the case is illustrative of a number of pertinent points. Blinding and castration are forms of punishment that feature prominently in medieval Eastern European history. Aside from being particularly fearsome forms of mutilation, the symbolism is significant, literally cutting off someone's family line and making them obsolete on the battlefield. Some historians suggest that such mutilations had particular significance in realms like Wallachia, where tradition forbade someone with such infirmities from becoming Voivode, making it a popular punishment for a potential rival to the throne. We'll go into the symbolic implications of the Impaler's favourite form of execution presently. The impact of using punishment as a form of display can't have gone unnoticed by the young Vlad. There can't have been a more public place for punishment than the Tailor's Tower, passed daily by most people entering or leaving Sighisoara.

While many of those punished would have been prosecuted under Sighisoara's Saxon council, no doubt some of those who met a premature end at the Tailor's Tower under Vlad Dracula's beady young eye did so under sentence from his father. The Dracula dynasty was something of an anomaly in Transylvania. Emperor Sigismund granted Vlad Dracul the right to mint his own currency in the town – around eight of the silver coins survive, stamped with the Wallachian eagle on side and Dracul's personal sigil of the dragon on the other. It was a great honour, a rare dispensation that not only showed the Holy Roman Emperor's approval, but also gave Vlad Dracul the financial means to begin assembling troops and equipment in order to realise his ultimate ambition and claim the Wallachian throne, which he believed rightfully his. Yet, despite housing a prominent Vlach lord like Dracul and his sons, Sighisoara observed the Unio Trium Nationum, the system that ensured Saxon dominance over all the town's trades and professions. Outside of the Dracula household, most of those speaking Romanian would have been powerless peasants.

The town's most impressive edifice is its gorgeous, baroque clock tower, positioned on another fortified entrance to the old town. At midnight, wooden figures emerge from the clock to strike the hour – seven Roman gods rotate representing the seven days of the week, each surmounted by an appropriate astrological symbol. It pays magical testament to Transylvania's rich heritage of Renaissance art and engineering, but also acts as a reminder of Romania's classical roots. The clock tower also housed a museum, displaying the miscellany of exhibits common to such provincial establishments the world over. Among the displays of Dacian pottery, medieval weaponry and renaissance apothecary's equipment was a vivid written record of the town's trials and tribulations. Whilst proud to have never fallen to siege, the record lists a sobering catalogue of the worst natural disasters that have blighted Sighisoara – a devastating fire in 1676, plague in 1709, an earthquake in 1738, a flood in 1777... The plague accounted for 1300 of the town's population of 3000, the fire destroying the vast majority of Sighisoara's wooden housing. While the citadel I visited was characterised by quaint Renaissance charm and picturesque suburban tranquillity, the undertones of strife and suffering weren't too far beneath the surface in Sighisoara. Clearly the disasters that have afflicted the town through the centuries have not left Sighisoara unscarred, and the narrow, shadowed and cobbled streets I wandered down have changed since a young Vlad played there some 550 years before.

Yet, it still felt like stepping back into the past, a potent jolt of that delicious shiver down the back of the neck when you feel you have truly connected with history, even for a brief moment or two. The sights, sounds, even smells of Sighisoara were evocative of days long past, and I left the unique Transylvanian citadel with powerful memories. Vlad Dracul left Sighisoara in the winter of 1436 in pursuit of the voivodeship of Wallachia, an ambition he finally realised the following year. His three sons, Mircea, Vlad and Radu – the latest addition to the dynasty – followed soon after, to join their father at his new palace in Tîrgovişte. It would open a new chapter in young Vlad's life, as he became accustomed to life as a prince in his new Wallachian home. This was a new world of international politics and Machiavellian schemes which would soon entangle the young prince. A world in which we will immerse ourselves in in the chapter to come…

CHAPTER III

Athletes of Christ

It is the autumn of 1415, in a village just over a day's ride west of Paris. An old man sits in front of a tavern. Tight, pale flesh clings onto a bowed frame that was once broad and powerful; he is the picture of broken man. Barely forty years of age, he could pass for double that with his thinning grey hair and worn face, lined by pain and care. In front of him, on his table, a hunk of stale, black bread, and an earthenware jug. Once a proud warrior, a knight of the King of France who feasted from silver plates with lords and ladies, boasting and laughing, he now greedily slurps the vinegary wine straight from the jug, his meagre food left forgotten. Each acrid, hungry gulp he vainly hopes might drown the feeling of appalling dread that is reaching up from his gut and tormenting his mind with unbidden memories...

For over a day now, messengers have been passing through the old knight's village with awful news. At first, it was a young lad on a sweat-slicked horse, his eyes wide and his tongue bursting with rumours of disaster as he paused to exchange his mount. There had been a terrible battle, he gabbled, many were dead, the English were triumphant, it might be but days before King Henry marched upon the capital itself. More messengers borne on ill winds soon passed through with similar tales to tell. France's finest warriors had been felled on a field near a village called Agincourt like so many corn stalks before the Great Leveller's scythe. Once these bearers of bad tidings reached Paris, however, they found a bitter welcome. The messengers were imprisoned before they could spread their stories to the Parisian suburbs. If their tales of disaster proved mere fables, they were to be drowned in the Seine as agents of the English.

That day, however, the first of the soldiers arrive – exhausted, battle-scarred, smeared in filth and blood – and the old knight knows that the stories are true, that the nightmare he has striven so hard to wash away with wine is rearing up before him once more. The soldiers had the strange distant looks on their faces of men who have been devoured by defeat, of those thrust into the hinterlands of Hell, who can now neither forget what they have seen, nor ever quite believe that they have truly escaped. It is the same mask that the old knight has been wearing for nearly twenty years, since his own brush with the worst fates the gods of war could inflict left him broken in mind, frame and soul. As the soldiers begin to recount the events of their fateful encounter on the field near Agincourt, he shudders, straining to hear every detail, though at the same time wishing with every beat of his heart that the shattered French warriors might keep their peace.

They tell of arriving in great splendour and good order, of charging the English lines like heroes from the Song of Roland. Then the storybook charge hits the wooden stakes and arrows of the murderous English peasants, and the soldier's tale transforms from an account of derring-do to a litany of casualties. Everyone in the village has heard of most of the lords whom the soldiers are listing as dead – indeed everyone in France is familiar with many of the names of the dukes and counts numbered among the fallen. The old knight is more familiar with them still – or at least he had been – their names briefly conjuring faces in his mind, of men who he had once rode beside. As the soldiers conclude their woeful narrative, they have saved the final horrific detail for last. With voices still quivering with shock and rage, the beaten French men-at-arms detail how the English put all of their prisoners to the sword, butchering their helpless captives with axe, dagger and mallet like so many farmyard hogs.

At this, the old knight can bear it no more. Tears streaming down his face, he gets to his feet, but his legs buckle beneath him. As he sinks to the floor, his memories flood back. They are visions of his own sojourn into despair, recollections that haunt his night hours, and leave him whimpering like an infant.

Like the brave knights who had taken the field at Agincourt, nearly twenty years earlier, in 1396, he and his fellows had ridden boldly onto the plains below the distant Turkish castle of Nicopolis, a veritable parade of burnished steel and heraldic colour. Like them, their valour was shattered in a few brief hours of bone-shattering shock, as the flower of French chivalry was swamped in a blizzard of Turkish fury. Horses fell beneath showers of arrows; heavily armoured knights were dragged to the ground, all around an infernal chaos of struggling, suffering, screaming flesh against iron. The knight's visor had filled with sweat and the unbearable heat of his own breath until he was just flailing blindly with his broadsword, as his horse stumbled, and he was immersed in welcome darkness.

The worst still awaited the French survivors of Nicopolis. The knight recovered his senses in the Turkish camp beneath the citadel. A comrade had dragged him from the battlefield in a daze rather than leave him to the knives of the heathen scavengers. He later heartily cursed this kindness. There must have been thousands of French and Burgundian prisoners corralled together that awful day, stripped of their armour and dignity, shivering in dread anticipation in their soiled shirts beneath a cold, heartless sun. First, the Turkish took the youngest among them, turbaned officials pointing and jabbering sharply in a tongue few of the terrified captives understood. Those who knew something of heathen ways said that the youths were destined for forced circumcision and conversion to the rites of Mohammed. Then the Turkish officers began leading the remaining Christian prisoners away in groups of a dozen or more.

Screams that suddenly pierced the windless sky left the remaining wretches in little doubt as to the fate that awaited those marched over the hill to the Sultan's tents.

For the first time the man next to the knight spoke. 'The Sultan has found out what they did to his own men,' he hissed bitterly. When the knight looked quizzical, his companion elaborated: 'Yesterday, the French Duke ordered all of the heathen prisoners killed – today the Sultan thirsts for Christian blood.' The knight could not be sure, but he thought his neighbour – a rough looking Hungarian – was smiling through his broken teeth and blood-matted beard. The executions continued for hours. File after file of battle-numbed Christians were herded before the Sultan to be hacked to the floor until terror and monotony threatened to merge. Surely every bloodlust has its limits, and if it does not, the muscles of the executioner's arm do, and the pungent rivers of blood and human waste from the hundreds slain was enough to glut or disgust even the most vengeful of hearts.

Once again the knight was forced to wonder if death might have been a blessing, as the remainder of the defeated army was mustered into a column, and marched east. Still dressed only in their filth-sodden shirts, the pride of Christian chivalry staggered across the plains, and over the mountains, ever towards the rising sun that roasted their flesh to welts in the day, and then cruelly deserted them in the bitter nights. Feet, rendered into bloody stumps of bone and blister, landed one after the other, and as only survival and avoiding the cruel whips of their captors became real, with everything else an illusion, many preferred to fall and welcome easeful death. Matters became easier when the Christians finally reached their destination deep in Turkish territory. Some of the wealthier captives even received gifts from sympathetic local lords, but the threat still remained – like a scimitar poised over their collective throats – that the Sultan's mood might change, and the slaughter begin anew.

After nearly a year of captivity, vast sums from Europe finally secured the release of the Sultan's remaining prisoners. Many did not make it. Those that did made a slow progress home, aware that what had happened on the field at

Nicopolis had traumatised not just them, but inflicted heavy wounds on the world to which they were returning. The old knight made it home, but he returned to a family ruined by his absence and the need to raise his ransom. He returned to recurring nightmares of the day he spent on the plain beneath Nicopolis, waiting to be summoned before the Sultan for butchery. Most of this proud warrior died on the days following the defeat at Nicopolis. Today, as the villagers discuss the defeat at Agincourt in urgent whispers, they are unaware that the old knight at their feet is not simply drunk again, but that he has finally abandoned his struggle with death with one rattling breath.

***

Though it was fought 35 years before he was born, in many important respects, the Battle of Nicopolis set the scene for the life of Vlad the Impaler. Agincourt was fought just 19 years after Nicopolis, though the two battlefields are almost a thousand miles apart. There are numerous similarities between the two battles, just as there are significant differences. Agincourt is certainly the more famous of the two, the subject of much study particularly among Anglophone historians. Yet Nicopolis was far and away the more significant. Agincourt made little real difference, even to the campaign in which it was fought. While the English won the battle, they ultimately lost the Hundred Years War. Nicopolis determined the fate of Eastern Europe for well over 400 years. Agincourt was unquestionably a remarkable victory against the odds, a celebrated triumph for the English that boosted support for the war at home and the reputation of their skill at arms abroad. But, compared to the cataclysmic clash between civilisations at Nicopolis in 1396, where the Christian world's military elite confronted their counterparts from the Islamic world, Agincourt was a mere skirmish, a local quarrel between rival dynasties with little lasting impact.

Yet, in the *Oxford Guide to Battles* by Richard Holmes and Martin Marix Evans, Nicopolis doesn't even warrant a mention, while the centuries of conflict between the Ottoman Empire and the European powers warrant only a page in the book's 400+ pages. By way of comparison, the Hundred Years War enjoys three pages of coverage, Agincourt occupying a full page on its own. This certainly doesn't reflect the relative importance of these conflicts in authentic historical terms, but it is an accurate reflection of their comparative significance in the eyes of most Western historians, however distorted and parochial that view may be.

In several respects, there are striking similarities between Nicopolis and Agincourt. Both featured the controversial execution of prisoners. Both established the reputations of their respective victors – Henry V of England and the Ottoman sultan Bayezid I – as war heroes. There are similarities in the strategy employed by both victors – using sharpened stakes driven into the ground to demolish opposing cavalry – to the extent that some believe that the English at Agincourt were inspired by reports of Turkish tactics at Nicopolis. In both cases, the mounted forces on the receiving end of the sharpened stakes were predominantly French. The battles have both been seen as emblematic. The losses suffered by the French aristocracy – who saw themselves as the embodiment of the medieval chivalric ideal – not only traumatised France, but fatally wounded the status of the knight. It has been described as a key moment in a 'Military Revolution' in medieval society, for anything that compromised the pre-eminence of the armoured aristocrat on the battlefield also threatened their privileged position as the warrior caste in the social hierarchy.

Some historians have challenged the Military Revolution theory, pointing out that well-motivated common infantry had defeated over-confident aristocratic heavy cavalry long before Agincourt. As early as 1176, Frederick Barbarossa's knights were humbled by a force of Milanese foot soldiers, known as the Company of Death, at the Battle of Legnano. Agincourt itself was the last of a trio of similar victories – preceded by Crécy in 1346 and Poitiers a decade later – where hard-bitten English professionalism had humbled superior French chivalric forces by employing infantry tactics. It's almost as if it was a brutal lesson the French aristocracy didn't want to learn. Military tactics were firmly enmeshed in medieval culture and social identity. To dismount for battle literally diminished a knight's status, according to chivalric logic, regardless of any tactical imperative. You might say the French aristocracy fell on the field at Agincourt in 1415 as much victims of their own snobbery as the arrows of Henry's famed longbowmen.

France's battlefield humiliations at Crécy, Poitiers and Agincourt certainly did not point to the obsolescence of the heavy cavalry, who continued to play a vital part on the battlefield long after such high profile military disasters. The contest between upper class horsemen wielding swords or lances, confronting lowly foot soldiers sheltering behind sharpened wooden stakes, pikes, or fixed bayonets, would be repeated countless times with differing results on battlefields over the next five centuries, and only definitively decided with the advent of the tank. (Prototypical tanks were already entering the battlefield in Dracula's era, courtesy of the battlewagons pioneered by the heretic rebel armies in the Hussite Wars that wracked Sigismund's Bohemian realms in the early 1400s – an innovation subsequently adopted by both Christian and Ottoman forces.)

Chivalry would also survive such humiliations, not least because of its ambivalent role in medieval society. In theory it was an attempt to muzzle the worst excesses of the era's warrior class by appealing to their vanity – creating an idealised archetype for the knight to aspire to – a hero bound by a romantic ethos of defending the weak and fighting fair. Chivalry was an appeal to aristocratic vanity with vague religious overtones, disseminated in the popular culture of the day. In practice, few adherents paid much attention to its codes as applied to the vulnerable. Rather it became what some historians have described as an insurance policy for medieval Europe's elite, whose exclusive entry requirements – the premiums if you will – were the expensive equipment and entourage required of a knight. Once encased in state-of-the-art steel, a knight was unlikely to be seriously injured in battle, and if captured, could rely upon his chivalric foe to keep him in comfort until his captor was rewarded with a ransom.

Unsurprisingly, such insurance actually encouraged combat among Europe's armoured elite, for whom war became akin to sport. This also helps explain why the French aristocracy were so reluctant to countenance the custom's demise, even in the face of the brutal lessons of Crécy and Poitiers. Improbable as it may seem considering his reputation for merciless savagery, chivalry was also indirectly responsible for the immortality of Vlad the Impaler, or at least his epithet Dracula. The most controversial aspect of Henry V's victory at Agincourt remains the execution of a large number of French prisoners during a lull in the battle. By any modern standards a war crime, contemporary apologists for the popular king are inclined to excuse it as a desperate measure, when Henry feared a fresh assault from the French might encourage their captured countrymen to overwhelm their guards, and envelop the English.

Subsequent to Henry's legendary victory, the atrocity did little to tarnish his chivalric reputation, according to contemporary opinion. Indeed, the following year the recently elected Holy Roman Emperor, Sigismund, came to the English court to congratulate him, and entreat Henry not to be too harsh on the humiliated French. It was a high profile meeting between the rising star of European politics – Sigismund then stood at the head of a vast empire – and a ruler who was now widely recognised as Christendom's most accomplished commander courtesy of his triumph at Agincourt. Playing host to such a powerful and esteemed guest was a great propaganda coup for Henry, who honoured Sigismund by initiating him into the Order of the Garter, an elite English chivalric brotherhood. His guest reciprocated by making Henry a member of the Order of the Dragon, a chivalric fraternity Sigismund had founded himself only a few years before.

The English Order has somewhat obscure origins, some suggesting inspiration stretching back as far as Richard I (another English king whose valour blinded most to his brutality) though it was actually founded in the mid-1300s. Similar orders proliferated across late medieval Europe, conscious attempts to harness the theoretical fraternity of chivalric brotherhood for specific causes, deliberate echoes of King Arthur's mythic Round Table. They came with the oaths, ritual and regalia that have made secretive gentlemen's clubs appealing throughout the ages – from the Freemasons to Yale's Skull and Bones society – with the additional duty that members were expected to support their brethren with their swordarm. Sigismund's initiation into the Order of the Garter signified an official endorsement of Henry's claim to the French crown. By initiating Henry as a Draconist, the Hungarian monarch hoped to secure English support in his own struggle against the Ottoman Turks.

The timing of this exchange of honours was far from coincidental. Sigismund was desperate for help. Just as Agincourt had put the English crown in the ascendant in Henry's conflict with France, Nicopolis had left the embattled Sigismund's vast but fragile empire – which embraced not just the Germanic realms of the Holy Roman Empire, but also the kingdoms of Hungary and Bohemia – perilously exposed to the aggressive Ottoman Empire. While some historians have judged Sigismund harshly for striking a deal with Henry in 1416, he might be excused for turning his back on his former French allies. The Emperor needed the best help Christendom could offer, and King Henry and his troops had proven themselves against the elite of France. On a personal level, Sigismund had bitter personal experiences of the limitations of the French military, only narrowly escaping with his life at Nicopolis 20 years before in a debacle most recognised as a consequence of the same arrogance that had cost France so dear at Agincourt.

If Agincourt was suggestive of a medieval Military Revolution, Nicopolis was indicative of many broader flaws in European society of the late Middle Ages, yawning cracks in the walls of medieval culture through which the light of the Renaissance would inexorably shine. The Crusades were emblematic of the best and worst in medieval Europe – illustrative of the astounding bravery and nauseating brutality that characterised the era, of its fervent piety and blind bigotry. Some Islamic militants contend that the war that began when European armies first crossed the Bosporus on their way to Jerusalem over 900 years ago is still being waged today. The 21st-century Taliban pointedly refers to NATO bases in Afghanistan as Crusader castles. But most historians date the end of the Crusades to the fall of the port of Acre in 1291 (described in the first of the Devil's Histories, *God's Assassins*), when the forces of Islam overthrew Europe's last major stronghold in the Middle East. The Battle of Nicopolis, over a century later, was the climax of a Crusade – one however that seldom warrants even a mention in most studies of the Crusades – almost as if the West is in collective denial over the episode, a last traumatic spasm of medievalism best forgotten.

In time-honoured style, this final Crusade was preached by the Papacy, offering special dispensations to those Christian warriors willing to head east, whereby spilling heathen blood in the holy cause would cleanse them of their sins. In this case, however, the call to arms was heard in stereo, as the Catholic Church had been split by the Western Schism of 1376, which resulted in two rival claimants, each denouncing the other as an unholy imposter. The man who took it upon himself to try and get these two rival Popes to sing from the same hymn sheet was Sigismund. Not then yet Holy Roman Emperor, Sigismund was crowned King of Hungary in 1387, taking control of a powerful nation turbulent with civil war. With a clarity of vision shared by few of his contemporaries, the new king recognised that he not only needed to promote unity in Hungary, but a unified Christian front, if Europe was to resist the implacable advance of the Ottoman Empire. Advancing rapidly through the Balkans, it had already swallowed Serbia and Bulgaria.

The next realm in the path of the Turkish juggernaut was Wallachia. Facing the onslaught was Dracula's grandfather, Mircea the Elder, who had been successfully repelling Ottoman incursions since 1390, winning a notable victory against the Muslim invaders at the Battle of Rovine in 1394. The following year, the Wallachian Voivode signed a treaty with Sigismund at Braşov (our touchy Romanian historians Mircea Dogaru and Mihail Zahariade pointedly insist that Voivode signed his anti-Ottoman pact with the Hungarian King 'under conditions of complete equality'.) The only enterprise likely to inspire any kind of unified European action further afield was a holy Crusade, and Sigismund toured Europe drumming up support for the venture, describing the terrible atrocities and indignities suffered by good Christians at the hands of the heathen Turkish hordes. Happily, the Hundred Years War had subsided into a truce in 1389, allowing the Hungarian king to solicit support from the battle-hardened knights of England, France and Burgundy.

While the English, under Henry IV, were largely deaf to the call, crusading fervour took hold among the French and Burgundian nobility, and a substantial force of the cream of Francophone knighthood assembled, pledging to strike back at the Ottoman threat. In the first indication of future problems, however, the Crusade's command fell to young, blue-blooded French and Burgundian lords – rank superseding ability and experience. Ultimate authority was invested in Jean de Nevers, oldest son of the powerful Duke of Burgundy. At 24 years of age, Jean was an untested warrior and not yet even a knight. (This underlines an issue that will echo throughout our story – is power better vested in the hands of a hereditary elite, or won by right of arms? The former promises consistency, the latter ability. Both could create bloody anarchy.)

Taxes were raised from the long-suffering populace to finance the campaign, while the clergy were energetic in soliciting funds from those who couldn't go, but craved the absolution from sin granted to Crusaders. Huge sums were raised, but in the second indication of future disaster – emblematic perhaps of medieval decadence – the Crusader commanders spent lavishly on splendid liveries for their retinues but gave little thought to the expenditure on mundane logistics required for a hard foreign campaign against a formidable foe. It was a parade of pomp and circumstance, a military display of conspicuous consumption aimed at the home crowd. A bespoke suit of armour from one of the famous workshops in Germany and Italy was both a work of art and a masterpiece of state-of-the-art engineering – a hugely expensive investment that could attract admiring glances just as it could deflect hostile weapons – top of the range Armani and a bullet-proof Mercedes rolled into one.

The Duke of Burgundy in particular, seized upon the Crusade as a propaganda opportunity, a chance to put on a dazzling display of wealth and power to impress potential allies and intimidate unfriendly neighbours. In April of 1396, the French and Burgundian force (henceforth referred to as French here, even though the two factions were far from united) set out from Dijon in a fanfare of chivalric magnificence, a cavalcade of the cream of European knighthood, their armour gleaming in the sun. In another ominous detail, suggestive of dark medievalist superstition and vendetta, reports later suggest that Bayezid was soon made aware of their progress. The Duke of Milan had a grudge based upon the terrible treatment his pretty daughter had received at the French court. Accused of bewitching the King by his jealous Queen, she was driven into ignominious exile. In response, the outraged Milanese duke secretly passed on details of French troop movements to the Ottoman Sultan.

The Crusader force made a leisurely progress through Germany towards the Hungarian capital of Buda, their ranks swelling with recruits as they went. Much to the disgust of the Christian holy men accompanying the army, the march resembled a mobile festival, the knights feasting and whoring as they went: hardly behaviour befitting a military pilgrimage. More distressingly for the local populace, the common soldiers, following standard medieval practice, helped themselves to wine and women, leaving a trail of rape and pillage in their wake. In the eyes of many pious observers, this Crusade was already spiritually compromised by the sinful behaviour of its leaders and men. They reached Buda in July, where the French army rendezvoused with the large Hungarian force raised by Sigismund. They were joined by a Venetian contingent providing naval power, and a substantial force of Hospitallers, members of the monastic military Order of St John, who had waged holy war against the Islamic infidel for nearly three centuries.

At fraught conferences held to discuss their campaign plan, Sigismund advised caution. If the Ottoman Sultan Bayezid plans to invade, let him come to us, suggested the Hungarian king, and let him fight upon our terms. Jean de Nevers reacted with disdain. They had not marched this far to cower before the Turks. Bayezid was a coward, his troops no match for the flower of French knighthood who would drive the Ottomans from European soil, before recovering Jerusalem. Sigismund had little choice but to follow his cocksure new allies. Pausing on the way only to collect Sigismund's Wallachian allies, they advanced towards the River Danube, the frontline between Christian territory and Bayezid's new Bulgarian provinces, crossing at the famous gorge known as the Iron Gate. Initial progress through enemy territory was good. The chief problem from Jean's perspective was the absence of resistance. Small garrisons with little loyalty to their new Ottoman masters surrendered swiftly, offering the French little opportunity to demonstrate their knightly prowess. Despite this, Jean de Nevers and

300 of his comrades were knighted after the capture of Vidin.

Friction between the French forces and their Eastern European allies intensified at the siege of Rachowa. Again, after a nominal defence the garrison surrendered. In a classic example of the thin veneer of chivalry, Jean de Nevers's troops refused to recognise the terms offered by Sigismund to the inhabitants, and butchered them, Ottoman Muslim and Bulgarian Christian alike. The next objective on the allied agenda was Nicopolis. This would prove a more challenging proposition – a strategic stronghold with a garrison resolved to resist – resolution strengthened, no doubt, by the fate that had befallen Rachowa. The besieged commander had received a message from the Ottoman Sultan: 'Hang on bravely, and I will look after you. You will see that I will be here like a flash of lightning!' Here the hubris of the Crusaders truly began to bite. Gold that might have been spent on siege engines had been frittered away on fine tents and fancy liveries. Without the equipment to successfully assault Nicopolis, the Crusader advance stalled, obliged to try and starve the defenders into submission.

Bayezid had earned the epithet of 'the thunderbolt' for his proven ability to mobilise his forces with frightening speed and efficiency, a master of medieval blitzkrieg tactics. The Sultan was as good as his word to the governor of Nicopolis. In the final week of September, the Crusaders found themselves caught between the city's garrison and a rapidly-advancing Ottoman relief force. Discussions in the Christian camp over strategy soon became heated. Sigismund, once again, urged caution. He proposed sending Mircea's Wallachian troops out in advance; these were nimble light cavalry and infantry skirmishers who could probe the Ottoman strength and disrupt their formations.

In contrast to his superiors who treated their Eastern Europeans allies with lofty disdain, the French knight Engueurrand de Coucy, a seasoned campaigner who had been sent to accompany Jean de Nevers as his advisor in the hope that his experience might mitigate the rash ebullience of the Crusade's inexperienced leadership, 'willingly kept by him the good companions of Wallachia who were well acquainted with Turkish customs and stratagems'. Jean de Nevers, however, had little interest in the cautious stratagems suggested by Sigismund or Mircea, accusing his allies of trying to cheat the French Crusaders of the glory of leading the charge. In vain, Sigismund attempted to convince the impetuous young Burgundian that the glory came not in landing the first blow, but delivering the knockout punch. In yet another indictment of medieval custom, however, de Coucy and the other French veterans deferred to their feudal superiors. The Christian army took to the field in the reverse of the battle plan suggested by the army's seasoned strategists. The French knights formed the vanguard, champing at the bit to trample the heathen, drunk on the promise of tomorrow's glory and last night's wine. Sigismund's contingent of Hungarians, alongside the German knights and Hospitallers, fell in reluctantly behind, with Mircea's Wallachian warriors bringing up the rear.

The French charged uphill on the morning of 25 September1396, straight at the heart of the Ottoman lines. The Turkish troops scattered before the full force of the chivalric might of the Crusaders, firing arrows and casting javelins before taking to their heels. Yet the French had only encountered the Azabs, Ottoman cannon-fodder, employed by the Turks as raiders and skirmishers. Over-confident Crusaders assumed they were putting the infidel army to flight, until they reached the crest of the hill.

Then the unstoppable force of a knightly charge met the immovable object of the Ottoman infantry elite, in the shape of the Janissaries, dug in behind sharpened stakes and trenches. The result was a bloody, cacophonous stalemate, as French horses were impaled upon wooden points, or broke their legs in the pits, throwing their riders to the ground. It was a stalemate that brought the Christian charge to a shuddering halt. The French knights were now forced to fight on foot, hacking their way through the Turkish defences with axe and sword, relying upon their fine armour to deflect the arrows, maces and scimitars of the Janissaries that beset them from every side.

Then Bayezid closed the jaws of his trap. He unleashed his own heavy cavalry, the mail-clad Sipahi, who loosed a stinging volley of arrows before falling upon the flanks of the embattled French with lances and sabres. Sigismund, overtaken by events, was left with little choice. The battle was running away from him and he launched his own charge to try and relieve his French allies, who were now enveloped, and otherwise doomed. The final act of the battle of Nicopolis was also emblematic, as Bayezid played his final trump card, sending another devastating cavalry charge into the flank of Sigismund's force of Hungarian, German and Hospitaller knights. A well-timed cavalry charge yields glory; an ill-considered one can cost a battle. At Nicopolis, the Crusaders provided a textbook example of bad medieval tactics, of how to waste the devastating hammer blow of a heavy cavalry charge, and then reap the consequences. Those consequences were disastrous.

In testament to the fighting spirit and excellent armour of the

Crusaders, they stubbornly hacked and bludgeoned their way through the Ottoman lines. Yet it was clearly a lost cause, and faced with making a final stand, the French threw themselves upon the mercy of their infidel foe. Some military historians speculate that had Sigismund's force successfully connected with the French knights, then the outcome would have been different and that, despite the failure of their initial charge, the dogged ferocity of the French had pushed the Ottoman line to breaking point. Perhaps... But Sigismund's valiant attempt to relieve his allies failed and, in a telling aspect of the battle, the troops who shattered Sigismund's relief attempt by unleashing a flanking charge were fellow Christians, Serbian lancers, under the despot Stefan Lazarevi. After years of struggle, the Serbs had been forced to accept Ottoman rule following their disastrous defeat at Kosovo in 1389 (this defeat at the 'Field of Crows', at which Serbia lost her independence is still a raw wound in the nation's psyche). It was perhaps testament to the disunity that beset the Crusades, that the final act was concluded with Christians slaying Christians.

As the Crusader army collapsed, Sigismund was dragged from the battlefield by his loyal retainers – his desperate retreat covered by Hungarian crossbowmen – only narrowly escaping on a fishing boat as swarms of Ottoman arrows whistled past the king's ears. What part, if any, Voivode Mircea's Wallachian rearguard played in the battle is difficult to say. They were, at least, well placed to flee the battlefield, to make their way home to prepare for the Ottoman counterattack that must surely follow. If any Christian comfort could be taken from the field at Nicopolis, the Crusader forces had inflicted crippling casualties on Bayezid's army. While it was unquestionably an Ottoman victory, it had been won at a horrific cost, and the Sultan's shattered forces were in no condition to take advantage of their triumph. Bayezid's brutal treatment of his Christian captives may have reflected his frustration at the heavy Ottoman casualties on the battlefield as much as his fury at the summary execution of Turkish prisoners ordered by the French before the battle.

In *Infidels*, his study of 'the conflict between Christendom and Islam 638-2002', the historian Andrew Wheatcroft offers another potential motive for Bayezid's post-battle brutality. In addition to the Ottoman Sultan's frustration and vengeful fury, he suggests, there was method in this mayhem, that 'this formal and ceremonial slaughter was an innovation, and different from the massacres that were commonplace after the capture of cities or in the immediate aftermath of a battle. The mass killings by Crusaders in 1099 had stemmed from an enraged bloodlust after battle. Bayezid by contrast intended a calculated and memorable act of cruelty, which ran counter to the normal customs of war: many of those killed were of noble birth, for whom a ransom would have been paid.' In other words, the Sultan was deliberately employing terror tactics in order to deter future Crusades. It is one of the many respects in which Nicopolis sets the stage for the future career of Vlad Dracula.

In Wheatcroft's estimation 'the Sultan's aim was achieved. The news of Nicopolis and its aftermath quickly became known throughout Europe and it proved very difficult to rouse any interest in the West for a new Crusade.' The sceptics who had condemned the Crusade from the start now seemed grimly prescient, as Paris was swamped in a sea of mourning black, the church bells tolling day and night to commemorate the fallen. Those in a position to say 'I told you so' included men like Albert, Duke of Bavaria and Count of Hainault (and Jean de Nevers's father-in-law) who had forbade his own son from joining the Crusade. Albert had condemned the whole project as vain folly, asking why they should 'seek arms upon a people and country that never did us any damage,' instructing his son to focus his military efforts on quarrels with their European neighbours.

In the decades to come, the kings and dukes of Western Europe would discuss launching another Crusade. As late as 1454, Philip the Good, Duke of Burgundy, hosted the famous Feast of the Pheasant, held to initiate a Crusade against the Ottomans. The event was a sumptuous triumph in culinary and cultural terms, but failed to launch a single ship east against the Turks. In *The Battle for Christendom*, Frank Welsh compares Western Europe's prevailing attitude to that taken by the British Prime Minister Neville Chamberlain in reaction to Nazi aggression in the 1930s, quoting his dismissal of the German seizure of Czech territory in 1938 as 'a quarrel in a faraway country between people of whom we know nothing'. (The same attitude was taken to the appropriation of Romanian territory under the Molotov–Ribbentrop Pact of the following year.)

This is not of course to equate the Ottoman Empire with the Third Reich, so much as to draw parallels between the action taken by the French and British governments towards burgeoning threats to European stability in the 1930s and the early-1400s. Just as Hitler had made his ambitions clear in *Mein Kampf*, Bayezid had promised to overrun Hungary, before conquering Rome, where the Sultan promised that he would plant the banners of Islam before feeding his horse on the altar of St Peter's. In both cases, the prevailing strategy in

Paris and London was to close their collective eyes and hope it all just went away. In the 20th century this approach led inexorably to World War 2 and Chamberlain's name being forever associated with the follies of a policy of appeasement towards a ruthlessly expansionist power.

Bizarrely enough, in the 15th century, however, this policy of blind optimism in the face of imminent disaster actually worked. This was, of course, due rather more to luck than judgement, as Bayezid's plans for European conquest had to be put on hold when he faced an imminent threat to his own eastern borders. Like Genghis Khan two centuries before, the warlord Tamerlane, or Timur the Lame, succeeded in uniting the fearsome Mongol clans of the arid Asian steppes, and led them in a devastating campaign of conquest, leaving a trail of skull pyramids and smouldering cities in his wake. By 1400, his armies reached the eastern borders of the Ottoman Empire, and after an exchange of insulting letters, Bayezid met Tamerlane on the battlefield at Ankara in the summer of 1402. It would be the Thunderbolt's only defeat. Outnumbered and outmanoeuvred, deserted by many of its allies, the Ottoman army was obliterated by Tamerlane's forces.

Bayezid himself was captured shortly afterwards. Accounts differ on the Ottoman Sultan's fate. Some suggest that his Mongol captor treated him with respect. Other accounts describe an ignominious end for the Turkish Sultan. Kept in a cage as a living trophy, Bayezid was obliged to watch as Tamerlane humiliated him, forcing his wife to serve at table naked. Tormented by shame, it is said, the proud Turk dashed his own brains out on the bars of his cage. Whatever the truth, the Ottoman Sultan was dead by 1402, triggering a bitter civil war in the Turkish Empire between rival candidates for the succession. It gave Eastern Europe a vital breathing space, taking the pressure off the mighty Eastern Orthodox metropolis of Byzantium which the Ottomans had been threatening for decades, and allowing Sigismund to lick his wounds and attempt to shore up his brittle European empire against the next crisis.

Mircea the Elder took astute advantage of the situation. His proven leadership against the Ottoman threat had already allowed him to expand the powers of the Wallachian Voivode at the expense of the boyars – the local landholding aristocracy – whose influence kept the realm in a state of perpetual instability. The Turkish incursions that followed Nicopolis underlined a need for unity which allowed Mircea to elevate the status of Wallachian Voivode from nominal leader of a loose confederation of local nobles during wartime, to that of nascent royalty. In the process, he laid down the legal and administrative framework that established Wallachia as a true nation, an achievement that helped earn him the epithet Mircea the Great, in some eyes the father of the Romanian state. In the wake of the Battle of Ankara, Mircea turned the tables and attempted to play kingmaker in the fractured Ottoman Empire, offering support to two of the warring Turkish factions, backed by a marriage alliance.

The Voivode was now playing out of his league and had backed the wrong horse. By 1413, Sultan Mehmet I crushed Mircea's favoured candidates for the Ottoman throne and secured overall control. With intimidating speed, the formidable Ottoman war machine was ready once more to turn its attentions upon its neighbours. The legacy of Nicopolis now returned to haunt Mircea. With little prospect of help from his former comrade-in-arms Sigismund, let alone assistance from the kings of Western Europe, the Voivode was now exhausted and alone. He had ruled his turbulent realm for nearly three decades, which must certainly have taken its toll on the venerable Voivode. In 1417, the fatigued ruler finally gave up the fight, agreeing to pay the Turks an annual tribute in return for peace and thereby effectively recognising his realm's subordination to the Ottoman Empire. Mircea died the following year.

In the decades to follow, his legacy would become the subject of a bitter struggle as his heirs competed for the throne, soliciting support from both the Hungarians and Turks, who in turn hoped to control the strategic Wallachian realm. They did not follow the Western European rule of primogeniture – whereby the oldest male heir inherits titles and property. Local custom demanded only that the heir be a male descendant, 'of the male royal bone' in the colourful terminology of the era. Mircea had several sons, only one of whom was born in wedlock, the rest offspring of courtesans and mistresses. The contemporary Greek chronicler Michael Ducas described Dracula's father as 'one of the many bastard sons of Mircea, the profligate voivode of Wallachia'. While Mircea's 'legitimate' heir would fade into the background, other limbs of his family tree would become entangled in a dynastic feud every bit as savage as the civil war that threatened to shatter the Ottoman Empire.

***

The long shadow of the Battle of Nicopolis fell over the life of Vlad the Impaler from an early age. His tutor at Sighisoara was a veteran of the battle, and the young Vlad must have heard tales of the disastrous battle, though no doubt given a Wallachian spin, just as the French had blamed the Eastern Europeans for the disaster, and Sigismund loomed large as a patron and mentor in the life of Vlad's father and namesake. As a consequence of the pact Mircea the Elder made with Sigismund at Braşov in 1395, Dracula's father was sent to the Hungarian court. Whether the young Wallachian went as Sigismund's protégé to enjoy the benefits of Hungarian hospitality or as a hostage to ensure that Mircea honoured the alliance isn't clear. It probably wasn't clear cut then either, though at the very least, Sigismund certainly hoped that educating the boy at the Hungarian court would create powerful cultural bonds between Dracula's father and the Christian cause. Mircea's son enjoyed the privileges of an education as a European noble. He trained to fight as a knight and was tutored in the art of government, witnessing the day-to-day running of the realm, accompanying Sigismund on his endless round of diplomatic tours from city to city as he attempted to unify a Christendom fractured by religious rivalry and dynastic conflicts.

Sigismund's primary power base in Hungary represented something of a crossroads between Eastern and Western Europe. 'The impression I had was that we were leaving the West and entering the East,' notes Jonathan Harker in Stoker's *Dracula*, passing through the Hungarian capital of Budapest on his way to Transylvania. Hungary was a Catholic country, unlike many of its neighbours like Wallachia, whose citizens were Eastern Orthodox Christians. Despite favouring the traditional moustache of the Eastern European warrior, many image-conscious medieval Hungarian nobles followed the fashions set in Paris and imported armour from the prestigious workshops of Italy and Germany. Only subtle details separated the Eastern European elite on the battlefield from their Western counterparts, such as favouring local trapezoid-shaped shields, or curved sabres over the traditional straight-edged sword of the clichéd knight. The rank and file that took to the field under the Hungarian banner were more distinctive, living reminders of the Magyar nation's roots as nomadic horsemen from the eastern steppes. A 15th-century French chronicler described typical Hungarian cavalry as carrying 'small bows of horn and tendons and crossbows with which they shoot, and they have good horses and are less armoured and light and do not descend happily on foot to fight'.

Some Romanian historians have suggested that Vlad senior found life as a courtier to Sigismund tiresome, though this may just reflect anti-Hungarian bias on their part. While a life of luxury compared to the existence endured by many, Sigismund's court was modest compared to the likes of the French, whose elite often looked down their collective noses at their eastern counterparts (a Hungarian delegation to England reported with puritanical dismay on the flamboyant styles favoured by the local aristocracy). By 1433, when he was elected Holy Roman Emperor, Sigismund ruled over a huge realm bordered by France to the west, Denmark to the north, Italy to the south and Poland to the east. Whilst in theory he literally owned Central Europe, in practice, revenues from Sigismund's sprawling, fragile empire scarcely covered the crippling expenses of maintaining his lavish travelling court, where keeping up appearances was a vital aspect of projecting power and status. The Emperor spent almost as much time securing funds from sympathetic fellow monarchs as soliciting support for his vision of a unified European front against the Ottoman threat.

Personal magnetism was a vital trait if Sigismund was to succeed, and there has been a tendency among historians to overlook this remarkable monarch or even write him out of the history books altogether. In *The Battle for Christendom*, Frank Welsh attempts to redress the balance: 'His portrait shows an impressive eagle beak of a nose, but his imperial temper was matched by a devastating charm; women were overwhelmed, a fact of which he took full advantage, but he had also the politician's gift of appearing to dedicate himself to other people's problems – and frequently did so. He could unaffectedly chat with tradesmen, and flirt with their wives or visit guests in their rooms for an early-morning chat, but it was foolish to take advantage of Sigismund's affability. His physical strength and endurance, inherited from his mother, had brought him through thirty years of wars and tournaments, but his most formidable characteristic was his single-minded ability to concentrate his energies, disregarding whatever other problems pestered him.'

Sigismund's energies were concentrated on the building Turkish threat on his south-eastern border, now focused upon the buffer state of Wallachia. Dracula's father represented a small but important playing piece in this crucial game which could decide the fate of Christendom. After Mircea the Elder's death, Wallachia had descended into civil war, comparable with the conflict that had consumed the Ottoman Empire subsequent to Bayezid's demise. As Vlad senior came of age in Sigismund's court during the 1420s, the Wallachian voivodeship changed hands numerous times in an increasingly bitter struggle between Mircea's kin, with Ottoman incursions throwing the realm deeper into chaos. The young Wallachian's thoughts increasingly turned to his own claim to the throne, and to when Sigismund might give his blessing to a campaign to claim his heritage. The Emperor deferred. With his own problems in suppressing religious and political dissent at home, Sigismund preferred to sit back and see what happened in Wallachia.

In frustration, with middle age approaching, Vlad finally deserted Sigismund's court in 1423, in the hope of securing support for his claim from the King of Poland. But he was intercepted at the border and escorted back to Buda. It was now clear to the astute Holy Roman Emperor however that he could not keep this restless war-dog chained forever, and that perhaps now it was time to loosen the leash. More importantly the current Voivode was showing increasing signs of favouring peace with the Ottomans over continued resistance. In 1431, Sigismund finally dispatched Vlad to the eastern front, charging him with guarding the border between Transylvania and Wallachia at the strategic fortified town of Sighisoara. It would prove a momentous year in Vlad's career. That same year his second son was born, and he was initiated into a society that would define his identity throughout history. His son, of course, is the subject of our book. The society was the Order of the Dragon, the organisation that would lend him the epithet Dracul, his faction the Draculestis, and his son the title Dracula.

Vlad senior took his vows in Nuremberg, henceforth adopting the Order's dragon insignia as his own, the symbol of the new Wallachian dynasty he planned to establish, taking on the name Vlad Dracul. The enthusiasm with which Vlad senior embraced this new honour is understandable. The chivalric orders that sprung up across medieval Europe thrived upon their exclusivity – members liked to be painted wearing the regalia just as modern royalty are photographed in military uniforms and medals. Becoming a Draconist not only signified Sigismund's support for his claim, but put Vlad among a very select crowd of the movers and shakers of 15th-century Eastern Europe, most of them royalty. He had arrived. From Sigismund's point of view, initiating Vlad bound this up-and-coming warlord to his cause, the sacred vows Vlad took compelling him to support the Hungarian crown against the foes of Christendom. Significantly, Sigismund had founded the Order of the Dragon as a specific response to the disaster at Nicopolis.

The curious cultural connection between the Order of the Dragon and one of Gothic fiction's most tenacious villains has made it the subject of particular study. The Order was only one of dozens of similar organisations established throughout the Middle Ages. It was, however, unusual in taking such a provocative motif. Orders of Saint George were comparatively common (an organisation of that name, founded in Hungary in the 14th century probably formed the prototype for Sigismund's order) yet a society that took the saint's serpentine foe as its emblem does, at least in retrospect, appear ambivalent. Look closely at the Draconist symbol, and the dragon in question is marked by a wound in the shape of a cross and is strangling itself with its own tail. But those unlucky enough to face either Vlad Dracul or his son Vlad Dracula on unfriendly terms might be forgiven for missing such details of the heraldic symbols emblazoned on their shields and surcoats.

The significance of the Order of the Dragon, particularly as it relates to Vlad Dracul and his son, has inspired differing interpretations among historians and Dracula scholars. Some suggest that as Dracul's son became Dracula, membership was handed from father to son, though this is dubious. Even more dubious is the supposition that one of the Order's ceremonial capes was black, inspiring Bram Stoker to equip his fictional vampire with his most famous fashion statement (standard regalia for Draconists was in fact red with a green mantle). On a broader historical level, in *Hungary and the Fall of Eastern Europe*, David Nicolle highlights the Order of the Dragon as evidence of Sigismund's desperation, a tacit admission by the Holy Roman Emperor that he was just a minor figure, while other historians identify the Order as evidence of Sigismund's power and influence, his ability to bind powerful figures to his own agenda. The redoubtable Dracula scholars Florescu and McNally cite Vlad Dracul's initiation as evidence that he had converted from the Eastern Orthodox faith of his fathers to Catholicism during his apprenticeship at Sigismund's court.

Other historians have taken the large number of inductees of the Eastern Orthodox faith to indicate that the Order of the Dragon was an ecumenical fraternity, blind to internal Christian schisms. There is powerful evidence for this. Among the first inductees at the Order's foundation in 1408 was Stefan Lazarevi. The Serbian despot was one of several early members whose fidelity to the Eastern Orthodox faith is difficult to dispute. Other aspects of Stefan's loyalty might be more open to question. He was the same Serbian leader who had commanded the cavalry charge against Sigismund at Nicopolis, shattering the Christian Crusade in 1396. His initiation as a Draconist just twelve years later is indicative of several points. One is Sigismund's pragmatism. In the messy politics of 14th-century Eastern Europe the Emperor's capacity for forgiveness was one of his strengths. Another is the significance of personalities. Stefan's loyalty had been to Bayezid, a ruler he liked and respected, not the Ottoman Empire. Our story is very much one of personal loyalty and animosity, a grand drama where a notable number of the protagonists had enjoyed the opportunity to literally stare each other in the eye.

Vlad Dracul's years at Sigismund's court led him to rub shoulders with many of Eastern Europe's most remarkable and powerful individuals. Florescu and McNally suggest that his instalment as a Draconist at Nuremberg facilitated a meeting with the man who would dominate the arena for the next 25 years, John Hunyadi (though in *Vlad the Impaler*, M. J. Trow argues that their paths crossed as early as 1408-9). Hunyadi would become a legend in his own lifetime, dubbed the White Knight of Wallachia, Eastern Europe's equivalent to *El Cid*, the Castilian knight revered for warring against the Muslims in 11th-century Spain and later immortalised in the 1961 Hollywood epic starring Charlton Heston. Like Vlad, John Hunyadi was a Vlach born in Transylvania, perhaps a few years before the future Voivode. Hunyadi was a cosmopolitan character compared to Vlad, who, for good or ill, remained true to his Wallachian roots.

We can't be sure of the identity of Vlad Dracul's mother – most likely also a Vlach – while Hunyadi's mother may well have been Magyar, and Hunyadi himself certainly chose a Hungarian as a bride. (It is perhaps a reflection of differing attitudes to women that Wallachian women remain such shadowy figures – seldom more than anonymous wives, mothers or mistresses – while Hungarian noblewomen played pivotal roles at a number of crucial points in the kingdom's history. While the small concessions made to sexual equality in Western Europe during the Middle Ages are surely laudable, scheming wives and ambitious mothers added an extra layer of chaos to politics, becoming leading protagonists in dynastic struggles – not least in Hungary – and giving ample ammunition to those theologians who preached that permitting women authority went against the will of God.)

Hunyadi, whilst a noble, had a more modest lineage than Vlad and he does not appear to have been initiated as a Draconist, though Sigismund rewarded Hunyadi's father for loyal service on the battlefield with the awe-inspiring Transylvanian fortress at Hunedoara, which John duly inherited. Hunedoara Castle's imposing Gothic character has led a few to refer to it as Castle Dracula, and others to misidentify it as the location where Vlad the Impaler was imprisoned. It certainly has a dark history, but one that betrays the iron running through Hunyadi's soul. The 60-foot well in the castle courtyard was dug by Turkish prisoners-of-war who were promised their freedom upon its completion – it took them nine long years, after which they were instead cast from the castle battlements to their deaths. While it is easy to see John Hunyadi as a heroic figure, he was very much a man shaped by troubled times.

There may also be something timeless in the characters of the ruthless and fascinating personages that make up the cast in the brutal drama of the Ottoman Wars which form the backdrop to the story of Vlad the Impaler. The 20th-century philosopher Sir Isaiah Berlin came up with a theory regarding what he described as 'borderlands syndrome' to explain the charismatic but unstable political figures that have made such an impact on history. Taking such leaders as Hitler, Napoleon and Stalin, Berlin speculates that their magnetic personae and fanatical views owe something to originating 'from outside the society that they led, or at any rate from its edges, the outer marches'. The philosopher speculates that this borderlands syndrome has a tendency to create 'men of fiery vision, whether noble or degraded, idealistic or perverted,' leaders who develop 'either exaggerated sentiment or contempt for the dominant majority, or else over-intense admiration or even worship of it [...] which leads both to unusual insights, and – born of overwrought sensibilities – a neurotic distortion of the facts'.

It's a description that fits the men of blood and iron who occupy the pages that follow – none more than Vlad the Impaler. Unusually for an up-and-coming noble of the era Hunyadi did not dedicate his growing wealth and power to personal ambition. While Vlad Dracul's eyes remained focused on his inheritance in Wallachia throughout his life, Hunyadi adopted the mantle of a Crusader who shared his patron Sigismund's broader vision: his single-minded quest to drive the Ottomans out of Europe. These differing priorities would colour the volatile relationship between Hunyadi and Vlad II. It would also impact upon the interaction between Hunyadi and Dracul's son, Dracula, though the Impaler's obsessions came much closer to those of the White Knight. Ironically, the two 15th-century Eastern European warlords whose ideals most closely followed the vows taken by initiates into the Order of the Dragon are the two whose status as authentic Draconists is most open to question.

John Hunyadi served his military apprenticeship in a number of local conflicts, most notably the Hussite Wars beginning in 1420, which divided Sigismund's Bohemian kingdom. In another sign of the

VLAD THE IMPALER

Medieval Military Revolution, the humble rebel army of the Hussite heretics successfully thwarted more powerful cavalry armies through the skilled use of early firearms and war-wagons. War-wagons were mobile, fortified platforms for handgunners and crossbowmen that could be employed in both defence and attack – in effect, horse-drawn tanks. Hunyadi learnt from his foe, employing Hussite tactics and mercenaries after Sigismund successfully brokered a peace in Bohemia. John Hunyadi himself served as a mercenary in Italy in the early-1430s, where constant feuding between the wealthy city-states ensured lucrative employment for talented soldiers-of-fortune.

In Italy, where mercantile profit was the bottom line, mercenary captains were known as condottieri – literally 'contractors' – success resting on mastering not just the art, but also the business of war. John Hunyadi came back from his foreign ventures a wealthy man, and soon made himself indispensable to Sigismund, not just as a military commander, but a banker, loaning his perpetually-insolvent liege large sums. These loans were often ultimately repaid in land grants, slowly making John Hunyadi one of the most powerful lords in Hungary. Beginning in the late-1430s, John Hunyadi led – and often financed – Christian forces that took the battle to the Turks. He suffered some serious setbacks, but also achieved some remarkable victories – often employing the tactics he had learnt in the Hussite Wars – triumphs which were greeted with great enthusiasm across Europe, used to hearing only bad news from the east since the dark days of Nicopolis.

***

Sigismund stationed Vlad Dracul on the Transylvanian border in 1431 as an implicit threat to the current Voivode of Wallachia, Alexandru Aldea, as much as a deterrent to raids into his own territory by Turkish troops. Holding the claimant to a contested foreign throne has long been a trump card in the game of international politics. Such a card might be held as a threat over the foreign nation in question, promising civil war, quietly disposed of to please a foreign faction, or played in the hope of placing a friendly monarch on the foreign throne. In 1434, Sigismund chose the latter option, as Alexandru's health was failing, promising yet more political turbulence in Wallachia. After years waiting in the wings, Vlad Dracul was given Imperial backing to invade, and gathered a force of mercenaries and sympathetic rebel Wallachians, and an arsenal – including cannons and firearms – from the industrious weapon-smiths of Transylvania.

After repelling Turkish forces determined to impose their own candidate and defeating boyars loyal to the rival Danesti faction, in December of 1436, Dracul entered Tîrgovişte as Vlad II, Voivode of Wallachia. Once he had taken the throne, now in his mid-40s, Vlad Dracul's problems were only just beginning. Wallachia was far from stable. The feud between his own Draculesti faction and the Danestis, who also claimed a bloodline from Mircea the Elder, was far from settled, and Vlad set about hacking at the roots of the Danesti family tree with a vengeance. The Ottoman Empire remained a looming threat on his border, and the treaties with Turks signed by his father Mircea the Elder still hung over his head. Meanwhile, after Vlad II had enjoyed his new throne for just a year, his patron Sigismund died in December of 1437, leaving a worrying political vacuum in Hungary.

Just months later, in the first of a series of political U-turns, Vlad Dracul travelled to the Turkish city of Bursa and, in a ceremony of some pomp and circumstance, paid fealty to the Ottoman Sultan Murad II. He agreed to honour the deals his father made, continuing the annual tribute Mircea had promised to the Turks. It was, perhaps, an offer he couldn't refuse – payment of protection money unavoidable if his fledgling regime were to survive as his Christian allies looked increasingly unstable. Dracul's actions the following year are more difficult to excuse. In the hope of placating the Ottomans, Vlad II undertook an action that didn't so much overlook the pledges he had made before Sigismund in Nuremberg seven years before, as trample them into the dust under heavy hooves. In the summer of 1438, the Wallachian Voivode joined Murad II on a raid into Transylvania, burning and looting through the realm as far as his old home in Sighisoara. Terrified Transylvanian civilians tried to surrender to Vlad in preference to his new Turkish ally, hopeful that his vaunted Draconist vows might at least move the Voivode to mercy towards Christian prisoners.

A pure pragmatist might see some virtue in Dracul's decision to throw in his lot with the Turkish Sultan. Murad had not only seen off all of the rival claimants to the Ottoman throne after the death of Mehmet I in 1421, but made good all of the damage done to the Empire by Tamerlane. He is widely credited with throwing the Turkish war-machine up a gear with a series of vigorous military reforms. Most significantly, he helped transform the Ottoman janissary corps – already a fearsome institution of indoctrinated infantry – into perhaps the first true modern army, complete with firearms and uniforms. John Hunyadi wasn't the only military visionary with a keen eye for burgeoning trends on the 15th-entury battlefield. Pragmatism aside, however, Hunyadi must have felt Vlad Dracul's stab in the back to the Christian cause particularly acutely. Paying tribute to the Turks was one thing, but joining them on an orgy of destruction, sending thousands of both Hunyadi and Dracul's Vlach countrymen to the Turkish slave-markets quite another. To make matters worse, the defence of Transylvania had become Hunyadi's direct responsibility – something Murad certainly knew – making Vlad's part in the raid a direct affront to the White Knight. Things were in danger of getting personal...

In the wake of Sigismund's death two years before, John Hunyadi had found himself in the role of kingmaker – desperate to suppress the anarchy brewing in Hungary by establishing a stable monarchy, while keeping the Turkish threat at bay. After several years of civil strife, in 1440, he established the pious, warlike young Polish King Vladislaus on the Hungarian throne, a monarch who Hunyadi felt confident had the spine to meet the Ottoman threat head on. With the position in Hungary finally stabilised, Hunyadi returned to his life's mission, and began planning his next assault upon the Turks. In 1441, in a meeting Vlad Dracul had no doubt dreaded, Hunyadi visited the Wallachian Voivode at Tîrgoviște and demanded he remember the vows he had made as a Draconist. In an echo of the situation when Dracul had been posted to Sighisoara by Sigismund, Hunyadi had installed the Danestis, rivals for Vlad's crown, in Transylvania, as an implicit threat. Faced with either honouring his Draconist vows or the treaties he had signed with the Turks, Dracul stalled. When Murad led an Ottoman army through Wallachia the following year to attack Hungary, he neither opposed nor joined them.

Such fence-sitting was a high risk strategy with few obvious returns, and it would sow the seeds of Vlad Dracul's eventual demise. In what became something of a pattern for Hunyadi, after suffering a defeat at Sântimbru on 18 March, 1442, five days later the Hungarian warlord, now officially Voivode of Transylvania, turned the tables on the Turks, inflicting the first of a series of crippling blows to the Ottoman invaders. The defeats sent shockwaves through the western provinces of Murad's Empire, particularly his new Christian vassals, who might now be tempted to reconsider accepting Ottoman sovereignty. So the Sultan sent for the two such leaders he considered most likely to defect to the Hungarians. These were Vlad Dracul and George Branković who had inherited the throne of Serbia from his uncle, the Draconist Stefan Lazarević in 1427. Like Vlad, Branković had tried to placate both Hunyadi and Murad, and as a consequence wasn't trusted by either.

The details of the meeting between Vlad Dracul and Murad at the

Turkish city of Gallipoli in 1442 are confused. Most suggest the Wallachian went willingly when summoned, others that he was captured by some sort of ruse. Branković turned down the invitation point blank, raising the drawbridges of his capital at Belgrade when the Turkish delegation arrived. However Vlad made the long journey east, accompanied by his two youngest sons. When the Turks asked why he hadn't brought all three of his sons, as instructed by the Sultan, Dracul lied and insisted that his eldest – named Mircea after Dracul's father – had recently died. This suggests that the Voivode was at least suspicious that his summons involved more than friendly discussions. Such suspicions were confirmed when the delegation reached Gallipoli and Vlad and his sons were put in chains. Suggestions that Vlad may have willingly sent his two sons to Turkey as hostages seem improbable, as the Voivode himself remained Murad's reluctant guest for nearly a year.

Vlad Dracul must have seethed with frustration from captivity as news came back to the Ottoman court of events in Wallachia. History repeated itself as John Hunyadi gave his blessing and military support to the Danesti pretender, Basarab II, to take advantage of the Voivode's weakness and claim the crown for himself, just as Sigismund had unleashed Dracul on his predecessor six years before. Happily for Vlad, his son Mircea was no pushover, anti-Hungarian sentiment was strong in Wallachia and many boyars remained loyal to the Draculesti regime. Inevitably, civil war ensued. Murad finally released Dracul to join the conflict in 1443 where he successfully reclaimed his throne from Basarab, but not before the Sultan obliged Vlad to swear upon both the Bible and Koran that he would henceforth be a loyal Ottoman vassal. Murad also increased the annual tribute Wallachia must pay and made the country subject to the Devşirme, whereby a human levy of 500 young Wallachian boys had to be sent each year, to convert to Islam and train as Janissaries or to serve in the Ottoman administration.

Vlad Dracul was also obliged to leave his own two sons behind as hostages to guarantee that this time he would abide by his promises. Again, history was repeating itself. Just as Dracul had been obliged to serve his adolescence at the Christian court of Sigismund as guarantor of his father's good behaviour, so his two young sons would find themselves the reluctant guests of Murad's Muslim court, to be tutored as the Ottoman Sultan thought best. Just as Sigismund hoped that the opportunity to educate Dracul might predispose him to loyalty (with decidedly mixed results), so the Sultan believed Turkish tutors would imbue his vulnerable young captives with Islamic values. Their position at the Ottoman court was ambivalent, a curious existence which hung between the duties imposed upon them by their new tutors, opulent Turkish luxury, and the omnipresent threat of torture or execution, should political expedience demand it. The brothers spent their formative years trapped almost literally between the terrors of the torture chamber and the pleasures of the harem – one would ultimately yield to the seductive lure of pleasure, the other to the siren song of terror.

They were educated as royalty alongside the Sultan's own sons and a small 'ex-pat' community of European boys, 'guests' of the Ottoman who must surely have clung together in this new world of unfamiliar customs and foreign tongues. The threat of violence was omnipresent. Two of George Brankovi's sons were blinded in 1441 while enjoying such Ottoman hospitality (which may well explain his reluctance to accompany Vlad Dracul the following year). Happily for the members of this curious clique of frightened young Eastern European nobles, isolated from their families – these strangers in a strange land – they had an older companion to look up to as a mentor. George Kastrioti was one of four Albanian princes taken as hostages by Bayezid decades ago. The Ottomans saw the older Albanian as a good influence on the youthful captives. He'd voluntarily converted to Islam and served in the Ottoman army with such success that the Turks dubbed him Iskander Bey – Lord Alexander – comparing him with the legendary Macedonian warlord Alexander the Great.

The reactions of the two young Wallachian princes to their confinement differed, reflecting not just their respective ages, but also different temperaments. Vlad was entering adolescence when he entered Turkish captivity, while Radu was several years his junior, making him more receptive to his Islamic tutors. While Radu would convert to Islam, Vlad was a less co-operative pupil, a wilful, volatile, even violent youth who some even say frightened his Turkish tutors. Time would prove that Vlad's attitude was more than mere teenage temper tantrums. His brother was growing up to be a very good-looking young man, earning himself the nickname Radu the Handsome. The Wallachian's good looks did not go unnoticed, catching the eye of Murad's son Mehmet. One account describes Radu hiding in the palace gardens from the amorous attentions of the bisexual future Sultan. In time, the handsome young Wallachian would become more amenable to Mehmed's advances, becoming one of his closest companions.

Meanwhile, events far to the west were moving apace, with consequences that threatened the lives of Vlad and Radu. In the wake of his successes against the Ottomans in Transylvania and Wallachia,

John Hunyadi made ready to take the battle to the Turks. In 1443, with his sovereign King Vladislaus, he assembled a multinational anti-Ottoman force the likes of which had not been seen since the heady days of Nicopolis. As before, Hunyadi reminded Vlad Dracul of his Draconist vows, demanding he bring a Wallachian army to join this new Crusade. To strengthen his argument, Hunyadi had the Pope personally absolve Dracul of any vows he had made to the Turkish Sultan. Once again, the Wallachian Voivode prevaricated, finally sending his son Mircea at the head of a small cavalry force. Faced with alienating either the Hungarians or Ottomans, he had made another unhappy compromise, one which he knew put the lives of his hostage sons in very real danger. One can only guess at the dread Dracula and Radu felt when they learnt of this new development, every mile the Christian army travelled bringing the prospect of death or mutilation closer to the two young Wallachian hostages.

Whilst it had received the appropriate Papal blessing, Hunyadi's expedition is seldom referred to as a Crusade but rather became known as the Long Campaign. The concept of Crusading had become heavily devalued by cynical overuse, and few Western warriors answered the call. This was perhaps its strength, as Hunyadi's victories demonstrated that Eastern Europe could engage with and defeat the might of the Ottoman Empire without assistance. Using his Hussite war-wagons, Hunyadi inflicted a series of crushing defeats upon Ottoman opponents, striking deep into Turkish territory in the Balkans. At the battle of Niš in November of 1442, he secured an unexpected ally when Iskander Bey and the Albanians under his command deserted the Ottoman army to join Hunyadi's forces, contributing to yet another Christian victory. After capturing Sofia and scattering an army commanded by Sultan Murad himself, in February of 1443, Hunyadi's advance slowly ground to a halt, as the bitter winter weather began to take a heavy toll.

Meanwhile, Iskander Bey took his small force of 300 Albanian horsemen back towards his ancestral homeland, riding hard to outdistance the news of his betrayal of his former masters. When he reached the Albanian fortress of Krujë, Iskander used a forged letter from the Sultan to gain entrance. Once inside the gates, his men fell upon the Ottoman garrison. The Turkish crescent was torn from the flagpole and replaced with his emblem of the double-headed eagle. In a significant detail, he had all of his Turkish prisoners impaled. When reports reached the Ottomans of their former hero's brutal treachery, it no doubt had the desired effect of sending a shudder of horror through the court. There may well have been one resident whose reaction was altogether different. Some have suggested that Dracula developed his sadistic taste for impalement from the Turks during his early years of confinement. Others insist that the Turks later emulated the Wallachian in adopting this vile form of execution. It seems at least as likely that the seed for Vlad's infamy as the Impaler were planted when he saw the effect that his erstwhile Albanian mentor's atrocity had upon his Ottoman captors.

Iskander Bey renounced Islam and would henceforth be known by the westernised version of his name, Skanderbeg, uniting Albanian resistance to the Ottoman occupying forces under his eagle banner. His subsequent, hugely successful guerilla campaign against the Turks would lead the Pope himself to style Skanderbeg an 'Athlete of Christ', a title that was also bestowed upon the Albanian's new ally John Hunyadi in recognition of his tireless campaigning against the Muslim threat to Europe's eastern borders. It's an awkward term to modern ears – resonant of the unconvincing humility of those sportsmen who credit their triumphs to divine favour – yet in the 15th century it carried true weight. As the Crusading ideal had withered on the vine, those few men still willing to put aside local feuds in order to dedicate themselves to the defence of Christian Europe were held in high regard.

Conversely, of course, they were demonised by the Ottomans, and Skanderbeg and Hunyadi were styled murderous villains by many Muslims and cast as the boogeymen Turkish mothers used to frighten their children into behaving. Only three warlords were officially honoured as Athletes of Christ – in addition to Hunyadi and Skanderbeg, the Moldavian ruler Stephen the Great – Dracula's cousin, who we shall encounter later. The title always eluded the Impaler himself, though as we shall see, the dread he stoked in Ottoman hearts easily eclipsed that engendered by Hunyadi or Skanderbeg. For now, however, we have left the young Vlad Dracula, at just thirteen years of age, grimly awaiting the violent fate that must surely await him and his brother Radu in the wake of their father's treachery, his teenaged mind seething with powerful emotions and dark thoughts that he could not openly express in front of his Ottoman 'hosts', but which would find fierce expression in the years to come...

CHAPTER IV

An Apprenticeship in Terror

You don't have to be a Freudian analyst to conclude that the experiences of Dracula's youth at the court of the Turkish Sultan would have had a seismic impact on his adult character. Long before psychiatrists were blaming adult misdemeanours on childhood trauma, basic common knowledge indicated that early experiences could leave indelible impressions on our personalities thereafter. This was why Sigismund invited Mircea the Elder to send his son Vlad Dracul to be educated at court, and why in turn Sultan Murad assembled his colourful collection of adolescent Eastern European princes. They were both hostages and potential protégés. Though as the career of Skanderbeg vividly illustrates, such attempts at shaping young minds could backfire in spectacular fashion. You might almost look upon the fates of the Christian princes kept in opulent confinement at the Ottoman court as the results of practical experiments testing the enduring debate over 'nature versus nurture'.

The elder Vlad seems to have suffered no known ill-effects as a consequence of playing a part in Sigismund's peripatetic court, whose travels stretched from Mitteleuropa to Rome. Indeed, it provided him with a cosmopolitan education he wouldn't have received, had he stayed within the provincial borders of Wallachia. A charitable interpretation of his later behaviour is that, in giving his sons to the Sultan, Vlad II may have thought that he was broadening his sons' horizons in a way for which they would one day be grateful. But in actuality their experience was very different: the Ottoman court was an alien place, and the culture shock of two young boys who had never set eyes on a Turk before can only be imagined.

And yet Radu seems to have been seduced by the Ottoman culture in a way that could never be claimed of his second elder brother. This seduction may have been quite literal (see previous chapter). The Ottoman reputation for homosexual behaviour has long been a persistent factor in Western writings and, even in the Empire's dying days during World War 1, T. E. Lawrence, fabled British military champion of the Arabs, claimed to experience the rapaciousness of the Empire when arrested on a spying mission in the town of Deraa by Turkish overlord Hacim Bey. According to his book of philosophical memoirs, *The Seven Pillars of Wisdom*, he was restrained, stripped and molested by the Bey and his men: 'I bore it for a little while, till he got too beastly; and then jerked my knee into him.' Over the ensuing decades, historical researchers have questioned the veracity of Lawrence of Arabia's account. According to them, heavy implications of his own masochistic homosexuality lend a suspect hue to the beating that supposedly followed, not least the passage that runs: 'I remembered smiling idly at him, for a delicious warmth, probably sexual, was swelling through me.' But whether in actuality or as an erotic fantasy, Lawrence was responding to that universal reputation of the Ottoman Turks as reinforced over the centuries.

Rather than resulting from any impious tolerance of perversion, the alleged sexual antics of the Ottomans were probably the result of a cultural pragmatism. Born into an empire that was the hub of power in the Islamic world, a young man's sense of worldly entitlement and his developing sexual feelings were circumscribed by the holy edicts of koranic culture. Their young female contemporaries may have been much desired, but the prohibitions against premarital coitus, and the devalued status of a woman known to have given herself to a man outside marriage, tended to divert the sexual impulse in a number of ways.

Some have challenged the Ottoman reputation for homosexuality as a myth born of Christian propaganda. If it is a mere myth, it is a notably tenacious one. In 1475, chronicles from Moldavia mention a raid upon Crimea by Ottoman forces where 150 young male prisoners were taken, doomed to fall victim to 'the filthy sodomy of the whoring Turk'. The English author and adventurer Thomas Sherley was captured by the Ottomans and held prisoner between 1603 and 1605. 'For their Sodommerye they use it soe publiquely and impudentlye as an honest Christian woulde shame to companye his wyffe as they do with their buggeringe boys,' he later wrote of his experiences of Turkish society (from an admittedly notably unsympathetic stance).

If homosexuality was tacitly tolerated in the Ottoman Empire, it would inevitably find most expression in all-male institutions such as the army, particularly the Janissaries, who were forbidden to take wives. In the mid-1700s, arguments over a particularly handsome young tellak (tellaks were bathhouse masseurs who also served as rent-boys) between two Janissary regiments threatened to descend into open warfare, until the Sultan settled the matter by having the tellak hanged. The threat of sexual violence was sometimes employed by Christian commanders to try and strengthen the resolve of their troops when fighting Ottoman foes – its usefulness as pre-battle propaganda perhaps another reason for the resilience of this particular rumour.

According to the author Parker Rossman, Sultan Mehmet II used the promise of homosexual conquest to motivate his own forces. 'The Sultan inspired his troops to more conquests by promising them beautiful boys, and in each captured city he gave the sons of middle-class parents to his troops, left the lower class children to do the work, and kept the sons and daughters of the aristocracy for his own pleasure and purposes. He has been described as a *"pederast heroique"* who celebrated his conquests in bed, and who spent most of his time in the company of boys under seventeen – except for his nights in the harem fathering children. As gifts to Muslim rulers in Africa and Asia he would often send as many as fifty young European boys at a time.'

In *The Jewel in the Lotus, A Historical Survey of the Sexual Culture of the East*, author Allen Edwardes relates a particularly grisly tradition of battlefield sexual violence by the Ottomans manifest in 19th-century conflicts with the Russians, writing that 'at the battles of Kars (Crimea) and Plevna (Russo-Turkish war) [Russian troops] got an unpleasant taste of the Bashi-Bazook [raiders who took over from the Azabs as the skirmishers in Ottoman armies] whose procedure on killing a man was to take full sexual advantage of the anal spasms. With horror the Russians beheld the familiar flagrancy of the Turkish battlefield, the "bestial Toorks", their pantaloons down, working heatedly upon the freshly slain. When hesitantly asked about this "horrible desecration of human beings" by a certain war correspondent, the indifferent Turk characteristically replied "It is, to be sure Effendi ['my Lord'], a most devilish matter of expert timing." '

The seduction of Radu, young son of Prince Vlad II, is highly likely to have possessed such an erotic component. But Radu's subsequent history shows that this was only part of the story. His empathy and admiration for Ottoman culture was such that he would stay away from his homeland until 1462, apparently making little protest, almost a full two decades after his father had offered him up as a hostage. Considering that he and elder brother Vlad held the status of captives, the younger boy's predicament smacks of the phenomenon we now know as 'Stockholm Syndrome'– though, like many such phenomena, its roots are age-old. In the Renaissance era, the entire Ottoman Empire had relied upon a variant of the Stockholm Syndrome. The notorious policy of Devşirme, was one of the chief engines of the Empire's expansion. It weakened the kingdoms on the Ottoman borders while ensuring a steady stream of fresh blood to the Empire. Ironically, it might in our context, be described as vampiric. The European youths absorbed into the Ottoman state in this fashion were ritually circumcised, then drafted into the service that best suited their talents. Brighter inductees became administrators, for example, while the stronger youths were conscripted into the Ottoman's famous Janissary regiments. The Janissaries – kidnapped as Christians of course, because Muslims cannot be made slaves according to koranic law – fought fanatically and devotedly for their captors.

***

Whilst this sort of devotion to one's captors may seem mystifying, there are many examples of similarly-mystifying behaviour in recent times. In late August 1973, bank robber Jan-Erik Olsson shot and seriously wounded a policeman in a foiled raid on a branch of Sweden's Kreditbanken. Instead of giving himself up to the law, Olsson took stock of his options and decided he'd do better by holing himself up in a vault with the four clerks on duty that day, using them as bargaining chips to negotiate his escape. So began six days of a knife-edge standoff. At one point the police threatened to fire tear gas into the bank, only to be deterred by Olsson coercing the four bank clerks into rope nooses and threatening to hang them. It was only after the cops agreed to the release from prison and entry to the bank of Olsson's friend (a fellow professional thief) that their final raid brought the bank robber's capitulation. To the amazement of law enforcement and the press, the four released captives expressed their relief by hugging and kissing the two robbers, calling out messages of support as the police took them into custody.

This sense of over-identification by captives with their captors was termed 'Stockholm Syndrome' by criminal psychologist Nils Bejerot, who assisted the police in their negotiations with Olsson. Cut off from the outside world and dependent on the armed robber (who claimed that he never seriously considered hurting them) for their survival, the bank clerks had come to regard the raids by the police as aggressive acts and to place their trust in Olsson – with whom they at least had a one-to-one human relationship.

Shortly after, in early 1974, American university co-ed Patty Hearst – granddaughter of newspaper tycoon William Randolph Hearst – was kidnapped from campus by a wannabe urban guerrilla grouping styling themselves the Symbionese Liberation Army. In this last-gasp flowering of Marxist action among the radicalised children of the US middle classes, the SLA had seen fit to assassinate a black superintendent of schools in Northern California, as a supposed traitor to his race and class. Kept prisoner at a number of apartments and safe houses, Ms Hearst was indoctrinated with Maoist and Black Power tracts (all but one of her guilt-ridden radical kidnappers was white) that prescribed revolution as the path to justice for 'the people'.

When the kidnappers' impossibly Utopian ransom demands – $400m worth of free food to be distributed to the poor by Patty's father – fell through, their captive naturally feared she was about to be executed. Instead, she survived within the fugitive group while some of its members died in shootouts with the authorities, by adopting the new identity of 'Tania', a gun-toting bank robber fighting for 'the people'. While she later insisted in her autobiography that she merely parroted the group's dogma as a survival technique, she also admitted, 'I had been trained and drilled ... just as soldiers are trained and drilled to obey an order under fire instinctively, without questioning it. By the time they finished with me I was in fact a soldier in the Symbionese Liberation Army.'

***

To return to the Ottoman court, Radu's indoctrination into the culture of his captors can therefore be seen as not merely successful, but as a textbook example of a widespread phenomenon of the time and one which retains its influence today. But what of Vlad, his seemingly stronger-willed brother?

In the 2009 documentary film, author Kim Newman (whose reputation as a Dracula scholar stems from his entertaining historical fantasy novel *Anno Dracula*) observes speculatively that, 'Vlad spent a great deal of his childhood in the hands of the Turks, and it's possible he was sexually abused by them.' 'I think it's quite likely he was sodomised by them,' concurs historian M. J. Trow in *Vlad the Impaler*. 'This was traditional practice in the whole of the Turkish court for many generations by then.' The elder princeling's later enmity with the Turks, and his merciless treatment of them, suggests he was never fully indoctrinated into either the prevailing Middle Eastern culture or the sexual practices of his hosts. But still, the lasting psychological impact of possible sexual coercion can only be guessed at. It is, perhaps, best left to a less refined voice of the early 20th century to laterally describe his predicament.

Carl Panzram, hanged in 1930, is posthumously infamous as one of the USA's most unrepentant felons. After running away from the impoverished family home as a child, his early life was spent as a vagrant and in youth reformatories, before the extensive crime spree that took him continually in and out of prison and finally terminated his existence, aged 38. The hardship Panzram experienced and the lack of mercy shown by, in the first instance, the adult world and, later, the penal authorities would crystallise into an unforgiving personal philosophy. His resultant hostility toward the entire human race (not even sparing himself) made him an icon of nihilism for the 'apocalypse culture' generation, whose poisonous flower came into bloom into the late 1980s – performers, writers and artists whose own anti-humanist philosophies seem largely informed by memories of being kicked around the schoolyard and labelled 'weirdos' by their contemporaries. The privations of Panzram were, by way of contrast, rather more severe.

In *Killer: A Journal of Murder*, the startling annotated memoir published four decades after the convict's death, the author recounts from his prison cell the experience of being gang-raped by four hobos, at a time when he rode the freight trains himself as a 13-year-old vagrant: 'I cried, begged, pleaded for mercy, pity, sympathy, but nothing I could say would sway them from their purpose.' The net effect of this and other, non-sexual, forms of violent abuse suffered in institutions and prisons was to leave Panzram continually lusting after a generalised form of vengeance: 'I began to think I would have my revenge as often as I could injure someone else. Anyone at all would do. If I couldn't injure those who had injured me, then I would injure someone else.'

By the time he had grown to full adulthood, the physically fearsome criminal regarded the abuse he had endured as within the natural order of things. In this world the strong always preyed on the weak, and that was the end of it. In the months before his 5 September 1930 execution for the killing of a prison worker, Carl Panzram made a full and unrepentant confession in his memoir: 'In my lifetime I have murdered 21 human beings. I have committed thousands of burglaries, robberies, larcenies, arsons and last but not least I have committed sodomy on more than 1,000 male human beings. For all of these things I am not the least bit sorry … I preyed upon the weak, the harmless and the unsuspecting. This lesson I was taught by others: might makes right.'

The young Vlad's experience of detainment, over 450 years before the American convict's birth, was of an altogether more pampered kind as a 'guest' of the Ottoman Empire. But if – as some have suggested – he was also subjected to the gross indignity of male-on-male rape, then it's easy to conceive of how his psychic survival depended on his acceptance of a world without mercy, as with the similarly strong-willed Panzram. And of how the sentiment 'might makes right' – which provided the title of a long-neglected Social Darwinist polemic published around the time of Panzram's birth, of which we shall hear more – is the credo that informed the lives of both.

***

Back in medieval Wallachia, the lives of Dracula and Radu hung by a thread. Every success of John Hunyadi's Long Campaign brought the prospect of mutilation or death at the hands of their Turkish hosts ever closer. When the Christian advance stalled in early 1444, many must have breathed a long sigh of relief. The Turkish Sultan was in the mood for compromise. Hunyadi's forces had inflicted a series of punishing defeats on the Turks, claiming substantial amounts of territory in the Balkans, and rekindling a spirit of resistance among many European realms who had previously assumed that the Ottoman juggernaut was unstoppable. Yet the hard-headed Hunyadi knew when to stop, when supply lines and the support of fickle allies had been stretched to breaking point. The vainglorious hotheads who believed every battle against the heathen ended in the conquest of Jerusalem must surely have all died in the plains below Nicopolis. So it was that the Treaty of Szeged was signed between King Vladislaus and Sultan Murad in the summer of 1444, confirming Christian conquests, and promising ten years of peace. It was a triumphal conclusion to Hunyadi's campaign, evidence that the tide was slowly turning against Ottoman expansion.

Inevitably, however, there were those who regarded the treaty as a wasted opportunity. If the Sultan was willing to make so many compromises, then the Christians must surely have their Ottoman foe on the ropes, and now was the time to deliver the knock-out blow, not pause to regroup. Loudest among such voices were those who knew nothing of the situation at the frontline, most notably the Pope, who absolved King Vladislaus of any vows made at Szeged on the iniquitous basis that no promise made with an infidel was binding. His energetic and charismatic envoy to the Hungarian court, Cardinal Julian Cesarini, put the Papal view strongly to the young King, playing on Vladislaus's pride in his building reputation as a heroic Crusader. Skanderbeg was also in favour of any military option that would take the pressure off his own guerilla fighters in Albania. Further strengthening the case for renewed hostilities was the news that Murad had abdicated as Ottoman Sultan, placing his adolescent son, Radu the Handsome's Turkish playmate Mehmet, in command. If the fearsome Murad was tired of ruling, then surely his Empire too must be approaching exhaustion, while Mehmet II wasn't old enough to grow a beard, let alone lead an Ottoman army to victory. The hawks at the Hungarian court prevailed, and John Hunyadi reluctantly began assembling the troops in the autumn of 1444 to relaunch his Long Campaign.

Hunyadi's scepticism was shared by many of his allies. While some of the Balkan leaders were enthusiastic over another offensive which might finally force the Turks from European soil, many others were more circumspect. Happy with the gains made and confirmed under the Treaty of Szeged, they were reluctant to roll the dice again, particularly in a project that began with an act of flagrant treachery, Papal dispensation notwithstanding. (Many, of course, were Eastern Orthodox Christians, meaning they put far more store in Murad's proven reputation for straight-dealing, than the power of a religious leader they didn't recognise to nullify sacred vows to suit his own purposes.) Typical of such sceptics was George Branković. Murad had returned his two blinded sons as part of his side of the treaty, which confirmed George as sovereign ruler of Serbia. Branković had no intention of breaking the promises he had made at Szeged, and refused to have any part of this underhand endeavour. Were Vlad Dracula and Radu also due to be released as a clause of the Treaty? It's quite probable that the Ottomans still weren't ready to relinquish the heirs to the Wallachian throne due to Vlad Dracul's proven duplicity, or equally, that preparations for their release were aborted when it became clear that the Voivode was among those prepared to tear up the Treaty of Szeged at the beheast of King Vladislaus.

Once again, Vlad II's enthusiasm for the renewed campaign was notably half-hearted. Rumours suggest that a Bulgarian soothsayer warned him that the omens for the endeavour were very bad. The Voivode was also unimpressed by the size of John Hunyadi's force. 'The Sultan goes on a mere hunting expedition with more troops than the Christians are bringing into battle,' he sneered, in an observation calculated to infuriate Hunyadi. Relations between the two men appear to have dipped several degrees below freezing. Dracul had a point. Not only had the reluctance of many previous allies – including many of Vladislaus's own Hungarian lords – to rejoin the Long Campaign led to a smaller army, it had also led to a lopsided force, strong in cavalry, but severely lacking in the infantry who were beginning to dominate the battlefield in the era. The Christian strategy relied on naval support from the Venetian and Papal navies to prevent the Ottomans from concentrating their forces. The plan looked a little too complicated for comfort. Whether the Wallachian Voivode had been warned of occult portents of disaster or not, he must have felt that the venue for his meeting with the Hungarian army was uniquely inauspicious. The summit was held at the city of Nicopolis.

Despite all of this, Dracul followed the same compromise he had previously followed, and sent his son Mircea in his stead at the head of a modest force of Wallachian horsemen. It's possible that this compromise actually reflected a building difference of opinion between Vlad and his son, who'd held the fort briefly as Voivode Mircea II during Dracul's confinement of 1442-3. Mircea doesn't appear to have approved of his father's policy of appeasement, and it seems possible that he joined King Vladislaus's army of his own volition, exercising his independence, ploughing his own furrow in anticipation of once again claiming the Voivodeship as Mircea II. Was Vlad Dracul deferring for fear of what might happen to his other two sons, hoping to distance himself from a project he saw as unwisely risky, or simply reluctant to fully commit himself to a conflict when there was no obvious benefit for himself?

Whatever motivated Vlad II to sit out the campaign of late 1444, his son Mircea acquitted himself well. Leading his force of Wallachian cavalry, supplemented by a mercenary infantry contingent, advancing in parallel to Hunyadi's column, Mircea captured the Bulgarian city of Petretz. While we know his father bought cannons and handguns from the Transylvanian gunsmiths, Petretz is the first time we know of Romanian forces actually employing gunpowder weapons on the battlefield, bringing the city walls down in a thunder of sulphurous smoke. In the grimly familiar pattern by now established in the Ottoman wars, Mircea threw his Turkish prisoners to their deaths from the battlements. Meanwhile, Hunyadi made good progress south of the Danube, bypassing a number of Ottoman strongholds in favour of a rapid advance. In contrast to the Franco-Burgundian Crusaders that had passed that way in 1396, Hunyadi's Polish and Hungarian troops did not indulge in a litany of looting and pillaging, and as a consequence his army were greeted as liberators, with a local contingent swelling their ranks. Yet the campaign plan was already unravelling. When Hunyadi's army rendezvoused with Mircea's men at the Black Sea port of Varna in November of 1444, they discovered that the Italian navies had failed to disrupt Ottoman mobilisation, and a Turkish army perhaps three times as large as the Christian force was fast approaching.

At its head was Murad II, once more in the saddle as Ottoman Sultan. As with the situation surrounding the Wallachian involvement in the campaign, there is some confusion over what transpired between the ruler and his son to determine who commanded the army. Some insist that when he saw the Christians mustering once more for war, the old Sultan feared his son wasn't up to the challenge – not unreasonably as Mehmet was barely a teenager – and seized the reins of power, displaying a lack of faith that dented his son's self-confidence, and ultimately contributed to Mehmet becoming such an aggressive over-achiever when he finally did sever the apron strings. Other accounts have a panic-stricken young Mehmet begging his reluctant father to come out of his restful retirement, eventually resorting to verbal trickery. If Murad was still Sultan, he was obliged to lead the Ottoman armies against this serious threat. If Mehmet was now Sultan, then he commanded Murad to lead the army. Whatever the true story behind the old Sultan reassuming the mantle of leadership, Murad clearly brought more than a little personal pique to the battlefield at Varna, brandishing a lance with a copy of the Treaty of Szeged skewered upon its point. King Vladislaus's treachery had turned the conflict into a grudge match.

In the Christian camp debate raged over the best strategy to employ in the imminent clash of arms. Cardinal Cesarini, the Papal representative who had done so much to launch the endeavour, favoured a rapid retreat. When he was advised by more experienced military voices that the army's current position – wedged between the Ottoman forces and Lake Varna, with the Black Sea at their back – made this suicidal, Cesarini proposed a defensive strategy, in the hope of holding out until the Italian navies could bring reinforcements. Hunyadi then pointed out that the composition of their army – primarily cavalry, with only a small force of war-wagons and artillery – made such a course equally impractical. Their only option was to attack, insisted the White Knight, and this time King Vladislaus took his advice.

On the morning of 10 November, the two armies began an exchange of cannon-fire, as the Turkish Azabs flooded forward, trying to goad their foes into a rash charge. They enjoyed some success, as Hunyadi's Croat cavalry on his left wing broke ranks to hurtle at the Turkish skirmishers through the clouds of gunpowder smoke. The inevitable happened, as Sultan Murad, commanding from the vantage point of an Ancient Thracian burial mound, sent a force of Sipahi heavy cavalry to envelope the Croat charge. Hunyadi's right wing, primarily composed of mercenaries, had a ringside seat for the slaughter befalling the Croats and began to waver. Despite Cardinal Cesarini's best efforts to rally them with promises of rewards in heaven, panic spread among their ranks, and they began to flee the field. Sipahi were soon hot on their heels, chasing them into the marshes surrounding Lake Varna, leaving a vast swathe of corpses studded with arrows bobbing in the shallow, dirty water.

It was now time for Hunyadi to make his move. With perfect timing, he signalled for Mircea to lead his troop of seasoned Wallachian cavalry into the flanks of Murad's triumphant Sipahi. They hit the Ottoman cavalry like a hammer, scattering the Turkish horsemen, who fled in frantic panic. Mircea followed as his quarry raced towards the Ottoman rear. By accident or design, this brought the Wallachian cavalry to the Ottoman camp. They'd hit the jackpot – the ill-defended encampment contained all of the Sultan's travelling expenses and supplies – and the Wallachians indulged in an orgy of looting, the battle forgotten. Meanwhile, against the odds, Hunyadi's heavy cavalry were slowly turning the tide against the Turkish centre, the duel between Christian knight and Ottoman Janissary starting to tip in his favour. The battle was on a knife-edge. If the Janissaries broke ranks or the knights lost momentum, the slaughter would begin.

Murad is said to have lost his nerve at this point, only for a bold Janissary to grab the bridle of the Sultan's horse and physically prevent him from fleeing. Vladislaus reacted in the opposite fashion. Thinking he saw a clear path through the roiling battlefield to the Sultan, the impetuous young King charged at the heart of the Ottoman centre, his heavily-armoured bodyguard obliged to join him in his rash race for glory. It was a catastrophic miscalculation. The Janissary line closed around the King's gallant party, the elite Ottoman infantry engulfing them, dragging the knights from their horses in a frenzied, brutal struggle. Hunyadi was soon apprised of the situation, but could do nothing to save his sovereign, unable to hack his way through the human wall of Turkish troops that had swallowed the King. The moment Vladislaus's head – still in its helmet – was stuck upon Murad's lance alongside the broken treaty, the battle was over.

It remained only for Hunyadi to use all of his tactical genius in an attempt to drag as much of his army from the jaws of the Ottoman war machine as he could, the Christian advance now rapidly reversing into an anarchic rout. The shattered remnants of the Hungarian and Polish force fled as best they could towards the safety of Wallachia, as Murad's victorious troops rounded up those unable to escape, living trophies to sell in the Turkish slave markets. Meanwhile, Mircea's men also made their way home to Wallachia, burdened with booty taken from the Sultan's camp. The catastrophic defeat at Varna was equal to the traumatic impact of the debacle at Nicopolis nearly 50 years earlier. As at Nicopolis, the only compensation was that the damage done to the Turkish army left the Ottomans in no position to take advantage of their victory. Inevitably, the disastrous defeat invited a post mortem in the theatre of Christian European public opinion, as recriminations for the tragedy began to spread.

In a letter to the Pope, John Hunyadi described Varna as 'an unequal battle… which was fiercely fought, and only the sunset stopped the carnage. But the battle became a losing one because of the continuous waves of an endlessly attacking multitude, from which we receded not so much defeated than rather overrun and separated from each other. Nevertheless, we saw it with our own eyes and know it from many documents, that we did not inflict fewer wounds to the enemy than we received. We left them with the remains of a bloody and funestuous victory… Our defeat was not caused by our weakness, or the superior bravery of the Turks, but it was divine justice which administered the defeat to us for we were ill equipped and almost unarmed; the barbarians won the day because of our sins.' Just as some had blamed the sinful behaviour of the Crusaders for the divine disfavour which doomed the Crusade at Nicopolis, Hunyadi evidently felt that the treachery that overshadowed the Long Campaign meant that it was destined, or even that it deserved, to fail. Others, however, were pointing the finger of blame at less abstract scapegoats.

On his weary way home, John Hunyadi was to receive a harsh welcome from the Voivode Vlad II. At a summit authors Florescu and McNally say was held in the Bulgarian city of Dobruja, while M. J. Trow locates it on Vlad's home turf at Tîrgovişte, Dracul made a sensational accusation, levelling the blame for Varna directly at Hunyadi, claiming his battlefield incompetence amounted to gross criminal negligence. It was no idle allegation. Clearly taking the

Voivode of Transylvania totally by surprise, Dracul took Hunyadi into custody by force, making dark threats that only death represented adequate punishment for the man who'd masterminded such a disaster for the Christian cause. What motivated Dracul to such radical action? Perhaps he hoped to deflect blame from closer to home. His own record of collaboration with the Ottomans was an ongoing scandal, compounded by his lukewarm support for the Long Campaign and Mircea's abandonment of the field at Varna. It's far from impossible that Vlad II hoped to court Ottoman favour by orchestrating the death of the Christian commander they dreaded most. If so, once again, Vlad vacillated. Faced with the enormity of killing the White Knight – still a hero despite Varna – Dracul balked, and released his eminent prisoner. Whether motivated by cynical ambition or personal spite, Vlad had taken a big risk in seizing a tiger by the tail, and took an even greater one by letting him go.

In 1445, taking advantage of the damage done to the Ottoman war machine the previous year, and hoping perhaps to improve his own tarnished image among his fellow Christian princes, Vlad II undertook his own bizarre miniature Crusade. It was a water-based operation, employing shipping to transport an army of Wallachian and French troops – the latter led by Jean de Wavrin, Burgundian knight, scholar and adventurer who had fought at Agincourt as a boy. As usual, Mircea took the principal role on the battlefield, his father joining the expedition only when it suited him. At the campaign's closing stages, they linked up with a Hungarian force under John Hunyadi, by which point Vlad had made himself scarce. The mission's macabre stated goal was the recovery of the remains of Cardinal Cesarini and King Vladislaus for Christian burial. In more practical terms, a number of Ottoman strongholds were taken (it probably goes without saying that Mircea treated captured Turkish garrisons with casual brutality), most significantly Giurgiu – a town fortified by Mircea the Elder to control traffic on the Danube – and Nicopolis. The capture of Nicopolis may have provided some salve to wounded Christian pride, though it was largely symbolic – these were skirmishes over border towns, not a decisive clash of civilisations which had taken place there in 1396.

The success of the mission's chief aim is similarly ambivalent. Some refused to believe that Cardinal Cesarini was dead – that like the elusive MIA GIs of the post-Vietnam War era, he languished behind enemy lines awaiting rescue. The more plausible theory, that he had fallen in the marshes by Lake Varna, where his body would have been picked clean of valuables by Azabs before being picked clean of flesh by natural scavengers, would give anybody hoping to recover his remains a year later even less cause for optimism. Similarly, if Turkish accounts are to be believed, King Vladislaus's remains had been preserved in honey, before being reunited with his severed head at the Ottoman capital and displayed as an object lesson to anyone tempted to betray the Sultan. If so then his remains were hardly likely, in such circumstances, to be recovered by a military expedition up the Danube. But this is, perhaps, to overlook the power of myth, and indeed the ability of history to continually offer surprises. (An enduring story has it that Vladislaus survived the battle, but tormented by the conviction that breaking his word had brought about disaster, became a pilgrim. After seeking absolution in Jerusalem, he supposedly made his home in Madeira, where the Portuguese King – who accepted this stranger as the disgraced Hungarian ruler – granted him land under his assumed name of Henry the German.)

By 1446, the fragility of the morale-boosting gains made in the bold Danube expedition were exposed, as one after another they were abandoned as Murad once again began applying military and diplomatic pressure on his western borders, finding little resistance from kingdoms still reeling from the defeat at Varna. In addition, Hunyadi was faced with once again steering the Hungarian succession away from the stormy waters of civil war. This time he took the role of Regent, the senior member of seven captains who would rule until the infant King came of age. In the summer of 1447, Vlad II joined the Ottoman Sultan at the negotiating table once more. It was an act of pre-Machiavellian diplomacy that would preserve Vlad II's tiny princedom and guarantee the safety of his sons. Or that, at least, was the intention. In reality it would cost Vlad and his bloodline dear.

The treaty with Murad obligated Vlad to give up the recently-taken strategic prize of Giurgiu, and to expel his Bulgarian refugees – valuable manpower, in the form of those who had migrated several thousand strong to the province of Wallachia in the wake of Mircea's successful capture of Nicopolis two years before. Such ruthless *realpolitik* was, in the eyes of Vlad II, necessary both for the survival of his country and perhaps that of his youngest sons, who remained favoured prisoners of the Ottomans but would live or die at the whim of the Sultan.

This was an uncomfortable fact of which the elder of the two children – the violently defiant young Dracula – can scarcely have been unaware. After all, they remained in luxurious captivity as a defence mechanism to ensure their father's compliance, but young Vlad must have heard the talk around the Ottoman court about his father's fickle politics. For all the cruelty of the Ottoman Empire, the continued survival of the two boys suggests that their near-contemporary Mehmet, the Sultan's son and heir, may have whispered discreet pleas for mercy in his father's ear. Whether such favouritism was based on sexual lechery or on a humane gesture that belies Mehmet's behaviour in later life (tyrants, like all human beings, may be capricious and inconsistent), Vlad the younger's instinct for survival must have told him to hold his tongue.

But Vlad the elder's slippery statesmanship was neither as subtle nor as cast-iron in its guarantees as he might have hoped. On European soil, to the Hungarian Regent John Hunyadi the treaty was yet more proof of the treacherous nature of the Voivode, the final straw in a political game that had gone beyond deadly serious. The time had come for a reckoning.

***

'For God and for Vladislav Danesti!'

Thus are fickle alliances yoked to the power of the Almighty. The boyar class which throngs the narrow lanes and streets of Tîrgoviște has been converted to the cause of Vlad Dan, one of several pretenders to the throne. 'A pox upon the house of Dracul!' There is no cause so fervent as that of self-interest. If power is bestowed from above, then to resist an alliance with the newly-rising power is virtually an act of heresy.

Is that not what men mean when they talk of the 'sanctity of God'? And is not the feckless servant who refuses to follow the flow of history's currents not disavowing His love and protection?

'Desist! Stay your hand or suffer a thousand deaths!'

The command is tremulously given. The threat is heartfelt but its quavering tone doubts its own authority. As the chill November night is illuminated by the malodorous glow of burning torches, Mircea Dracula, his adjutants and vassals, find themselves in the ungentle grasp of the mob.

'Save your orders for the Devil, son of the dragon! See how he honours you when you stray into his domain!'

Their conversion came suddenly, the betrayal falling upon Mircea and his men with ruthless stealth. The Voivode himself has already stolen east, alert to the air of disquiet among a mob that suspects his alliance with the Mohammedan heathen. It leaves his elder son to defend the power and the honour of his dynasty, an onerous duty to bequeath in these uncertain times.

'Unhand your ruler, or every hand shall lie in a mound of its severed brethren!'

The threat elicits only laughter. For who can be said to rule in this modest Carpathian enclave of less than half a million souls, when the duplicitous traitor that takes his orders from the circumcised dogs east of the Danube has fled?

The prince who would be king is dragged by the chain that holds the Order of the Dragon's medallion about his neck. It is all his errant father has bequeathed to him, its silver links chafing his throat like the leash of some hapless tormented bear. None of his small coterie of guards and servants dares to second his bravado. Their sword sheaths held at their side, they know the price of defiance in the face of an armed mob. Several of their comrades lie disembowelled, their throats cut, on the outskirts of the city, the only distinction between those who live and those who died being that the dead unsheathed their blades first.

Marched back into the royal palace of Tîrgovişte, with its Orthodox church-inspired decor, Mircea has returned home a prisoner. And there, at the head of the banqueting table in the royal dining hall, he is met by a familiar solid visage.

'Hunyadi …'

Both the elder and younger man regard each other with a tensely muted respect, but without deference.

'My lord Mircea…' The humbled white knight of Christendom accuses with his tone.

'Am I brought back to my father's palace for my humiliation?'

The bulky elder man shifts and rises from his seat at the table. The Wallachian prince holds no power to harm him, but the inference of ignoble motive causes discomfort.

'I have brought you to the palace of the ruler of Wallachia, Vladislav I of the Danesti dynasty, to give you the opportunity of swearing your allegiance.' He approaches his captive in battle-worn armour that shows signs of corrosion.

'Hah! I should sooner swear allegiance to a castrated hog!' The defiance is real but so is the slight breathlessness, the fatal anticipation. 'And if I do not, shall I die?'

Hunyadi studies the sallow features of the young man intently. He is not here to play games with him, but to punish. To punish rightly and justly, as he sees it.

'If you choose not to swear allegiance, you shall die the death of a traitor.'

Now that the words are spoken, a calm defiance comes over Mircea. His breathing is at once deeper, more measured. He no longer stands rigid against the talon-like grasps of those who grip him by his arms, his hair. He ceases trying to recoil from them: in his fatalistic acceptance, he will remain their superior.

'And if I choose to swear allegiance to this "Vladislav"?'

'Then you shall die quickly.'

Mircea spits contemptuously at the knight's steel boot. The missile is misjudged, splattering against the lower breastplate of the knight's armour.

'Then so be it. A coward dies many times. I am a warrior – I can perish only once.'

Hunyadi averts his gaze from his former comrade-in-arms, whether in dismissal or acknowledgement of the last vestiges of camaraderie. He rises to his feet and walks slowly down the hall, as the young warrior nobleman falls deeper into the clutches of the treacherous boyars and their cronies.

John Hunyadi will not look back. Mircea will not lower his burning gaze. Both are imprisoned by the violent inevitability of what will follow. Both burn with the self-justifying indignation that remains after the bloody debacle of Varna.

'Die only once, eh, Dracula?'

'And yet this pig threatens to make us all die a thousand times!'

'Then let us teach him what it is to wish to die, before God or the Devil stakes their claims on his last breath!'

In this darkened hallway where only a few candles flicker, the half-glimpsed faces of Wallachia's farm owners and administrators evince a loathsome singularity. To those born to rule, the mob is always the same in its collective courage and mass cowardice – its howls and shrieks of allegiance are always impassioned but ever fickle, its ugliness born from the intoxicating moment when their squalid numbers overpower their natural leaders.

They have his limbs pinioned hard, held down like a common thief. 'Our young master does not wish to see the ascendance of Dan to the throne? Then let him never live to see it!'

The imperial Romans called it tormentum *– the infliction of pain and torment as a prologue to the death penalty. At first only slaves had been subject to its protracted indignities; later,* tormentum *was inflicted on freemen for only the worst of crimes. But here, halfway through the second millennium of the Christian messiah, no such decorum reigns.*

'No! Let him see – let him see clearly once, and then see nothing evermore!'

The swathes of rag wrapped tightly around the wooden stakes are reignited with pitch, their choking flames serving to heat the iron stakes held at their epicentre.

There is no greater impetus to cruelty than moral righteousness. It is now that young Mircea, son of the esteemed Draconist Vlad II, knows that his former valour in combat counts as nothing. The greatest challenge he has ever faced is now, to try to hold his composure as the mob reduces him to mere quivering flesh.

But Mircea cries out.

The red-hot glow of the metal has not touched his face, yet he feels its scalding power evaporating the moisture from his eyes as it comes slowly closer.

'Where's the sanctity of a soldier's death now, Dracula?'

The mob cackles hard at its own witless taunts. To Mircea, all words are now lost. He responds merely as a reactive mass of nerve endings. His eyelids seek to stay closed, to make a last futile defence, but still they twitch and flicker as the iron rods finally connect.

VLAD THE IMPALER

The young warrior gives out a scream such as few have ever heard on the battlefield. His orbs pulsate and blacken, the blood and aqueous humour boiling together within his eye sockets.

'Out, vile jelly!' taunts one of the tormentors. Others in the crowd are sobered by the spectacle, hoping only for the endgame that will put paid to it. It is they who cajole Mircea along, binding his wrists with an abrasive cord, keen to see an end to it all.

Their blinded prisoner is compliant now, pitched into a world of darkness and pain. His aquiline face is aged a thousand years by the deep black pits burnt into it.

'Let us dig a grave for yesterday's hero. Wallachia shall bury its past.' The words may mock, but they bespeak a hope to be free of the parochial wars that have split the region and switched its alliances with bewildering regularity. It is a hope without hope.

'It is here.' In the forests at the edge of Tîrgovişte, night devours the scene. All is blackness. This is truer for Mircea than for anyone else present. Led by knotted cord, propelled by hostile hands, he stumbles against the distended roots of trees and is scratched by nettles and bracken.

But for him the encroaching night is the only mercy. As they draw to a halt, in his sightlessness he steels himself for the moment when all his senses shall be eclipsed. One moment of total darkness, before he is delivered unto his maker.

It never comes.

'Get ye into the earth, princeling!'

There are no more hands to coerce him or to break his fall, as he plunges forward as if into the Abyss. The sharp impact of wood against his forehead would induce stars, if there were any light left in the night sky or within his flame-gouged eyes.

As Mircea Dracula scrambles desperately to raise himself upright within his makeshift tomb, he hears only the voices of his executioners. Those who have descended several feet into the earth to seal the coffin's lid, within which the mutilated young warrior scratches with bloody nails and gulps at the precious air that will soon become scarce …

***

Dracul, the Dragon of Wallachia, has made his escape before. But this time, he is fleeing the consequences of a gamble which has backfired. In using his younger sons as pawns in negotiations with the Turks, he has behaved more calculatingly than the 'mad queen' chess players starting to appear in Europe's more cosmopolitan quarters. But his fair-weather allies among the Ottomans are his only hope, now that the treacherous Hungarians and their champion Hunyadi have instigated a revolt in his kingdom.

His mud-stained white horse whinnies as it loses its footing in the boggy marshes. 'Stay aloft, nag, or I'll whip you till you're fit for the slaughter!'

It is no use, as the Voivode scrabbles to find his own feet in the mud, fearful of slipping into the murk atop his steed. Fear permeates the air breathed by Vlad II and his mount. Having broken free of his outriders just as surely as he left his elder son to defend the throne of Tîrgovişte, he is now bogged down in the wilds outside the provincial city of Bucharest.

'Who goes there?'

An insolent silence is all that he hears, besides the crackling and splashing of dismounted riders. 'I am your liege, the Voivode of Wallachia, I demand a reply!'

This time the response is hearty laughter, from a confederacy of bulky shadows that have started to group together.

'And who grants you the right to speak on behalf of "our liege", fugitive?'

It is a question loaded with menace. Vlad has stalemated himself, desperate to invoke his authority but too fearful of the consequences to admit his own identity.

There is a neighing shriek as his bedraggled white stallion is jolted by a rope noose around its neck, then splashes heavily down in the water on its left flank.

Prince Vlad is knocked off his own footing, but is sure enough of his anger.

'Whosoever harms a hair of my horse's mane will have his head displayed on a pike!'

As a surly gaggle of equerries pull the frightened steed back up onto its hooves, one chain-vested insurgent makes a quiet assessment. 'You swear retribution with great assurance, Draculesti.'

The charade is over. As a contingent of blade-wielding warriors step forward, there is greater ignominy in pretence than there is in death. 'This is so, Danesti …'

The warrior, a swarthy Hun-like figure who might have commingled with Vlad's allies the Turks, regards his quarry at close hand. 'I see you do not wear the sign of the Dragon, oh Prince? But still, you are unmistakable to me.'

The mighty stallion gives out a snorting retort. Vlad turns away from his confronter.

'That horse is worth more than all of your families combined!'

Blades are drawn in anticipation of the Prince's last stand.

'Stand as you are!' commands the Hun. 'The prize is mine!' His own battleaxe is withdrawn from its scabbard.

Before Vlad can hurl any further threats, the matted lower locks of his hair are clasped. They are jerked violently forward till his upper vertebra gives an audible click.

His neck is bared.

The axe traces a mighty downward arc.

VLAD THE IMPALER

The severance of the trachea from the upper spinal cord is as quick and clean as circumstances allow. As the Hun holds the Voivode's head aloft and his comrades wrap the body in a makeshift blanket shroud, the nobleman's eyes seem still to roll in rage as dark blood drips from the vessels in his bisected throat. This is the most valuable currency that can be taken back to the Danesti: proof that Vlad II has genuinely vacated his throne. Dethroned and decapitated.

The severed head is virtually the crowning symbol of 15th-century Europe, and it will remain so throughout and beyond the intermittent reign of Vlad's infamous son.

'Men willingly change their ruler, expecting to fare better,' Niccolo Machiavelli, the Florentine 'prophet of force', will observe early in the following century. 'This expectation induces them to take up arms against him; but they only deceive themselves, and they learn from experience that they have made matters worse. This follows from another common and natural necessity: a prince is always compelled to injure those who have made him the new ruler, subjecting them to the troops and imposing the endless other hardships which his new conquest entails. As a result, you are opposed by all those you have injured in occupying the principality, and you cannot keep the friendship of those who have put you there.'

Across the Adriatic Sea that separates Hungary and the fringes of the Ottoman Empire from the principalities and republics of Italy, such a cynically rational philosophy is seen at work in the provincial outposts of Wallachia. Eighteen years separate the ascendance to the throne of Mircea the Elder and the reign of his son, Vlad II, now reaching its end in the year 1447 AD. Though native-born rather than foreign conquerors, the constant bloody struggles and switches of allegiance that permeate the Draculesti's *rule provide a framework through which late medieval Europe power politics may be seen.*

***

The above imaginings of the deaths of Vlad Dracul and Mircea Dracula are based on the commonplace (indeed, casual) instances of extreme cruelty in the late Middle Ages. The details are speculative. Was John Hunyadi present to witness the fate of his erstwhile comrade-in-arms Mircea? Some insist he was – it certainly makes for a more satisfying dramatic conclusion – but other historians believe that the White Knight merely sanctioned or facilitated the regime change that left the Wallachian heir and his father living on borrowed time. The cruel act itself however is less speculative: indeed, this method of execution runs like a seam through history, even finding an outlet in the canon of William Shakespeare. Writing just over a century after the death of Vlad the Impaler, Shakespeare dooms Aaron, the villainous Moor in *Titus Andronicus*, his first performed tragedy, to the punishment of burial alive: 'Set him breast-deep in earth, and famish him; / There let him stand, and rave, and cry for food ...'

(Though *Titus* is actually set early in the first millennium, during the declining years of the Roman Empire, the Holy Inquisition also sanctioned premature burial as the occasional punishment for heretics who refused to recant. The last known victim was Dutchwoman Anne van de Hoor who, like the fictional Aaron, was only partially buried in earth – in her case up to her chin, though her end was hastened by the gravediggers continuing to heap the soil onto her head until she suffocated. Mircea, as far as can be known, seems to have had full entombment inflicted on him – like those unfortunate souls whose disinterment and evident efforts to escape their coffins fed the Mittel-European vampire myth.)

There have been more than a few academics prepared to challenge the fact that Shakespeare, the most pragmatically adaptable playwright of his age, wrote an early play like *Titus* which teems with such atrocities. So the argument goes, how can a poet also capable of celebrating romantic chivalry, patriotic jingoism and rustic buffoonery – to name some other aspects of his *oeuvre* – also empathise with the bloodthirsty and the tyrannical? There may be some crossover here with those who dispute that a Midlands leather merchant's son of little academic education could be so well acquainted with the human condition, seeking a more 'likely' candidate for the plays' authorship according to their own prejudices. However, perusal of a later tragedy like *King Lear* only compounds the fact that the Bard had as much of an insight into atavistic savagery as he had a taste for silly frivolity. Its blinding of Gloucester also echoes the savagery of the punishments inflicted on Mircea, giving the sense that cruelty was merely a tragic fact of life among the rulers and the ruled.

Indeed, if one were able to comprehensively catalogue all the violent deaths, torture and torments of the Middle Ages (impossible, in that most of the individual incidents are surely unknown to us), one might be left with a worldview not too far removed from that of young Vlad Dracula – who would soon be burdened with the traumatic news that his father and brother had now met their own violent ends. From here on, Vlad the younger was the eldest of his surviving bloodline, left alone to fend for himself in a chaotically violent world. It doesn't seem overly cynical to mention at this point that, for both Dracula and Radu the Handsome, the death of relatives who played fast and loose with both of their lives might easily be interpreted as good news.

As a testament to the complex times, and to the attitudes held by Vlad Dracul's contemporaries, it appears that he enjoyed enthusiastic eulogies after his untimely demise in a swamp near Bucharest. 'The impact of Vlad Dracul's death was like that of a thunderbolt out of a clear blue sky,' according to Dracula historians Florescu and McNally. 'He had, after all, been one of the mainstays of the Christian resistance, a most effective crusader, the only member of the Dragon Order who remained loyal to his oath, at least in fighting the Turks.' The duo quote a couple of contemporary sources who paid fulsome tribute to the Voivode as a fallen hero. Antonio Bonfini, the Italian scholar who became official historian at the Hungarian court, hailed him as 'a righteous and unconquerable man, the mightiest and bravest in battle, since with only a few men at his disposal and due solely to his own heart and wisdom, he waged a long war with the Turks, supported by his soldiers, who proved to be valiant beyond belief and without any foreign help, and the war was such that even all the Christians put together could hardly have faced'. The Burgundian Jean de Wavrin concurred that Dracul had been 'very famous for his bravery and his wisdom'.

It's touching stuff, scarcely borne out by the facts. As Florescu and McNally themselves admit, when Vlad II was captured and killed, he was on his way east to try and solicit help from the Turks, something it might be hard to square with his Draconist vows. In truth, Dracul had as much Christian blood on his hands as Turkish, had expended as much ink signing treaties with the Ottomans as with his European allies and, wherever possible, preferred not to get his hands dirty at all. While his son Mircea could claim some success on the battlefield against the Turks, Vlad himself only appears to have been eager to take the field in pursuit of his own ambitions. The closest he came to having a substantial impact on the broader picture was when he toyed with executing John Hunyadi – who truly was 'an effective crusader' – something which would have had a catastrophic effect on the Christian cause. He left Wallachia paying a more substantial tribute to the Turkish Sultan, with the added burden of the Devşirme, bringing his realm a substantial step closer to becoming an Ottoman vassal. The best spin you can put on the career of Vlad II was that he clung onto power for eleven years – no small span in this turbulent era – and resisted the efforts of his Islamic and Catholic neighbours to reduce Wallachia to a puppet state.

He also left his dynasty with both a name – the Draculesti – and something to fight for. Florescu and McNally quote a local Romanian tradition that says that one of Dracul's last acts was to despatch his former chancellor, a boyar named Cazan, with his Draconist regalia, to pass it on to his oldest surviving son. According to this story, Dracula received the items emblazoned with the symbol of the Order of the Dragon – a gold collar and a sword fashioned by the famous Spanish weaponsmiths of Toledo – with great reverence and rage, swearing a solemn oath to avenge his father or die trying. As even the tellers of this tale admit, however, the only witness to this scene of filial devotion was Cazan, and it may well be that this is just one of the legends beginning to cohere around the intense young Wallachian. Whatever he truly felt about his father, if Dracula wished to claim his inheritance, he was obliged to declare war upon Dracul's Danesti assassins, something the prince undertook with bloodthirsty gusto.

CHAPTER V

The Blood-Slicked Path to Power

Before we look at the later reign of Vlad Dracula, we must turn to the mighty Ottoman Empire for the cultural grounding that gives it context. Did the Impaler, for example, develop his appetite for impalement while a youthful hostage of the Ottomans, or did the Turkish Empire embrace the brutal form of execution in emulation of the Wallachian Voivode? Were Vlad's worst excesses excused, even justified, by the need to oppose a merciless foreign invader at any cost, and by any means necessary? Answering such questions requires an examination of the Ottoman Empire, not just as a historical entity, but also a mythic power that exists as much in the mind as on the map. Dracula's relationship with the Turks in many respects defines the ruler, both as a psychological key to his personality, and a clue to why some regarded the Voivode in a heroic light, and still do.

Reading descriptions of the Turks issued by their European foes in the centuries following the events central to our study reveals the evolution of an archetype of peculiar potency, a figure of morbid fascination and fear in the Western imagination. History is, of course, often highly subjective. The lens through which we view the past distorts as it illuminates, refracted as it is through the prism of prejudice and fashion that accumulates over the decades, centuries and millennia to separate the historian from their subject. In such accounts, the Ottoman Empire sometimes seems closer to a fabled domain of transcendent evil and gloating depravity, to a fictional evil kingdom rather than a real historical realm with all of the moral complexity and cultural achievement common to a functional state. Attitudes to Vlad the Impaler, an implacable foe to the Turks throughout most of his life, must inevitably fall beneath such a shadow.

In Bram Stoker's novel *Dracula*, the author allows his vampire villain a lengthy heroic speech in the third chapter, when the English solicitor questions the Count about local history. 'Who was it but one of my own race who as Voivode crossed the Danube and beat the Turk on his own ground? This was a Dracula indeed!' he boasts (relating his own deeds as those of an ancestor in order to avoid alerting his guest to his own immortality). 'Was it not this Dracula, indeed, who inspired that other of his race who in a later age again and again brought his forces over the great river into Turkeyland, who, when he was beaten back, came again, and again, though he had to come alone from the bloody field where his troops were being slaughtered, since he knew that he alone could ultimately triumph!' It's stirring stuff. Even his most dogged opponent, Professor Van Helsing, later concedes that Dracula 'was in life a most wonderful man. Soldier, statesman, and alchemist.' It is only the latter unholy experiments, according to the novel, that debased the man, turning him into an undying monster.

Some students of Stoker's text present this as further evidence that he was unaware of the historical Dracula's infamy as the Impaler. It is also possible, however, to read further depth into this biographical detail the author puts into the mouth of his supernatural villain. Might the fact that Vlad had fought the Turks – still a foe of almost metaphysical evil in many Victorian imaginations – have lent the Count a certain dark nobility in Stoker's mind? In the 1870s, Bulgaria – site of so many of the bloody 15th-century battles we have already touched upon – rose against its Ottoman overlords. The revolution captured the collective imagination of the European and US media, the ruthless response of the Turks inspiring popular outrage, akin perhaps to the popular Western reaction to the war crimes committed during the Bosnian conflict 120 years later. In Britain, many shocked citizens challenged their government's diplomatic ties with the Turks, suggesting that no civilised nation should have any truck with a state capable of such atrocities.

Most famously, the Liberal politician William Gladstone – then in opposition – issued a pamphlet in 1876 entitled 'Bulgarian Horrors and the Question of the East', condemning the savagery of the Ottoman troops: 'There is not a criminal in a European jail, there is not a criminal in the South Sea Islands, whose indignation would not rise and over-boil at the recital of that which has been done, which has too late been examined, but which remains unavenged, which has left behind all the foul and all the fierce passions which produced it and which may again spring up in another murderous harvest from the soil soaked and reeking with blood and in the air tainted with every imaginable deed of crime and shame.'

Moreover, Gladstone was in no doubt that the bloodcurdling

reports of massacre, rape and torture coming back from Bulgaria were a chilling reflection of the character of not just the Ottoman Empire, but the people who founded it over five centuries before: 'Let me endeavour, very briefly to sketch, in the rudest outline what the Turkish race was and what it is. It is not a question of Mohammedanism simply, but of Mohammedanism compounded with the peculiar character of a race. They are not the mild Mohammedans of India, nor the chivalrous Saladins of Syria, nor the cultured Moors of Spain. They were, upon the whole, from the black day when they first entered Europe, the one great anti-human specimen of humanity. Wherever they went a broad line of blood marked the track behind them, and, as far as their dominion reached, civilization vanished from view.'

This is not, of course, the kind of language one might expect from a modern Western politician. We have, happily, matured and largely exiled such rabid, racist rhetoric beyond the outer fringes of acceptability. Yet Gladstone was no maverick demagogue. His pamphlet sold 24,000 copies on its first day of publication, going on to sell some 100,000 in total. He served as British Prime Minister four times (still a record) and while scoring points against his domestic political foes with the pamphlet, by accusing them of indifference in the face of an international outrage, Gladstone was also articulating a popular attitude of the day, or at least hitting a nerve. It was an attitude that also had a dark underbelly of prurient fascination. *The Lustful Turk* is one of the most notorious pornographic novels of the 19th century, first published in 1828, but not widely circulated until the 1890s. In it, two virginal English roses are kidnapped by a Turkish lord as his sex slaves. The sadomasochistic fantasy is particularly preoccupied with anal sex and the idea that, once initiated into the realms of sexual deviance, the girls themselves become addicted to depravity. A little, one might observe, like the virginal innocents who fall victim to the Count's unholy kiss in *Dracula*. We don't know if Bram Stoker had a copy of *The Lustful Turk* hidden under his mattress, but he can't have been unaware of the dark reputation of the Ottomans. It came to the fore in international controversies like the Bulgarian wars, which dominated headlines during the years Stoker first began to write professionally, with lurid descriptions of Islamic war crimes against European innocents. Of course Stoker didn't choose to make his most famous creation a Turk, but was rather inspired by a warlord who made his name fighting the Turks.

The Turk's image as an international bogeyman, manifest in documents like Gladstone's bestselling pamphlet, had its roots, as we have already suggested, in the aftermath of the Battle of Nicopolis in 1396. Sultan Bayezid's butchery of the Crusaders began a cycle of savagery – a landmark act in the waging of sadistic psychological warfare that thereafter became a defining feature of the ensuing centuries of conflict in south-eastern Europe. In *Infidels*, Andrew Wheatcroft suggests that the mid-1400s – Vlad's lifetime – saw the struggle descending inexorably further into a bloodthirsty mire of ruthless brutality. 'There was a new intensity to these wars in the Balkans. Hitherto, the Mongols had been unique in their relentless cruelty, but now it seemed that both Christians and Muslims vied with each other for the scale and ingenuity of their atrocities.' Inevitably, perhaps, Wheatcroft cites Dracula as the outstanding exemplar of this trend, but he also notes that Vlad's Ottoman nemesis Mehmet II was just as capable of cynical sadism on a breathtaking scale. 'Earlier centuries had seen many isolated examples of deliberate savagery, but from the fifteenth century barbarity reached new levels.'

The centuries of Turkish dominance of south-eastern Europe that began in the late Middle Ages lit a fire under the region that has intermittently erupted into startling acts of ethnic violence, which have destabilised the Balkans ever since. A direct line can be drawn between many of the medieval atrocities detailed in this book, and subsequent conflicts. The Great War of 1914-18 had its roots in bitter Balkan grudges from centuries past, as did the Bosnian War which shocked the world between 1992 and 1995. Ever places on the frontier, whether Transylvania and Wallachia qualify as part of the Balkan peninsula, or are just beyond its northern borders, remains a point of some controversy. (In her essay on 'The Image of Transylvania in English Literature', the Romanian academic Carmen Andras blames the ominous stereotypes and clichés concerning her homeland propagated in novels like *Dracula* on the fact 'that in English literature and even in historiography, Romania is often pushed towards the "Balkan" area with its inherently negative connotations'.) Even if you choose to exclude modern Romania from the Balkan peninsula, in Vlad's lifetime Wallachia was fighting to avoid the fate that had befallen its Balkan neighbours to the south, swallowed whole by the voracious Ottoman war machine.

'The definition of the Ottoman occupation of the Balkans as a period of darkness, slavery, and oppression evolved in the nineteenth century and crystallised in the first half of the twentieth century,' writes André Gerolymatos (who does regard Romania as Balkan) in *The Balkan Wars*. 'This negative record was in part a natural reaction to foreign domination and the cycle of repression, massacres and reprisals that characterised the wars of liberation fought by the Balkan peoples, first against the Ottoman Turks and later against each other. [Modern historian L. S.] Stavrianos summed up the notion of five hundred years of slavery and darkness as "part of the folklore of Balkan nationalism. Turkish rule in the early period was in many respects commendable. It provided the Balkan peoples with a degree of peace and security that previously had been conspicuously absent. It permitted them to practice their faith and to conduct their communal affairs with a minimum of intervention and taxation." This type of folklore so often distorts the historical reality. But that doesn't mean myths and legends offer no insight into the past.'

This book is concerned in no small part with the role of myth and legend in shaping history. Not least how it can paradoxically render a historical figure like Vlad the Impaler as both a heroic figure and an embodiment of evil. The crucial factor here is the part Dracula played in the Ottoman wars that were still simmering fiercely in the background when Bram Stoker penned his immortal Gothic chiller some 400 years later. It seems pertinent here to take a closer look at Vlad's Turkish adversaries. Not just as the historical rulers who provided 'peace and security' in south-eastern Europe for much of that span according to Stavrianos, but also 'the Great Turk' whose epic iniquity justified Vlad's savage brutality in the eyes of many patriotic Romanians. So, just who were the Turks and what – if anything – did the Ottoman Empire do to inspire such indelible horror and hostility among their European foes?

***

While 'Turk' today largely refers to a nationality, for many centuries it referred to the Turkic tribes – a people scattered across the vast Asian steppes, sharing a family of languages and a nomadic, horse-based lifestyle. It was a background that proved excellent training for the battlefield, and the Turks largely intrude upon medieval world history as mounted raiders, swooping down upon their settled neighbours from the east like a malevolent force of nature. It was when Turkish tribes decided to conquer the fertile lands to the west rather than simply to pillage them, that the Turks began making a lasting impact upon the political map of Europe and the Middle East. The Magyars, who would found the Hungarian nation – later among the Ottoman Empire's most determined Christian opponents – were identified as Turk raiders when they invaded Europe in the 9th century on their tough, nimble little horses (though their exact ethnicity is controversial). Many Turks also came west as mercenaries; widely recognised as the ablest warriors in the Islamic world, they had little trouble finding employment. In the words of the 15th-century European literary compendium *Tractatus*, the Turks were believed to 'come together for war as if they had been invited to a wedding'. In time, several of the most accomplished and ambitious Turkish generals staged coups, establishing themselves as progenitors of some of the most powerful Islamic dynasties of the Middle Ages. Most notably the Seljuks, who seized power in the 11th century, and became the principal opponents of both the Crusaders from Western Europe, and the Byzantine Empire, the last remnant of the mighty Roman Empire, ruled from the fabulously wealthy metropolis of Constantinople.

The Ottoman Dynasty began with Osman (who lent his name to the dynasty and empire), ruler of a small Turkish realm on the eastern fringes of the Islamic world at the end of the 13th century. He had the good fortune to find himself at this pivotal location just as the power of the Byzantines to his west and the Seljuks to the east were waning, and Osman took full advantage of the opportunity to lay the foundations for his empire. The fledgling Ottoman Empire was a Ghazi State – 'Ghazi' being a term meaning 'raider' with religious overtones, denoting a holy warrior who spread the word to the infidel with fire and steel – in many respects the Islamic equivalent of 'Crusader'. The Empire's early successes, most notably Nicopolis which established the Ottomans as a world power, attracted a growing influx of eager ghazi warriors keen to exploit opportunities to pillage the heathen territory opened up by the Sultan's victories. The Ghazis were exploited in turn by the burgeoning Islamic empire to soften up their European neighbours. Like their Christian Crusader equivalents, a mixture of religious zeal and personal greed motivated Islam's Ghazi warriors, who could expect both loot in this world and salvation in the next as their reward for shedding the blood of the infidel.

A similar ambivalence between the carnal and spiritual marked the fierce expansion of the Ottomans. Much of the territory swallowed by the hungry young Empire was Christian. Rather than depopulate the land, which would have had disastrous consequences for the local economy, the new Turkish overlords preferred a policy of absorbing new populations into their growing Sultanate, alongside aspects of native culture. Eastern Orthodox Christian leaders were allowed to continue to minister to their flocks, so long as they also preached loyalty to the new regime. The Greek officials who administered the

Byzantine territories the Ottomans conquered were also encouraged to retain their posts, so long as they did so as unquestioning vassals of their new Islamic masters. The Ottoman Empire was a curious compromise between Jihadist zeal and secular pragmatism that proved devastatingly effective in capturing hostile territory and, crucially, holding it as a vital source of revenue and manpower.

In his infamously incendiary pamphlet of 1876, William Gladstone gives an unsympathetic assessment of the Ottoman achievement, portraying the Turks as Islamic cuckoos in the Christian nests which they usurped, brutes incapable of imitating the sophisticated societies they conquered. 'They represented everywhere government by force as opposed to government by law.—Yet a government by force can not be maintained without the aid of an intellectual element.— Hence there grew up, what has been rare in the history of the world, a kind of tolerance in the midst of cruelty, tyranny and rapine. Much of Christian life was contemptuously left alone and a race of Greeks was attracted to [the Ottoman court] which has all along made up, in some degree, the deficiencies of Turkish Islam in the element of mind!'

André Gerolymatos gives a rather more sober assessment of the Ottoman achievement, painting a picture of an Empire of striking contrasts: 'In point of fact the Ottoman Empire was the first multiethnic state that practised a degree of toleration for minorities, which would have been unimaginable in medieval Europe – and for that matter, in many parts of the world at the end of the millennium. At the same time, however, the Ottoman Turks were not averse to subjecting towns, villages, and cities to the sword, which translated into mass killings, torture, rape, mutilation, forcible conversion and wonted destruction for its own sake. In the end, it is not so much the excesses of Turkish atrocities but rather the particular brand of suffering endured by the Balkan peoples during the Ottoman period.' Gerolymatos is referring to the contrast between the enlightened aspects of the Turkish regime and its propensity for shocking barbarity. 'This inexplicable and paradoxical behaviour permeates both the European and the Muslim accounts of Ottoman presence in the Balkans until the beginning of the twentieth century.' He adds: 'It is then reintroduced in the 1990s. A rational approach to the Ottoman period in the Balkans, consequently, has meant coming to terms with a host of contradictions and fallacies in order to provide some explanation for such unspeakable human cruelty.'

To understand the dark reputation of the Ottomans – which far eclipsed Vlad the Impaler's infamy until he was resurrected as a fictional villain by Bram Stoker – we must start at the top. Mehmet II, who became acquainted with Dracula during the Impaler's confinement at the Ottoman court and later became the Voivode's sworn enemy, was of the Osman bloodline. He was every inch the archetypal Ottoman Sultan, a frightening viper's nest of contradictions – cultured and vindictive, noble and debauched – a remarkable man to be both admired and despised. When Mehmet finally secured the Sultan's crown after a series of setbacks and disappointments he attempted to prevent the chaos that came with a contested succession by decreeing that the Sultan had the right to commit fratricide in support of a lineage of strong leadership. At the Ottoman court, brutality begins at home. This was Social Darwinism within the family, long before the phrase was coined. The new law, the *Zanannameh*, was decreed as follows: 'The majority of legists have declared that those of my illustrious children and grandchildren who shall ascend the throne shall have the right to execute their brothers, in order to ensure the peace of the world; they are to act comfortably.'

The method of dispatch would be strangely poetical: strangulation with a silk bowstring by the deaf-mute servants who attended the palaces. Thus began a fratricidal dynasty to outstrip the notorious Borgias, with fewer restraints upon their internecine plotting.

In the time of the Sultans, greatness often became synonymous with great cruelty, and it is hard to extricate these two characteristics. Mehmet II's grandson, Selim, would become known as Yavuz – 'the Grim'; the implications of such a title seem obvious, but to the Turks it implied 'strong', 'unfaltering', 'tough'. Born in 1470 (six years before the fall of Vlad, 11 years before the death of Mehmet), this great Ottoman leader would order the deaths of thousands of heretics.

But before this, his will of iron was demonstrated by Selim's ascendancy to the Sultanate throne. Deposing his own father, Bayezid (named after the 'Thunderbolt', victor of Nicopolis, but lacking his namesake's resolve) in 1512, Selim would interpret the fratricidal policies of Mehmet for his own ruthless ends. Neither of his two brothers, Ahmet nor Korkut, was the type of moral weakling that the Conqueror sought to bar from the throne; indeed, both had much military support. This did not prevent Selim, with the aid of the Janissaries, from strangling Ahmet and his son in 1513, after defeating his brother's aim to become Sultan of Anatolia supported by an army of Turkish nomads. To eradicate his own potentially vengeful bloodline, he had Ahmet and Korkut's five surviving sons brought to the Grand Seraglio – the imperial palace compound in Constantinople built by Mehmet II – to be strangled; Korkut himself was assassinated at his own palace.

For all his treachery, Selim the Grim was seen by many Muslims as the great Ottoman champion of the faith. His brief reign was largely spent in military campaigns, particularly against the Mamelukes (descendants of a former soldier-slave caste) who had ruled Egypt for 300 years; Selim's war of attrition against them took 50,000 Mameluke lives. Despite the fact that they were ostensibly his Sunni Muslim brothers, Selim was able to denounce them as non-Turkish foreigners; this, and his war against the forces of the Safavid Ismail, the heretical Persian Shiite who claimed descent from Muhammad, earned Selim the sword and mantle of the Prophet, both supposedly preserved in Constantinople. For all his grandiosity and heroic status, his administrators had few illusions about him. 'May you be Selim's vizier,' ran one piece of gallows humour, in line with the Confucian curse, 'May you live in interesting times' – both equating with a violent death.

The tyrant widely regarded as the last great Ottoman Sultan succeeded Selim in 1520. Suleiman the Magnificent continued the Empire's conquest of Eastern Europe with his incursion into Belgrade in 1521 and Hungary in 1526. According to contemporary accounts 200,000 Hungarians died, and 2000 prisoners-of-war were slaughtered before the Sultan's eyes for his entertainment. His siege of Vienna in 1529 – attended by 250,000 Ottoman troops and 300 cannons – provided a supply of Austrian girls taken as slaves for the Ottoman harems, where the Sultan and his adjutants took full advantage of a polygamous (indeed, promiscuous) lifestyle; his merciless massacre by fire of the city's peasantry also provided a grim echo of the 'social cleansing' of Wallachia by Vlad the Impaler decades earlier (see Chapter Seven.) For this is the Middle Ages culture that had once inculcated its behaviour into the Turks' young captive prince regent, and the unchecked power of the Ottoman Empire would ensure it survived into the modern age – both as an anachronism and as a portent of other tyrannies yet to come. If we could witness the recurring events of history on a screen, we would find that much of it consisted of an unending tape loop of atrocities – a 'video nasty', to coin the phrase of the censorious, underlining both the savagery and the valour of human conflict.

Suleiman is also infamous in Ottoman history for paving the way for his favoured son's succession by having the mute guards strangle his elder son, Mustafa – before decreeing three days of mourning in Mustafa's honour. The ascension to the Sultan's throne of Suleiman's favourite, Selim II, preordained the modern history of a Cyprus divided between warring Greeks and Turks. For the new Selim was a decadent sensualist and a drunkard, the schisms in Ottoman society between pious muftis and self-indulgent rulers creating a tolerance to alcohol (both cultural and physiological) unprecedented in other Muslim societies – despite early clerical punishments for drunkenness that ranged from whipping the soles of the feet (bastinado) to being forced to drink molten lead. (This inherited tolerance also makes the modern Turk a far more convivial counterpart than his co-religionists to most Westerners, with our culture's long tradition of alcohol as a social lubricant.)

Selim II's own two-year siege of Famagusta in Cyprus was, legend has it, inspired by his love of the grape and the city's reputation for fine wine production. Despite its hedonistic origin, it reached much the same climax as other Ottoman military adventures: the city's surrendering garrison, having been promised they would be spared, were slaughtered; their commander was flayed alive, the skin removed bloodily wholesale from his bones as he screamed his death agonies. In the final post-mortem humiliation, his organs and viscera were removed to be replaced with straw, and the stuffed soldier-mannequin was paraded in front of the appreciative Ottoman troops.

At the height of the Ottoman Empire, in the late 16th century, the Turks ruled over the Balkan region and Eastern Europe, as well as the entire Middle East and regions of North Africa. It was one of the most successful imperial powers the world has seen, and the departure from the global stage of parochial nationalist heroes like John Hunyadi and Vlad III left its progress unchecked.

But alongside the grandeur was the horror. When Mehmet III, son of the drunkard Selim, ascended the throne in 1595, he eliminated any further claims to succession by murdering 19 of his own brothers, all under the age of 11, after calling them to undergo a traditional Muslim circumcision. (This was at the urging of his ruthless mother, Sofia Baffo, who, as with a number of Ottoman women, exercised her influence from within the harem. She too would later be strangled in her bed. The mothers of the murdered boys were instructed to grieve in private, as any open display would carry an instant death penalty.) As if fearful of his own bastard progeny, he also had seven pregnant concubines tied up in a sack and drowned in the Bosporus.

After Mehmet III, the Sultanate court reversed the ruthless fratricidal edict of Mehmet the Conqueror by rearing the Sultan's heirs in pampered seclusion in the Grand Seraglio's *Kafes* ('the Cage'), a luxurious prison, attended only by the mute slaves and concubines. It was a kind of Social Darwinism in reverse, with the isolation and unworldliness of the subsequent Sultans making them increasingly unfit to rule – if not outright insane.

The last great Ottoman conqueror of this period was Murad IV, who became Sultan in 1623. Murad was perhaps the most formidable warrior of his age, a fearless leader who often fought at the head of his troops. But his excesses were extreme and he exceeded any of the past Sultans' reputations for sadism, as we shall see. Murad IV resembles less a character from *The Thousand and One Nights of Scheherazade* than one of the cruel, authoritarian libertines in de Sade's *The 120 Days of Sodom*. His prolific list of punishments is also said to have included impalement – a punishment meted out to a Frenchman the Sultan discovered in a liaison with a Turkish girl. But this was no innovation of his, as it was long established in the Ottoman repertoire of sadism. Bocaretto, an Italian travelling through 18th-century Turkey, would later write of the barbaric penalties he saw inflicted on anyone who transgressed against the decaying empire: 'The other morning I saw a pyramid of human heads on the left side of the principal entrance to the Imperial Palace ... You can see from the road, naked and still living men, caught on long spikes, where they will have to remain until death delivers them.'

Three hundred years after the time of Vlad the Impaler, impalement was still one of the myriad tortures and torments of the Ottoman Empire. We will return later to the vexed question of exactly who taught who this charming technique.

There was also a canny worldliness to Murad's terror tactics that was geared toward holding his empire together. When the formerly loyal Janissaries, conscious of their status as the backbone of the Ottoman army, pressured Murad into executing 17 of his handpicked administrators, he restored equilibrium by having 600 of their number strangled in their own barracks.

Murad ruled with a will of iron that Vlad III would have recognised. As former newspaper foreign correspondent Noel Barber describes in *Lords of the Golden Horn*, his history of the decline of the Ottoman Empire:

> 'Murad quickly found a panacea for the ills of the country. He cut off the head of any man who came under the slightest suspicion. In 1637 he executed 25,000 subjects in the name of justice, many by his own hand.

His maxim was, 'Vengeance never grows decrepit though she may grow grey.' He executed the Grand Mufti because he was dissatisfied with the state of the roads. He beheaded his chief musician for playing a Persian air.'

Under the religious *sharia* law of the Muslims, the Turkish muftis forbade torture as an instrument to procure a suspect's confession – in sharp contrast to much of Europe, where the inhumane instruments of law were granted *laissez-faire* by a Church that benignly nodded compliance with the torturers of the Inquisition. This, however, shows the divergence between the religious doctrines inculcated into the indigenous subjects of the Ottomans, and the largely secular will of the Sultans who behaved as a law unto themselves.

Murad, as with many other tyrants of the age, undoubtedly saw the will and voice of God as inseparable from his own sense of self. Assured that he ruled by divine right, such a psychotic egotist would have little reason to discern between the wrathful deity and the unquestionable assurance that all of his despotic actions were righteous and just. Thus it is with the rulers and the ruled throughout history – from the British Prime Minister in our own age who, in the name of liberal interventionism, refuses to be judged by anyone but God (the imaginary friend in his own mind who offers unbending moral support) for unilaterally committing his nation to the invasion of Iraq (former Ottoman territory), to Prince Vlad III of Wallachia, who, in the name of defending Christendom, seems to have acted with the unrestrained sadistic relish of the Devil.

***

'Do not fear, precious jewel! We will soon be delivered unto Paradise.'

Mustafa the royal gardener implores his terror-stricken wife to have faith. Dressed in pale robes of contrition, the trembling couple await the summary justice of their pious Sultan, Murad. Murad, whose clandestine nocturnal wanderings into the taverns of the city's lower neighbourhoods bring him into contact with much lowly and disreputable behaviour. Murad, the exemplar of justice. Murad, the voice of Allah.

Elma weeps, shaking, as the muftis and imperial administrators emotionlessly assess their plight. Bound to the trees beyond the royal gardens where her husband has spent much of his life, they await the judgement of their Sultan. Their transgression has been one of carelessness; their penalty will be severe.

'You have been found guilty by His Imperial Excellency, Sultan Murad IV, of indulgence in the forbidden infidel vice of tobacco.'

The words are read aloud from a scroll of golden-leafed script. All is propriety here.

'It is therefore the most pious and just judgement of the Sultan that your lives shall be forfeit and your souls surrendered unto Allah, the most wise, the most merciful.'

The justice minister's quiet words rain down hammer blows that smash all hope. For the Sultan is a most pious man who, in his nightly wanderings, discovered Mustafa and his wife partaking of the filthy shisha pipe. Their sensual vices have been their own undoing.

Barely raising their eyes from the ground in front of them, they know that Murad's unforgiving eyes are upon them. As the chief executioner unsheathes his scimitar, Mustafa mutters implorations to Elma to have faith and trust in her deliverance.

His Imperial Excellency watches the execution of sentence with great satisfaction. Did not the Sheik-ul-Islam say that imbibing of the rank weed was haram, *and should be remedied by the utmost sanctions?*

Of course, the great sheik was answered by those pedants who insist that the Holy Koran makes no mention of tobacco at all. Let them quibble. If Murad does not act now, then who knows what inroads this vice shall make into the land of the Ottomans? Will there one day be Turkish farms that grow the prohibited plant? And might the Turkish people, Heaven forefend, take this filthy stuff to their bosoms?

The gardener and his wife hang their quivering heads forward, in anticipation of the executioner's blows. As Elma sobs, Mustafa is silent, but he shakes as if about to succumb to a freezing temperature on this hot night.

Their hair is pulled back sharply, preventing them from offering the bared backs of their necks. Startled, daring not to hope for reprieve, they realise too late what is about to happen as the executioner's assistants tear back the fabric of their pantaloons and skirt to just above the knee, placing wooden blocks beneath their naked legs to support them.

The crescent blade rises, sweeps downward and strikes.

Then it strikes again, and again, as it must. Until the blade has bitten through skin, sinew and vein, until the agonised sinner and his corrupted wife are bereft of both their legs and the couple's screams cry out to Heaven to deliver them from their earthly sufferings.

It is a pleasing spectacle. Murad inspects his punitive innovation with satisfaction. The gardener's face is as bleached and colourless now as that of his wife. They gibber and their teeth chatter as the fresh blood squirts relentlessly through their exposed femoral arteries. They will be left to die out in the open, as an example to all the others. The manner of their demise will take a little time, and for Murad this is all the more gratifying.

***

Murad's 1638 siege of Baghdad, then the Persian capital, climaxed in a typical orgy of vengeance when an accidental ammunition explosion killed Turkish troops. In return, he reportedly ordered the slaughter of 30,000 Persian men, women and children. However, this was amongst the last of the successful Ottoman imperial adventures, although the bloodshed was a long while in subsiding. Murad was succeeded to the throne by his brother Ibrahim, an effete weakling who dwelled in the Cage in fear of his elder sibling and declared, 'The Butcher of the Empire is dead at last,' on hearing of his demise.

Despite his apparent distaste for bloodshed, Ibrahim followed a familiar pattern of petty tyranny. Suspecting one of his many concubines of cheating on him with one of the court's black eunuch slaves (some still apparently capable of sexual activity after the amputation of their testicles – or in some cases their penises), he had all 280 of his women drowned together in the Bosporus. A diver's testimony of the time spoke of 'a great number of bowing sacks, each containing the body of a dead woman standing upright on the weighted end and swaying to and fro with the current'. Ibrahim himself would be strangled with the silk bow, after an unusual *fatwa* issued by the Grand Mufti when he discovered the Sultan had seduced his daughter.

For the next two centuries, weak leadership and bloody regional rebellions would force the Ottomans further back into their native geographical borders. In 1821, their old enemies the Greeks – for long an occupied people in their native land – rose up against the Turks, massacring up to 8000 of the Turkish men, women and children who made Greece their colonial home. True to historical pattern, the oppressed had become the vengeful oppressors. ('Greek historians have recoiled from telling of these barbarities,' noted English historian George Finlay in his 1877 *History of Greece*, 'while they have been loud in denouncing those of the Turks.') The backlash was predictably severe. In 1826, Sultan Mahmud had the rebellious Janissaries slaughtered in battle, shooting and drowning up to 10,000 of the adopted warrior caste that the Ottoman Empire had previously depended on.

VLAD THE IMPALER

By 1876, very little of the Empire remained. It was widely regarded as what Tsar Nicholas I had described 25 years prior as 'a very sick man'. It was then that the rebellion in Bulgaria – which inspired Gladstone's outraged pamphlet – led to the burning of 60 villages and the slaughter of 15,000 men, women and children under Sultan Abdul Aziz. The atrocities were committed in part by Circassian mercenaries, whom Turkish troops allowed to run amok in return for whatever they could loot. London *Daily News* correspondent J. A. MacGahan described the sights that awaited him in the Bulgarian town of Batak, in the aftermath:

> 'On every side were skulls and skeletons charred among the ruins, or lying entire where they fell in their clothing. They were skeletons of girls and women with long black hair hanging to their skulls ... I never imagined anything so fearful. There were 3000 bodies in the churchyard and church ... In the school, a fine building, 200 women and children had been burnt alive.'

The international reaction led to the deposal of the senile Sultan, who was followed by a quick succession of rulers – the most supposedly progressive of whom, Abdul Hamid II, was imposed on the Ottomans in the months following the Bulgarian massacre by reforming politicians who saw him as a force for change. While it's true that he introduced more pluralistic Western standards of education for the privileged elite and the military officer class, he also fell in line with what the philosopher Nietzsche described as history's 'law of eternal recurrence', when he ended the centuries-old Ottoman Empire with one of its bloodiest acts.

In 1894, with the Empire diminishing within its ever-contracting borders, Abdul turned the powers of the Ottoman state against its latest ethnic scapegoat, the Christian Armenian minority whose leaders were seeking political reform (tantamount to revolution, according to the Sultan). Their persecution was enacted in a surreal scenario, suggestive of the 'two-minutes' hate' in Orwell's *1984* expanded onto a grotesquely extravagant canvas.

At the dawn clarion call of a military bugle, Turkish troops and civilian mobs were turned loose on the populations within the Empire's Armenian quarters. Property was destroyed and businesses looted. Men were killed and women raped. Children were not spared. By imperial decree, within the time frame afforded by two reports of the bugle, the

Armenians were fair game for the violence of the dominant Turks. In the town of Trebizond, every Christian family had its home ransacked before their throats were cut. In Urfa, 3000 of all ages and both genders were burned alive as they sought sanctuary in the cathedral. At the second bugle call, at twilight, the Turks returned to their barracks and homes while the lives of their Armenian neighbours lay in bloody ruins. At the end of several days of this perversely ordered ritual, more than 100,000 were dead.

Revulsion in the West at the massacres earned Abdul Hamid II the soubriquet 'the Red Sultan', as coined by the French President. Most tellingly, he became known as 'Abdul the Damned' among those Turks who regarded the atrocities with shame. His behaviour as a medieval despot in modern times would hasten the end of Abdul's reign, but even the military coup by the 'Young Turks' and their political movement's steps toward modern democracy could not halt the final horror.

In 1915, when the Turkish nation fought alongside Germany in World War 1, Enver Bey, one of Turkey's new political leaders, ordered a massacre of the rebellious Armenians on the basis that some were fighting on the Russian side in the conflict. What followed even eclipsed the mass murder of 1894.

The populations of more than 80 Armenian villages were rounded up for shooting. Rape was endemic. According to Henry Morgenthau, then U.S. Ambassador to the Ottoman Empire, one of the Turkish torturers admitted he'd 'delved into the records of the Spanish Inquisition and adopted all the suggestions found there'. Another was known as 'the Blacksmith' for his crude innovation of horseshoes nailed to the feet (although it should be pointed out that apologists for the Ottomans decry Morgenthau's testimony as deliberately embellished for political reasons of his own). What is certain is that 18,000 Armenians of all ages were forced to march across the Syrian Desert to the city of Aleppo. En route they were ambushed by Kurdish tribesmen, alerted by the Turks; today the Kurds are seen as victims rather than victimisers, having endured years of marginalisation and repression in modern Turkey and the genocide perpetrated against them by Saddam Hussein; seen in the light of 1915, we have a tragic reminder that all human tribal groupings are potentially capable of becoming xenophobic and murderous, directing their atavistic rage against 'the others'.

By the time the bedraggled Armenian survivors arrived in Aleppo, not many more than 150 naked, starved and dehydrated women and children had been spared, while all their menfolk had been massacred by the Kurds. The mass murder of a conservatively-estimated 600,000 Armenians has since been acknowledged by Jewish historians as the precursor of the Holocaust. It would have a further grotesque sequel at the end of empire, in September 1922 – the time of the rise of Ataturk, father of modern Turkey. In the chaos of the fire of Smyrna, on the Aegean Coast, vengeful Turkish troops perpetrated atrocities against their close neighbours and traditional enemies, the Greeks and Armenians. Noel Barber relates that, during the carnage, the elderly Patriarch of the Greek Orthodox Church had his eyes gouged out and was torn to pieces by a baying mob.

Such was the now fallen empire that infused Vlad III with his lifelong lust for revenge, and perhaps inspired him with its ever more innovative methods of torture and execution. While no longer a byword for despotic global power in our modern age, in its lifetime their empire was one of the most formidable and ruthless the world has yet seen. From our modern perspective, the problem we have in discerning the motivation for Vlad's most extreme actions is similar to that we face with the Sultans: was all the cruelty committed out of political expediency? Was it solely the product of ensuring survival in savage, desperate times? Or was there a level of personal gratification to be gained from acts which must have seemed gratuitous even in the era when they were committed?

***

Back in the 15th century, the Ottoman Empire was reaching the height of its power. The strange blend of luxury and terror evolving at the Sultan's court left its young hostage Radu cowed and compliant. His elder brother Vlad, however, reacts differently. Initially violently defiant, the older Wallachian finally learns to hold his tongue. Has he, as his captors believe, finally accepted the futility of resistance? Or are there darker thoughts passing through the mind of the brooding prince? As the future shade of convict Carl Panzram (see previous chapter) informs us, a schooling in terror can create monsters. All of the wrongs done to him during a youth in captivity built up inside the young Carl until they erupted in the behaviour of the pathological adult. Such is the origin (or the rationalisation) of the criminal misdeeds of all who endure an early institutionalisation – and so it will be with Vlad …

Vlad and Radu's survival in Ottoman captivity intact, despite the treachery of their father, is regarded as little short of a miracle by many Dracula historians. Vlad's release in 1448 is almost as surprising. It suggests that he had gained the trust of his captors, who had trained the young Wallachian in the Turkish arts of war, even making him an officer in the army. This wasn't so unusual. There were numerous Eastern Orthodox Christians fighting for the Ottomans. Men who had found themselves there by circumstance or in the hope of fighting for the winning side, as the tides of war certainly seemed to favour the Turks in the wake of the victory at Varna. Many Orthodox Christians hated the Catholics far more than the Muslims – the phrase 'Better the Sultan's turban than the cardinal's hat' echoed across Eastern Europe throughout the 15th century. The region's dominant Catholic nations, Hungary and Poland, had been complicit in generations of prejudice and persecution towards their Eastern Orthodox neighbours, while the brutality of the Crusades from the west towards Eastern Europe's native population had sown deep seeds of mistrust and hatred. For many Orthodox Christians, the light hand of a pragmatic Ottoman governor must have seemed far preferable to the mailed fist frequently employed by the servants of the Papacy.

Vlad had more reason than most to throw his lot in with the Turks. While the men who murdered his father and buried his brother alive were fellow Wallachians – supporters of the Danesti faction – his Ottoman captors must have emphasised the role the Catholic warlord John Hunyadi probably played in the bloody episode. The Greek chronicler Demetrios Chalcocondylis described the new Danesti Voivode Vladislav II as John Hunyadi's 'great friend, the one whom he had brought to the Dacian land because of his hatred towards Dracula'. Even if Dracula had been able to put his personal feelings aside, he had no realistic prospect of claiming the throne of Wallachia from Vladislav II, who enjoyed the support of the Hungarian crown, without the assistance of the Ottoman Empire. Despite his best attempts to leash his vicious side, Dracula was clearly growing into a man who had trouble putting his personal feelings aside.

The Turks admired ruthlessness and ferocity in their warriors; unlike his pretty young brother Radu, the teenaged Vlad evinced both qualities in abundance, and was beginning to show every sign of being a loyal vassal to the Ottoman cause, charmed by Turkish luxury, finally tamed by harsh Ottoman discipline. But, as Machiavelli observes in *The Prince*, 'Everyone sees what you appear to be, few know what you are' – and Vlad had been playing things close to his chest. 'Being brutalised at a very young age takes its toll: feeling powerless, vulnerable,' observes Laura Richards, a contemporary criminal behavioural psychologist. 'Certainly what I know about powerless people is that at some point they will try to take the power back.'

For Vlad's captors, however, the time seemed ripe to unleash their angry young asset to reclaim his legacy and take revenge upon the hated Danesti clan. From the Turkish point of view, this would finally install a staunch anti-Hungarian Voivode in the border state of Wallachia, bringing Ottoman power another crucial step further onto European soil. The timing was not accidental. In the autumn of 1448, John Hunyadi launched another offensive against the Ottomans through Serbia. He summoned as many allies as he could, including Vladislav II, who brought a modest contingent of Wallachian cavalry to join the ranks assembling for the march south. With both the Wallachian Voivode and John Hunyadi fully occupied on campaign it was an ideal opportunity for Dracula to stage a coup. Backed by Turkish troops loaned to him by the Ottoman Sultan, the teenage warlord seized the crown in a lightning campaign.

Resistance was probably minimal as confusion reigned in Wallachia. Not only was Voivode Vladislav II and his powerful patron John Hunyadi absent, but nobody seemed sure where they were. The news filtering back from the frontline had not been good for some time. The friction that had built up between Hunyadi and the Serbian despot George Branković during the ill-fated Long Campaign had once more blossomed into open hostility. Once more, personal animosity threatened to determine the fate of nations. To Hunyadi, the Serb ruler was a traitor, an ingrate and a coward – Branković saw the White Knight of Transylvania as an upstart, a fanatic and a fool. George Branković not only turned down John Hunyadi's request to join the campaign, but refused to grant the Christian force permission to cross Serbian territory. The enraged White Knight responded by treating Serbia as enemy territory, giving his men free rein to loot and pillage as they marched. In turn, the incensed Serbian ruler passed on detailed reports of Christian troop movements to the Ottoman Sultan, Murad II, allowing the Turks ample opportunity to prepare a response to Hunyadi's advance. Even more damagingly for Christian prospects, the Serbs were also successful in delaying Hunyadi's most important ally, Skanderbeg, whose fierce Albanian freedom fighters had proven themselves against the Turks time and again.

John Hunyadi's forces finally clashed with Sultan Murad's army at Kosovo on 17 October, at the Field of Crows, where the Ottomans delivered a crippling blow to Serbian independence nearly 60 years earlier. (The name of Kosovo would gain even greater infamy in 1995, when the Kosovo War between ethnic Serbs and Albanian separatists inspired a series of atrocities that finally convinced NATO to try and bomb the belligerents to the negotiating table in 1999.) The terrible refrain of history set at Nicopolis echoed in a chorus of blood in the autumn of 1448, as once again the steel wave of Christian knights broke against the solid rocks of disciplined Janissary infantry. This time the terrible toll stretched over days, as the cannons thundered and men, screaming in rage and pain, fell upon each other with sword, spear and mace. When the clouds of gunpowder smoke finally lifted, the Christians were once more in full retreat. Once again, the sheer scale of slaughter stopped the Ottomans in their tracks; the cost of the victory was high, and rather than try and muster his forces for pursuit, Murad paused to bury his many dead. The old Sultan was tired of battle, ready to try again to pass the burden of command to his son Mehmet, who had enjoyed his first taste of battle at Kosovo.

In the final echo of past tragedy, Hunyadi and Skanderbeg now found themselves forced to try and make their way back through Serbia, the army's violent previous advance ensuring that this was now decidedly hostile territory. George Branković took advantage of the White Knight's distress, and once again John Hunyadi found himself the captive of a former ally with a grudge. Hunyadi no doubt experienced a powerful sense of *déjà vu*. Just as he had been at the mercy of Vlad Dracul four years before following the disaster at Varna, he was now the reluctant guest of Branković, his life once more hanging by a thread. News of the disaster at Kosovo took its time filtering back to Wallachia.

In Wallachia, as Dracula set about securing the foundations of his new regime, the letters he sent soliciting support from local boyars and the councils of Transylvania were met with decidedly guarded responses. Was his new regime sanctioned by John Hunyadi? More pertinently, where was John Hunyadi – was he still alive? Where indeed was the former Voivode Vladislav II? Such questions received a pointed response before the end of 1448, when Vladislav returned to Wallachia with the remnants of the Hungarian army, driving Dracula's force of Ottoman mercenaries and opportunists out as quickly as they had arrived. His reign had lasted barely two months.

Happily for Hunyadi, like Vlad's father Dracul, George Branković proved pragmatic. Placated with promises of property, and wary of executing an 'Athlete of Christ', the Serbian despot finally released his eminent prisoner. Hunyadi's status in Hungary was severely damaged by the defeat at Kosovo, and he had much urgent work to do at home to counter the machinations of his enemies at the Hungarian court. He did, however, find time to write to the council at Braşov, where Dracula had sought refuge among exiled Wallachian boyars hostile to the Danesti clan. Hunyadi instructed the Braşovians to remove this impudent new puppet of the Ottomans, permanently if possible. While Hunyadi's enemies at the Hungarian court had officially stripped him of the title of Voivode of Transylvania, his influence was damaged but far from destroyed, and so Vlad found himself a fugitive.

This period in Dracula's career is somewhat obscure. With his bold stab at the Wallachian throne thwarted, the teenage warlord was fast running out of options. Some accounts suggest he headed back east in the hope of securing additional support from the Ottomans. If so, it was a futile hope. Murad's attention was focused upon threats to his eastern front from Tamerlane's son and the increasingly damaging revolt led by Skanderbeg in Albania. The Sultan had little time or interest to dedicate to events in Wallachia. A more plausible version of events, considering Vlad's future career, has Dracula remaining in the region in hiding whilst pursued by assassins, escaping the fate that befell his father by a combination of cunning and good luck.

By the end of 1449, however, we know that Vlad had sought asylum at the Moldavian court. The medieval principality of Moldavia was located to the east of Transylvania and Wallachia, and with them now constitutes modern Romania (though the eastern part is now the independent Republic of Moldavia, while other parts of the original principality are now under Ukrainian control). The Vlach principality of Moldova shared not just a border with Wallachia, but had a lot of other things in common with its neighbour. Like Wallachia, Moldavia had struggled for decades against domination by the powerful Catholic kingdoms of Hungary and Poland to the north and the constant threat of the Ottoman Ghazis from the south and east. Their ruling dynasties also shared a common bloodline, something Dracula no doubt hoped might guarantee him safe haven. The Moldavian Voivode Bogdan II was not only Dracula's uncle, but had been given asylum by Vlad's father Dracul some years before, no doubt predisposing Bogdan to be sympathetic to the young fugitive, and he was welcomed to the Moldavian capital of Suceava with open arms.

While in Suceava the young Dracula, now entering his 20s, made one of the most significant relationships of his life when he befriended the Voivode's son Stefan, who was a few years younger than the Wallachian. It's important as perhaps the sole clear example we have of human warmth or weakness from Dracula, his friendship with his cousin Stefan perhaps the only time the future Impaler let his guard down. (With depressing predictability, it was a friendship ultimately destined to be tainted by betrayal.) The two friends rode together in the summer of 1450, helping to repel a Polish invasion, and made a solemn pact. If either needed help in reaching their respective thrones, the first to achieve power would lend military assistance to the other.

Vlad's happy days at Suceava were brought to an abrupt end in October of 1451, when Stefan's father Bogdan was the victim of a brutal assassination by his own step-brother, who ambushed the Voivode at a wedding, beheading him. Once again Vlad was obliged to flee with the prospect of imprisonment or worse breathing hard down his neck, though at least this time he had a companion in the shape of Stefan, who also needed to escape the plotters who had butchered his father. The pair must have thought long and hard about where to run. The Ottoman court was always an option, though it seems unlikely that Vlad entertained such a possibility for long, if at all. Recalling his years sheltering with sympathetic boyars in Braşov, Vlad decided to risk the wrath of John Hunyadi, and headed for the Transylvanian border.

It was a gamble, certainly, but one where Dracula must surely have carefully calculated the odds. Much had happened in the years since he had been chased from Transylvania with his tail between his legs, and Vlad must have been a keen student of current affairs during his stay at Suceava. Sultan Murad had fallen gravely ill in the winter of 1450, dying early the following year. The much-vaunted friendship between Hunyadi and the Wallachian Voivode Vladislav II appeared to be souring fast. After the series of false starts that plagued his early reign, Mehmet was finally crowned Sultan of the Ottoman Empire in January of 1451. Vladislav sent a delegation of Wallachian worthies to the coronation to congratulate the new Sultan, something Hunyadi interpreted as a prelude to treachery. To punish his former protégé, and hopefully bring him to heel, Hunyadi seized a number of Vladislav's estates.

Dracula must have calculated that, as the former alliance began to degenerate towards open conflict, the White Knight might require a new candidate for Voivode. He was taking a chance. Hunyadi's men were still looking for Vlad when he reached Braşov, and he was obliged to keep moving in order to avoid the fate of his father. Might Hunyadi take a gamble on Vlad, now very much the wild card in the deadly game of Wallachian politics? Hunyadi's own fortunes were at a low ebb. His rivals had taken advantage of the White Knight's defeats against the Ottomans to challenge his position at the Hungarian court, while Mehmet showed every sign of having learned by his own humiliations, and looked ready to spring into action against the divided Christians. Dracula decided to take the plunge, swallow any feelings of resentment he may have felt about Hunyadi's rumoured role in the deaths of his father and brother (if indeed he had any) and head for the White Knight's headquarters at Hunedoara, effectively throwing himself upon John Hunyadi's mercy.

Thankfully, Vlad Dracula's substantial gamble paid off. Hunyadi greeted the refugee Voivode with open arms – not only accepting him as a fellow leader, but allowing access to some of the estates his father, Vlad Dracul, had once owned. It was during his stay with Hunyadi that Dracula met Hunyadi's son and heir, Matthias Corvinus, who will become a significant figure in his future career, and learned the arts of European war and statesmanship at the court of their undisputed master.

Hunyadi has his reasons for such magnanimity. The Voivode he has installed on the Wallachian throne has proven unreliable, signing a pact with the Ottoman Sultan; his treachery costs Hunyadi the Battle of Kosovo. The astute Hungarian general is satisfied that Vlad's hatred, on the other hand, is firmly directed at his erstwhile Ottoman captors and declares his support for Dracula's ascendance to the Wallachian throne.

For his part, Vlad evidently doesn't hold Hunyadi responsible for his father's death, directing his burning thirst for vengeance at those closer to home …

CHAPTER VI

The Light of The World is Extinguished

*'As long as mankind shall continue to bestow more liberal
applause on their destroyers than on their benefactors, the
thirst of military glory will ever be the vice of the most
exalted characters.' Edward Gibbon.*

*If there was ever a building that carried its owner's mark, an imposing edifice
that incarnated its master's spirit in stone, it is Hunedoara Castle. With its
broad, unyielding walls and proud, unassailable towers, the colourful roofs and
ornate windows are the friendly face upon a fortress that stands like a tireless
sentry, perched, immovable, over the Zlasti River. As Vlad Dracula crosses
the long raised path towards the drawbridge, the only entrance to John
Hunyadi's inner sanctum, he glances nervously at the dizzying drop either
side. His mount snorts, and he wonders for a moment if the steps his horse is
taking are leading him over a threshold with no way back. But no – for the
young Wallachian, he has already made his choices – had his choices made for
him by something deep within his own soul. Honour, revenge, power? Or
something deeper or darker still, it doesn't matter. This hunger has brought
him here, and Vlad urges his horse on, eyes forward, with a steady pace.*

*Once in the courtyard he dismounts. With a gesture he has two boyars who
have accompanied him do the same, then step back as Vlad is ushered up the
stone steps to the Knight's Hall. While the castle is far from the front line,
everywhere the place seems ready for war – the guards in full armour clasp
their halberds, the cannons are charged – Vlad feels curiously at home. But he
has much to unsettle his carefully guarded demeanour. Dracula is slowly
walking into the lion's den, each echoing footstep carrying him closer to the
man many say ordered the assassination of his father and the death of his
brother in circumstances that had made some of his Turkish captors blanch,
and others smirk, in their repetition. But this is no time for feelings, no time
for open faces – it is a time that a man needs to be a man, needs to wear the*

iron mask of a ruler, should his hunger ever be sated…

Beneath the imposing stone arches of the Knight's Hall, John Hunyadi is in conference with his knights. They clearly haven't broken their council for food, and the detritus of their previous meal is scattered all over the huge chamber. Several stout oaken tables have been drawn together, the dying sunlight supplemented by candles and torches to illuminate a large map spread over the tables. As Vlad approaches, his entry is acknowledged by cold glares from many of those stood around the table. Most, like him, betray the traits of an Eastern European noble: the long hair and heavy moustache, the ornate clothing influenced by fashions in Byzantium rather than Paris. Others are more Germanic, even Italian in their garb. All emanate suspicion as they look up from their charts to scrutinise the Wallachian, who does his best to ignore every eye, save that of his host.

John Hunyadi is simply dressed. The man who is known across Europe for his silver-embossed armour wears a smock that, were it not so finely tailored, could easily be on the shoulders of a Transylvanian merchant or petty official. Yet there is no mistaking the bearing of this man. Those shoulders frame a powerful physique, supplanted by a broad, noble face, divided, like Vlad's, by the proud moustache of a Vlach warrior. His expression is not guarded, but welcoming. 'Greetings,' he smiles. 'We are surveying our situation, pray join us.' Hunyadi's hand sweeps across the maps in front of them, which Dracula sees depict the regions of Eastern Europe, the Balkans, and the Ottoman territories to the east. The charts are held flat by plates and jugs, though there are also items of food – fruit, meat, and bread – dotted across the paper. 'We have been talking since last night,' offers Hunyadi, noticing Vlad's quizzical gaze. 'These morsels serve as reminders of the armies and men who are moving across our maps.'

'Now,' he adds, picking up a mutton bone, his smile freezing, 'one of our pieces is amongst us.' At that, a knight to Hunyadi's left interjects. 'Is there not a little too much meat on that for this Wallachian whelp? Have we not something smaller – a grape perhaps? Without a Turkish army at his back there isn't much to…' The knight's words stop in their tracks with just a glare from Hunyadi. Dracula's emotions are wavering between rage and fear. He stares at the knight and, with well-tested restraint, simply lowers his head slightly and commits the face to memory. 'It isn't about who is behind you, though' is it, my young dragon,' Hunyadi says, taking a bite from the hunk of meat. 'It's about blood, isn't it? Isn't it? Come, speak, that is why you came here surely?'

Dracula suddenly feels curiously aware of his surroundings. The dour stone arches over the echoing chamber – the stench of cooked meat and sour wine that soaks the straw at his feet – a trio of hounds chewing lazily at bones beneath *the table. For a moment his mind spins back to the world of his youth, of the perfumed court of the Sultan, of the elegant Ottoman cage where his brother Radu remains an eager, pampered captive. 'I am here to offer my fealty to you Lord Hunyadi,' offers Dracula, with what he hopes sounds a deferential tone. 'And you have questions to ask?' responds Hunyadi, rising, and looking Dracula full in the eye. 'Questions?' responds Vlad, unsure of the correct response. 'About your father,' continues Hunyadi. 'I fought beside your father...' 'But not for long,' Vlad spits back, momentarily forgetting himself.*

'No, not for long,' concedes Hunyadi, and for the first time anger tinges his tone. Somehow Dracula finds that reassuring. 'I didn't lay a hand upon your Dracul or Mircea,' Hunyadi adds, regaining his composure, but turning his back to the table. 'Betrayal is an ugly thing, and I never betrayed your father.' With that, Hunyadi turns to stare Dracula in the face once more, and then goes silent for a few heavy seconds. 'Do you love Christ our lord?' whispers Hunyadi with sudden insistence, his face close to Vlad's. 'I do my lord,' nods Dracula. 'And do you hate the Turk?' Hunyadi says, stepping backward. 'I do,' spits Vlad. Hunyadi turns his back again. 'Do you love Christ more than you hate the Turk?' Dracula waits until Hunyadi has turned to face him again, before declaring, 'Isn't loving Christ and hating the Turk the same thing?' Laughter erupts around the table, as Hunyadi gestures for Dracula to join them. But Vlad Dracula isn't laughing, nor, he notices as he takes his place at Hunyadi's shoulder, is Hunyadi himself...

***

Whatever truly happened behind closed doors at Hunedoara, Vlad Dracula and John Hunyadi managed to strike a deal. Vlad was clearly able to overcome any reservations over the man some blamed for the murder of his father and older brother. Hunyadi was willing to trust the son of the man who had once threatened to execute him on a trumped up charge of treachery. Dracula was offered much the same deal his father was given the year of his birth. He was charged with guarding the Transylvanian border, his presence serving as an implicit threat to the current incumbent, whose loyalty was becoming increasingly suspect. Hunyadi must have hoped his latest prospect for the voivodeship of Wallachia might prove more satisfactory than the previous candidates he had sponsored, all of whom had buckled beneath the pressure of the Ottomans on their doorstep.

The importance of a Christian warlord with a spine in the buffer realm of Wallachia had never been greater from the White Knight's perspective. He had serious problems at home. His influence at court as effective regent of Hungary was waning. The new King of Hungary, Ladislaus Posthumous (a title reflecting the fact that he was born after his father's death) was coming of age and asserting his independence. The boy monarch was expressing his building confidence by kicking against his most powerful advisor and mentor and challenging the policy of focusing upon the threat of the Ottoman Empire. Hunyadi had been honoured by the Pope himself in 1448 with titles and a gold chain, but many now remembered the White Knight's catastrophic defeats at Varna and Kosovo more vividly than his many victories, making Hunyadi's status as the champion of Christendom increasingly precarious, the Athlete of Christ depicted as yesterday's man by his many rivals in Buda.

As the wheels of treachery spun once more, John Hunyadi's breach with Vladislaus II now looked increasingly permanent, the Voivode moving ever closer to Ottoman appeasement as the White Knight's influence waned. There may have been a personal component to the schism. While he excelled in a crisis, and was clearly much loved and respected by his men, the middle-aged warlord often struggled to be treated as an equal by the elite of Eastern Europe. His background was comparatively humble and, like Vlad, he was a Vlach, even if he had embraced the Catholic faith of the Hungarian court. Hunyadi worked well with warriors, but the intricacies of court politics often frustrated him. Meanwhile, Mehmet had much to prove after his own humiliatingly abortive early career as an adolescent Sultan, and was showing the first signs of being an aggressive and able leader. Something serious was afoot, and once again, it seemed like only John Hunyadi appreciated the threat. But perhaps, just perhaps, he had finally found his man, a Wallachian Voivode who shared his dedication to the cause, a warlord just as implacable and single-minded as himself...

Hunyadi took Vlad Dracula under his wing, and did what he could to further his cause at the Hungarian court. He solicited the blessing of Ladislaus Posthumous for the Wallachian's new posting in Transylvania, this time in the fortified city of Sibiu, even closer to the Wallachian border than his birthplace in Sighisoara, where Vlad's father had awaited his own opportunity to seize the crown some two decades before. Some have speculated that John Hunyadi became something of a mentor to the young Vlad Dracula, completing his education in the finer arts of war on the Ottoman borders. Hunyadi probably had just as much to learn from his new protégé. Dracula knew the new Ottoman Sultan personally (though how intimately remains controversial) and could give firsthand insight into the inner workings of the Turkish war machine. Dracula had also, of course, known that other Athlete of Christ, Skanderbeg, during his years at the Ottoman court, and the celebrated Albanian leader no doubt proved inspirational to Vlad. In 1450, Skanderbeg had spurned a large Turkish bribe and aggressively resisted a formidable Ottoman invasion force, obliging Mehmet's father Murad to retreat from Albania, marking a sad end to the old Sultan's career.

Mehmet, however, had bigger fish to fry – or, to put it another way, an apple to pluck. The city of Constantinople was the original 'big apple' – colloquially known as the 'red apple' by Turks, a ripe prize, forever just out of reach. The city, otherwise known as Byzantium, was a fabulously wealthy metropolis that bestrode the Bosporus, dividing Asia and Europe, perfectly placed to profit by both the mercantile riches and exchange of ideas that came with dominating such a significant axis. At least as important as its dazzling wealth, however, was what the city signified. It was the last outpost of classical sophistication and opulence, a stronghold of civilisation that stood while the rest Europe fell beneath the wave of barbarian invasions that heralded the Dark Ages. The city took its name from the Roman Emperor Constantine, though many still knew it by its Greek name Byzantium. Constantine chose the city as his capital in AD324, turning his back upon Rome, opening a new chapter in the history of the Roman Empire. In many respects, it was to be the final one.

The Emperor earned the epithet Constantine the Great by virtue of adopting Christianity as the state religion of the Roman Empire, effectively establishing the faith as Europe's dominant creed thereafter. Not every historian is so convinced of the wisdom of Constantine's conversion. In his landmark history, *The Decline and Fall of the Roman Empire*, Edward Gibbon suggested that the adoption of Christianity contributed to the ultimate collapse of the Empire. It was a suggestion that proved inflammatory upon the publication of the book's first volume in 1776, and its author was denounced from church pulpits across Europe. None, however, could deny that the Roman Empire did decline and fall, though the date of its demise remains open to debate. Rome itself crumbled beneath the assaults of a merciless wave of Germanic warlords in the 5th century, and many historians end their histories of the Empire then. Gibbon, however, continued his history long after, detailing a further thousand years in the following five volumes, which he completed in 1789, writing in Switzerland to avoid the controversy that dogged him in London.

VLAD THE IMPALER

The final volume covers some of the same territory to be found in this book – Chapter 67 includes brief accounts of the careers of John Hunyadi and Skanderbeg – though these sections are almost invariably cut from the epic study in modern abridged versions. Gibbon also discusses the Crusades at some length. Just as most conventional histories of the Crusades stop at the fall of Acre in 1291, despite the Papacy continuing vainly to call Crusades up to the disaster at Nicopolis in 1396 and beyond, the history of the Roman Empire continued in the east well into the 1400s. The Byzantine Emperors considered themselves the legitimate inheritors of the Roman legacy, governing the remaining eastern provinces in Asia and Eastern Europe as well as parts of Italy and Greece, and were accepted as such by most contemporaries. Inevitably, the character of the Empire changed. Educated Romans had long revered Greek culture, and the Greeks dominated the Byzantine Empire, which became a byword for lavish refinement. 'Byzantine' also survives as an adjective implying deviousness and intricacy, suggesting the complex web of diplomatic intrigues the Empire had to undertake to survive.

The history of the Byzantine Empire is a thousand-year saga of a sophisticated classical relic attempting to endure in the face of aggressive neighbours at every side and dynastic rivalry within. Its trump cards were wealth and political skill, though these did not always prove enough, and by the 11th century the Empire was crumbling under the pressure of Islamic incursions from the Middle East. In particular, a disastrous defeat at the hands of the Seljuk Turks in 1071 had far-reaching implications. It not only delivered a shattering blow to Byzantium's fragile military power, but also convinced the Byzantine Emperor to send envoys to the Pope in Rome appealing for military assistance. When the Roman Empire divided into Eastern and Western entities in the 4th century, it prompted a similar schism in European Christianity. By the 11th century, the situation was solidifying into an increasingly bitter rivalry between the Eastern Orthodox creed, centred upon Constantinople, and the Catholic faith, which bowed to the authority of the Pope in Rome. When the desperate Byzantine Emperor entreated Rome for assistance in 1071, he was opening a substantial can of worms.

The Emperor was hoping for a contingent of Western European knights to help him contain the Seljuk threat. What he got was a full-scale invasion force of religious fanatics, hell-bent on capturing Jerusalem and everything on their path to the Holy City. He had inadvertently triggered the Crusades. It wasn't the first or last time that

Byzantine attempts to supplement irs waning military power with diplomacy had disastrous future consequences. In 1202, the Pope launched the Fourth Crusade, which foundered after funds to transport the army to the Middle East could not be found. The Crusaders diverted their attentions to Eastern Orthodox targets, climaxing with a successful assault upon Constantinople itself in 1204, a siege given the crucial edge by treachery. The Catholic troops sacked the city with great violence, adding insult to injury by parading a prostitute on the Patriarchal throne, sacred to the Orthodox faith. When word reached the Pope of the Crusade's ignominious outcome, he was justifiably outraged, disowning the enterprise in no uncertain terms:

'How, indeed, will the church of the Greeks, no matter how severely she is beset with afflictions and persecutions, return into ecclesiastical union and to a devotion for the Apostolic See, when she has seen in the Latins only an example of perdition and the works of darkness, so that she now, and with reason, detests the Latins more than dogs? As for those who were supposed to be seeking the ends of Jesus Christ, not their own ends, who made their swords, which they were supposed to use against the pagans, drip with Christian blood, they have spared neither religion, nor age, nor sex. They have committed incest, adultery, and fornication before the eyes of men. They have exposed both matrons and virgins, even those dedicated to God, to the sordid lusts of boys. Not satisfied with breaking open the imperial treasury and plundering the goods of princes and lesser men, they also laid their hands on the treasures of the churches and, what is more serious, on their very possessions. They have even ripped silver plates from the altars and have hacked them to pieces among themselves. They violated the holy places and have carried off crosses and relics.'

The Crusaders elected one of their own as Byzantine Emperor, and while the Greeks were able to reclaim Constantinople in 1261, the damage done – both to the Empire and relations between Catholic and Orthodox Christians – was irreparable. The new Greek Emperor was ruling over a sprawling realm held together by a dying ethos and fragile alliances, with subject Balkan leaders attempting to break away to assert their independence with demoralising regularity, stretching Byzantium's military power to breaking point. It was fertile territory for able and ambitious Ghazi warlords like Osman to establish themselves. Osman's name translates as 'bone-breaker', also associated with the royal vulture, a species of bird symbolising power in the same way Western culture uses the eagle as an emblem. It's an apt symbol for the Turk leader, picking mercilessly at the bones of the Byzantine Empire, seizing one poorly defended outpost after another, every success luring more Ghazis from Asia to the Ottoman banner, lured by the prospect of pillage in the name of the Prophet.

His son Orhan consolidated the fledgling Ottoman Empire's territory in a fashion typical of Byzantine weakness, when he was invited to provide troops for the embattled Byzantine Emperor, who offered his daughter in marriage to seal the deal. In 1354, Orhan exploited the relationship to establish a base in the European port of Gallipoli – recently evacuated due to an earthquake – simply ignoring his Byzantine counterpart's pleas to leave. The Ottoman Empire now had a crucial toehold in Europe, all but invited over the threshold by the Byzantine Emperor. Over the following century the hungry young Ottoman Empire chewed away at Byzantine territory, gradually developing the appetite and confidence to attempt to seize Constantinople itself. But the 'red apple' always remained just out of reach. While Byzantium's waning power left its military resources stretched to the limit, the city itself remained impregnable. Generations of wealth had been invested in three rings of indomitable defensive walls – reckoned by many to be the most formidable in the medieval world – while its location on a promontory made it difficult to attack by land whilst easy to reinforce by sea.

For a Sultan with something to prove, like the young Mehmet, it represented an irresistible challenge. His dead father's political advisors – particularly the Grand Vizier Chandarli – made no secret of their opposition to the plan, dismissing it as folly, a prize that had consistently eluded his formidable forebears. But this was a red rag to this driven young Ottoman bull. These were the same men who had helped shame Mehmet during his humiliating abortive reign in the 1440s, before he was obliged to reluctantly hand the reins of power back to the old Sultan when faced with the fury of John Hunyadi. Capturing Constantinople would not only wipe the stain of failure from his pubescent reign, but deliver a blow to the prestige of the sceptical Chandarli, who still posed a threat to Mehmet's authority at court. Most importantly, however, the ruler of Byzantium could claim the legacy of Ancient Rome, effectively taking on the mantle of Caesar. The Islamic world was just as conscious of the lost glories of the classical world as its Christian counterparts.

The achievements of the Roman Empire, which had successfully brought stability and prosperity to so much of the world, have remained an aspiration for leaders for centuries. The Empire was emblematic of not just military glory, but a standard of living that would long remain the envy of future generations. It's a point wittily expressed in the controversial film *Monty Python's Life of Brian*, which satirised the situation in Judea at the time of Christ's birth. In one scene the Jewish revolutionary Reg, played by comedian John Cleese, is attempting to stoke up anti-Roman feeling among his fellow freedom fighters with a stirring speech asking, 'What have the Romans ever done for us?' It's a task made increasingly difficult by reminders from his fellow revolutionaries that their hated Roman oppressors have actually been responsible for numerous positive contributions to their lives. Reg is finally obliged to conclude that, 'apart from better sanitation and medicine and education and irrigation and public health and roads and a freshwater system and baths and public order... what have the Romans done for us?'

Romania named their state in a deliberate reference to their origins as descendants of the Dacian tribes who, subsequent to conquest, became enthusiastic Roman citizens. The Papacy consciously modelled its spiritual empire on Rome, adopting imperial purple for its robes of office and Latin as its ritual tongue. The medieval Holy Roman Emperors – who counted Hunyadi's patron Sigismund among their number – styled themselves the heirs of the Western Roman Empire (though, as many have observed, the ungainly confederacy of Germanic states was no more holy than it was Roman). When the British established their own empire in the 1700s, it was during an Augustan Age, establishing Pax Britannica – conscious references to Roman Imperial glory. The history of Europe's empires is littered with titles – Kaisers in Germany, Tsars in Russia – that translate as Caesar. Only in the 20th century, when the doctrines of Marxist socialism and capitalist democracy rebranded imperialism as a synonym for exploitation rather than civilisation, did the iconic status of Rome as the idealised empire begin to pall.

The Islamic world wasn't immune to the allure of the Roman model and the Ottomans in particular saw their imperialistic ambitions in classical terms. They were better qualified than many of Europe's aspirational imperialists to claim the legacy, even if Islam was conceived over a century after Rome's fall in the West. The Ottoman policy, whereby local beliefs were tolerated so long as they didn't challenge the supremacy of the state, mirrored the Roman recipe for imperial success (until Christian intolerance began to hold sway). The Janissaries were arguably the first disciplined, professional infantry force to take to the field since the legionnaires marched the Empire's long straight roads that criss-crossed the known world. Like his better-educated European contemporaries, Mehmet II was a keen student of Roman history and tactics, and he recognised that establishing a lasting empire required taking advantage of the sophisticated administrative sinews of government left by the dwindling remnants of the Eastern Roman Empire. The Ottomans knew the region that they were taking as the heartland of their new empire – encompassing modern Turkey, the Balkans and Wallachia – as Rumelia, 'Land of the Romans'.

Yet, though his Ghazis constantly eroded the borders of the Byzantine Empire, the capital itself, mighty Constantinople, remained defiant behind its ancient walls. The Byzantine Emperors paid tribute to the Ottomans, but even as their Empire shrank back to the walls of the city itself, they would not yield sovereignty. The beginning of Mehmet's reign as adult Sultan was taken up with preparations for a conquest which many of his dead father's advisors still regarded as impossible. The Sultan's plans were as meticulous and innovative as they were ambitious. They had to be. In the circumstances, failure could well spell deposition which, in an environment he had codified in law, would likely prove fatal. The Byzantine Emperor was vigorously lobbying support from Eastern Europe – particularly the Athletes of Christ, Hunyadi and Skanderbeg. Western Europe had largely lost interest in the fate of its eastern borders after Nicopolis. Only the powerful Italian mercantile empires of Venice and Genoa with their formidable navies were obliged by their trading interests to remain involved in the fate of Byzantium, but their policy was swayed more by profit than politics or religion.

Mehmet began by isolating his target. Military assaults on Byzantium's remaining Greek allies neutralised any prospect of reinforcement by land. He also set about building fortresses on either side of the Bosporus, one on the site of a fort erected by his predecessor Bayezid I, the other on the site of an old Roman fortification. The latter was nicknamed Bo azkesen – which can translate as 'strait-cutter' or 'throat-cutter' – both vivid descriptions of the role of the fortifications in severing Constantinople's crucial artery to the Mediterranean. The forts are significant in two very different fashions, one of which illustrates the increasing sophistication of the Ottoman war machine, the other with a more immediate significance to our story. In contrast with medieval fortifications, designed to give lofty defences which challenge the attacker to scale them while providing the defender with tall platforms from which to harry their foe, Mehmet's are broad, squat buildings. They were built around the power of gunpowder, designed to defend cannon batteries and give maximal defence against return fire, more akin to modern gun-emplacements than the crenellated fortifications of the Middle Ages.

Among their first victims was a Venetian ship which made the mistake of trying to run the gauntlet. A volley of cannon-fire quickly rendered the vessel helpless. 'Those sailors who survived the cannonade were initially imprisoned,' writes Barnaby Rogerson in *The Last Crusaders*. 'Later they were taken down to the water's edge and held down while a pointed fence post was driven into the rectum and up through their guts. The posts were hoisted up into place. Eventually the wriggling of the half-impaled victim allowed the sharpened stake to penetrate further, pierce the chest cavity and put an end to his agony. It was a cheaper method of execution than crucifixion for it required no nails or crossbar, and also involved the added psychological humiliation of inflicting death by anal penetration.' It's also a scenario that will become queasily familiar in this book – powerful evidence for those who suggest that Dracula inherited his taste for impalement from his former Turkish captors.

Mehmet planned his attack with a combination of dogged determination and creative foresight. A small fleet of ships was literally dragged across an inconvenient peninsula to give the Ottomans naval superiority in Byzantium's immediate vicinity. The Sultan secured the services of an eminent Hungarian gunsmith named Urban to manufacture the most devastating artillery battery the world had seen. Urban had initially offered his services to the Byzantine Emperor, but he couldn't meet the Hungarian's price. Just as in the Cold War, decided by economics as much as military might, cold hard cash was a pivotal factor. Opinion differs on the efficacy of Urban's masterpiece. A terrifying cast iron monster of 19 tons that could fire its 800 pound ammunition only a few times a day, it arrived late to the siege because it required a team of 60 oxen to drag it to the battlefield. Yet the rest of the devastating arsenal Urban provided for his new patron provided ample proof that the cannon was no longer a new fangled novelty, but the future of warfare.

For those watching events within the walls of Constantinople, there was little scope for optimism. The only concrete support had come from a Genoese captain named Giovanni Giustiniani Longo who brought a force of 700 troops to assist in the city's defence. The rest of Europe remained complacent, content to stand by and watch. Giovanni was entrusted with co-ordinating Constantinople's garrison against the oncoming Ottoman onslaught by the Byzantine Emperor Constantine XI. The city's impressive defences proved a problem in themselves.

Centuries of decline had diminished Byzantium's population, and the Genoese commander was faced with manning twelve miles of walls and towers with an inadequate ad hoc force of soldiers of fortune, Byzantine regular troops and local militia. As ever in this period, numbers are wide open to question, but a fair estimate is that Giovanni had well under 10,000 men at his command, outnumbered by his Ottoman opponent by something like ten to one. For all of that, Byzantium had weathered numerous such storms: its defences had always humbled the Turkish barbarians whenever they had dared to hammer at the gates of Rome's last bastion.

On the morning of the 5 April 1453, Mehmet's guns began their thunderous assault upon the walls of Byzantium. Giovanni set the locals to repairing every breach in the city's ancient defences, while Mehmet's teams of sappers tunnelled ever closer, inch by inch, digging trenches to give the Ottoman infantry shelter in striking distance of the enemy, burrowing beneath the walls in the hope of undermining them. The siege dragged on for nearly two months before the Sultan's patience began to dwindle. His cannons had done terrible damage to the walls, but the ancient defences of Byzantium still refused to crumble beneath the insistent pummelling of gunpowder. Mehmet could not wait forever. He had enemies, not only in Europe but among his own court, who anticipated his failure with relish. At a war council on 26 May, the Sultan decided to take the walls by frontal assault – his men must do or die in his name – the final roll of the dice. After two days of preparation and prayer, the Ottoman army made their fateful last surge towards the walls before the sun rose on the morning of the 28th.

It was textbook Ottoman tactics. The initial assault consisted of Ghazi rabble – Azabs or Bashi-Bazooks – lightly-armed cannon-fodder to soften and tire the opposition. Behind them were the regular infantry drawn from the Ottoman provinces, with explicit instructions to cut down any of the first wave retreating from the front. In reserve were the Janissaries, the Ottoman elite who could be counted upon to push home any attack. The first assault quickly faltered – capable at hit and run tactics, the Azabs were no match for the volleys of stones, arrows, javelins and bullets raining down from the dogged Byzantine defenders. The second wave fared little better, stalling before the walls, unable to take advantage of the breaches which Urban's artillery had punched in the Byzantine defences. Mehmet finally unleashed his finest soldiers, as the Janissaries joined the fray, advancing grimly through the chaos of gunpowder smoke and fallen men.

The Turkish historian Tursun Bey, who was present at the siege, gives this vivid (and somewhat confused) description of the brutal confusion of the struggle at the walls, as the tide of battle ebbed and flowed. 'And from the furthest reaches below to the top-most parts, and from the upper heights down to the ground level, hand-to-hand combat and charging were being joined with a clashing and plunging of arms and hooked pikes and halberd in the breaches amidst the ruin wrought by the cannon. On the outside the Champions of Islam and on the inside the "wayward ones", pike to pike in true combat, hand-to-hand; now advancing, now feinting, guns firing and arms drawn, countless heads were severed from their trunks... presented to the bastion their hooked pikes, drawn, they were knocking to the ground the engaged warriors; as if struck in the deepest bedrock by the digging of a tunnel, it seemed that in places the city-walls had been pierced from below.'

The fortunes of war can turn on a pinhead, and so one version goes, a contingent of Janissaries chanced upon a side-gate that had been carelessly left unbarred and undefended. The defenders successfully isolated and killed the small force of Turks who made their way through the unexpected breach, but not before the Genoese general Giovanni sustained a serious wound, most likely from a crossbow bolt. Despite desperate entreaties from Emperor Constantine to stay, Giovanni's appetite for battle was ebbing with his life-blood, and the stricken warrior fled the city by boat. With the architect of Constantinople's defences fleeing, the morale of the defenders collapsed, and Constantine made a last heroic stand against the Ottoman troops swarming through the walls as the city fell, reportedly begging his fellow Christians to behead him in preference to being captured. With that, the victorious Turks fell upon the defenceless population in the orgy of rape, murder and pillage that almost inevitably followed the successful siege of a medieval city that had refused to surrender.

Michael Critobulus, a Greek civil servant serving under Mehmet at the time, wrote a detailed account of the siege, describing the horrible aftermath of the Ottoman victory. 'Then a great slaughter occurred of those who happened to be there: some of them were on the streets, for they had already left the houses and were running toward the tumult when they fell unexpectedly on the swords of the soldiers; others were in their own homes and fell victims to the violence of the Janissaries and other soldiers, without any rhyme or reason; others were resisting, relying on their own courage; still, others were fleeing to the churches and making supplication – men, women, and children, everyone, for there was no quarter given. The soldiers fell on them with anger and great wrath. For one thing, they were actuated by the hardships of the siege. For another, some foolish people had hurled taunts and curses at them from the battlements all through the siege. Now, in general they killed so as to frighten all the City, and to terrorize and enslave all by the slaughter.'

Critobulus is unsurprisingly sympathetic to his patron, and depicts Mehmet as appalled by the damage his armies have inflicted upon Byzantium, describing how 'the Sultan entered the City and looked about to see its great size, its situation, its grandeur and beauty, its teeming population, its loveliness, and the costliness of its churches and public buildings and of the private houses and community houses and of those of the officials. He also saw the setting of the harbour and of the arsenals, and how skilfully and ingeniously they had everything arranged in the City – in a word, all the construction and adornment of it. When he saw what a large number had been killed, and the ruin of the buildings, and the wholesale ruin and destruction of the City, he was filled with compassion and repented not a little at the destruction and plundering. Tears fell from his eyes as he groaned deeply and passionately: "What a city we have given over to plunder and destruction!"'

You might plausibly argue that the appalling atrocities suffered by the defenders and citizens of Constantinople were no worse than those inflicted upon the populations of many captured towns throughout this brutal period. Mehmet's apologists insist he reined in his troops as far as he reasonably could – his hands tied by Islamic law which decreed that victorious Ghazis were entitled to their spoils, and the need to reward his victorious warriors – not least because a city depopulated of its artisans, merchants and labourers would be an empty shell. A poor place for a new capital, and the Sultan planned to make the metropolis – thenceforth to be known by its Turkish name of Istanbul – the seat from which he would rule as an Islamic Caesar. Yet accounts of the wanton Turkish violence and sadism in Byzantium captured the popular imagination in Europe, just as the reports of the savage suppression of the Bulgarian rebellion would in the 1870s.

While his victory established Mehmet as the Conqueror in Islamic eyes, the bloody aftermath of the fall of Constantinople in 1453 became a recurring theme in anti-Ottoman literature. An early example of the emotive tone taken by accounts comes from Cardinal Bessarion, writing to the Doge of Venice just two months after the fall of the city. 'A city which was so flourishing... the splendour and glory of the

East... the refuge of all good things, has been captured, despoiled, ravaged and completely sacked by the most inhuman barbarians... by the fiercest of wild beasts. Men have been butchered like cattle, women abducted, virgins ravished, and children snatched from the arms of their parents... Much danger threatens Italy, not to mention other lands, if the violent assaults of the most ferocious barbarians are not checked...'

Western dismay over the violent extinction of the last beacon of classical glory in Europe at the hands of the bloodthirsty Turks became increasingly tinged perhaps with a sense of guilt. 'The fall of Constantinople is, after the Crucifixion, the greatest human calamity to have befallen Christianity,' writes Paul Fregosi in *Jihad in the West*, a modern text that still seethes with outrage over the episode. 'Poor theology, I know. The Crucifixion was the inevitable prelude to the Resurrection. But it's good imagery, and it conveys the feelings of Christians at the time. Today, more than half a millennium later, if one is a Western European, one can still cringe in shame when one remembers how this bastion, however flawed, of European civilisation, religious tradition, and culture, in spite of its desperate calls to Christendom for help, was allowed by the rest of Europe to disappear into the maw of a then cruel nation while the West wrung its hands and twiddled its thumbs.'

To be fair, John Hunyadi was hardly twiddling his thumbs. His own situation in Hungary was becoming increasingly fragile, as Hunyadi's rivals obliged him to relinquish any claim to act as regent to the callow young king Ladislaus Posthumous, who was following an increasingly inward-looking policy under their influence. The fall of Constantinople in some ways strengthened Hunyadi's position. The shock waves that rippled westward at the fall of mighty Byzantium to the infidel, lent weight to the White Knight's argument that those European leaders who chose to ignore or appease the Ottomans were effectively signing the death warrant of Christian Europe. Yet, despite flamboyant displays of mourning and shock – the Pope declared that 'the light of Christianity had suddenly gone out' – the response in most European courts amounted to little more than talk. The Hungarian and Polish nobility continued to jockey for position at home, while most of the Balkan Voivodes seemed resigned to a future as Ottoman vassals.

Happily for Hunyadi, not everybody was reconciled or blind to Mehmet the Conqueror's ambitions. The Mayor of the Transylvanian town of Sibiu, where Dracula was now stationed, had received reports suggesting that his town was next on the Sultan's agenda. He joined a popular call for action among the region's churchmen and common folk against the looming Turkish threat. The only leader to heed the call was John Hunyadi. Despite a catalogue of defeats, Hunyadi had always got back on his feet and returned to the fray. In the punishing arena of Eastern European warfare in the 15th century, Hunyadi distinguished himself by his endurance and dedication – the seasoned fighter who always beat the count and rose to fight another round. He was also an acute strategist. Hunyadi correctly predicted that the Sultan's next move wouldn't be another advance through Wallachia to attack Transylvania's network of well-defended towns, but a drive up the Danube through Serbia, converting the region from a vassal state into an Ottoman province, culminating in an assault on the old Serbian capital of Belgrade.

If Belgrade fell – known as 'the Gate to Hungary' – it would leave the whole of Eastern Europe open to Mehmet's Ghazis. George Branković had given the keys of the Serbian capital to John Hunyadi in 1420, recognising its value to the Turks, and reasoning that Hungary stood a better chance of defending the city than he did. Hunyadi had his back against the wall as he prepared to counter the Ottoman advance at the end of 1455, outnumbered and outgunned, faced with accusations of negligence and sedition by rivals at the Hungarian court. If the aristocracy of Europe needed any further excuse to decline Hunyadi's entreaties to join his campaign against the Turks, in the summer of 1456, in an act of inadvertent biological warfare the Ottoman army brought the plague with them. The plains around the Danube soon became a very unhealthy place to be, and any Eastern European noble who could – including King Ladislaus Posthumous – made for the comparative safety and clean air of their mountain estates.

Estimates of the size of Mehmet's invasion force ranged upwards of 100,000 men, their morale boosted by the capture of Constantinople. Hunyadi, deprived of the support of the Hungarian and Polish nobility, struggled to muster half as many men, most of them ill-equipped amateurs, inspired by the White Knight's call-to-arms against the infidel. Even if his reputation was in tatters among Eastern Europe's inward-looking elite, Hunyadi was still the White Knight of Transylvania, Athlete of Christ in the eyes of many ordinary Eastern Europeans. He found an unlikely ally in the Franciscan priest John of Capistrano, a septuagenarian Catholic zealot entrusted by the Pope with preaching a Crusade against both the Turks and Eastern Orthodox Christians. The aged cleric succeeded in raising a small army in his progress towards Belgrade from Frankfurt which, although primarily peasants armed with improvised weapons, proved a valuable addition to Hunyadi's meagre forces, in numbers at least.

The Christian army had to fight their way through the Muslim lines to reach Belgrade, which had fallen under fire from Mehmet's cannons on 29 June 1456. Hunyadi's relief force didn't reach Belgrade until 11 June, something of an achievement in itself in the face of stiff resistance from Mehmet's rearguard, successfully breaking the Ottoman naval blockade to transport much needed reinforcements and supplies to Belgrade's beleaguered defenders. The stage was now set for a climactic battle between the Sultan's hungry war machine – bristling with Janissary arquebuses, belching death from his batteries of artillery – and the ad hoc Christian army, whose chief strengths came from the fervour of John of Capistrano and the valour of the White Knight. The odds were stacked against the Europeans, the smart money on a repeat of Constantinople, of Kosovo, of Varna – another example of the unstoppable Ottoman juggernaut rolling inexorably westward. This time, Hunyadi did not even have his steel ranks of proud knights to rely upon. Perhaps he preferred it that way. At least at Belgrade he was fighting upon his own terms, to his own plans, unhampered by the chivalrous arrogance of haughty allies.

John Hunyadi did not campaign wholly alone. At the same time he was mustering his forces as swiftly as he could, Hunyadi's newest ally, Vlad Dracula, was formulating his own battle plans. Once again, the weaponsmiths of Transylvania were busy forging the armoury needed to equip an invasion force to take Wallachia. The last thing Hunyadi needed was a Wallachian army under the treacherous Danesti Voivode Vladislav II attacking him in the flank. It was time to unleash Dracula. It was perhaps too much to hope for that an attack on Wallachia would divert Turkish forces from their advance into Serbia, but it would at least deter Vladislav from taking any part in the Turkish campaign. In June of 1456, Vlad Dracula led a force of loyal boyars, soldiers of fortune and Hungarian troops through the pass guarded by Castle Bran, into Wallachia. By the end of July, he was triumphant. According to most accounts, Dracula's campaign climaxed in a direct confrontation with Ladislav, an encounter which concluded with the Danesti Voivode being hacked to death. The death of the man responsible for the murder of his brother and father must have been sweet revenge for Dracula, something he was definitely developing a taste for…

Meanwhile, at Belgrade, events were also reaching a crescendo. By

21 July, Mehmet's patience had once again worn thin. The city's formidable defences were now cratered with holes by his peerless artillery corps, while Ottoman engineers had successfully filled in much of the moat, allowing his infantry a clear run at the walls. As darkness fell, the Sultan ordered the attack. This time, he decided to open with his strongest troops, and the Janissaries made easy progress through Belgrade's outer defences. Too easy. Once the first wave was safely within the walls, Hunyadi sprung his trap. Men on the walls showered the moat with torches and burning oil, igniting the flammable materials that had been cast there in preparation. The moat became a burning deathtrap separating the Turkish vanguard from the rest of the Ottoman army, and Hunyadi's men sprang from hiding to fall upon the isolated Janissaries, wiping out the best of the Sultan's forces.

Come the morning, it was time to take stock and bury the dead. The Christian commanders began supervising the repair of Belgrade's crumbling defences, while the Sultan assessed the damage done to his army during the preceding night's abortive assault. Yet armies don't always conform to the will of their superiors, particularly when their forces contain a large contingent of volatile volunteers such as the peasant force John of Capistrano had brought to Belgrade. Despite explicit orders to remain within the walls, a contingent of defenders filed out of the city toward the Turkish encampment, intoxicated by the previous night's victory, intent upon shedding more Islamic blood. Both John of Capistrano and Hunyadi were horrified at the development. It was the sort of indiscipline from which defeats were forged, and the aged cleric ran among the building wave of Christian volunteers surging toward the Ottoman lines, entreating them to stop and turn back.

It was to no avail, and events began to develop their own momentum beyond the control of the commanders, as the skirmish developed into an engagement, and then a full-fledged recommencement of battle. John of Capistrano finally despaired of halting the human tide, and decided to go with the flow, bellowing 'The Lord who made the beginning will take care of the finish!' Watching half of his garrison pouring out onto the plains from the walls of Belgrade, Hunyadi had little choice but to join the impromptu assault, hurriedly donning his armour and leading his own forces on a chaotic charge towards the Ottoman lines. The rash attack caught the Turks wholly by surprise, and the shocked Ottoman army began to disintegrate beneath the Christian tide. The remainder of the Janissary corps attempted to rally and mount a counterattack, their furious Sultan at their front, slashing at his fleeing troops with his scimitar. It was a futile gesture. In the ensuing melee, Mehmet was wounded in the leg and passed out, and it was all his bodyguards could do to drag him to safety.

When the dust cleared, the Christians had won a remarkable victory. The Pope declared it a miracle. He had previously ordered that church bells be rung at noon every day as a signal to pray for the souls of the beleaguered defenders of Belgrade. His order hadn't reached many churches before news of Hunyadi's triumph, and the Pope retroactively changed the tolling of the bells at midday as a celebration of the victory. Many churches still ring the Noon Bell in Hunyadi's honour to this day. John Hunyadi's hero status was now unassailable, an Athlete of Christ who had turned the Ottoman advance against the odds. While his Hungarian rivals had bickered over power, the White Knight had drawn his sword and defended the faith. In less than a month, however, John Hunyadi was dead. On 11 August, the White Knight succumbed to the plague blighting the region. John of Capistrano paid tribute to his dead comrade with the words 'The Light of the World is extinguished.' The disease also claimed the ageing priest shortly thereafter, later canonised as the 'Soldier Saint'.

According to popular tradition, Hunyadi gave a stirring patriotic address as his final words, sentiments that encapsulate his career: 'Defend, my friends, Christendom and Hungary from all enemies... Do not quarrel among yourselves. If you should waste your energies in altercations, you will seal your own fate as well as dig the grave of our country.' His loss was keenly felt across Europe, tardy recognition for a warlord who, almost alone among his peers, fought for an ideal. Even Mehmet paid tribute to a worthy opponent: 'Although he was my enemy I feel grief over his death, because the world has never seen such a man.' What did Vlad Dracula feel when he heard the news of Hunyadi's demise? Grief at the loss of a comrade-in-arms, perhaps even a mentor? Satisfaction at the demise of a man who had been instrumental in the deaths of his father and brother? Simple indifference to another casualty of the brutal arena of Eastern European conflict? We don't know, but we do know that Dracula was about to carve his own unique, cruel mark into the skin of history...

CHAPTER VII

Class War - Transylvanian Style

As autumn loomed in Wallachia in 1456, Vlad Dracula was once again installed in Tîrgovişte as Voivode. He was an older, wiser man than the teenager who had seized power at the head of a small force sponsored by the Ottoman Sultan eight years before, losing his grip on power after only weeks on the throne. Now 25, Vlad also faced a very different world. John Hunyadi had averted disaster for the Christian cause in Eastern Europe, but Hunyadi was dead, and only soothsayers were willing to predict what future awaited the unstable kingdoms of Hungary and Poland. The threat of civil war lurked omnipresent in the wings, like a vulture ready to tear the tattered spirit of European resistance to the Ottoman Empire to shreds. Despite his humiliation at Belgrade – rumour insisted that the Sultan had first toyed with taking poison on the journey back to his new capital of Istanbul, before venting his frustrations upon his generals with his scimitar – Mehmet was still the Conqueror. The final, shocking fall of the Byzantine Empire had redrawn the map, changed the rules of the game, and nothing would ever be the same again. A daunting prospect for Vlad, who now found himself at the helm of a principality poised directly in the path of Ottoman expansion, and his only significant European ally a victim of the plague.

The new Voivode was faced with a near impossible balancing act if he hoped to maintain Wallachia as an independent realm, avoiding the fate of the Balkan countries to the south, which had, one after another, fallen under the Ottoman crescent. In common with most empires, while Ottoman expansion may appear to have followed a coherent strategy, in reality it was a more ad hoc, even organic process. The Empire began as a small Ghazi state, and Ghazi raiders remained central to its growth for a long period. Religiously-sanctioned Islamic freebooters were encouraged to congregate on the Ottoman Empire's western borders, where they made life hell for their European neighbours. Constant raids sapped the strength and credibility of unstable regions, devastating harvests and placing increasing burdens on local leaders who struggled to meet the military demands of defending their realms. Inevitably, an offer of protection from the Sultan – of paying an annual tribute in return for freedom from the Ghazi raids – became an increasingly attractive proposition to beleaguered Balkan despots and Voivodes. It was a protection racket on a grand scale. As the Christian princes fell further under Ottoman influence, the demands would increase. Then Devşirme would be imposed, whereby the young men of the realm would join the gold flowing eastward to the Turkish Empire, further weakening the vassal kingdom. Once the subject realm was truly on its knees, the Sultan would move to convert the vassal state into another province of the Ottoman Empire, replacing local leaders with Turkish appointees. The comparative tolerance of the Ottoman regime (they largely left Eastern Orthodox religious authorities in place) and low taxes (peasants in Ottoman vassal states were supporting both the local regime and the Ottoman tribute) meant that the transition from Christian vassal to Ottoman province was seldom resisted by the realm's population, regardless of their religious affiliation.

With his own education at the Ottoman court, Vlad was no doubt aware of this, but equally aware of the precariousness of his position. As far as the Ottoman Empire was concerned, the treaty his grandfather Mircea had signed, promising annual tribute to the Sultan in gold, still stood, as did his father's settlement, which not only increased the tribute, but also bound Wallachia to the hated Devşirme. When the first Turkish delegation arrived at Tîrgovişte demanding that Dracula honour his obligations to the Sultan, the new Voivode was amenable. On the subject of the Devşirme, he appears to have been more evasive and – understandably, considering his own experiences – Vlad politely declined the Sultan's invitation to deliver the tribute in person at the new Ottoman court in Istanbul. Any vengeful resentment Dracula may have felt towards the Turkish delegation had to be curtailed in the interests of preserving his fledgling regime. At least for the time being...

Vlad III had more pressing issues to concern him, relating to more immediate issues of domestic policy. His rule in Wallachia would establish Dracula as a byword for brutality. In a letter to the mayor of Braşov, written in 1457, the new Voivode observed: 'Pray, think that when a man or prince is powerful or strong at home, then he will be able to do as he wills. But when he is without power, another one more powerful than he will overwhelm him and do as he wishes.' His position at home remained worryingly precarious. Almost without exception, medieval rulers had to keep a keen eye on their own aristocracy, who were always conspiring to strengthen their own power, often at the expense of their liege. The consequences for the stability of the state, should such challenges to the authority of the head of state remain unchallenged, could be devastating. Medieval history is littered with nations riven by civil war, or which succumbed to outside invasion, when a weak monarch failed to keep his most powerful subjects in check. Eastern Europe, with its unstable dynasties and constant friction between Catholic and Orthodox – forever beneath the shadow of the Ottoman threat – was particularly vulnerable. Wallachia had practically become a basket case by the 14th century. Its agricultural economy was in tatters, battered by the ravages of war and the demands for Turkish tribute, while the local nobility – the boyars – had been able to exploit the region's chronic instability, backing one candidate for Voivode or another, according to whichever offered most potential personal advantage for themselves and their families. In the process, the status of Voivode, diligently built up by Vlad's forefathers, was steadily eroded.

It was a situation that Dracula could not condone. Only a unified nation stood any hope of standing up to the pressure from Wallachia's powerful Catholic and Islamic neighbours. More pressingly, his own position – and life – was always under threat when local lords felt comfortable sheltering, or even supporting his rivals from the hated Danesti clan, who still laid claim to the Wallachian throne. Vlad's solution to the problem was emblematic of the new Voivode's approach to government, both in its savagery and brutal simplicity. Some might even suggest an element of sadistic humour in Dracula's actions. Demonic humour aside, the episode also suggests the other three psychological interpretations that can be applied to many of the acts that would transform Dracula from the ruler of a tiny Eastern European principality into the dark legend that is still with us today. Was he motivated by simple pragmatism, employing fear as his only effective weapon against impossible odds? Was it revenge that ate away at his heart, making real terrible fantasies of retribution he had concocted during his long years of incarceration, every day marked by the constant threat of imminent execution, his youth blighted by news of the terrible ends met by his father and brother? Or, as some of his foes contended, was Dracula simply a 'bloodthirsty madman' for whom the painful deaths of those around him represented an end in itself? Of course, none of these interpretations are mutually exclusive.

In the spring of 1457, Vlad convened his first major royal conference at his palace in Tîrgovişte. The great and the good were summoned from across the principality to attend the Easter feast being held by their new Voivode, an opportunity for them to get the measure of their ruler, to lobby for any causes close to their heart, and ingratiate themselves with the new regime. It was also a social occasion, and an opportunity for the principality's leading families to flaunt their wealth before their peers in their most flamboyant finery and richest jewels. Some must have felt a certain foreboding at the occasion, as more than one boyar dynasty had been implicated in the violent end of the last Draculesti regime. Yet the air of frivolity at the sprawling Wallachian capital soon put minds at rest, as the guests began to relax and let their hair down in the city which was still the jewel in the Wallachian crown, a centre of culture and worship which one Venetian traveller compared to a 'vast gaudy flower house'.

If they had known how Vlad had been occupying his time recently, they might not have felt quite so secure. So some accounts have it, Dracula had been making vigorous enquiries into the fate of his older brother, an investigation which finally led him to the site of Mircea's grave. The sight that greeted him when he disinterred his sibling would have chilled most hearts. The corpse's eyes still bore the marks of the torture that prefaced his burial, the contorted state of the body paying mute tribute to the fact that the prince had been buried alive. It would have been enough to move many to uncontrollable rage or speechless horror, but Vlad was used to horror, well-acquainted with the virtue of sublimating his emotions until the time was ripe.

The Voivode who presided over Tîrgovişte Easter feast of 1457 did so as the consummate host to his distinguished gathering of 200 or more guests. After a prodigious and convivial repast to celebrate the Resurrection, the assembled company of boyars and bishops, their wives and families, sleepy with wine and too much rich food, listened as their new Voivode addressed them in a friendly, even jocular tone. 'How many reigns have you, my loyal subjects, personally experienced in your lifetime?' Dracula asked his assembled nobility. 'Since your grandfather, my liege, there have been no fewer than 20 princes,' answered one forthright boyar after a brief pause. 'I have survived them all.' The boyar's peers soon chimed in with their own recollections of times past, wondering at the many rulers who they had seen come and go in Tîrgovişte during their days. Such matter-of-factness, with its slight taint of pride, is what sealed the fate of the speaker and all his compatriots at the feast.

VLAD THE IMPALER

'Prince Vlad punished the boyars who were often conniving with the Turks or did not behave honestly with people such as us,' recalls one Romanian peasant tale, passed down to this day. 'On one occasion, in order to trip them up more easily, he gave a great feast, and also summoned those boyars against whom he also bore a grudge. But when they came, he impaled them.' Just how many of his aristocracy he had his men drag from the hall at Tîrgovişte and execute remains controversial, as does the fate of the survivors. Melodramatic accounts imagine him exterminating his own aristocracy in one fell swoop, rounding up the survivors to serve as his slaves unto death, like some kind of medieval Pol Pot. Sceptical scholars doubt the Wallachian state could have survived such a brutal purge, and point to continuity between lists of leading boyars in records before and after that fateful Easter Sunday in 1457. None, however, seriously contest that Dracula chose the holy day as a pretext to summon the most powerful men in his realm, before having them murdered in one of the most painful and humiliating methods ever conceived.

The historical basis for the tales surrounding Vlad's excesses after taking the principality of Wallachia comes from the pamphlets distributed in Mittel europa, in the years preceding and following his death, such as the above with its obvious wild inaccuracy of '20 princes'. But still, they give the first instance of the barbarically refined method of mass execution which gave Vlad III his soubriquet Tepeş – 'the Impaler'. 'Impaling is kind of a cheap technique,' describes Dr Mark Benecke, eminent forensic biologist (and Consul of the Rhine Parts for the Transylvanian Society of Dracula), in the *Real Horror* 'Dracula' documentary, 'as long as you have trees, small trees, the tree must not be too thick and not too thin, and then you just remove all the little branches and in the end you just have a stake. The stake is not pointed too much, because then it will easily rupture the vessels and then the person will die too fast. And you don't want that, you want them to die slowly.'

This prosaic acknowledgement of the Voivode's cruelty prefaces a scene of his *armas* – Vlad's squad of torturers and executioners – applying animal fat to a stake, and then ramming it up the bagged pantaloons of the screaming boyar. 'Then grease is put on top and the person is put on the floor, and it's inserted anally as far as you can,' Benecke matter-of-factly describes, 'and then you just lift up the person. Then the person will slowly slide down usually. In the better situation the person dies from circulatory shock, which means the circulation shuts down and then you cannot survive that. This is a relatively quick death. In other cases people will just stay there and die slowly.' The weight of the victim's body propelled him or her slowly down to an agonising death, via the solid pointed wooden stake that entered their abdomen or anus. (In the case of women, the spikes often exited their breasts.) As with the more powerful 20th-century despots Stalin, Hitler and Pol Pot, the victims of Vlad's cruelty died not by his hand but under the auspices of his state death squads. Unlike those ideological tyrants, however, Vlad's presence at the protracted executions suggests a personal relish for the way in which his enemies were eliminated.

The British TV documentary depicts the impalement of the first boyar as an agonised anal crucifixion. Though described more by suggestion than graphic gore, it's still very strong, bloody stuff for the television medium. (Unlike other episodes in the *Real Horror* series – such as 'Werewolf', similarly directed by newcomer Ben Chanan – 'Dracula' was relegated to 4am rather than the pre-midnight slot.)

Such was the fate of the boyars and their families in 1456, the year of the first recorded instance of Vlad's idiosyncratic sadism, and such a hellish tableau surely requires logistical planning. The drama-doc's eye-watering focus on the mechanics of impalement – as opposed to the usual shtick of seeking parallels between Vlad and Bram Stoker's vampire archetype – passes over some of its obvious problems. If we are to assume that entire families were put to the stake at a time, then for every three or four of the *armas* that bound, impaled and raised aloft the condemned, there must have been a couple more keeping order among the terrified onlookers awaiting their own end. As fellow interviewee Mei Trow points out in his own book on the Impaler, Benecke's functional view of impalement overlooks the difficulty in 'insert[ing] the wood through the tough sphincter muscle, yards of twisted gut and the even more formidable diaphragm'. Particularly given how much of the natural foliage of what is now Romania consists of pine and beech trees – with lightweight trunks prone to splinter when placed under the pressure of weight.

As to how the slender sharpened tree trunks may have borne the weight of the human form, perhaps the answer lies in the parallels with the Roman penalty of crucifixion – which also left the condemned prisoner exposed up in the air, at least until he or she had given up the ghost and was starting to rot. 'Crosses were not all of one kind,' claims the Roman stoic Seneca in *De Consolatione* (*Consolations*), his three volumes of philosophical musings and letters, 'but differently made by different people. Some there are who hang the criminal head downwards, while others drive a stake through his entrails, and others again stretched out his arms on a forked gallows.' Seneca wrote his *Consolations* over the years AD 40-44, straddling the period when he was exiled for adultery with the Emperor Caligula's sister Livilla (whose bed-hopping, it was rumoured, included that of her decadent brother) and within a decade of the crucifixion of the Nazarene Jesus. The momentum of driving a stake upwards through the unfortunate offender's (or heretic's) entrails seems to be impalement by any other name. As with crucifixion, it is the battle between the body held precariously aloft on the cross or stake with the force of gravity that provides the victim's protracted agony.

('In its earliest form in Persia, the victim was either tied to a tree or was tied to or impaled on an upright post, usually to keep the guilty victim's feet from touching holy ground,' writes pathologist William D. Edwards, Methodist minister Wesley J. Gabel and biological illustrator Floyd Hosmer of crucifixion in 'On the Physical Death of Jesus Christ', an essay published in the *American Medical Journal*. Again, its close relationship with impalement is very apparent.)

The natural inclination of the punctured human form to sink to the ground is defied by the vertical wooden plinth with which the body has become one, blocking its descent in a process that causes trauma to every major organ. Dr Benecke's descriptions acknowledge that – despite the TV programme's fixation on the more sexually sadistic aspects of impalement – the punished were also likely to be forced downward onto a spike that penetrated their abdomen or intestines, rather than entering through the anus or vagina. If we look at Matthias Hupnuff's famous 1500 wood carving of the boyars' massacre, we see how two of the most prominent of the impaled lay horizontally sprawled over sharpened stakes that run through their belly or chest. 'Sometimes the stake exits somewhere,' describes Benecke, 'either it will not pop out at all or it will pop out of the back, in the sides or in the front. It was a technique that would put people on display, make them look very helpless and stupid, and so it's not just killing the person, it's showing everybody who sees that: "I'm in power, this person is so *not* in power, forget it."'

'I think Vlad realised that his attitude, the fact that he really doesn't mind who dies, is an important weapon,' seconds Trow. 'It's a psychological tool that he can use to instil terror into his enemies.' As with the Romans, the sight of rows of offenders bound to stakes like an unholy triptych of pain would provide Vlad Tepeş with a psychological weapon against a formidable enemy. But, as Mei Trow suggests, in the first instance this ruthless exhibitionism was practised on the bodies of his fellow countrymen.

The cruelty of the method is oft attributed to Vlad's sadistic ingeniousness. But, as can be seen in Seneca, there is little in the field of man's inhumanity to man that doesn't acquire a universal status. And while the origins of impalement as punishment may pre-date the Roman Empire, its contemporary use seems to coincide with Vlad's personal history. In *De Cruciabatus*, the vivid 1591 martyrology by Catholic priest the Reverend Antonio Gallonio – a similarly popular work to John Foxe's 1563 *Book of Martyrs*, published during the English Protestant reformation that Gallonio and his co-religionists regarded as heresy – the author makes reference to Seneca's description of an alternate form of crucifixion: 'While one form of cross was like those we commonly designate by the word *cross*, another resembled the sharp stakes which at the present day the Turks employ for executing criminals, driving them through the victims' middle up to the head.'

The possibility exists that the Ottomans adopted elements of their former esteemed captive's cruel ingenuity. But the Reverend Gallonio makes us aware of another gorily prurient detail of Christian martyrdom: 'It is a fact, moreover, that the Turks impaled on stakes Hadrian of the Order of St. Dominic and 26 others, his companions; and the like punishment is spoken of by Procopius[...]' The sixth-century military historian Procopius was writing of the martyrdom of St Hadrian in AD 306, a Roman soldier whose conversion in the time of the merciless Emperor Diocletian was supposedly punished by having his 'member broken' and his body burned alive. Although his wife is said to have carried his remains for burial in Byzantium, the suggestion that he was impaled by the Turks is historically dubious – though reference is also made in *The Roman Martyrology*, confusingly, to a Hadrian of Nicomedia who was supposedly martyred in the same year. Nonetheless, if the assertion has any basis in fact, then the Ottoman Empire might have been using this little documented form of capital punishment not only in the decades and centuries immediately following Vlad III's reign (see previous chapter), but may have pre-empted him in their sadistic innovation by a full millennium. Their young esteemed captive's festering desire for revenge – on the Turks, and perhaps on humanity on general – may well have been inculcated with knowledge of their repertoire of punishments.

All the above parallels with crucifixion are drawn from *De Cruciabatus*, available in a visceral modern edition entitled *Tortures and Torments of the Christian Martyrs*, published by US literary heretics

Feral House. The English title, coined in 1903, implicitly acknowledges that the term 'torture' itself had come to mean the generalised torments oft inflicted by sadistic despots like Vlad.

(Historian Edward Peters describes the original pedantic Roman definition in his 1983 study *Torture*: 'By *quaestio* [torture] we are to understand the torment and suffering of the body in order to elicit the truth.' In other words, if it was not part of a legal inquisitorial process then it wasn't 'torture', but merely the infliction of a painful torment. By the time of the December 1975 United Nations Declaration against Torture, it was more widely redefined thus: 'Any act by which severe pain or suffering, whether physical or mental, is intentionally inflicted by or at the instigation of a public official on a person for such purposes as obtaining from him or a third person information or confession, punishing him for an act he has committed, or intimidating him or other persons.' In any case, the horrors of 'torture' and 'torment' had long since become synonymous in the common vernacular.)

The text, scanned from the 1903 English edition of the martyrology, contains the following statement in the translator's introduction: 'Men have changed: the old tigerish instinct has been conjured and subdued. Men are more humane, and the sight of blood, the thought of pain and cruelty, is abhorrent to all who live in the great centres of Christian civilisation.'

When we consider the generalised truth of this sweeping statement (as it refers to the industrialised rather than the developing world, at least), we should remember that Vlad the Impaler, the exemplar of late-Medieval cruelty, sometimes believed himself to be acting in defence of this same Christian civilisation when he was at his worst.

***

'What good is a man who lives upon the sweat of others?'

The words of their warlord strike like lightning balm, igniting the self-esteem of the newly-elevated peasantry of Wallachia. Murmurs of approval are muted, but there can be no doubt of the pride breaking through on the faces of the new ruling class, this ragtag militia with their shapeless clothes and pitchforks for weaponry, soon to be bedecked in the colours of the Voivode's army.

From diggers of ditches to tax administrators; from shovellers of shit to sergeants at arms, the lowly of the peasant class have effortlessly supplanted those once above them. In the aftermath of the massacre of the boyars, any survivors have been put forcibly to work renovating the Voivode's castle at

Poenari, on the outer ring of the Transylvanian Alps – like the slave builders who erected pyramids for the Pharaoh.

At a time when inner power struggles are almost invariably between monarchs and the nobility, Vlad has cut the Gordian knot by simply eliminating his aristocracy and replacing them with men from his army. Wallachian peasants gaze in wonder at the trudging lines of the nation's wealthiest lords, still dressed in their Easter finery, marching in chains as Vlad employs them to build his new stronghold.

Their inscrutably pragmatic prince, having been forced to obey the strictures of the Koran for much of his exiled youth, has returned to the Christian orthodoxies of the Church; like all rulers of Europe in the Middle Ages (apart from those hereditary heirs crippled by self-doubt), his certainty that he rules by the Divine Right bestowed by God is unshakeable.

This, then, is no devout follower of the Christ giving away his all, from his money to his robes, to ensure righteous entry to Heaven. Nor is he some prototype communard, committing treason against his own class to rouse the dispossessed to the barricades.

'We are with you, o liege.' The elder man with a weather-beaten complexion and specks of muddy soil engrained around his eyes dares to speak, with only a slight tremor in his voice. 'Lead and we follow; to victory or to death, our loyalty is yours.'

Those around him murmur their assent, and the Voivode, who has brought this delegation of the new boyar class to his ancestral house, smiles. Like all sons of the Devil who become heroes of the people, he knows that his will shall not be done without the mass compliance of the mob.

By humiliating their haughty former lords, Dracula has won the loyalty of many ordinary Wallachians. For Prince Vlad III has not established an early 'dictatorship of the proletariat', but has instead channelled the sublimated will of the people and their segregated sense of identity.

***

'Therefore if your illustrious House wants to emulate those eminent men who saved their countries, before all else it is essential for it, as the right basis for every campaign, to raise a citizen army; for there can be no more loyal, more true, or better troops' – Niccolo Machiavelli, *The Prince*.

It seems likely that Vlad's cousin Stefan was in attendance at the infamous Easter feast of 1457, where Dracula first demonstrated his legendary appetite for impalement. If so, the Moldavian prince's reaction to the savage demonstration of brute power is not recorded.

VLAD THE IMPALER

On the face of it, the saintly image Stefan later acquired might suggest that he would have been disgusted by his host's bloodthirsty display, but as we shall see, Stefan was far from above getting his own hands bloody in the pursuit of his ends. In one of the most significant acts of his reign, in 1457, Vlad honoured the pact he had made with his cousin at Suceava, and loaned Stefan a large force of Wallachian cavalry with which to seize the Moldavian throne from Petru Aron. Stefan made good use of the troops, crushing his rival and driving him into exile, and by the end of the year Stefan was crowned Voivode of Moldavia. While it risked provoking a response from the Turks, this first stroke of foreign policy proved an astute move by Vlad, dislodging a potential Ottoman ally from his eastern border, and replacing him with a friendly ruler.

Despite his ruthless display at Tîrgovişte in the Easter of 1457, brutally rooting out potential subversives among the Wallachian aristocracy, Dracula had still not fully secured his throne. His boyars had been cowed but not tamed, and rival claimants remained. They lurked just over the border in Transylvania, gathering support and plotting a coup sheltering in the principality's formidable fortified towns, just as Dracul himself and his father Dracul had done before them. Local traditions of royal inheritance meant each of Vlad's three potential foes enjoyed theoretically equal claim to the Wallachian throne. Dracula's half-brother and namesake, whose piety earned him the nickname Vlad the Monk, took refuge in the Transylvanian duchy of Amlas, soliciting support from the city of Sibiu. Braşov gave succour and shelter to Dan, whose brother, the Voivode Vladislav II, Dracula had slain in single combat in the summer of 1456. The heir apparent in the eyes of most supporters of the Danesti dynasty, Dan went as far as to have himself crowned, setting up a rival court on Mount Timpa which overlooked the walls of the Transylvanian city. The wild card was Basarab, another member of the Danesti family, a cultured man who few regarded as a plausible contender. All three attempted to bolster their candidacies by both courting Wallachian dissidents – made more numerous by the savage start to Dracula's reign – and attempting to solicit support among Transylvania's powerful Saxon population, the mercantile caste who they wooed with promises of commercial concessions once they took power.

It was clearly a situation Dracula couldn't tolerate if he hoped to hold the crown this time. When Vlad, and his father before him, plotted to seize the Wallachian throne from the safety of Transylvania, they did so largely unmolested. He didn't plan to allow his own rivals so much breathing space. Transylvania, still a Hungarian province, was experiencing its share of political turmoil. The death of John Hunyadi had further shaken the foundations of the Hungarian state, creating shockwaves that could be felt in Transylvania. Dracula endeavoured to maintain good relations with the councils that ran Transylvania's fortified cities, while establishing an alliance with Mihaly Szilagy, John Hunyadi's brother-in-law, a seasoned Hungarian warlord whom Hunyadi had left as military overlord of Transylvania. Factionalism at the Hungarian court in Buda put Szilagy and the Saxon councils of Transylvania on opposing sides of a developing civil war. Dracula could try and employ diplomacy to convince the powerful Saxon merchants to hand over the trio of his relatives plotting his downfall from Transylvania, or throw in his lot with the Hungarian, and achieve his ends by brute force of arms. Curiously, for those who would dismiss Dracula as little more than a bloodthirsty thug, the Voivode attempted to steer a middle path.

Transylvania is, of course, forever associated with Dracula, even though he regarded himself as a Wallachian. This association goes further than the geographical and historical confusion caused by a Victorian horror story. He was born in Transylvania, spent many years of his life there, and attempted to maintain cordial – even warm – relations with the realm throughout his career. This somehow makes it more shocking that this was also the setting of his most infamous atrocities, the outrages depicted in the Germanic woodcuts now so familiar via reproduction in countless modern texts on the vampire myth. While separate realms, the fates of Wallachia and Transylvania (and indeed Moldavia) were entwined long before they were united to form modern Romania. Though still ultimately under Hungarian sovereignty, the two Transylvanian duchies of Amlas and Faragas had become traditional estates of the Wallachian Voivode since the days of Mircea the Elder. John Hunyadi had finalised his break with Vladislav II when he confiscated the duchies in retaliation for the Voivode's scheming with the Ottomans, and signalled his support for Dracula by conferring them upon him. Amlas and Faragas would later be the sites of some of Vlad's most vicious atrocities.

While Transylvania's busy commercial centres and rich mineral resources were vital for Wallachia's prosperity, the dark, fertile soil of Wallachia's plains provided the grain that would not grow in Transylvania's mountainous terrain. Transylvania's industrious towns forged the modern weapons necessary to wage effective war, but it was largely Wallachia's ranks of hardy warriors who took to the field in the

Ottoman Wars. In a sense, Transylvania provided the burgeoning middle class of merchants and artisans – then becoming integral to a successful society across Europe – which Wallachia's agricultural economy lacked. However, division between the two realms was determined not just by social, political and geographical boundaries, but religious and racial divides. The Unio Trium Nationum, the system of apartheid formalised in 1438, set generations of prejudice in stone, condemning Vlachs to life as second-class citizens within Hungarian territory. Ambitious Vlachs could rise above this medieval 'glass ceiling', as John Hunyadi did, but only by abandoning the Eastern Orthodox faith and embracing Hungarian culture. (Hunyadi's humble, obscure beginnings and subsequent heroic career have provoked numerous scholarly challenges to the authenticity of his ethnicity, claimed as a national icon by Hungarian and Romanian alike.) Suffice to say, the relationship between Transylvania and Wallachia in Dracula's era provided fertile ground for class, religious and ethnic strife, something that Vlad as a Romanian-speaking Vlach of the Eastern Orthodox faith would have been well aware of, and as a ruthless politician must have considered exploiting.

The Transylvanian atrocities which immortalised Dracula's infamy have often been portrayed as the arbitrary massacres of a sadistic tyrant inflicted upon his innocent population, but this is only part of a complicated picture at best. Lengthy negotiations between Vlad and the Transylvanian cities giving shelter and support to his Wallachian rivals were getting nowhere. He had tried economic sanctions, cutting off the trading rights Wallachia had negotiated with Transylvania's network of Saxon merchants, then subjecting them to increasingly punitive regulations when trading within his borders, eventually setting prices for Germanic traders that compelled them to sell at a loss. Some have interpreted this as an attempt by the Voivode to stimulate a thriving mercantile class among his own population – a tall order, as success in international commerce demanded not just large quantities of capital, but the experience and contacts only acquired by generations in trade. If Dracula simply hoped to drive the Saxon councils of Transylvania to expel his enemies by hitting them in the wallet, this also proved largely futile. In the familiar fashion, merchants faced with increasingly burdensome regulations and duties simply found increasingly creative ways around them.

By 1458, Dracula's patience was wearing thin. Military intervention in Transylvania would technically represent a violation of Hungarian territory, yet the issue was more complicated than that. Amlas and

Faragas could be interpreted as grey areas, as both duchies were technically under his jurisdiction, while it might be argued that Braşov and Sibiu were guilty of serious diplomatic transgressions by harbouring traitors. Contrary to the impression given by many histories of medieval warfare of a bloody free-for-all where anything went, war in the Middle Ages was governed by laws every bit as binding (though abused just as often) as today's Geneva Conventions. 'Four types of war were recognised,' writes Sean McGlynn in *By Sword and Fire*: '*guerre mortelle*, war to the death, in which a captured enemy could expect either slavery or death; *bellum hostile*, open or public war, in which Christian princes were ranged against each other and knights could plunder and expect to be ransomed; *guerre couverte*, feudal or covered war, in which killing and wounding were acceptable, but not burning or the taking of prisoners and spoil; and truce, a momentary hiatus in hostilities'. As the most potentially profitable and least hazardous to their own safety, most nobles preferred to wage *bellum hostile* or *guerre couverte*, but many circumstances arose to encourage the merciless absence of rules of a state of *guerre mortelle*.

There were no crimes worse in medieval Europe than treason or heresy, and when forces regarded the other as traitors or heretics, *guerre mortelle* almost invariably applied. Civil wars and religious wars are almost invariably the most brutal under any rules. In the 20th century, ideologies came to replace religion to an extent. The savagery of the Eastern Front in World War 2 owed something to the conflict between two fanatical ideologies – Nazism and Stalinism – which actively attempted to ape and replace religion in their efforts to indoctrinate adherents. Some might contend that the most savage of the Cold War era conflicts – most notably America's Vietnam War – also contained elements of conflicting ideologies that contributed to the breakdown of discipline and basic human decency at the battlefront. In the 21st century, however, religion is once again rearing its ugly head as the chief contributory factor in conflicts where the opposing factions dehumanise their opponent as a preface to declaring a modern state of *guerre mortelle*. In Vlad's era, religion had long been established as ample justification for atrocities between Christian and Muslim forces, and indeed for the war crimes committed by Catholic Crusaders on both Jewish and Eastern Orthodox non-combatants.

In the case of Dracula's invasion of Transylvania in 1458, religion may have been an aggravating factor – the Voivode appears to have regarded Catholics with a great deal of suspicion – but the chief justification for a state of *guerre mortelle* was treason. The targets of his blitzkrieg strike across the mountains into the heart of Transylvania were Saxon merchants and dissident boyars, though the local populace bore the brunt of his wrath. By the brutal law of *guerre mortelle*, the combatant was entitled to exterminate his foe with extreme prejudice, wherever he found him. Dracula's theoretical sovereignty over Amlas and Faragas made their populations' support of his rivals treasonous, and the policy of not just killing traitors, but making an example of them, was certainly nothing new. Leaf through the pages of any history of torture and execution, and the most harrowing and inhumanly brutal examples detailed are almost invariably perpetrated on prisoners found guilty of treason.

Yet the small cavalry force Vlad led through the Transylvanian passes just as the spring sun was melting the snow in 1458 was no travelling court of law. His small army headed first to Amlas, where Vlad the Monk's supporters were gathering, then swept through to the region surrounding Braşov, where Dan had set up his shadow court on Mount Timpa. The slaughter of Transylvania's ordinary Vlachs represented collateral damage; devastating the land and the people who worked it was the most effective way of delivering a body blow to the region's prosperity, a tactic sanctioned under *guerre mortelle*. Vlad planned a campaign of medieval 'shock and awe', a mission designed to punish not just his opponents and their sympathisers, but also to terrorise anybody who dared challenge his status as arbiter over life and death in his embattled realm.

***

'Open up the grain store!'

The axes that crack through the merchants' reserves in the small town of Bod are wielded by members of a freshly elevated boyar class; battle-hardened mercenaries rub shoulders with the ennobled peasantry of Wallachia – guardians of the new social order. For who has more to lose from the erosion of the new power structure imposed by Prince Vlad? Who will defend it more vociferously, or more savagely?

Cries of 'Thieves!' and 'Bandits!' fall like tributes on the ears of the Impaler's troops. The resentment of the merchants – those supercilious, Germanic-speaking Saxons – is a source of amusement to the armed mob, imbued with the sense of its own righteous power. The merchants may gesture and throw curses, but not one dares to unsheathe a blade and step forward. Many step back into the implied protection of their womenfolk, most of whose protestations are a good deal more forthright.

'Take what you will, but leave a little for our livelihood!' the merchant's wife implores of the Draculesti's troops, as cloth sacks of grain are split open or tossed aside carelessly.

Her protest is met with gap-toothed amusement by the captain of the guard. As a native Vlach-speaker, he barely comprehends her words but her tone is clear. The Saxons have misunderstood the nature of their mission; their Voivode has entrusted them not with the theft of grain, wheat and corn, but with retribution against the disloyal.

As the sacks are dumped in a heap, and the lit torches begin to ignite them, the merchants and their families retreat in a collective cringing huddle. The flames that lick at their stalls and warehouses will soon spread to their homes, for the Wallachian troops are not here to plunder. Their purpose is to destroy.

***

As a pertinent point of comparison with the modern age, we can look to the actions of American soldiers during the Vietnam conflict. On 16 March 1968, the US Army in Vietnam was in the midst of an operation that sought to counter the Viet Cong's 'Tet Offensive' that had erupted at the beginning of the year. Years later, enlisted soldier Frederick Whitmer would describe what happened when he entered the My Lai region as a part of Taskforce Barker: 'Before going down there we were told that anybody there would be considered VC or VC sympathisers, and would be dealt with as such. We were on a search-and-destroy mission and we were told that anything from housing, food, people were to be destroyed, because that's what a search-and-destroy mission was.'

Ron Haberley was a US Army photographer at the time, who also later gave his own account: 'So, after that, we started moving into the village and it was just real carnage, just unreal scenes happening: hooches [bamboo shacks] were burning, there were dead people laying in the hooches, people on the trail. I think the weirdest thing was some of the soldiers were jumping on the animals, the water buffalos, with their bayonets, trying to stab 'em, it was just a complete freak-out scene. Still, to this day, I can't really figure it out.'

***

'May Mary and Jesu preserve us!'

As the picturesque town of Talmes is devoured by red and yellow tongues of flame, its people cry to the divine for preservation. Their words make no emotional impact on the soldiers of the Voivode. In their unfamiliarity with the mother tongue, they recognise only the names of the Christ and His Holy Mother. Even this is a source of disdainful amusement – are they not, after all, acting in the name of the divinely-ordained prince, the defender of Orthodox Christianity?

'Spare my … spare my family …' The axe blows rain down upon the bleeding merchant. His fur-collared robe is besmirched with his own dark blood and the skin unevenly cleaved away from his face.

'Spare me …' In his dying moments, as he sinks into the bloodstained cobblestones, the focus of his plea changes from his family to himself. For he can no longer see his wife and children among the huddled mass of the town square, and knows in his leaden heart that all is hopeless. None shall survive.

***

Military journalist Jonathan Shell had reported from Qang Ni province, where the My Lai massacre of March 1968 took place: 'Another very, very important aspect of all of this is that great areas of the province had been declared on the ground as being "free-fire zones". What that meant was that there was just a ceaseless, ceaseless barrage of military fire going into those regions. Everybody and everything that moved was considered to be 'the enemy', so the idea that you could kill civilians was hardly anything original or novel. And in fact I personally witnessed just village after village being ground up in ground operations …'

Private Leonard Gonzalez of Charlie Company gave testimony after the event to the Pentagon inquiry headed by one General Piers: 'That day was a massacre, just plain, right-on wiping out people. When you get the order, the command to kill anything and everything, that's what it is, you're just wiping it off the map.'

Piers: 'It's been suggested by some people that the killing was just committed by some members of the company.'

Gonzalez: 'No, nah.'

Piers: 'Why did they do it?'

Gonzalez: 'Revenge. To me, the way we hear it, we figured that the VCs, the Viet Cong, were there with their supporters. But when we were sweeping out the area, we didn't find nothin' but the civilian people.'

(Gonzalez was one of the few soldiers to resist participating in the massacre.)

***

The portly merchant has enriched himself by a lifetime of canny trading between the towns and hamlets of the Transylvanian region. Now he sweats out every last moist drop of self-indulgence through the burning pores of his skin.

In his scalding agony, he smells his own life juices like boiled cabbage water – the bland fare of the Carpathians returning to haunt his dying senses. As the Vlachs jeer and heap coals on the flames which heat the iron cooking cauldron, the boiling merchant perceives his fellow townspeople hacked about 'like cabbage' – the metaphor that will return again and again in German accounts of Vlad the Impaler's reign.

He see husbands, wives, children – even farm animals, dogs and cats – staked, semi-crucified, paraded aloft at the side of the road. The vision is a phantasmagoria and, in his burning agony, the merchant no longer knows if he can trust the evidence of his own senses. He only knows that, in this tableau of bloodshed, indifference and cruel amusement, the people of the town have been identified as the enemy, the wrongdoers, the evil ones, and the Vlach invaders inflict their torments with a clear conscience and a cheerful heart ...

***

In his rooting out of the supporters of the pretender Dan III, Vlad's troops sack the towns of Bod and Benesti, outside of Braşov, the Danesti's stronghold. 'He had a big family uprooted,' reads one of the German propaganda pamphlets that will follow Vlad's reign, 'from the smallest to the largest, children, friends, brothers, sisters, and he had them all impaled.' This is the family of Albert the Great, another regional warlord – and by this account Vlad pays them the tribute of personally attending their executions.

The city of Braşov has been rash enough to host the 'coronation' of Dan, who was crowned Prince of Wallachia – irrespective of how Vlad already occupies the throne – in the city's Russian Orthodox cathedral. By the late summer of 1460, the Impaler's retributive attacks on Braşov's satellite towns give it the feel of a city under siege.

In the town of Sercaia, the invading armas *take particular joy in their work. The tongue of the patriarchal head of a prominent household distends agonised and purplish as he splutters on his own blood. He hangs, impaled, from a meathook his servants formerly used for the smoking and curing of pigs.*

In the lanes and streets beyond, the conscientious novices adapt their prince's emblematic sadism to their own improvised methods. Women are impaled against the sides of houses by pitchforks driven through their belly or breasts; their crying children, tearfully urging their hapless mothers to somehow escape their torments and return to them, are cut down before the eyes of those who bore and nurtured them.

It is little wonder, perhaps, that Braşov will opt to strike a peace treaty with Vlad III on 1 October 1460. Among the conditions set are that the city will hand over all the boyars and merchants within its walls that have supported the Danesti, to be punished by Vlad as he sees fit.

***

Frederick Whitmer described one of his own actions in the My Lai massacre thus: 'I was walking down the trail and a young boy came around the corner, he was probably about eight years old. He had one arm, part of his arm, and his guts were hanging out, someone had previously shot him and he'd survived. I shot and killed him. You could say my justification was that it was a mercy killing, because I knew he would not be given any treatment or taken out of that situation, due to the mission we were on.'

Helicopter pilot Hugh Thompson gave the following testimony to the Piers Inquiry: 'When I saw the bodies in the ditch, I flew around and saw that some of them were still alive. So I set down on the ground then and talked to, I'm pretty sure it was a sergeant, a coloured sergeant, I told him there were women and kids over there, they were wounded and could he help 'em? And he made something of a remark that the only way he could help 'em was to kill 'em. I thought he was joking, I didn't take him seriously, and I took off again, and as I took off again my crew chief told me he could see a guy shooting into the ditch. I could a see guy holding a weapon ...'

Both Whitmer and the sergeant described by Thompson had – with vastly differing levels of moral squeamishness – cut through the illusions of modern warfare with a single atrocious action. It was this shadow between moral intent and deed that screenwriter John Milius comments on in *Apocalypse Now*, when he has Captain Willard plug a wounded Vietnamese family point blank because 'we cut 'em in half with a machinegun and give 'em a band-aid. It was a lie.'

The centuries separating Vlad's parochial wars from Vietnam had seen the introduction of many safeguards relating to the treatment of civilians, not least the Geneva Convention signed by Western countries in the early 20th century. However, the atrocities at My Lai demonstrate – as do the intermittently reported incidents from the recent US-led wars in Iraq and Afghanistan – that the group psychology of troops remains much the same: such simple characteristics as speaking a foreign language, or inhabiting unfamiliar territory, may turn a civilian population into the unrecognisable 'other' in their eyes. All empathy ('fellow-feeling') for another human being diminishes. When the adrenaline of fear or exhilaration is added to the sanctioned remit to inflict pain that Harvard psychologist Stanley Milgram described in his landmark study *Obedience to Authority*, then the outcome may be sadistic impulses in otherwise 'average guys'. 'I was personally responsible for killing between 20-25 people,' another soldier at My Lai later confessed, 'for cutting their throats, scalping 'em, cutting off their hands and cutting out their tongue. I just started killing any kind of way I could kill.'

504 villagers – including many women and children – lost their lives in My Lai, with many female casualties suffering sexual mutilations including bayoneting through the vagina. The US military investigation indicted only five soldiers for the atrocities, all members of Charlie Company, which had destroyed one single hamlet in the region. Their commanding officer on the day, Lieutenant William Calley, was the only man convicted. Calley pleaded mitigation in a carefully prepared courtroom statement: 'When my troops were getting massacred by an enemy I couldn't see, I couldn't feel and I couldn't touch, that nobody in the military system ever described as anything other than communism, they didn't give it a race, they didn't give it a sex, they didn't give it an age, they never let me believe it was just a philosophy in a man's mind. That was my enemy out there.'

Lieutenant Calley's prison sentence was commuted early on by President Nixon; he ultimately served just over two years under private house arrest. Soon after his conviction, he was celebrated as an all-American hero in a hit single called 'The Battle Hymn of Lt. Calley', set to the tune of 'The Battle Hymn of the Republic'.

***

Just as the 'heroes' of My Lai had their apologists – even supporters – Dracula's atrocities at Braşov have been the subject of sympathetic re-evaluation in certain quarters. Among the more plausible champions of Dracula's historical reputation is the eminent Romanian historian Professor Constantin Rezachevici. In his essay 'Punishments with Vlad Tepeş – Punishments in Europe: Common and Differentiating Traits' the Professor argues that Dracula was a fair, even comparatively lenient ruler by the standards of his day. 'Vlad Tepeş ruled with a difference,' writes Rezachevici: 'he applied to foreign offenders the kind of punishment used in their country of origin rather than those provided by Romanian feudal law. Those kinds of punishments were detailed in the *Altenberger Codex* (chronicle) brought from Vienna to Sibiu in Transylvania at 1453. The Codex enumerated the punishments provided by laws in the South of Germany, the Law of Magdeburg – also used by the Saxons of Moldova, and the Law of Iglau – applied by the Saxons in Sibiu and in south-eastern Transylvania. Besides, for commercial offenses in Transylvania, the law allowed beheading, blinding, cutting of limbs, death by the wheel; Vlad employed all but the last against the Saxon merchants who ignored his trading rules in Wallachia.'

On the subject of the punishment that earned Vlad his immortal epithet, the Professor maintains that Dracula actually borrowed the practice of impalement from Transylvania, which subsequently inspired the Turks to adopt this hideous method of execution. 'It was not Vlad who started the impalements of the Saxons of Braşov,' he insists. 'It was these Saxons who, together with fugitive adversaries of Vlad, impaled Vlad's followers who had fallen into their captivity. In a letter to the Braşovians, who supported the claims to Vlad's throne of Dan III after December 1456, dignitary Neagu asked: "Remember, who started the impalements? The fugitives and yourselves, because you embraced Dan's cause. Then voivode Vlad angered about it and harmed you a lot, impaling people and setting you on fire." Vlad reacted, not acted, employing the same kind of punishment – their own, as stipulated in their local law. Thus this form of punishment, of German-Transylvanian origin was for the first time introduced in Wallachia by Vlad Tepeş. There are no known records regarding its use before.' It's an intriguing argument, but ignores Vlad's infamous purge at Tîrgovişte in the Easter of 1457, as well as accounts of Turkish impalement that pre-date Dracula's Transylvanian atrocities, such as the Venetian sailors impaled by the Ottomans for attempting to run their blockade of the Danube. Furthermore, might not Neagu's letter be suggesting that the citizens of Braşov were responsible for their own fate by angering Dracula, not that they impaled Vlad's followers, hence inspiring the Voivode to answer in kind?

Rezachevici has an interesting theory as to why he believes it likely Transylvanian Saxons inspired Dracula's later infamous proclivity for impaling: 'Vlad employed impalement from the legal provisions of the

Saxon towns in Transylvania, which, in the fifteenth century officially endorsed this type of punishment. In Transylvania, impalement was done according to various German laws, mentioned in the Altenberg Codex – for killing of babies, rape, killing of relatives and adultery (when both partners shared one stake). Vlad punished by impalement citizens of Sibiu for baby-killing and adultery.' This leaves us with the somewhat improbable vision of Dracula's force chancing upon a best of rapists, adulterers and baby-killers upon arriving in Transylvania, then deciding to subject them to summary local justice. It's an intriguing defence of a national hero by a Romanian patriot, if not a particularly convincing one.

Some have also cast Dracula as a medieval class warrior, an interpretation particularly popular among Romanian historians during the nation's Communist era, when the regime sponsored positive portrayals of the national heroes of Romania's turbulent past. Might Vlad have purged Wallachia's nobility and persecuted the middle classes of neighbouring Transylvania as part of a deliberate policy to support the cause of his realm's peasant population? Yet Dracula did not exempt the peasantry from his terror campaigns. He may well have felt some sympathy for the locals who shared his Romanian language and Eastern Orthodox faith, but this proved little barrier to his more brutal side. In common with most rulers of the day, he treated them as chattels, massacring them mercilessly during his attempts to inflict collateral damage on his opponents. John Hunyadi's triumphant final stand at Belgrade was ample proof of the military potential of humble armies when well-motivated and well-led. It remains doubtful that Vlad's choice to employ men from the lower orders in his administration and armies reflected any proto-socialist agenda. More likely, a desperate situation obliged him to find men he could trust wherever he could, something made particularly difficult by his ruthless purges of Wallachia's upper classes.

Vlad's Transylvanian campaign reached a climax in 1460. Dan, who styled himself Voivode Dan III, had successfully fled Braşov before Dracula's forces reached the city, and had evaded capture ever since. He employed reports of Vlad's atrocities as part of a vigorous propaganda campaign, also accusing Dracula of being a puppet of the Turks, hoping to drum up enough support to raise a force capable of counterattacking. In March he believed he had assembled enough men to defeat Dracula on the field. He was wrong. In a battle on the Wallachian border his army was soundly defeated, only seven of his boyars escaping the rout. Inevitably, Vlad impaled all of the boyars he captured. He had something special in mind for Dan however. Dan was treated to a funeral service fit for a king, with the unorthodox aspect that 'the dearly departed' was still alive during the service, obliged at sword-point to dig his own grave. Once the service was complete, Dracula beheaded Dan himself, the lifeless corpse tumbling into the freshly dug pit. Was this Vlad giving due respect to a noble opponent – sparing him the horrors of impalement – as his apologists have suggested? An attempt by Dracula to refine a new form of psychological torture perhaps? Maybe even an example of the bizarre sense of psychopathic humour that occasionally leaks through in some of the accounts of the Impaler's atrocities? Witnesses of the day may well have struggled to be certain, as Vlad had developed a Machiavellian mask that made him both inscrutable and unpredictable in the eyes of his increasingly numerous enemies.

Whichever interpretation of this sinister episode is most accurate, it's clear that, once he had dealt with the pretenders to the throne, the Voivode attempted to build bridges with Transylvania, offering to return relations to their original footing. His success suggests that either his terror campaign bore fruit, and the Transylvanians had little stomach for further conflict with the Impaler, or that his sadism was more selective than most accounts suggest and that there was a pragmatic acceptance that there was some method to his madness. Either way, the apparent return to business as usual with the Saxon merchants fatally weakens the idea of a proto-socialist Voivode championing the rights of the downtrodden against their bourgeois oppressors.

Yet there is a strange but tortuous indirect lineage between Dracula and the totalitarian rule of communism, though one that links with the Soviet cult of Stalinism more comfortably than the ideologies of Karl Marx. Among those who disseminated the legends of Vlad the Impaler was one Fedor Kuritsyn, envoy to the Hungarian court on behalf of Ivan III, Grand Duke of Muscovy (Moscow). Kuritsyn reached Buda in 1482, six years after the death of the Impaler (and a year after the demise of his close contemporary, Mehmet the Conqueror). Kuritsyn soon became captivated by stories of the city's esteemed former reluctant guest, Vlad Dracula (of which more presently). At court, the Russian became acquainted with Vlad's widow and his eldest son from a previous marriage (subsequently known as Mihnea the Bad); his curiosity took him further afield, to Transylvania, the Impaler's birthplace, and to his former principality of Wallachia.

Kuritsyn also travelled to Braşov, former stronghold of Dan III, where its people were well acquainted with the terror tactics employed by the

Voivode; in Suceava, he met with Vlad's cousin and confidant Stefan the Great, as well as his niece, the daughter of younger brother Radu. He even went as far as to interview the ten soldiers who served as Vlad's bodyguard in Bucharest, during his final years.

The outcome of all this fact-finding was a Russian pamphlet entitled *Povesty o Mutyanskom Voyevode Drakule* ('The Story of the Wallachian Warlord Dracula') that rivals its Saxon counterparts as a source on the life and crimes of the Impaler. Composed in the late 1480s, its actual author was 'Elfrosin the Sinner', a Russian monk whose horror at Vlad's atrocities may have counterbalanced Kuritsyn's obvious admiration for his audacious heroics. The booklet would become a well-thumbed favourite of the Russian court of Ivan III.

In 1533, the late Grand Duke's grandson, the orphaned Ivan IV, would inherit the throne from his late father Vasily. Moscow was then a feudal society ruled by the boyars, whose periodic switches of allegiance influenced the balance of power even more so than in Vlad's old principality. The young boy's emerging psychology was moulded by the imperial backstabbing at court – particularly the poisoning murder of his mother Elena, the reigning regent, when he was seven. Their treachery was compounded by the flaying alive of her close consort (possibly also her lover), whose skinned body was left to hang and suffer in Moscow's central square (later Red Square). In this sense, it can be argued that the entire career of Ivan Grozny ('Ivan the Terrible' – as with the Ottoman Sultan Selim the Grim, the soubriquet is as suggestive of awe in its original language as of horror) was a protracted act of revenge against the boyars – or indeed against his nation as a whole, in the latter part of his reign when his sanity and self-control began to crumble. His first killing, of a plotting courtier known as Prince Shuisky, occurred when he was 13 and he had the executed man's body thrown to the dogs.

But the reign of Ivan the Terrible, as well as being an object lesson in vengeful tyranny, is a textbook case of an iron-willed autocrat uniting a nation. When he had himself crowned Tsar ('Caesar' of Russia – the 'third Rome', after Byzantium) in 1547, at the age of 17, Muscovy was then considered a cultural backwater straddling Eastern Europe and Asia.

In the beginning, Ivan had a reputation as a fair-minded and just ruler who was open to consultation by delegations of peasants. In the tradition of the more openly brutal Vlad, he was given to promoting men from the lower orders to positions of influence while displaying a quiet hostility toward the boyars. He also invaded the regions of Kazan and Astrakhan, deterring any further attack from those quarters and paving the way for his imperial dream of a greater Russia.

VLAD THE IMPALER

It was this era that established Ivan in the Russian national consciousness as a hero of the people and a highly cultured Renaissance man. But the patron of the arts who could debate theology with leadings Catholics and Protestants alike was also possessed of ruthless autocratic tendencies. After the capitulation of Kazan, the devout Ivan gave praise to his divine guidance by ordering the grandiose St Basil's Cathedral to be built in the centre of Moscow. Once completed, he had the architects blinded so that they could never repeat their monumental work elsewhere.

In many ways, the reign of Ivan the Terrible may be seen as a salutary lesson in the excesses of autocracy. However, when Soviet filmmaker Sergei Eisenstein commenced an intended trilogy of biopics in the mid-20th century, his chief patron had no such perspective. For Josef Stalin, the 'Red Tsar', Eisenstein's films on Ivan were never intended as a critique but as a tribute to the despot who created imperial Russia.

IVAN THE TERRIBLE: The First Tale

A film written and directed by Sergei Eisenstein, with music by Prokofiev. Ivan portrayed by Nikolai Cherkasov.

'This film is about the man who united Russia in the 16th century.' It glorifies the 'autocrat of all Russia'. 'What is our land now but a body with severed limbs?' lament the Russian court's nationalists, who declare Moscow as a 'third Rome' (Byzantium being the second).

The effete, androgynous boyars are depicted as inherently suspect, while Ivan is supported by the bearded, earthier relatives of his wife Anastasia Romanov. There's a solemnly religious tone to Eisenstein's epic, despite its production in an avowedly atheistic state. Its opulent style, costumes and huge cast seem to belie the fact that it was filmed in the early-to-mid-1940s, when a besieged Soviet Union was only just turning the tide in World War 2. Its baroque sets and melodramatic acting are enhanced by Eisenstein's ponderously slow-moving but beautifully grotesque expressionist style.

Ivan is a 'People's Tsar', before whom the peasantry prostrate themselves when they come to complain that the boyar class 'sprinkle the floor with blood'. 'We will cut off their heads mercilessly,' Ivan heroically promises the invading mob – and they loyally follow him into his wars against neighbouring regions.

The execution of young Kazan fighters evokes the martyrdom of St Sebastian, with arrows fired into their naked torsos. Ivan, who chides his executioners for their mindless brutality, is warned, 'Beware princes and boyars more than arrows.' He is very much the centre of a religious personality cult – 'Behold, the Tsar of all Russia' – and is healed on his sickbed when his head is enclosed in a huge ornate bible.

The boyars' treachery is made to justify Ivan's vengeful rage. They refuse to swear allegiance to his baby son – which, in his feverish trance, he claims as the only safeguard against Tartar, Polish and Livonian invasion – while the plotters seek to put androgynous and malleable idiot boy Vladimir on the throne, 'to do the will of the boyars'.

Ivan's supposedly close friend Prince Kurbsky tries to seduce Anastasia to make her his tsarina, when Ivan appears to be on his death bed. 'The Tsar, risen from his sickbed, trusts no one,' confides one cloaked boyar with a scarred face. 'He displaces boyars and promotes commoners.' Kurbsky takes refuge in Livonia, and Anastasia is poisoned by Ivan's sinister, black-hatted aunt, the mother of Vladimir.

***

The film's poisoning of Anastasia, while not Ivan's responsibility, may be a partial Stalinist rewriting of history in that it neglects to acknowledge later, similar crimes committed by the Tsar himself. It's also a turning point at which he seems to lose all self-control. (In fact there's no conclusive proof that Anastasia did not die from natural causes. But it's symptomatic of the internecine plotting of Ivan's world that he suspected two of his closest advisors, including a priest named Father Silvestr, and banished them.) One short-lived wife, named Maria, was drowned after her wedding day when it was discovered she was not a virgin. (Ivan's self-righteous wrath again mirrors that of Vlad – see the possibly apocryphal account of his mistress's murder in Chapter 13.) But it's the fate of the adulterous Anna Koltovskaya's lover that draws the dramatic parallel. While Anna herself was effectively banished to a convent for the rest of her life, the man who cuckolded Ivan suffered the far harsher punishment of impalement. In a society where this ultimate barbarity was not formerly used as a punitive measure (though, as we've seen, there is no culture that admits to any punitive use and it may simply be a case of reluctance to record their own worst excesses), his fate has been described as to be 'drawn upon a long sharp-made stake, which entered the lower part of his body and came out of his neck; upon which he survived for 15 hours …'

Other savage aspects of legend include the punishment of disrespectful ambassadors who refused to doff their caps – and were tortured by having them nailed to their heads. Some have suggested this is too close to the tale of Vlad similarly abusing Ottoman ambassadors (see Chapter Nine) to be anything but apocryphal; others have mused on whether the story of Prince Dracula may have entered the culture of Muscovy to such an extent that Ivan may have found it inspirational.

***

Ivan becomes obsessively driven post-illness, though what history records as his fit-like tantrums amount to no more than throwing a silver tray. (History records his later tendencies to beat his forehead on the cathedral steps to the point of concussion, ranting all the while.) His sympathies are now clear-cut: 'The princes and the boyars, who have gained much wealth, care neither for the sovereign nor the kingdom.' This 'first tale' ends with the line, 'For the sake of the great Russian kingdom!'

***

IVAN THE TERRIBLE – The Second Tale: The Boyars Plot

The boyars are presented as 'the enemies of Russia', while Ivan's secret police, the Oprichniki, are heroic, Ivan's 'backbone'. The heavily hirsute Oprichniki first appear on horseback like the Dark Riders from The Lord of the Rings. 'Protect Russia's frontiers – and suppress sedition', they are commanded.

***

Sixteenth-century Russia was placed under the totalitarian watch of his secret police force, the Oprichnina; formed in 1565, its ruthless horsemen had the thuggish efficacy of Vlad's *armas*, but the absolute power and terror tactics they indulged in with the Tsar's blessing went far further. Riding black horses, carrying brooms and dog's heads as an emblem of how they were to make a clean sweep of Russian society, they were beyond reproach and out of control. Although their initial targets were the distrusted boyars, whose estates they could confiscate, no sector of society high or low was safe from the Oprichniki. When an outspoken group of noblemen protested, Ivan had 50 of them whipped in public and a number of their tongues cut out. The peasantry also suffered terribly under the Oprichniki, who made random purges and restricted their movement under pain of death.

The Oprichniki are known to have purged 4,000 aristocrats and boyars, holding dominion over the Russian territories which were too remote for Ivan to exert total control. In 1497 the Tsar's grandfather,

Left: A copy of the most famous portrait of Vlad the Impaler – paintings have subsequently surfaced, though debate rages as to how accurate any of these depictions might be...

AN

ACCOUNT

OF

THE PRINCIPALITIES

OF

WALLACHIA AND MOLDAVIA:

WITH

VARIOUS POLITICAL OBSERVATIONS

RELATING TO THEM.

BY WILLIAM WILKINSON, Esq.

LATE BRITISH CONSUL RESIDENT AT BUKOREST.

Dobbiamo considerare queste due provincie, Wallachia e Moldavia a
guisa di due nave in un mar' tempestoso, dove rare volte si gode la
tranquilita e la calma.   DELCHIARO—*Revolusione di Wallachia.*

LONDON:

PRINTED FOR LONGMAN, HURST, REES, ORME, AND BROWN,
PATERNOSTER-ROW.

1820.

Left: The title page from the Victorian volume many believe introduced author Bram Stoker to the name of his famous character, Dracula.

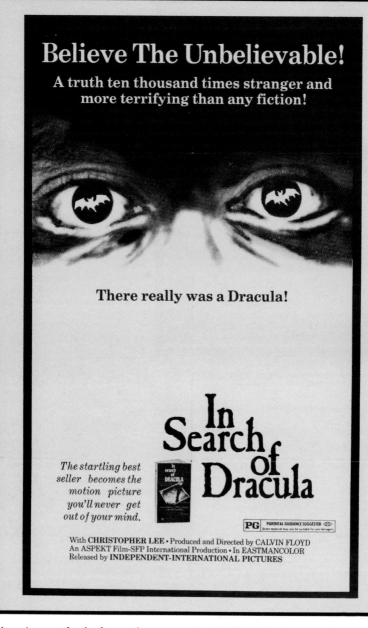

Above: A poster for the feature documentary inspired by Radu Florescu and Raymond McNally's classic 1972 book of the same name, which first popularised the link between the fictional Dracula and his historical namesake.

Above: Mount Timpa, identified by modern experts as the place where Vlad impaled his victims at the infamous Braşov massacre.

Below left: Vlad is depicted in this 1500 German woodcut, enjoying a meal among the impaled corpses of his victims at Braşov.

Below right: The actor Christopher Lee adopts the mantle of Vlad Dracula in the courtyard of Castle Bran, for the documentary In Search of Dracula.

Left: Co-author Gavin Baddeley investigates the interior of Castle Bran.

Below: The exterior of Castle Bran, long thought a fraudulent Castle Dracula aimed at tourists, but subsequently suggested as an authentic model for Bram Stoker's mythic fortress.

Left: The sigil of the Order of the Dragon, recreated as a pendant by the leading UK Gothic jewellery studio Alchemy.

Below: The Draconist symbol, as adapted by English metal band Cradle of Filth for their Order of the Dragon fan club.

Below: Sighisoara – Vlad the Impaler's birthplace–the best-preserved inhabited medieval citadel in Eastern Europe.

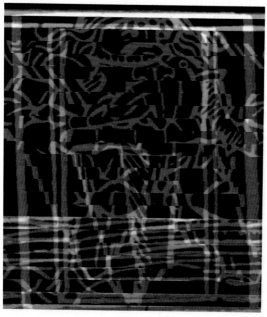

Above: The house in Sighisoara in which Dracula was born.

Left: A contemporary woodcut of Janos Hunyadi, the raven king who clipped Vlad Dracula's wings.

Above: A 15th-century illustration depicting soldiers leading a captive from a captured city – the armour is somewhat fanciful, but the scenario, whereby hostages were taken by conquering armies, was a familiar feature of medieval warfare. *Courtesy: Dover Pubs*

Above: Turkish Janissaries unleash a lethal volley of cannon-fire – the Ottoman army made effective use of gunpowder weapons in the 15th century.

Above: A selection of Transylvanian firearms from Dracula's era – Transylvania was a centre for arms production at the time.

Left: Medieval European armour, probably Italian-made – elite warriors of the era, Dracula included, would likely have worn something similar into battle.

Left: Turkish heavy cavalry equipment as worn by the Ottoman Empire's fearsome sipahi regiments – among Vlad's most formidable opponents.

Above: A French knight confronts the Turks in Sebastien Mamerot's 1470s account of the Crusades – though French enthusiasm for crusading waned after the disastrous defeat at Nicopolis in 1396. *Courtesy: Dover Pubs*

Left: The statue of the Hungarian king Matthias Corvinus in Cluj – the archaeological excavations to the front were interpreted by some as a ruse to remove the statue by the city's nationalistic Romanian mayor.

Left: Turkish troops assault a city – the seemingly unstoppable march of the Ottoman Empire justified extreme measures in some eyes, including the excesses of Vlad the Impaler.

Left: A bust of Vlad Dracula from Transylvania – the ruler is celebrated as a hero by many Romanians.

Above: A Czech poster for the sympathetic 1979 Romanian Vlad the Impaler biopic, made with communist state backing.

Above: A selection of the Vlad and vampire souvenirs co-author Gavin Baddeley brought back from his trip to Transylvania.

Right: An impalement scene from a Spanish chamber of horrors – impalement remains one of the most savagely iconic forms of execution.

Below: From the Renaissance onwards, Vlad's reputation assured him a place in chambers of horrors – this is behind the scenes at the London Dungeon, where the Impaler tableau has been retired – note the Dracula hat on the random dummy.

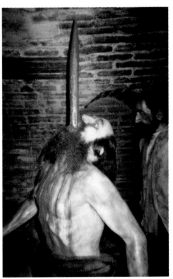

Above: Vlad confronts the Ottoman Sultan's envoys, prior to having their headgear nailed to their heads. The image is from a Romanian postcard; the stamp commemorates Dracula's role in the foundation of Bucharest.

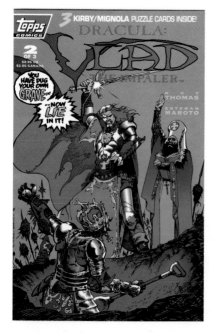

Left: The episode where Vlad literally obliges the rival Danesti voivode Dan III to dig his own grave, imagined on the cover of a 1993 comic. © *Topps Comics*

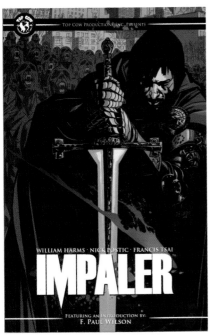

Left: In one of the more radical re-imaginings of Dracula, he is reinvented as a ruthless immortal vampire-hunter in this graphic novel by Daniel Harms. © *Top Cow*

Left: The scene is set in medieval Wallachia by artists Nick Postic and Nick Marinkovich for the Daniel Harms' *Impaler*.

Above: The Dance, a painting by artist War Arrow (Lawrence Burton), pastiching Matisse's *The Dancers* and inspired by the atrocities of Vlad the Impaler. It's said Dracula enjoyed watching his victims die, amused at how they twitched like frogs.
© *Lawrence Burton*

Right: Industrial music pioneer Boyd Rice, who has kept the Impaler's dark spirit alive in his provocative lyrics.

Ivan III, had introduced the *Sudebnik* code which allowed torture to be used against 'suspects of bad repute'. By the time of the Oprichniki no such reservations were in place; everybody was fair game now that these dark riders had total power delegated to them.

***

In a flashback sequence, the child Ivan resolves to rule over the boyars and become tsar (Caesar) after a villainous boyar accuses his mother of being a 'bitch' and sneering, 'There's no telling who sired you.'

Against the almost surreal expressionist décor of Ivan's court, the Tsar laments, 'I am all alone … no one to share my sorrows and joys.' For Anastasia is dead, but the film gives no hint of Ivan's subsequent rapaciousness.'

***

The historical Ivan veered between the religious piety he shared with Vlad and a rapacious sexual compulsion. (The English trader Sir Jerome Horsey noted Ivan's 'boasting of a thousand virgins he had deflowered and thousands of children of his begetting destroyed'.) The extremes of his dualistic nature were long thought to be the result of a brain fever endured shortly before his worst wave of atrocities. This 1553 bout of serious illness, followed by the death of his wife in 1560, are oft cited as the factors that tipped a relatively benign post-Renaissance ruler over into the psychology of a merciless autocrat.

However, Mei Trow notes how a 20th-century exhumation of the imperial skeleton revealed that the first tsar was suffering from osteoarthritis. It's at least possible that the almost constant pain from this incurable bone condition was displaced into some of Ivan's acts of hysteria and extreme cruelty. But it's also feasible that Ivan developed sadistic tendencies during his disturbed childhood; anecdotal accounts of him hurling cats from the upper battlements of the Kremlin resonate with similar stories of Vlad as an adult in captivity (see Chapter 13).

***

'I lean on the shoulders of the people,' Ivan tells the proletarian advisor he elevated to the rank of courtier. This voice of the people urges him, 'You must use power, use force!'

Much of the film is laden with the same religiosity as its progenitor; indeed, the solemnly devout tone of some scenes reflects the conviction of Ivan – and indeed of Vlad the Impaler – that he ruled by divine right and was an instrument of the will of God. Ivan reacts piously to the execution of the first treacherous boyars (for conspiring with Sigismund of Poland), as if it were not of his instigation. But his genuine tyranny is foreshadowed by the comment, 'Not nearly enough!'

The Orthodox Church is also implicated as being in part responsible for the escalating imperial backlash when Philip, the Metropolitan of Moscow, refuses to bless the Tsar and promises to curb Ivan's powers on behalf of the boyars. 'Why do you serve a satanic king, who bathes in the blood of the people?' sings an Orthodox boys' choir like an angelic Greek chorus. 'I shall be Ivan the Terrible,' resolves the Tsar in return, while a conniving old prelate opines that Philip will be more use to the church as an executed martyr than as a living opponent of the Tsar. (In actuality, Philip would be butchered by the Oprichniki.)

In a Pythonesque sequence, the feeble Vladimir's mother (evoking Terry Jones in drag) frightens her son with a song about hunters skinning a beaver, and urges him to assassinate his cousin the Tsar. Following a single colour choreographed Cossack dance scene that seems to anticipate some of Powell-Pressburger's more fanciful films (such as The Red Shoes, *1948), a knife-wielding assassin is tricked into killing Ivan's effete cousin instead of himself (Vladimir having drunkenly given the game away).*

The Oprichniki swear a subsequent vow to Ivan, with religious overtones: 'I vow to shed the blood of the guilty, sparing neither myself nor others.' The film closes on a colour sequence of a brooding but triumphant Ivan, promising to use the sword against any traitors: 'Russia must be protected.' A foretaste, perhaps, of the climactic third tale which would never appear?

***

The second part of Eisenstein's *Ivan the Terrible* would not see release until 1958 – five years after Josef Stalin's death and ten years after that of its writer/director. Its suppression seems to have been due to the suggestions of darkness in Ivan's psyche, the inference that – despite the film's otherwise hagiographic nature – the first tsar was not merely a beleaguered and benign leader reacting justly to outside pressure, but in part at least its instigator. This must have been particularly galling to Stalin – who, for all his Marxist-Leninist dogma, was in thrall to Ivan as a Russian nationalist hero. Like his imperial antecedent, he had developed the tactic of posturing as if to save the Russian people from disasters often of his own making, just as the Orthodox Church honoured the Byzantine tradition of 'the sacred mission of the imperial power' by blaming all Ivan's excesses on his overzealous underlings.

Eisenstein was fortunate in that, being the creator of the revered Soviet cine-polemics *Battleship Potemkin* and *October*, his omnipotent mentor refrained from having him imprisoned in the gulags. (The filmmaker was merely obliged to apologise for his 'formalist errors' in the making of the second tale of Ivan.)

If Eisenstein had lived to complete his intended third tale (he died of a heart attack in the early days of production), and if the Red Tsar himself had allowed it to be screened, there can be little doubt that Ivan's 1570 massacre of Great Novgorod would appear as an act of heroism. For this was a ruthless crushing of perceived sedition, justified by how Ivan believed the populace to be conspiring with the Poles. In the actuality it was an unfettered atrocity: walls were built around the city and, for five weeks, Novgorodian men, women and children alike were subjected to torture by castration, or having their tongues or noses cut off, before drowning in the River Volkhov. Married couples were forced to watch as their family members – often including their children – were tortured before their eyes. Women were impaled on revolving spears, and roasted alive as they spun like the Christian martyr St Catherine of the Wheel. According to the testimony of one German mercenary, Ivan played a hands-on role in the atrocities akin to that of the Impaler himself: 'Mounting a horse and brandishing a spear, he charged in and ran people through ...'

In its monstrously grand scale (64,000 deaths has been the highest estimated total – though Soviet historians, whose communist regime once overthrew the hated tsars, tried to scale it down to as few as 2,000), it is closer to the Turks' 'final solution of the Armenian problem' than to even Vlad's worst excesses – or perhaps to Stalin's wholesale starvation and execution of millions of Kulak peasant farmers, their families and co-workers. The monolithic Soviet leader – the champion of the proletariat who purged the Kulaks as ruthlessly as he did his Party comrades – believed for his part that, in eventually disbanding the Oprichniki (in 1572, after their secret police tactics proved of little use against the invading Tartars), Ivan simply did not take his policies far enough. For the dark horsemen and their unrestrained methods seem to have provided the model for the original Soviet secret police, the Cheka, whose director, Feliks Dzerzhinsky, asserted: 'We stand for organised terror – this should be frankly stated – terror being absolutely indispensable in current revolutionary conditions.' In his study *The Cheka: Lenin's Political Police*, historian George Leggett describes their methods of torture: 'Scalping and hand-flaying; some of the Voronezh Cheka's victims were thrust naked into an internally nail-studded barrel and were rolled around in it; others had their forehead branded with a five-pointed star, whilst members of the clergy were "crowned" with barbed wire.' Stalin would replace the Cheka with the more subtle but equally ruthless NKVD, under the directorship of serial rapist Lavrentiy Beria.

It is a brutal pragmatism, claiming comradeship with the masses while extending no greater mercy toward them than to one's avowed enemies. And this more extreme school of Machiavellian philosophy hangs like a shadow over the eastern fringes of Europe, written in blood since the days of Vlad the Impaler. But then, as Stalin once famously explained, 'A single death is a tragedy; a million deaths are a statistic.'

In the final years of Ivan the Terrible, the Tsar's bursts of intense rage became uncontrollable. A beating administered to his pregnant daughter-in-law for being inappropriately dressed caused her to miscarry; in the subsequent row with his son, Ivan beat him to death with his iron-tipped cane. His ensuing contrition entailed creating lists of everyone he could recall who had suffered – directly or indirectly – at his hands, literally thousands of names, to be mailed to Orthodox monasteries in the hope of saving his immortal soul.

Ivan Grozny devoted the end of his life to a holy order, under the adopted name of 'Jonah the Monk'. At the same time, it's also been suggested that he continued his rapacious double life, forcing himself on the Russian women he regarded as rightfully his. His death in March 1584 left his nation without effective leadership in a time of national crisis, until his first wife's family, the Romanovs, eventually imposed an imperial dynasty. He also bequeathed to the Russians an emergency measure which left the peasants he once supposedly championed locked in feudal serfdom for centuries.

Sir Jerome Horsey described at the time how 'the emperor began grievously to swell in his cods', suggesting syphilis. But legends persist that Ivan the Terrible died not from natural causes but from poisoning, after the attempted rapes of the wife and sister of two close advisors. This, of course, may be just the wishful thinking of those who long to see moral order imposed on the affairs of man – just as there are those who theorise that Stalin's 1953 demise was due not to a series of strokes but to a poisoning conspiracy within the Politburo, or that Vlad III died not as a war hero but as the target of assassination by his own soldiers.

In the 1972 treatise *The Dracula Myth*, cultural historian Gabriel Ronay translates the Russian Dracula pamphlet thus: 'There was a monarch of Greek Christian persuasion, called Dracula in the Latin tongue, but Devil in the Russian language. He was evil but wise, of angry disposition, who did not pardon or spare anyone, and who punished evil by quick death.' (According to Soviet researchers of the time, there were a total of 22 different versions of the Vlad Dracula legend in the Russian language.) This tone, slightly begrudging in its admiration of Vlad's dual morality, finds further expression in the following passage: 'And hating to see evil on his land, none of those committing any evil, wickedness, highway robbery, or the telling of lies will he allow to live. Be he mighty boyar, or priest, or monk, or simpleton, or rich man, he cannot escape death, for so terrible was he.'

The idea of 'Vlad the Terrible' as a blueprint for the reign of Ivan the Terrible is an interesting conceit that has been conjectured upon by several writers. Ronay, however, seems certain of it. To him, both rulers symbolise the old Russian Orthodox principle of autocracy by divine right, the idea that 'justice cannot be established in the land without such terrors', to quote 16th-century Russian chronicler I. S. Persvetov. According to Ronay's own research, 'In the texts written in Ivan the Terrible's time and after his death, Dracula becomes the "*tsar grozny*" – the "Terrible tsar" – and Muscovites begin to refer to Ivan the Terrible as "the Russian Dracula".'

None of which proves that Ivan regarded Vlad as a personal role model. But comparison does suggest certain behavioural parallels – even if what we know of Vlad, his psychology and personality remains largely educated guesswork, compared to the better-documented Ivan.

According to *The Dracula Myth*, it was this duality of personality and purpose that found acceptance in 15th/16th-century Russia: 'The inference is clear – the ruler is always right. As his power is of divine origin, his deeds cannot be judged by ordinary mortals. The Russian Dracula stories duly underline this basic tenet of Russian autocracy.' By the time of the later 16th-century versions of the story, it seems that the Voivode was no longer the ambiguously cruel but just figure he was first presented as, but an outright heroic figure – just as filmmaker Eisenstein would later lionise Ivan IV. But it is as *both* a fearless defender of his culture *and* a cruel tyrant that Vlad starts to appear less of a relic from the Middle Ages, and more of a precursor to the centuries that were to follow.

CHAPTER VIII

Better to be Feared Than Loved

'The souls of emperors and cobblers are all cast in one same mould. Considering the importance of princes' actions, and their weight, we persuade ourselves they are brought forth by some as weighty and important causes; we are deceived: they are moved, stirred and removed in their motions by the same springs and wards as we are in ours. The same reason that makes us chide and brawl and fall out with any of our neighbours, causeth a war to follow between princes; the same reason that makes us whip or beat a lackey maketh a prince (if he apprehend it) to spoil and waste a whole province. They have as easy a will as we, but they can do much more. Alike desires perturb both a skin-worm as an elephant.' Essays, Michel de Montaigne (1580).

'It is far better to be feared than loved if you cannot be both,' observed Niccolo Machiavelli in *The Prince*, 'since some men love as they please but fear when the prince pleases, a wise prince should rely on what he controls.' Of course many conspire to be both feared and loved – princes and cobblers alike – and for many, inspiring love comes easier than cultivating fear. Vlad was proving himself a consummate artist in the creation and manipulation of fear, but there were still many who regarded the Voivode with respect, even affection. As already noted in these pages, there still are. Among the natives of the bucolic backwaters of Dracula's former realms, stories and songs still circulate that portray the long dead Impaler as a heroic, even benevolent figure.

Yet such Romanian peasants are unlikely to be seeing the medieval Voivode through the red-tinted spectacles of socialist ideology, but with rather a more romantic, even mythic perspective. Yet the gangster analogy is a more useful one when trying to unravel the intricacies of medieval European politics. Indeed, it is the case that many casual readers first encounter Vlad the Impaler through reading 'true crime' books – books which anthologise the most extreme examples of history's despots, gangsters and tyrants – those figures, like those in the vignettes to follow, who are renowned for their brutality and their practice of government by fear. All of these figures are active advocates of the Machiavellian dictum, 'It is better to be feared than loved.' Anarchists have long suggested that all governments are basically racketeers, a riff more recently taken up by right-wing ideologues in the US: we pay our various taxes in return for security and a quiet life, or ultimately, they will 'send the boys around'. Such radical perspectives certainly seem to hold water in the context of medieval Europe. The aristocracy demanded the obedience, produce and labour of the local populace by strength of arms, in return for protection, though the chief threats came from other local lords, or indeed their 'protector' himself, should they fail to satisfy his demands. There is a yawning gap between the image of the chivalric knight of Arthurian myth and the authentic medieval warlord, the racketeers in chainmail who presided over much of Europe for a millennium. Many of Vlad the Impaler's atrocities against his own people may have been considered excessive by his contemporaries, but by no means explicitly illegitimate by the standards of the day.

Another intriguing possible analogy between modern gangsters and medieval politics comes from the concept of dynasties. Medieval and Renaissance politics can appear particularly bewildering to the modern eye because of the constantly shifting alliances. Factions shift from one side of a conflict to another with startling rapidity throughout the era. Religious affiliation and ethnic factors offered a stabilising influence, but overall, personal loyalty was the glue that held society together. Within that context, family was all-important, and the ideological framework that underlies our understanding of most modern conflicts seldom applied. The history of nationalism – just when most people identified themselves as citizens of a specific country – is widely debated. Some historians doubt that the idea took hold until the 1700s, though others maintain its roots stretch back far earlier. Regardless, it's easy to see Europe in the Middle Ages as a territory carved up by dynasties – akin to the Mafia families who divided the rich pickings of the underbelly of 20th-century America according to their own private codes.

Such Mafiosi codes embraced notions of ethnicity – early gangster conflicts reflected tensions between the Italian, Irish and Jewish immigrant communities – and even religious elements, as the Mafia embraced Catholicism in contrast to the Protestant faith dominating America's ruling elite. Yet the overriding ethos was family values, and the rival Mafia organisations became known as the 'Five Families', with a power structure built around concepts of inheritance and family honour that would have been wholly familiar to the powerbrokers of medieval Europe. The history of the Middle Ages can be baffling if seen as an account of wars between rival nations. As a succession of feuds between rival dynasties – Mafioso families if you will – it starts to make much more sense. Certainly, some medieval leaders tried to rise above such cynical dynastic rivalry – to see a bigger picture – idealists in their fashion, willing to look beyond the interests of themselves or their clan. Athletes of Christ like John Hunyadi who fought for more than simple power, or Emperor Sigismund, who had visions of a unified Europe. Some include Vlad Dracula in such a list, a leader whose ambitions stretched beyond simply securing his own power to embrace the nobler cause of securing the future of his homeland as an independent Christian nation. Even if we accept this version of Vlad as a patriotic hero, motivated by nascent nationalism, there is little denying that his methods put him among the ranks of history's most brutal gangsters…

***

'I give my personal address to you, the people of Kronstadt …'

The fresh evening air is tickled by warm plumes of flame as Vlad the Impaler barks his speech at the local populace – the craftsmen, boyars, wives and children corralled from their homes onto the common ground adjoining the burning church of St Jacob outside the walls of the citadel the Vlachs call Braşov. Displaying his education unostentatiously, he talks in a competent if broken version of their native Teutonic tongue.

'… In solemn thanks for your aiding the house of Draculesti's stand against the Turkish menace. Without your personal sacrifice, it is doubtful that Wallachia may have resisted for as long as it has. For is it not the case,' he sneers at the downturned faces that dare not meet his own, 'that nothing harries a people toward self-defence quicker than desertion? And is not the urgency of the fight hastened by the knowledge that one stands alone?'

The populace of Braşov – for it is they, the Germanic name of 'Kronstadt' hurled back at their city in a spirit of vengefulness and mockery – have been roused from their workaday business by the unexpected arrival of the Voivode. Only a few have set eyes on him before. All as one regret that they have not lived out their lives in a perpetual state of obscurity, without reason or occasion to meet their esteemed lord.

On this day of April 1459, the warlord's campaigns against his most troublesome provinces will culminate in a holocaust. Friends and neighbours who are truly loved, *Vlad had addressed his futile implorations to the Saxon settlers for 200 men to bolster his army against Mehmet's invasion force. Now they cannot meet his eyes. The measure of his wrath is that he regards his presence as imperative, unlike those occasions when his* armas *levelled Braşov's neighbouring towns.*

The Vlach chickens are come home to roost.

Untold of in any biblical prophecy, this is the immigrant craftsmen's Armageddon. Endlessly recurring throughout the murderous annals of human history, it will be Vlad III's My Lai.

'In the spirit of our agreement that you be allowed to trade freely with the cities of my principality, I have come to exact payment in kind.' The first screams are piercing the air. Their inevitability is such that the town elders and boyars do not avert their defeated gaze from the ground in front of them.

'In the name of the Draculesti, I am here to tell you that your renegade behaviour gave the deepest *offence.' The otherwise impassive Voivode seethes the words. All escape is impossible now. The wooden bridge that offers the only way to the safety of the city's stone walls has been stormed by Vlad's troops. 'With respect to your 'liberators' the Danesti,' Tepeş mocks, 'I pray you have the fortitude to endure the fate to which they have abandoned you.'*

The stockade that housed the armoury of the pretender Dan III crackles and spits its black smoke to the sky. Such was to be the protection against the coming of Dracula. But the Danesti are long gone, as if a preternatural sense had warned them of the blitzkrieg *raid that was about to take place.*

On Mount Timpa, which looms over the battlements of the city of Braşov, the mechanisms of death are all in position. Chief among Vlad's adjutants is the man deemed the 'Stake Master'. For what use is vengeance if it does not announce the extent of your wrath to a tremulous world?

***

'When people are afraid of you, you can do anything.'

So ran the bastardised Machiavellian tagline for the 1990 Brit-gangster movie, *The Krays*. We need not dwell long on the Kray twins: two well-dressed London thugs whose most gratuitous crimes – one murder each committed by themselves, and one carried out by their associates – only quieted the tongues of witnesses until such time as they were taken off the streets. Once the law had remanded them to prison on another offence, the floodgates of information opened as all felt free to speak. It was a fantasy of 1960s London as equivalent to Prohibition Chicago that doomed them; in London, the long-term success of a criminal depends on keeping a low profile. Extremes of lawlessness are not necessarily a threat to the chief perpetrators' liberty, as long as they do not court the attentions of the media.

In becoming celebrity villains, 'the Twins' were seeking to emulate the Hollywood images of Paul Muni in *Scarface* and Rod Steiger in *Al Capone*. But these were pulp-fictionalised versions of the facts. In its early 20th-century context, when the cities of America were still the new frontiers of capitalism and organised crime, the life of 'Big Al' was a textbook prototype for anyone who aspired to be a local celebrity, gutter-level politician or Machiavellian monster.

The contrast between the real deal and the play-acting Brits is clearest in events that took place one night in May 1929 – culminating in a triple murder for which Capone would never be arrested, let alone convicted.

Alphonse Capone, the charismatic Italian-American venture capitalist, was then at the height of his powers, raking in annual profits that would place him easily in the billionaire bracket today. His profile as a popular public figure had been shaken a little by the St Valentine's Day Massacre several months earlier – when a small group of hoods disguised as Chicago policemen had raided a garage used as HQ by the rival North Side Gang, executing five of them and two unfortunate civilians by lining them against the wall and riddling them with machinegun bullets. Capone was hundreds of miles away at the time, but few with an ear to the ground or an eye on the headlines doubted that he'd given the orders.

But still, the *bon viveur* owed the balance of terror that made him the kingpin to *goombahs* like the Sicilian hitmen John Scalise, Albert Anselmi and Joe Giunta, all of whom were believed to be behind the Valentine's Day killings. It was to show his respect and gratitude that Big Al invited them to a meeting of the Unione Siciliana at a Midwestern roadhouse in Hammond, Indiana. He himself, of Neapolitan descent, was only an honorary patron of the supposedly Cosa Nostra-linked organisation, but the real purpose was to eat, drink and make merry, for tomorrow ...

***

The best whiskey and beer flowed, in defiance of the Prohibition laws that allowed Capone his power and above the standard of some of the rotgut that bootleggers pushed into speakeasies. Pasta and meatballs; stuffed cannelloni and fattening, creamy cannoli; there was no indulgence that backslapping, fleshy-faced Al wouldn't grant his boys – except perhaps for the usual broads, who were mostly notable by their absence ...

***

While popular culture has played a part in reinventing the gangster as an improbable antihero, for most, the term remains a slur. Gangsterism is the practice of securing authority by brute force, the charge of being a 'gangster government' one levelled at corrupt regimes to challenge their legitimacy, a smear upon those leaders who rule by virtue of fear alone. Gangsterism is, perhaps, in the eye of the beholder. The 20th-century regime most frequently condemned as a gangster government is Adolf Hitler's Fascist regime. For his own part, the Führer is reported to have based a low opinion of America's military capabilities on viewing Hollywood gangster flicks. At a Cabinet Meeting in 1942, the British Prime Minister Winston Churchill dismissed American ideas that Hitler, 'the mainspring of evil', deserved a fair trial as a war criminal should he be defeated and detained. Instead, only half in jest, Churchill suggested leasing Old Sparky, the electric chair infamous for ending the lives of many of America's most notorious criminals, as the only appropriate end for 'a gangster' like the German Führer.

Churchill was far from alone in comparing Hitler's Nazi Party to racketeers. The previous year, the celebrated German playwright Bertolt Brecht – an exile from the Nazi State – wrote *The Resistible Rise of Arturo Ui*. The modernist play was an explicit satire of the Third Reich, Hitler represented by the hoodlum Arturo Ui, a gangster who was attempting to gain power in 1930s Chicago by gaining control of the cauliflower racket. The 1944 Hollywood movie *The Hitler Gang* depicted the Führer's rise to power in the style of a classic gangster film, while by way of contrast, the 1942 film *Hitler – Dead or Alive* depicted a trio of American gangsters, hired for a million bucks to execute a hit on the Führer.

The idea wasn't wholly fanciful. In one of many details that tarnish the fringes of the image of World War 2 as a modern crusade of good against evil, the American government struck a deal with the Mafia in order to protect US dockyards against union agitation and foreign subversion. Before the American underworld became dominated by Italian families, Jewish mobsters were enthusiastic recruits to the Allied cause. Meyer Lansky was among the Jewish gangsters who played an active part in opposing Nazi sympathisers in the US. 'The stage was decorated with a swastika and a picture of Adolf Hitler,' he later recalled of a visit to a fascist rally in Manhattan. 'The speakers started ranting. There were only fifteen of us, but we went into action. We threw some of them out the windows. Most of the Nazis panicked and ran out. We chased them and beat them up. We wanted to show them that Jews would not always sit back and accept insults.'

The Mafia overall had good reason to hope for an Allied victory. Hitler's Italian ally Benito Mussolini sent the 'Iron Prefect' Cesare Mori to break the Mafia in their traditional Sicilian heartland of Sicily in the 1920s. An organised crime network that had proven immune to previous attempts at suppression withered beneath Cesare's ruthless tactics. 'The music changed. Mafiosi had a hard life...' reflected one Mafiosi. 'After the war the Mafia hardly existed anymore. The Sicilian Families had all been broken up.' Many Mafiosi fled to America, to resume their activities, and then the Allied victory opened the way for the Mob to stage a comeback in Italy. Some have argued that the ingrained criminality of the Italian Mafia could only yield to the even greater institutionalised criminality of the Italian Fascists. Like the distinction between terrorist and freedom fighter, perhaps the distinction between organised criminality and unfettered authority can prove elusive to the cynical observer. While, to most modern observers, Vlad the Impaler looks like the worst kind of gangster when he terrorised the Saxon merchants of Braşov, in his own eyes – and most of his contemporaries – the Voivode was simply laying down the law in an uncompromising style during highly volatile times.

In the years following the fall of the Third Reich, numerous regimes have been tarred with the brush of gangsterism by their opponents, typically dictatorships whose methods seemed excessive, their corruption or reliance upon brute force too pronounced or overt by the standards of the international community. Josef Stalin began his career as a bandit and gangster, a mode of operation many contend he continued after seizing power in the Soviet Union in 1924. Nicolae Ceauşescu turned the government of Communist Romania into a dynastic affair, installing indolent members of his own family in positions of power in a fashion reminiscent of a Mafioso family. Numerous Middle Eastern and South American regimes have invited accusations of gangsterism by their flagrant nepotism and ready resort to state brutality. But nowhere has the level of raw corruption and naked violence been so pronounced as in the troubled continent of

Africa, where government according to the rule of the ruthless racketeer became almost endemic in the late 20th century. If there is one modern ruler who exemplifies the worst of this trend, a man who embodied the leader as an immoral opportunist, a thug driven beyond the brink of insanity by the intoxication of power, it is Idi Amin...

***

Welcome to the palace of His Excellency President for Life of Uganda. Field Marshal Al Hadji Doctor Idi Amin, VC, DSO, MC. Lord of All the Beasts of the Earth and Fishes of the Sea, Conqueror of the British Empire in Africa in General and Uganda in Particular.

General Idi Amin Dada, the almighty absolute ruler of our glorious East African kingdom, has invited you to his Entebbe villa to celebrate one and a half years of his rule and ten years of liberation from the white oppressor, Allah be praised. You, O most privileged guest, shall dine on the most succulent traditional African fare that the palace cooks have prepared for you and take an aperitif or two of the finest Scotch whisky. (For remember that our generous host also holds the honourable title of the Last King of Scotland.)

And then we have girls for you, my friend. The finest big-breasted young women from the bosom of Mother Africa, who General Amin will allow to bestow their favours on you once he has selected who is to be his own wife for the night – or perhaps who will join his retinue of adored fulltime spouses, if fortune truly smiles upon her.

I see that you have been a little nervous since you arrived here, and perhaps you are uneasy to be in the place that is also the heart of our state security system? Or maybe, my friend, you are at heart a supporter of the deposed former leader whose name we shall not speak? Maybe even a friend of the imperial white devil, who would seek to impose his will again were it not for the fearsome might of General Idi Amin Dada?

But do not be so alarmed, I am merely joshing with you! You are safe here, my friend, your presence places you among the inner circle of Ugandan patriots. We have much to celebrate: our great nation has rid itself of the Asian maggots who siphoned off our riches and were profiteering from what is truly a black man's country, and a black man's economy; how wealthy we shall be when we are in control of all the businesses and stores they left behind, in their anxiety to flee!

Even now, as we take refreshment and relax in these luxurious surroundings, the Public Safety Unit and the State Research Bureau are active in the streets of Kampala and Entebbe, rooting out our nation's enemies. They will make dinner for the crocodiles. Listen carefully at night as the air grows quiet and you can hear the cracks of gunfire, broken only by the calls of nightbirds. And listen too to our great leader, General Idi himself.

'You are a damn fool, Suleiman! You gave away your chance to be a part of the new Uganda, the new Africa!'

Hear him now, out in the kitchen. Notice how everybody has drawn away and grown silent. Even the servants and the cooks keep their distance. Our leader is a most huge and intimidating man, is he not, my friend? This is how he demands respect. But I think you will agree he is also a most amusing man!

'Come and tell us, Suleiman, how damn clever you were! How you and your soldiers aimed to overthrow the constitutionally elected Grand Emperor of Uganda!'

I see now that your eyes are wide with fright, though your stare is not as wide as that of Brigadier Suleiman Hussein. But then, he has been such a long time in the refrigerator that there are icicles beneath his eyelids.

Do not be afraid, my friend. General Amin Dada sometimes retrieves the head of the Brigadier at dinner, after he has had a drink or two. See how he rants at the dead man and accuses straight into his eyes?

I see too that you are having trouble swallowing your yam. But do not be alarmed. This is how the General demands respect.

***

'Ain't this great, guys, this thing of ours?'

Big Al and his three Sicilian goombahs *were getting a little pie-eyed for a while, once the bottles of good vino from the old country had been broken out of the crates. But now it seems like Al has sobered up – maybe via some strong espresso, maybe even from a little of the flapper girl's nose powder.*

'I mean,' he motions around him, administering a backhanded slap to a flinching Johnny Scalise, 'all of this, huh? Only in America!' 'This' is just a steak and near-beer joint, but Capone's sense of proprietorship gives it a special magic.

'Sure, it's okay. I mean, it's nice.' Joey Giunta answers for them all, sensing the change in Big Al's mood.

'Nice?' The big boss considers the term. 'Yeah. It's-a-nice-a!' Brooklyn-born Al mocks the ice-cream salesman tones of the Sicilian 'Moustache Pete'. 'But you know what ain't so nice?'

Scalise and Anselmi shake their heads almost imperceptibly, their faces immobile. They know something's afoot and they know the doors are locked. They handed their pieces in at the cloakroom in a spirit of goodwill.

'It's how my feelings get hurt when some dirty sonofabitch *takes a shot*

behind my back!'

A shot was what they were expecting. But not the clean sweep of curved wood, connecting bang-splat with Johnny's nose.

'Dirty, traitorous sonsofbitches!'

Paranoiac and self-righteous, Big Al brings an Indian juggling club down again and again like a baseball bat on the gunsel's skull, like the wrath of God wielded by Babe Ruth. As he reduces the upper body to bone splinters and blood, his boys hold Giunta's alarmed compadres at gunpoint, to await their turn.

When the bat hits your eye like a big pizza pie, that's la morte.

All three men, battered and broken among the dinner plates, will be finished with a gunshot to the back of the neck and left in the underbrush at the side of the road. Speculation about the motive for revenge ranges from conspiracy with Chicago hood Johnny Aiello to assassinate Big Al to the heat called down by the otherwise faithful Scalise and Anselmi, when they autonomously decided to shoot all those saps on Valentine's Day.

***

When the massacre is later immortalised in pop culture – in movies like *The Untouchables* and even in comic books – the toll of victims will most often be downplayed to a single treacherous 'Moustache Pete'. After all, it's one thing for a man to have his skull caved in amidst the hospitality of the dinner table, but to do it to three men at a time seems a little excessive …

***

'You may approach the throne of the Emperor …'

The bespectacled Justice Minister steps lightly into the echoing dining hall. Seated at the end of a long table, Jean-Bédel Bokassa is propped stiff-backed in a velvet-lined chair, centred in a giant golden representation of the Napoleonic eagle.

'I've received further telegrams from the French embassy, your Excellency.' The nervous apparatchik addresses the head of the Central African Republic. The French-trained soldier, holder of the Croix de Guerre and the Légion d'honneur, is of only slightly greater physical stature than was Bonaparte himself. He cocks a curious brow, wordlessly enquiring of the nature of their concern.

'It is the question of the schoolchildren, Excellency.' Still, there is no response. 'They wish to confirm that the account they have of the detentions is accurate.'

VLAD THE IMPALER

Bokassa, the imperial face of post-colonial Africa, is no anti-western revolutionary but the grandiose product of every influence that ever touched him: Napoleonic military honour; Third World Marxism; Islam – these latter two now relinquished in favour of the papal baptism which, according to the Central African emperor, has made him not only a Roman Catholic but the Thirteenth Apostle of the Holy Mother Church.

This sacred monster has been taking holy communion in his own singular fashion.

'Our children lack discipline. You must tell the ambassador that the detainments are necessary to breed a stronger Africa. Pupils who attend school improperly dressed lack the necessary seriousness for their studies.'

The Emperor waves away his former military masters' concerns, removing the silver lid from a serving tray. Steam from the lightly grilled meat and baked vegetables rises toward the ceiling and dissipates.

'But it is the numbers, Excellency ...' *The minister is hesitant in his reproach.* 'They claim it is unprecedented to detain children in adult prisons en masse. And then,' *he swallows back his caution,* 'there are the parents ...'

Bokassa regards his ministerial minion quizzically. 'And what is their complaint, these 'parents'?' *His fork impales what appears to be a chunk of pork garnished with haricot beans.*

'Their complaint is ... their claim is that they cannot trace some of the children,' *the minister corrects himself.* 'Even the prison authorities say they have no record of certain names from the schools register.'

His master ruminates quietly for a moment, then pushes some of the large plates towards his politician. 'Eat,' *he invites.*

'Thank you, your Excellency, but I will take my evening meal after work. For now I must respond to the embassy ...'

'Eat,' *comes the more emphatic command.* 'Your emperor invites you to eat at his table.'

The Justice Minister watches his master's expression intently. There is no sign of aggression, no malice. But he will broach no argument. Hesitantly, gulping back any reflexive nausea, the minister bends his legs to be seated at the table. Under the emperor's insistent gaze, he takes the serving prongs and reaches directly for the simmering meat in the centre of the table.

If he is to be made party to this crime, then so be it: better to consume the meat knowingly and willingly than to be shocked by the discovery that – like Tamora, the queen in Shakespeare's Titus Andronicus *– you have inadvertently feasted on the flesh of your children. If becoming a cannibal is what is required to survive in this empire of fear, then it is surely better to eat than to be eaten ...*

***

If one man could offer competition to Idi Amin as Africa's most appalling dictator it was Jean-Bédel Bokassa, who seized power in the Central African Republic in 1966, declaring himself Emperor a decade later. Like Amin, Bokassa was a decorated career soldier under European colonial rule (Bokassa fought for the French, Amin the British) before staging a coup in their newly-liberated homelands. Both men had been underestimated by their opponents as too stupid to orchestrate a takeover. In common with Vlad Dracula, Bokassa adopted the role of an enemy of idleness and immorality once he took power, setting up 'morality brigades' and taking ruthless action against beggars and the unemployed. There are also stories about both leaders subjecting their victims to enforced cannibalism – Dracula, for example, is said to have obliged some gypsies, who lobbied for the release of one of their fellows accused of theft, to eat the accused as a penance for their presumption. (After being deposed in a 1979 coup, Bokassa, while convicted of murder, embezzlement and treason, was acquitted of cannibalism during his trial in 1987.) Separated by centuries of time, thousands of miles of space, the Voivode of Wallachia and the Emperor of Central Africa are clearly very different creatures. Yet certain nagging details suggest patterns in history's endless catalogue of horrors, of terrible echoes that sound when men of blood achieve unfettered power…

***

As Prince Vlad reaches the end of his meal, a fur-clad and capped figure presents himself on the periphery of his vision. Aware of the presence, the Prince does not switch his attention from the twitching, convulsing, defecating, bleeding spectacle before him.

'Voivode …'

As if in answer, the Impaler expels a rich jet of gas from his glutted oesophagus, and then relaxes with the gratified sensation of a full belly. In these desperate times, it is a rare luxury for even one such as he – a man of royal blood and predatory bloodlust.

'Voivode, I …'

'Yes, I know. You have been sent by my great ally Corvinus, have you not?'

The Hungarian emissary, still not as long in the tooth as in his moustache, is given a surge of bumptious confidence by the ease with which the Impaler receives him.

'His Majesty had bid me to speak most urgently with you on the fate of Braşov, my Voivode.'

'The fate of Braşov!' echoes Vlad with amusement. 'Look around you,' he gestures, mocking Matthias's messenger and with him the whole of humanity, 'do you not see the city of Braşov impaled as if on one single stake?'

The emissary regrets to admit that he does. As twilight begins to fade into night, the eruption of burning torches turns the agonised shapes into twisted silhouettes. He tries to stare through them, as if they were nightmare visions from a dose of ergot poisoning.

'The King has stressed to me that time is of the essence ...'

The Prince, half-glutted by the wine, pushes the remainder of the carafe toward his visitor. 'Drink ...'

The emissary does not require much encouragement. He is already gulping down the heady dark ferment in agitated breaths before he realises he is drinking from the Voivode's own goblet. The Prince's askance smile tells him he has not transgressed, so he sups a little more.

'Eat ...' Vlad proffers the reminder of the swine that took pride of place on his table, offering up a remaining chunk of belly and crackling.

The emissary almost chokes on the thought of having to digest food in these circumstances. The pitiful mewling and puking. The blood that drips continually down like sap flowing from a eucalyptus tree. The profane visions and vile odours. All this is promised in the Roman papist visions of eternal damnation. To see it all here, now, is to know a world out of kilter.

'Eat,' comes the more emphatic command. 'Your Voivode invites you to eat at his table ...'

The emissary's distress is palpable. He looks to his host for a reprieve. For one moment, it seems as if he has found it.

'You are not able to stomach such rich food in the midst of all this human suffering – is that it?'

The Magyar nods his head emphatically, as if in appreciation. 'It is the terrible sights, my Voivode. And those infernal sounds. And o sweet Jesu, the noxious stench!'

'Guards!' The Impaler barks an order, his moderation abandoned. Risen to his feet, he points in accusation. 'Take this bilious wretch and throw him on the spikes! This messenger boy cannot bear the odours of blood and shit, so raise him high above the stink!'

The armaş are quick to respond. Their servitude is all that guarantees their survival, and one more human life is as nothing against safeguarding their own. As the disbelieving emissary from the court of Matthias Corvinus goes wide-eyed and sobbing to his fate, the Voivode's indignation begins to calm.

Vlad walks in wonderment beneath the grim hilltop tableau that, for him, never loses its fascination. The Hungarian messenger is stripped naked. In semi-darkness, he is raised by ladder onto stakes that are already occupied. Screaming like an agonised beast, he is left dangling awkwardly on the spike that punctures his bowel, shooting a stream of blood onto the heads of the craftsmen labouring below.

Restored to a state of calm, the Voivode reaches for a last scrap of the pig meat with which to mop up the human blood that spills onto his plate, giving it the flavour of a rich kishka.

***

The above imagining is based on versions of the Impaler legends that conflate the 'epicurean massacre' outside Braşov with the story of the dignitary who died for his culinary sensitivities. The vampiric dessert is believed to be a later embellishment – possibly originating after Bram Stoker, moving the Wallachian prince closer to the fictional count that assumed his family name of Dracula.

So it is with all tales of Vlad III: the broader military campaigns are well documented in regional history, relating to the ebb and flow of the Ottoman invasions and the parochial Eastern European squabbles of the time. The atrocities are more problematic. Printed in varying sensational accounts in several different languages, at times they seem to be engaged in a competition to outdo each other in terms of gruesomeness (but not realism, given the rather dreamy idiom of the folk tale that many of these accounts adopt).

All that can be known for sure is that Vlad developed a reputation for inhuman behaviour; the records of his crimes (if indeed they can be called 'crimes', given that his was the law of the land) are often contradictory but still, after hundreds of years, leave an impression of lingering dread. For who does not fear the man who maintains his healthy appetite in the midst of mass murder?

And for a despot to truly put the fear of God into his populace, he must have both the reputation and the arrogance of a living deity, with absolute power over life and death. Such power may only be expressed callously and arbitrarily, for power compromised – even by convention or common decency – is still power diminished.

CHAPTER IX

A Model Prince?

> *'So, as a prince is forced to know how to act like a beast, he
> must learn from the fox and the lion … one must be a fox in
> order to recognise traps, and a lion to frighten off wolves.'*
> – Niccolo Machiavelli, The Prince.

By the summer of 1460, Vlad Dracula had largely secured his position
at home. Potential rivals had been eliminated or scattered, the
merchants of Transylvania cowed with suitable display of power and
intent, his own court and armed forces purged, staffed with men whose
loyalty he could rely upon, and his eastern neighbour, Moldavia, under
the control of his old comrade and cousin Stefan. There was now time
to dedicate to domestic policy, for the new Voivode to try and fashion
Wallachia in the image he saw fit. Most historians agree that Dracula
was an energetic ruler in comparison to most of his predecessors and
successors, a Voivode determined to put his own stamp on the realm.
He established new villages to try and bolster Wallachia's war-torn
agrarian economy, guarded by what defences fragile local finances
could provide. He founded Eastern Orthodox monasteries and
churches – such religious institutions served not just to guard the
Voivode's immortal soul, but also helped provide a vital administrative
framework. Above all, bizarre as it may sound, Vlad was remembered
for instituting a moral revolution in Wallachia, personally establishing
a new ethos in his realm designed to stamp out the lawlessness and lax
morality that frequently plague embattled kingdoms.

An admiring Russian source explained that 'he so hated evil in his
land, that whenever someone did evil, a crime or robbery, or lied, or
was guilty of an injustice, then he was not allowed to live. Neither great
boyars or priests or monks or ordinary people or those owning great

wealth could save themselves from death with money, and that is how fearful he was. He had a water source and a well in a certain place and many travellers from many countries came to this well because the water there was cold and sweet. And he placed a great and wondrous golden cup in an empty place by the well so that anyone who wanted to drink the water could drink it with that cup and put it back again. And however much time passed no-one dared to steal the cup.' Just as Mussolini's 'Iron Prefect' Cesare Mori had proved that single-minded ruthlessness could defeat even the Mafia on their home turf, Dracula brought law and order to Wallachia with a similar recipe of merciless determination and draconian justice.

Meanwhile, time had not stood still on the international stage. Hungary was once again threatened by the spectre of civil war. Ladislaus Posthumous died in 1457 – though there were rumours of poison, most accepted that the Hungarian King was claimed by the plague which had killed John Hunyadi the previous year (recent research suggests Vladislaus actually died of leukaemia). Fearing the prospect of imminent anarchy, the Hungarian aristocracy elected John Hunyadi's second son Matthias (his oldest having been beheaded at Vladislaus's order) as their new monarch in 1458. The new King, who took the name Matthias Corvinus, was only 15, and many of the country's leading lords hoped he would prove a weak and pliant leader. They would be proven wrong.

Meanwhile, Skanderbeg had been keeping the Ottoman forces at bay in Albania with a series of brilliant victories, establishing his tough Stradioti cavalry as among the most sought-after mercenaries in Europe. In the process, the Albanian hero gave Mehmet an enduring headache, earning himself the accolade of Athlete of Christ from a grateful Pope who was still trying to muster support for yet another Crusade against the infidel Turk. There was a notable lack of interest among the crowned heads of Europe, most of whom preferred to regard the Ottomans as somebody else's problem. There was some enthusiasm at the prospect of raising the funds for such an endeavour, though this was more to do with a potential new source of revenue for corrupt administrators than any true intention to mount a military campaign.

Dracula could not afford to ignore the Ottoman situation on his doorstep. In one of the most momentous decisions of his reign, in 1459, Vlad ceased all tributes to the Turkish Sultan. His decision may have been triggered by renewed Ottoman demands that Wallachia honour the Devşirme, dispatching Wallachian youths to be re-educated as Muslims, something that would surely have struck a painful chord with Dracula. When Mehmet's envoys arrived in Tîrgovişte demanding the Voivode visit the Ottoman court in person with the overdue payments, Dracula played for time, insisting his war-torn kingdom couldn't afford the sums and that he couldn't leave Wallachia for fear of his rivals taking the throne, but promising lavish gifts in the future. Meanwhile he maintained a secret correspondence with Matthias Corvinus and the Transylvanian councils, soliciting support for an alliance against the Ottomans. Mehmet's spies intercepted enough of the letters to make the Sultan aware of Vlad's building confidence and belligerence. Dracula's brother Radu the Handsome was still a guest of the Ottoman court, and the Turks were no doubt already grooming him as the wilful Voivode's successor. The situation between Wallachia and the Ottoman Empire was moving once more steadily towards war, something Dracula evidently regarded as inevitable, perhaps even relished...

'He was a man of his day because he was fully conversant in the mentality and realities of his age,' observes John Bianchi in *Vlad the Impaler*, 'and yet many of his actions denote a visionary nature. His accent on psychological warfare, predilection for collective punishment as an instrument of waging this war, perception of Romania as a nation and not feudal states, as well as a Machiavellian approach to power and politics, are indications of this. He was among the first to use the concept of a "war-orientated economy", and in his conception, the State was the Voivode, and the Voivode was the image of his armed forces. He understood that without military power, there was no way to survive in the 15th century Balkans.' Bianchi's book is primarily a manual aimed at wargamers who wish to recreate this fascinating era in tabletop battles, yet his emphasis on Dracula's military policy is appropriate in a broader sense. It's probably fair to say that every Balkan leader was aware of the importance of military power. What is interesting is the way in which this may have influenced Vlad's radical social policies.

In military terms, the Impaler's primary resource was manpower, specifically Wallachia's warlike peasantry and yeomen, as his purges had decimated the indigenous aristocracy. Skilled military professionals could be hired as mercenaries and state-of-the-art Transylvanian arms could be bought – though this required the income provided by a healthy economy, which in his agricultural state also required a healthy peasant class. Dracula's domestic policy evidently reflected this, though the extent to which the puritanical aspects of his rule represented a deliberate attempt to create a strong, stable State, or simply reflected his own character, is wide open to interpretation. The idea that someone who favoured the slow execution of prisoners by the insertion of wooden poles into the most intimate areas of their anatomy was also a puritan seems incongruous. Yet Vlad would not be the first politician or ideologue to combine a ruthlessly vindictive, even sexually sadistic personality with a rigid moral code, at least as far as it governed others. He was clearly a very complex, conflicted character. A man whose own survival had often hinged upon his ability to conceal his true feelings, Vlad despised liars. Brought up in the sexually decadent environs of the Ottoman court, Dracula was a fanatical advocate of traditional domestic values among his people, incensed by indolence and sexual immorality.

One popular story about his rule illustrates the curious combination of traditional values and pathological cruelty that defined the Voivode's character. This version is taken from Russian accounts, generally sympathetic to Vlad's radical 'firm but fair' approach. 'One day Dracula was travelling on a journey and he saw a certain poor man in a worn and torn shirt. And he asked him: "Do you have a wife?" and the man replied "I have, Sire", so then he responded, "Bring me to your house so that I can see her," and he saw that the wife was young and healthy and he asked her husband, "Have you not sowed any flax?" and he responded, "Sire, I have much flax," and he showed him much flax. And then Dracula told the wife, "So why are you lazy and do not care for your husband? He must sow and plough and look after you, so you must make your husband clothes which are light and nice – and you do not even want to make him a shirt, though you are healthy in your body. You are guilty, not your husband. If your husband had not sown flax then he would have been guilty." So he ordered that her hands be cut off and her body be impaled.'

Other versions conclude the tale by adding that Vlad then offered the bereaved peasant a replacement bride. Well aware of her predecessor's fate, the new wife worked so hard to please her husband that she barely had time to eat. It's scarcely a feminist fable, though a vivid illustration of the policies the Voivode was enforcing in order to promote the type of domestic order he believed was not only morally right, but also perhaps essential for his realm's strength, a land where order and industry are imposed by a culture of fear. It's a vision that chimes with some radical conservatives even now. A Romanian peasant who related the story in 1935, suffixed it with an ambivalent observation: 'It is just as well that Dracula does not rule our country today, for he would have to expend many stakes, which might have eliminated from our land the innumerable drones who wither the very grass on which they sit.' It's a sinister sentiment expressed at a time when fascist parties – who shared Dracula's passion for obedience and industriousness – were rising to power across Europe, not least in Romania. Another, arguably even more shocking, story is often recounted as indicative of Dracula's style of rule, one even more ominously prescient of the atrocities that scarred Europe in the 1930s…

***

There was never before such a united confederacy of the wretched. Hobbling gingerly along as if they cannot believe their luck, the cripples with gangrenous stumps rub shoulders with the scabbed, the scurvy-ridden and the feeble, some of whom have, as the result of nature's caprices, entered into sexual relationships and borne children whose twofold feeblemindedness is their parents' only legacy.

'Our master bids you enter his house, of your own free will.'

This brotherhood of bad fortune, whose isolated lifestyles of begging and scavenging for survival have rarely crossed, are struck dumb and left bug-eyed. The small but luxurious house, its narrow confines barely containing this throng of several dozens, is a welcome change from woodland shrub or derelict woodpile. The Prince's administrators who rounded them up seem to have delivered them to the Kingdom of Heaven for a day.

'You must come, o dread Impaler, compound them to your care …'

The dark-maned figure is visible at the end of the shadowy dining hall, its large rectangular windows shuttered to blot out the sun. He regards them all with an aloof curiosity. For it is a rarity in the utmost to contain all the unfortunate of the principality of Wallachia under one roof. And they too are overwhelmed by the unexpectedness of the occasion.

Spit-roasted suckling pigs and goblets filled with the darkest crimson wine adorn the long dining table. Many of the beggars hesitate, frozen in trepidation, as their fearsome Voivode rises from his chair to approach them. Those who are hungriest and most simple-minded are already picking feverishly at the greasy swine flesh. Malnourished children who know no social etiquette or protocol are the most amused by the novelty of it all.

A Model Prince?

'Split them in two partitions, here the fools, the rascals there ...'

He passes among them, close at hand yet aloof and imperious. He exchanges no words with the poor of his kingdom, though his benevolent silence tells them all is well. It is as the Prince's courtiers told the beggars when they came to offer them passage to their liege's royal abode at Tîrgovişte: they are his honoured guests; the Voivode is their benefactor and patron.

Vlad III takes his leave of the least privileged of his domain with a last curious glance and the almost imperceptible raising of an eyebrow. Even those ragged men and syphilitic women who doubted their good fortune are put sufficiently at ease to gulp and gorge and enjoy the bacchanals.

Then their prince is gone, and his courtiers are vanished with him. The sensual indulgence of the underprivileged continues unimpeded, the beggars filling their faces as if they have never before eaten a full repast and never shall again. There is much good-natured grasping and groping at flesh, both the roasted flesh of animals and the wanton flesh of the uncouth, as the Wallachian underclass revel in this rare indulgence.

Then the key turns in the lock at the end of the hallway.

Those who were the last to join in the feasting are the first to realise the precariousness of the situation. Accustomed as they are to bad fortune and distrusting all else, the audible turn of the key is to them the twist that seals their fate.

'Shove them into two enclosures, from the broad daylight enisle 'em / Then set fire to the prison and the lunatic asylum.'

Those still glutting themselves till they belch or vomit are the last to perceive how the wood-panelled doors at the end of the hall are already sparking and crackling. It makes no difference. On the other side of the doors, the armas *who set their torches to the wood withdraw as the doorframes start to pulsate and bulge with the weight of the humanity enclosed within. Given time, the doors may burst open – but time is what the vagabonds and cripples do not have.*

As the black smoke rises to pollute the clean air of this bright day, within the burning house it begins to smother and suffocate. The strongest of the infirm have dropped their crutches and trampled over their benighted brothers and sisters, only for their lungs to fill and their bodies to seize up in asphyxiation.

If ever a benign and merciful god had ears, he might have offered up some miraculous method of escape. Or at least a sudden end for the pitiful wretches trapped inside.

VLAD THE IMPALER

But, existence being what it is, their extinction is agonised and protracted. Oafs that had previously trampled over the womenfolk to beat their fists at the door find their strength exhausted. Scabrous women cling to strangers, choking, in the vain hope of salvation and the absence of any saviour. The handful of small children cry until it hurts their lungs to do so, then drop exhausted at the feet of this huddle of desperate humanity.

The doomed conjoin in a dance of death. Prefiguring the huddles of bodies in the showers of the death camps by five centuries, they cling to each other for final consolation in bleak recognition that the path to escape is closed. Those who have not already suffocated will burn. All will be ashes.

Outside the burning house, their Prince the Impaler watches the eruptions of yellow flame amidst the black smoke with satisfaction, recognising that the structure of the building will soon implode.

'What good is a man who lives upon the sweat of others?' Vlad often repeats this rhetorical question, as to the guards who join him in watching the blaze. They nod sagely in approval of their warlord's words. For the veil of inscrutability that history has draped over the visage of Vlad the Impaler seems always to have been there, and they know no answer at all is safer than the wrong answer.

'Your job is accomplished, and you have done it well,' Vlad says to all and no one. As the screams and choking gasps from inside cease, he dares to step forward to where the tongues of flame lick out from within the windows. 'I thank you for your participation in the social cleansing of Wallachia,' he says with a modest bow, and it becomes clear that his words are addressed to the already charring bones within.

***

'You must know why I'm doing it,' Vlad the Impaler announces of the burning of the beggars in the first Russian version of his story, *Povesty o Mutyanskom Voyevode Drakule*. 'First of all, so that they do not burden my people and to rid the country of the poor; and secondly to save them from the suffering, poverty and miseries of this world.'

As already noted, the Russian Dracula pamphlets have a distinct tendency to view Vlad's autocracy with admiration, and were surely putting words in his mouth to try and give these harrowing narratives some kind of moral. That said, off setting the Voivode's ruthlessness against what appears to be a compassionate rationalisation of his actions may be an astute reading of an inscrutable nature. As ever with this extraordinary human being, it finds its echoes throughout history.

'Those who are physically and mentally unhealthy and unfit must not perpetuate their sufferings in the bodies of their children,' wrote another autocratic ruler in the 20th century, in the years preceding his reign. In Adolf Hitler's personal polemic of 1925, *Mein Kampf*, the street agitator and demagogue articulates the essence of his 'compassion' for those he considers unworthy of life. 'Illness is not a disgrace but a misfortune for which people are to be pitied, yet at the same time [...] it is a crime and a disgrace to make this affliction the worse by passing it on to innocent creatures out of a merely egotistic yearning.' Hitler's propagandising here is on behalf of eugenics, the science of Darwinian natural selection aided by engineered breeding. (The main plank of *Mein Kampf*'s philosophy is of course its anti-Semitism and its adherence to the racial folklore that attached to Europe's Jewry – some of which makes 'the Jew' of myth more of a blueprint for the gothic vampire than Vlad III.)

It might be argued (as it is in the Russian Dracula story) that Vlad's concern was simply the wretchedness of late-medieval poverty, but his method and rationale have a definite pre-eugenic bias. How else could he have believed he was eradicating poverty in his domain unless he believed it to have a hereditary – rather than social or purely arbitrary – origin? To kill a couple of generations of paupers would otherwise be no guarantee that circumstances would not give rise to more such unfortunates in the same state. And then of course there is a similarity of method. Despite Hitler's seemingly rational argument, his own peculiar forms of compassion led to much the same place as Vlad's – an inferno of choking vapours and, later, flame, albeit administered on a more efficiently industrial scale.

In the early part of the modern age, however, it became popular, almost voguish, for many intellectuals to visualise eliminating society's 'undesirables' by similarly radical means. The verse quoted in our imagined version of the burning of the beggars (skilfully translated to rhyme, scan and retain its startling meaning) is from Mihai Eminescu, the 19th-century Romanian romantic/nationalist poet; Eminescu's evocation of Vlad's massacre by conflagration was actually an extreme purgative recommended for the government of his day, in his poem 'Scrisoarea a III-a' ('Letter 3-a'). His urging that the policy of immolation should also be extended to 'the prison and the lunatic asylum' evinces how popular the idea of social cleansing by extermination had become, even if only in an imaginative sense. Its authentic apotheosis would follow later.

In the decades immediately preceding the revelation of the death camps, the region that once contained Wallachia was undergoing some of the characteristic tumult of the age, fed by the nationalistic sentiments of passionate patriots like Eminescu. In the nation of Romania – its capital, Bucharest, which Vlad III would come to favour as his capital – a young Orthodox Christian mystic named Corneliu Codreanu had formed the Legion of the Archangel Michael in 1927. While its dramatic emblem depicted the archangel as a heroic archer defending Christianity, the paramilitary nature of the Legion and the stern aesthetics of its dark green-shirted legionaries echoed that of Mussolini's Fascist Italy. The Legion became synonymous with its paramilitary wing – the *Garda de Fier*, or Iron Guard – whose own symbol, the stark but effective black triple cross, symbolised how Codreanu expected his Legion to risk their freedom and their lives in the name of their beliefs.

In his own *Mein Kampf*-style polemic, translated as *For My Legionaries: The Iron Guard*, Codreanu writes, 'What I want is that you, soldiers of other Romanian horizons [...] fill your hearts with fire and stand firm in the difficult and righteous struggle in which you are engaged and out of which we all have the command to emerge either victorious or dead. I think of you as I write. Of you who will have to die, receiving the baptism of death with the serenity of our ancestral Thracians. [While the name of Romania suggests its inhabitants' descent from the Romans, Codreanu and fellow nationalists pointed toward the Roman Empire's Balkan outpost of Thrace.] And of you who will have to step over the dead and their tombs ...'

Like Vlad III, Codreanu considered it imperative to kill or be killed in the defence of Christendom. But his words and actions evince a less Machiavellian nature, an almost Gnostic mystical conviction that it was virtuous to risk eternal damnation of the soul in the name of the Christians' Prince of Peace. As to who the enemies of Christendom might be, at this juncture of history Codreanu had no invading armies to contend with; as with Hitler, who admiringly called the Romanian 'the father of European nationalism', he found his enemies in the sons and daughters of Judaism.

The Jews had established their own communities throughout Eastern Europe in the centuries that followed Vlad's conflicts with the Muslims. Still then essentially a people without a homeland (despite Zionist ambitions), their adapt-and-survive techniques led many of them to thrive in banking or usury, financial professions once dogmatically closed to the gentiles by the Christian Church. Although many Jews worked in other industries, it was largely this that made 'the Jew' a popular scapegoat for many put-upon people during the world financial recession of the 1920s and 30s – whether westernised and assimilated, or bearded and be-hatted in the style of the Polish Hassids, they were regarded in much the same way as the Saxon merchants Vlad III had persecuted in the name of nationalism.

In Hitler's Germany, the one-sided war between National Socialist and Jew was not authentically religious but dogmatic; 'the Jew' was not just a racial/religious minority but a mythical figure representing all of the Third Reich's perceived enemies in one, magically reconciling the polar opposites of international communism and unfettered capitalism. (Hitler's own anti-capitalism was half-hearted at best. Once he'd eliminated the left wing of the Nazi Party, the Brownshirts, he courted the support of big business whenever it was convenient.) Mussolini's Italy initially had no such truck with anti-Semitism, the early *Fascisti* even containing Jewish members. It was only his Axis ally Hitler's later bullying which turned 'Il Duce', supposedly a man of iron, into someone prepared to give up Italy's Jews to the extermination camps.

In the Romania of the 1930s, the era's anti-Semitism played out against a mystical rationalisation that evoked such perennial ultranationalist touchstones as 'the blood of the people'. (Drawing, imbibing and writing in blood were key components in the Iron Guard's religiously hued rituals.) Codreanu's 'New Man' was a more atavistic being than his counterpart in Fascist Italy – whose upper echelons, at least, contained modernist and futurist philosophers or artists. For the Iron Guard and their supporters, symbol, blood and deed were mystically entwined and were not to be separated. And their enemy 'the Jew' didn't necessarily have to be kosher – it was simply a label applied to all who deviated from the one true path.

One such was the liberal Prime Minister Ion Duca, whose political clampdown on the Legion was regarded as the work of Zionism. His assassination by the Iron Guard at the end of 1933 put in motion a war-of-attrition strategy that culminated in Codreanu's April 1938 detention. It was then that the Romanian government revealed itself as not quite so liberal: the leading legionary and several of his comrades were strangled by their guards, then pumped with bullets to give the impression they had tried to escape.

Codreanu's martyrdom to his cause seems only to have inspired his followers with further zeal. In March 1939 the Legion assassinated the new prime minister; the 1940 rise of Horia Sima to the position of Iron Guard leader coincided with the early months of World War 2 and the Romanian government's pragmatic alliance with the Axis powers. One member of the new coalition government was also an activist in the

Legion of the Archangel Michael, and the background of the Nazi Holocaust allowed the legionaries to pursue their anti-Semitic crusade under a cloak of legitimacy. The deportation of Romania's Jews was conducted with a fervour and brutality that even some Nazis were reputed to find excessive.

If there ever was such a period as 'Codreanu's Romania', then it existed posthumously to the Iron Guard founder, from September 1940 to January 1941. It was then that the nation's new military leader, General Ion Antonescu, announced a National Legionary State that would rule with the collaboration and compliance of the Legion itself. For a short time, it looked as if the 'New Romania' had come to pass. But by 21 January an alleged *coup d'état* conspiracy by the Legion led to its banning and three days of open civil war that purged Romania of the legionaries and their guard.

It was then that the Iron Guard's participation in the Holocaust reached its grim climax. Bloodier in their hands-on approach than the Nazi industrial death machine, the legionaries impaled the bodies of their murdered Jewish victims on the meat-hooks of a Bucharest slaughterhouse. In a stroke of last-gasp gallows humour before their own purging (although many legionaries would survive – like Sima, who fled to Nazi Germany), it was supposedly a parody of the kosher *shochet* slaughter ritual.

***

Prince Vlad sits inscrutably on a makeshift wooden throne, atop Mount Timpa. His aloofness of manner and sanguine expression offer no greater glimpse of his inner workings than when he addressed the Saxon merchants and their kin. If he is distracted by the infernal spectacle before him, then his focus belies it. Never did a man appear so at ease in the presence of great suffering and death.

The Stake Master and his apprentices are hard at work, almost unable to keep up with the endless procession of the damned, harried and jostled towards their end by the armas. *They form a robotic carpenter's production line, steeling themselves to the screams, the blood, the stench of death. The division and repetition of labour inures them to the injury they are inflicting, freezing the emotions as it corrodes the soul. A length of sharpened pike is rapidly inserted straight up into a struggling woman, entering at the pudenda and exiting the breast, her weak thrashing easily pinned down by the apprentice who grips her by the shoulders.*

Her menfolk surrender less easily, though all to no avail. The Saxon gunmaker (where are his mighty cannons now?) who refuses to capitulate is stripped, gripped at each joint of the limbs and pitched without mercy onto the spikes, where his slow descent will make larger the gaping red wounds over the hours it takes him to die. Surreptitiously, one of the armas *breaks the neck of the weeping little girl-child who goes to join them upon a stake, unwilling to hear another child's rattling timbre added to the choir of the damned.*

The act is quietly performed, for mercy has no currency here. Each of the Prince's production-line of death knows that squeamishness or neglecting his duty will only ensure his broken body ends atop his own handiwork. The maintenance of fear is all-important, and each has his role to play in promoting fear of a hell on earth.

And the Voivode feasts upon his makeshift wooden dining table. He chews slowly, swishing the last morsels of roasted pork and cabbage leaves around his mouth with a few drops of red wine. He is almost motionless in the midst of this epicurean massacre, but he is hypnotised (not repulsed) by the masses of writhing bodies that are suffering and dying before him.

Truly, no man ever found a stranger stimulus for his appetite.

***

In their day, the Legion of the Archangel Michael utilised the 'volkisch' art (to co-opt the Nazi term) that emphasised the Romanian national identity that had developed over the centuries following Ottoman withdrawal. Folk song and martial music, in particular, were their means of uniting largely illiterate rural peasant followers. The cultural references do not seem to have included Vlad III, but there's no doubt that Codreanu was at least aware of him. (In *For My Legionaries*, he describes being unimpressed by an early 1930s encounter with a member of a nationalist group called the Vlad Tepeş League, regarding them as poseurs who 'seemed to lack earnestness'.) One of the Romanian folk heroes venerated by the Iron Guard, however, was Stefan the Great (Vlad's cousin and ally), in the marching song 'Stefan Voda'.

But it is in Vlad and Codreanu's religious convictions that we find a strange commingling of attitudes. The Impaler was a pragmatist whose Orthodox roots were (in the eyes of some of his contemporaries) betrayed by a temporary conversion to Catholicism; for the sake of survival, he may also have paid lip service to the tenets of Islam during his time in captivity. Corneliu Codreanu was, as we have seen, an Orthodox mystic prepared to die for his interpretation of the faith. What they have in common are personal concepts of God and

Christianity which have little to do with universal love, forgivness or turning the other cheek.

To both of these ruthless Romanian nationalists, God equated with Will.

While the Ottoman Sultan is concerned with problems on his eastern borders, it is only a matter of time before Mehmet the Conqueror turns his attentions to his impertinent Wallachian neighbour. For some time, the border has been simmering at a heat approaching open conflict. Turkish Ghazis have been raiding Wallachian territory with increasing confidence. This was a tried-and-tested prelude to invasion, and Dracula knew it; a method of probing enemy positions while sapping their strength. In a further escalation, in response to Vlad's defiance of the Devşirme, regular Turkish troops had begun crossing the Danube to seize Wallachian youths by force. Dracula's men countered such Ottoman incursions where they could, with any Ottoman warriors captured no doubt sent back to Tîrgovişte to face their Voivode's inimitable brand of pointed justice. More worryingly, Turkish assaults had steadily grown increasingly serious; raiding parties were building into small invasion forces, culminating in the capture of a number of significant Wallachian towns on the border, most significantly the port of Giurgiu, an important strategic stronghold fortified by Vlad's forebears to control traffic on the Danube.

Things were clearly coming to a head, and Mehmet offered Dracula one last chance for peace, suggesting a summit at Giurgiu, where the Voivode could make his case to the Sultan's appointed ambassadors. Mehmet dispatched a diplomatic delegation to Tîrgovişte to escort the Voivode to Giurgiu. According to several accounts, the Sultan picked his representatives with care, assigning men known for their persuasiveness and cunning to the task of bringing the recalcitrant Wallachian to the conference. It was a trap. Once they were confident that Dracula was vulnerable, the Turks planned to summon local forces to ambush the party and bring Vlad back dead or in chains. Whether warned by informers, or relying simply on understandable paranoia, Dracula anticipated the attempt, and had their party shadowed by a squad of his own best men. When the Turkish envoys attempted to spring their trap as they approached Giurgiu, the tables were quickly turned, and Dracula secured his would-be captors as his prisoners.

The delegation continued on the road to Giurgiu, but now with a rather different mission in mind. The Turkish garrison commander was expecting a contingent from Wallachia, so wasn't suspicious when

Vlad's men arrived at the gates. Suspicions were further allayed when Dracula demanded entrance in fluent Turkish, and welcomed Vlad's small force within the walls, some perhaps disguised in Ottoman armour taken from their fallen foe. Once inside, his troops unleashed a devastating surprise assault upon the unsuspecting Ottoman garrison, taking the fortress in a brief one-sided fight. Once they had butchered the inhabitants, Dracula's men looted then torched the place.

Vlad was almost literally burning his bridges. His guerrilla strike represented open warfare against the Turks. At this point of no return, Dracula must have pondered his position. The sham of negotiation with the Sultan was at an end, and whilst Mehmet was still occupied in Asia, he could not now ignore the implicit challenge Dracula had made at Giurgiu. The Voivode could now, hopefully, be confident of the support of his own people in the coming conflict. But alone, against the fearsome Ottoman war machine, Wallachia stood little chance. Might John Hunyadi's son Matthias follow in his father's footsteps and bring a mighty Crusading force to face the infidel threat? Much rested upon the Pope, whose support was crucial if there was to be any chance of Christendom uniting to face the Ottomans.

If there was any less a Christ-like defender of Christendom in the 15th century than Vlad, his personage probably resided in the Vatican. It would provide the unlikely backdrop for the historical dramas that inspired a certain Signor Machiavelli to pen his poisonous masterpiece, the 1513 manual on cynical statecraft entitled *The Prince*, which in turn influenced such leaders as Napoleon, Mussolini and Stalin. Florescu and McNally based much of their groundbreaking investigation into Dracula's paradoxical personality on the conclusion that the Voivode was not simply the 'bloodthirsty madman' of the Saxon pamphlets, but a calculating politician whose pitiless methods foreshadowed those recommended by Machiavelli. In *Dracula: Prince of Many Faces*, they stop short of suggesting Vlad III actually inspired the Italian's infamous work, but do suggest that Dracula's actions 'made him an ideal model for Machiavelli's future *Prince*'.

So, how does the Voivode compare to the Italian politicians generally accepted with actually inspiring Machiavelli's legendary text on securing and maintaining power by any means necessary? In the years immediately following the Impaler's death on the battlefield, the Papacy was functioning as a kind of ecclesiastical Mafia, engaged in the territorial wars and power grabs which characterised the city states of Renaissance Italy – just across the Adriatic Sea, but exerting a Europe-wide influence that placed smaller regions like Wallachia (whose leader had arguably been one of the true direct defenders of the faith) in the shade.

By the time of the return of the influential patrician Medici family to power in early 16th-century Florence, the younger Lorenzo de Medici (named after his illustrious grandfather) received a singular tribute from the out-of-favour Machiavelli, who, having given much of his working life to the Soderini government previously in power, had been imprisoned, tortured and then left unemployed as a result of his former loyalties. Machiavelli dedicated his amoral treatise on the art of Renaissance statesmanship, *The Prince*, to the young Lorenzo, leading recent mass-media historians to suggest that the model for the titular figure was his grandfather, Lorenzo the Great.

The Prince, however, is a compellingly straightforward work that has often confounded readers by being exactly what it appears to be – not a warning against autocracy, or even a satire of it, but a historically-rooted primer on surviving the politics of the age that Machiavelli had lived through. 'I composed a little book, *De Principatibus*,' noted the author, 'where I delve as deeply as I can into thoughts on this subject, discussing what a principality is, what kinds they are, how they are acquired, how they are maintained, why they are lost.' His Prince is a kind of 'Every Ruler' of the time, identified not by specific name or principality, but by the cynical politicking and occasional coldblooded slaughter which the author himself witnessed at a remove. As such, *The Prince* is not modelled on any individual leader – although the text reserves much of its praise for the most infamous figure of the Renaissance period, whose ruthlessness, the author claims, might once have united the divided city states of Italy and averted chaos.

The epitome of the Renaissance Popes ('the Bad Popes', to cite E. R. Chamberlin's popular study) was Alexander VI. More so than any other, he resembles less the pious pontiffs of modern times – railing against contraception in the overpopulated Third World, while leaving priestly pederasts to the tender mercy of their own conscience – than a Mafia don figure like Carlo Gambino. An unashamed power broker and earthly sensualist who made little pretence at celibacy, Alexander – or Rodrigo Borgia, to give this Spanish Pope his christened name – sired three children by his mistress: the soldier Giovanni; the prelate Cesare; and the desirable and promiscuous Lucrezia, whose rumoured incestuous liaisons were said to include not only both brothers but also her Holy Father (giving a faint air of the pagan emperor Caligula to the Christian Pope).

For our purposes, it is the power-hungry Cesare who makes a most informative contrast to the power red-in-tooth-and-claw of Vlad III, having been born in 1476, the year of the Impaler's death. When Rodrigo became Pope in 1492, his 16-year-old son – who had been rapidly made both Archbishop and Cardinal of Valencia – took off his priestly vestments and rode around the city of Rome, fully armed, in an ostentatious display of belligerence. With no piety, false or otherwise, in his nature, the youngest Borgia son made his resentment of his brother's positioning at the head of the papal army all too clear. The continuing conflict with the French gave Cesare ample opportunity to show his propensity for bloodshed. In January 1495, the French King Charles VIII's army en route to Naples began to sack Rome. Against Charles's orders, their Swiss mercenaries looted the houses of some of the richer citizenry – including that of Vannozza dei Cattanei, the Pope's mistress and Cesare's mother. Her son later exacted revenge on the looters (or at least on those accused of the offence) in a display of wrath worthy of Vlad, torturing them unto death.

In an aftermath which has echoes of the predicament of the younger Dracula brothers, Pope Alexander was forced to sue for peace with Charles VIII and used his youngest son as a bargaining chip. But it was to have an outcome more comical than poignant. Joining Charles's entourage to Naples as an esteemed captive, with a procession of 17 velvet-covered wagon coaches supposedly containing his clothes and possessions, Cesare quickly decamped and returned to Rome. (His coaches were all found to be empty.)

Back on his old stamping ground, Cesare was bereaved by the murder of his elder brother Giovanni in June 1497 – or at least, that was the perception at the time. When the body of the elder Borgia sibling was dragged from the Tiber with multiple stab wounds, it was believed he'd most likely fallen victim to one of the powerful families who rivalled the Borgias. But the death released Cesare from his priestly duties and granted him the soldierly status (and power) he'd long desired. It was only after the Pope had formed an alliance of convenience with Charles VIII's successor, Louis XII, and Cesare was granted the French title of the Duke of Valence, that the Roman populace began to detect a pattern in his behaviour. Men who had been his rivals in Louis's court were found murdered; his homosexual consorts and confidants also turned up dead in the river, or died suddenly of poisoning after eating at his table. (Legend has bestowed a reputation as a poisoner on his sister Lucrezia, but it's her brother who seems the much more likely culprit.)

As an unpredictably capricious military leader, Cesare soon became feared throughout Italy. His regional conquests included the city of Forli, where he raped and captured the detested local ruler, Caterina Sforza, and urged the local citizenry to petition the Pope for his son to take her place. (For all his cruel excesses, Cesare seems to have been a competent and fair-minded leader when the circumstances didn't cry out for murder.) In Faenza, his troops stormed the city after being alerted to a weakness in its defences by a traitor, whom Cesare promptly hanged. He procured the surrender of the 18-year-old prince, Astorre Manfredi, by promising he would be spared; once in the army's hands he was sent to Rome, where he was later found floating in the river.

Cesare lived by a policy of subterfuge and backstabbing far removed from the overt bloodshed of his near-contemporary, Vlad. True, the similarly youthful Wallachian prince had to pursue an early policy of stealth and deceptiveness in order not to alert his Turkish captors to his intentions. But once his power was established, it could only be maintained by open displays designed to strike terror in the hearts of all opponents. By way of contrast, the Machiavellian 'Prince' – as Cesare is recognised by most students of the Florentine 'prophet of force' – used clandestine intimidation and assassination as a climbing aid for the greasy pole of ambition. A conspiracy between deposed princes and his own lieutenants was nipped in the bud when they were invited to a banquet in the town of Senigallia, where those who betrayed the duke were garrotted. It was important that rivals and enemies realised the extent of his ruthlessness and power, but not to the point where he could be denounced for his actions.

It's also unlikely that the outwardly pious Vlad could have tolerated Cesare's more cosmopolitan sexual tastes. While the Impaler seems to have shared the general sexual licentiousness of his era's autocrats (such as Ivan the Terrible), Borgia's bisexuality might have earned him a sharp length of splintering wood – particularly given Vlad's memories of Ottoman hospitality. His equally voracious taste for young women was also said to include his sister Lucrezia, whose cloistering in a convent had not stopped her giving birth to a son. (Guesses as to the father include both Cesare and his father Rodrigo, suggestive perhaps of the debauched times they lived in.) In the Holy Roman Catholic jubilee celebrations of 1500 Cesare organised public orgies; the application of rouge to his formerly handsome features was the result of the pox then beginning to blight Europe and a life lived in the realm of the senses, far away from the edicts of the Christian Church. For despite his ecclesiastical background, a man like Cesare would have little call for

God until such a time as he was dying. This in itself would not be too long in coming, although Borgia's ruthlessness and unpredictability deferred the event in the short term. Apparently jealous of Lucrezia's marriage to King Alphonso of Naples (who drove Mehmet II's troops from Otranto), he made a brazen confession to strangling his brother-in-law as the Neapolitan king lay recovering from a mysterious knife attack on the streets of Rome.

When he threatened to sack Florence with the Papal army in 1502, the Florentine diplomat Machiavelli was sent to negotiate payment of gold in lieu. Fascinated, the statesman accompanied Borgia on some of his regional adventures, to gain a priceless lesson in amoral self-serving power. (It's notable, however, that his observations were published much later, in 1516, giving the author ample distance from events which, his dispatches of the time suggest, had initially rather appalled him.) When Cesare conquered his father's intended Roman buffer state of Romagna to the south of Venice, Machiavelli describes his method of establishing his rule with approval, if not outright relish: 'Now, the duke [of Valence] had won control of the Romagna and found that it had previously been ruled by weak overlords, quicker to despoil their subjects than to govern them well. They had given them cause for anarchy rather than union, to such an extent that the province was rife with brigandage [banditry], factions, and every sort of abuse. He decided therefore that it needed good government to pacify it and make it obedient to the sovereign authority. So he placed there Remirro de Orco, a cruel, efficient man, to whom he entrusted the fullest powers. In a short time this Remirro unified and pacified the Romagna, winning great credit for himself. Then the duke decided that there was no need for this excessive authority, which might grow intolerable, and he established in the centre of the province a civil tribunal, under an eminent president, on which every city had its own representative. Knowing also that the severities of the past had earned him a certain amount of hatred, to purge the minds of the people and to win them over completely he determined to show that if cruelties had been inflicted they were not his doing but prompted by the harsh nature of his minister. This gave Cesare a pretext; then, one morning, Remirro's body was found cut in two pieces on the piazza at Cesena, with a block of wood and a bloody knife beside it. The brutality of this spectacle kept the people of the Romagna at once appeased and stupefied.'

It's almost as if Vlad the Impaler had imposed order on one of the more rebellious of his provinces, then made a show of appeasement by cutting off his own vicious right hand. But, in Cesare's more subtle form of butchery, there are also echoes of Vlad's sacrifice of his own subjects in the face of Turkish invasion (much disputed – as we shall see). If he can inflict this on his own, asks the affrighted inner conscience, then what might he be capable of doing to *me*?

In Cesare's capture of Capua, his uncharacteristic massacre of 6000 men, women and children was redolent of the merciless Ottoman leaders. On his home territory, the climate of terror was no less pronounced. 'All Rome is trembling for fear of being destroyed by the duke Cesare,' reported the Venetian ambassador. Another contemporary claimed (perhaps exaggeratedly) that Borgia 'surpassed the bestiality and savagery of Nero and Caligula'. Rumours that he used prisoners for target practice in the grounds of his father's fortress also evoked the cruellest of the Sultans.

With his more rarefied, slippery subtlety, a tyrant like Cesare Borgia was able to switch allegiances at the drop of a hat – indeed, his turncoat tendencies suggest he might have led an even more precarious existence than the ever-struggling Prince of Wallachia, had he not the power of the Papacy behind him. But this would not last forever. In August 1503, both Cesare and his father, Pope Alexander, were stricken with apparent malaria at a cardinal's villa just outside the eternal city. The coincidence of them both falling seriously ill led to conjecture that the cardinal regarded himself as a likely victim for Cesare's poisoning and decided to strike first. Whatever the truth of the matter was, the fact remains that the young duke recovered over the space of several weeks, whilst his father the Pope died.

Even restored to health, it can only have been a matter of time before Borgia realised that life as he knew it was over. After another of the customary interim periods where an old and ailing Pope barely survived his coronation, the next ascendant to the Papal throne, Julius II, was a familial adversary of the Borgias. Fleeing house arrest in Rome to find sanctuary with the Spanish occupiers of Naples, Cesare's flight was interrupted by the forces of Ferdinand II of Spain, who imprisoned him on the island of Ischia. Pressured into giving up his conquered territories, his next short period of freedom was interrupted by the widow of his brother Giovanni, who had him imprisoned for murder.

The elusive Cesare broke prison again in 1506, joining forces with his wife's brother, the King of Navarre, who was engaged in a Spanish territorial war. Entrusted with the command of a garrison of a hundred, the former general would die, like Vlad III, on the battlefield – in Cesare's case at the age of 30, while laying siege to the town of Viana.

Unlike the ambiguous circumstances which surround Vlad's demise, there can be little doubt that the soldiers who stripped the mortally wounded Borgia naked and left him to dehydrate were on the enemy side. Besides his mother and sister, the only other mourner at his funeral is reputed to have been Niccolo Machiavelli.

'Cesare Borgia, commonly called Duke Valentino, acquired his state through the good fortune of his father, and lost it when that disappeared,' Machiavelli later conceded of his Renaissance role model, 'and this happened even though he used the same ways and means any prudent and capable prince would to consolidate his power in the states he had won by the arms and fortune of others … I know no better precepts to give a new prince than ones derived from Cesare's actions; and if what he instituted was of no avail, this was not his fault but arose from the extraordinary and inordinate malice of fortune…And he himself said to me, the day Julius II was elected, that he had thought of everything that could happen when his father died, and found a remedy for everything except that he never thought that when he did so he himself would be at the point of death.'

In *The Prince*, Machiavelli lists princely 'virtues' that are morally neutral and purely pragmatic; loosely adhering to conventional morality (though, like many of his era, he seems divorced from the prevailing Catholic dogmas), he concedes that wholesale slaughter can never be described as 'virtuous' in and of itself: 'I believe that here it is a question of cruelty used well or badly. We can say that cruelty is used well (if it is permissible to talk in this way of what is evil) when it is employed once for all, and one's safety depends on it, and then it is not persisted in … Violence must be inflicted once for all; people will then forget what it tastes like and so be less resentful.'

For all this, it's a contention of this book that Prince Vlad III offers an alternative European identity for the faceless archetype of *The Prince* just as profound as that of the Renaissance duke Cesare – albeit much cruder. For Cesare's downfall was due not merely to ill fortune but ill will; when his power base rapidly disintegrated upon his father's death, there was nothing to protect him from those he had betrayed and abused, or their surviving relatives. In contrast and in hindsight, the death of Vlad II announced the rise of his son like a Wagnerian thunderclap, an iron-willed terror whose regional power was commensurate with the dark depths of his psyche.

'So a new prince cannot find more recent examples than those set by the duke [Valentino],' Machiavelli claims, 'if he thinks it necessary to secure himself against his enemies, win friends, conquer either by force or by stratagem, make himself both loved and feared by his subjects, followed and respected by his soldiers, if he determines to destroy those who can and will injure him … be severe yet loved, magnanimous and generous, and if he decides to destroy disloyal troops and create a new standing army, maintaining such relations with kings and princes that they have either to help him graciously or go carefully in doing him harm.'

Given the chequered history of his rule, it could almost be a verse in the Tepeş primer to maintaining power – though Vlad's almost theatrical excesses exceed the Florentine's experience and imagination, and were played out against a volatile Eastern European flashpoint. Most pertinent to the Voivode, perhaps, is a guideline for maintaining the balance of terror between ruler and ruled: 'It has to be noted that men must be either pampered or crushed, because they can get revenge for small injuries but not for grievous ones. So any injury that a prince does a man should be of such a kind that there is no fear of revenge.' In comparison with Vlad, Machiavelli hardly knew of what he spoke; his rogue Italian adventurers and conquerors were masters of the assassin's subterfuge, but to the east of their country, penalties were routinely inflicted from which body and mind never recovered.

Ultimately, the Florentine's admonitions against the excesses of autocracy could apply to either Cesare or Vlad: 'A new prince, of all rulers, finds it impossible to avoid a reputation for cruelty, because of the abundant dangers inherent in a newly won state.' He goes on to quote Dido in the Roman poet Virgil's *Aeneid*: 'Harsh necessity, and the newness of my kingdom, forced me to do such things and to guard my frontiers everywhere.' 'None the less, a prince must be slow to believe allegations and to take action … his behaviour must be tempered by humanity and prudence so that over-confidence does not make him rash nor excessive distrust make him unbearable.' We cannot know whether Vlad perished at the hands of an assassin within his own ranks, but still perhaps, every tyrant may carry within him the seeds of his own destruction.

In the decades and centuries that followed the Renaissance, Cesare Borgia would remain the archetype of the amoral yet charismatic autocrat, while Vlad remained an obscure figure outside Central and Eastern Europe, or Russia. (This was prior to his own personal renaissance in the late 20th century, when scholars were keen to identify the lineage between him and Stoker's Dracula.) The Prussian philosopher Friedrich Nietzsche, who prophesied modern man's psychological development before dying at the dawn of the 20th century, would write of his own blueprint for a higher type of man in *Thus Spoke Zarathustra*: 'Courageous, untroubled, mocking, violent – that is what wisdom wants us to be: wisdom is a woman and loves only a warrior.'

A prophet without honour in the fatherland during his own lifetime, the physically enfeebled syphilitic espoused the great health and pitiless strength which remained out of reach to him. Nietzsche's celebratory amoralism placed him in opposition to the Christianity which repressed natural instincts; his espousal of a condition 'beyond good and evil' caused him to be regarded as a crank – at best – by the academic establishment of his day.

In *Twilight of the Idols*, he writes of the outraged reaction to his earliest works and makes clear the Machiavellian inspiration behind his wish for human nature to take the gloves off: 'I was invited to reflect on the "undeniable superiority" of our age in moral judgement, our real *advance* in this respect: compared with *us*, a Cesare Borgia was certainly not to be set up as a "higher man", as a kind of *superman*, in the way I set him up ... What is certain is that we would not dare to place ourselves in Renaissance circumstances, or even imagine ourselves in them: our nerves could not endure that reality, not to speak of our muscles.'

Writing most profoundly as a psychologist and a poet, rather than any kind of thin-blooded PhD, Nietzsche received little credit at the time for his analysis of how both humanity and morality evolved: 'In the history of mankind, the most savage forces beat a path, and are mainly destructive; but their work was nonetheless necessary, in order that a later gentler civilisation might raise its house,' he writes in *Human, All Too Human*. Among such barbaric trailblazers he might have cited Vlad the Impaler, defender of Christendom against the East – though, despite his iconoclastic temperament, Nietzsche would have been more familiar with history and culture as taught in the universities of the 19th century, and less so with its wilder offshoots.

As such, it's uncertain as to whether the self-styled Antichrist even knew the Voivode's name. But is he not detectable in the following description of a joyful tyrant in *The Genealogy of Morals*?: 'They *go back* to the innocence of the beast-of-prey conscience, as rejoicing monsters who perhaps make off from a hideous succession of murders, conflagrations, rapes and torturings in high spirits and equanimity of soul as if they had been engaged in nothing more than a student prank.' Nietzsche continues, his rejection of Christian morality becoming more explicit: 'Those fearful bulwarks with which the social organisation protected itself against the old instincts of freedom – punishment is the chief among them – brought it about that all those instincts of wild, free, prowling man turned backwards *against man himself*. Enmity, cruelty, joy in persecuting, in attacking, in change, in destruction – all this turned against the possessors of such instincts: *that* is the origin of the "bad conscience".'

But how would the herald of the *übermensch* (the self-overcoming man, or 'superman') have regarded a man possessed of all such instincts who used them in defence of Christianity and its kingdoms?

This is perhaps best imagined via Nietzsche's pagan poeticising of the most powerful and destructive forces in nature. As a university student in 1865, he wrote to a friend about trying to find shelter during a violent storm and witnessing a rustic scene that might normally turn the stomach: 'At the top I found a hut, where a man was killing two kids while his son watched him. The storm broke with a tremendous crash, discharging thunder and hail, and I had an indescribable sense of well-being and zest … Lightning and tempest are different worlds, free powers, without morality. Pure Will.' Thus would be regarded a man like the Impaler: pure will with no qualms of moral conscience or self-doubt, an elemental force of nature. The atheist Nietzsche, despite his stated intent to tear up Christianity by the roots, was the religiously-inclined son of a Lutheran cleric. His rejection of what he termed 'slave morality' was sincere and profoundly expressed, but his lionisation of a cynical materialist like Borgia only tells part of the story. Elsewhere, the violent man with a clear conscience and the gleefully rapacious warrior are described in romantic prose that takes its imagery from Europe's pagan past and the Buddhist East. In this context, Vlad III would form a natural part of the lineage, shedding blood not for the Nazarene Prince of Peace but to preserve his own power, in defence of that which he called 'God'.

Nietzsche has often been posthumously disparaged as the philosopher and prophet of Nazism. But it's also the case that, while reflecting the pro-European racial prejudices of his age, Nietzsche protested, 'I am a stranger in my deeper instincts to everything German,' and even broke with his early idol and mentor, Wagner, over the latter's anti-Semitism. Against this has to be balanced the fact that his philosophy of eternal yea-saying to all things, whether inspiringly beautiful or hideous, would have compelled him to say 'yea' to the Nazi Holocaust – a manifold industrialisation of mass murder which puts Vlad III's impalements into historical perspective.

The very bare bones of racial supremacy and eugenic selection – a subject of which he can have known relatively little – can also be picked from Nietzsche's philosophy. In *Twilight of the Idols*, he writes of '*Aryan* humanity, quite pure, quite primordial … the concept "pure blood" is the opposite of a harmless concept,' and later of 'the higher breeding of humanity' and of 'that *which ought to perish*' – though he was speaking of hereditary weaknesses rather than human beings.

In the final reckoning, Friedrich Nietzsche was a mild-mannered soul, not given to personal argument outside the pages of his work. While he praised the thunder, glory and forward evolutionary drive of warfare, he had served as a non-combatant stretcher carrier in the Franco-Prussian War of 1870 and quietly asserted that he, personally, could never kill. And yet still, there's no doubting that in his self-coined tragic philosophy, he gained an insight into mankind's scarcely hidden atavistic depths. In *Beyond Good and Evil*, he writes: 'What the Roman in the arena, the Christian in the ecstasies of the Cross, the Spaniard watching burnings or bullfights, the Japanese of today crowding in to the tragedy, the Parisian workman who has a nostalgia for bloody revolutions … what all of these enjoy and look with secret ardour to imbibe is the spicy potion of the great Circe "cruelty".'

The God which unites the Orthodox Christian tyrant Vlad, the murderous Roman Catholic Borgia, the moral pragmatist Machiavelli and the antichristian prophet Nietzsche is encapsulated in one Nietzschean phrase: 'the will to power'. Whether believing in a deity or not, their God was not an admonitory figure urging 'thou shalt not' and threatening eternal damnation but – and this seems most true in Vlad's case – an inner voice urging them onward to greater extremes and greater victories. As with all successful rulers and politicians, God was the voice of the Will. It is a conception found in the dualistic Christian heresies of Gnosticism, and is outlined in negative (via God's absence) by Nietzsche in *Beyond Good and Evil*: 'Of what consequence would be a God who knew nothing of anger, revengefulness, envy, mockery, cunning, acts of violence? To who even the rapturous *ardeurs* of victory and destruction were unknown?'

CHAPTER X

Campaigns of Vengeance

In the chaotic political arena of Eastern Europe during the 15th century's Ottoman Wars, the situation is seldom clear-cut. The complex interplay of shifting alliances, contested cities and rival claimants to the patchwork of principalities left by the collapse of the Byzantine Empire, exacerbated by the interference of exterior powers such as the Papacy and the mercantile empires of Venice and Genoa, makes for a maddeningly perplexing picture. Many Balkan lords found themselves pledging loyalty to both the Christian and Turkish cause out of the raw necessity of survival as much as Machiavellian duplicity, taking two simultaneous 'offers they couldn't refuse', then facing the consequences when circumstances made such double-dealing untenable. Borders fluctuated as the balance of power ebbed and flowed. Accepting Ottoman sovereignty did not offer a Christian realm automatic immunity from Ghazi raids, while border clashes between supposed allies were endemic throughout the region.

Dracula's seizure of the fortress of Giurgiu and his summary execution of the high-ranking Ottoman officials sent to bring him back to Constantinople was an effective declaration of war in many eyes, and several historians date the Wallachian Voivode's campaign against the Turks to that first blow dealt by Dracula in late 1461. Before we shift our attention to this burgeoning Ottoman-Wallachian War, there is another of the famous tales of Dracula's barbarity to consider. It is a popular account of the Impaler's legendary bloodlust which presents us with several questions, but is too well-entrenched in almost all of our accounts of his reign to be easily dismissed as folklore. The story concerns the fate of a diplomatic delegation sent to the court at Tîrgovişte – a high-risk occupation by any measure – of whom the Voivode decides to make an example. One puzzle concerns the identity of the diplomats whilst another concerns the date of the incident, and Dracula's motives provide the final question. The Russian account of the grisly episode is as follows...

'On one occasion there came to him ambassadors sent by the Turkish ruler. Entering and bowing according to their custom, they did not take their hats off their heads. So he asked them: "Why do you behave thus, you have come to a great ruler and yet you show me such dishonour?" And they replied: "That is our custom, Sire, and it is observed in our land." And he said to them: "I want to confirm your custom, so that you keep to it resolutely." And he ordered that their hats should be nailed to their heads with small iron nails. Then he let them go, saying: "Go and tell your ruler that he may be used to such dishonour from you, but we are not used to it, so he should not spread such a custom among other kings, who do not want to observe it. Instead let him keep to it at home."'

German versions of the incident identify the diplomats as 'Westerners' and the offending headgear as brown or red berets, the episode appearing at the end of the Saxon account of the Voivode's excesses, implying that it occurred late in Dracula's career. Whilst some have suggested that the victims themselves were Saxons – a further atrocity to add to the catalogue perpetrated against the recalcitrant merchants of Transylvania – it seems more likely that this version indicates that the stubborn envoys hailed from Venice or one of the other mercantile empires with interests in Eastern Europe. The Russian suggestion that the ill-fated diplomats were Turkish is both more plausible from a historical perspective, and confirmed in Romanian accounts of the episode. Interestingly, Russian history records it as one of the punishments later meted out by Ivan the Terrible to disrespectful ambassadors (see Chapter Seven). As this would have occurred over half a century after dissemination of the Russian Dracula stories, it poses once again the intriguing question of whether the older, maddened Ivan was influenced by the pamphlets he may have read in his youth.

Whilst the idea of Dracula subjecting Ottoman envoys to such humiliating and painful treatment makes sense, the timing is problematic. Florescu and McNally theorise that the episode may have occurred as early as 1460. However, the Russian source insists that it was this sadistic insult to the Sultan's representatives which finally triggered the war between Vlad and Mehmet, suggesting that it may have been one last attempt by the Sultan to avert, or more likely delay, open war on his western frontier, something rebutted in no uncertain terms by Dracula, most likely some time in 1461. If so, it represents a further example of the Voivode ordering an atrocity that appears to be an act of arbitrary sadism, but which also has deeper political, even psychological, undertones. In this light, it is clearly a defiant statement of independence and sovereignty, declaring in no uncertain terms that Islamic customs had no place on Wallachian soil, and that the Voivode was every inch the equal of the Ottoman Sultan. It's easy to imagine Vlad realising a scenario he had enacted in his imagination a thousand times while captive at the Turkish court in his youth, now that he was able to treat his Islamic guests with the contempt which Muslims had shown their Christian hostages all those years before.

The symbolism of mocking Islamic customs regarding headgear is also likely far from arbitrary. Dracula would have been well aware of the religious and cultural insult implied by his bloody gesture (indeed, the potential for head-covering garb to provide a symbolic trigger for cultural conflict is still very much with us in the controversies surrounding Islamic veils in Europe today). Above all, nailing the turbans of Mehmet's envoys to their heads was a calculated slight, a public display of contempt for both the Sultan's authority and his faith. The nails hammered into the skulls of the Ottomans were also driven with equal force into the coffin of any hope for peace between Vlad and Mehmet. There could no longer be any game of diplomatic cat-and-mouse between the Conqueror and the Impaler – it was now a fight to the death.

The question remains as to why Dracula chose such a radical path, when most of his contemporaries preferred to try and placate their powerful neighbours wherever possible. Wallachia was a struggling David next to the voracious Goliath of the Ottoman Empire. The Voivode's old mentor Skanderbeg had enjoyed notable success and international acclaim fighting the Turks under similar odds, and this may well have proven an inspiration, yet even the redoubtable Albanian had signed a temporary ceasefire with Mehmet in 1461. The Pope had endeavoured to stir up enthusiasm for a Crusade in 1459, presenting survivors of the Ottoman invasions in the Balkans to give testimony during an impassioned address where he tried to convince an eminent audience of delegates from the courts of Europe of the imminent threat posed by the Conqueror Sultan. 'Every victory for him will be a stepping-stone to another, until subjecting all the Christians of the west, he will have destroyed the Gospel of Christ and imposed that of his false prophet over the entire world!' Such words would have been music to Dracula's ears, if the reports ever reached him in Wallachia, but few of the delegates actually in the audience seemed moved by the Pope's call-to-arms to do much more than make statements of support.

A Hungarian delegation was in attendance, and made the appropriate sympathetic noises but gave no firm commitments to action. It was Matthias Corvinus, more than anyone else, on whom Dracula was pinning his hopes for military assistance. Yet the intentions of the new Hungarian King remained maddeningly opaque. Vlad evidently hoped Matthias might be swayed by the continuing calls to crusade emanating from the Vatican, that perhaps the Hunyadi blood coursing through the veins of the young King might be stirred into mounting his own campaign eastwards by a grand Wallachian gesture against the traditional foe, and to follow in the footsteps of his heroic father, becoming another Athlete of Christ. It's also possible that it was simply blind revenge – the result of decades of resentment built up since his years of humiliating captivity by the Turks – that motivated the Voivode to lead his small army over the frozen Danube, deep into Ottoman territory, in the winter of 1461.

If it was a campaign largely fuelled by fury, Dracula was careful to cloak it in strategic terms. His progress may have been a brutal succession of massacres, but according to the Voivode it was not an aimless rampage. Vlad's bloody blitzkrieg extended into Ottoman-held Bulgaria but stopped at the port of Vidin, because he said 'from that point on onwards the Turks can do no great damage'. He later boasted that his wave of carnage had crippled Ottoman infrastructure, that 'had the Turks wished to bring their ships from Constantinople to the Danube they no longer have fording points, because I burned, destroyed, and laid waste their towns'. All of which suggests that, yet again, there was method to the Voivode's apparent madness. He clearly believed that an Ottoman invasion of Wallachia was inevitable – even if it was his own belligerence that had made it so – and planned to do as much damage to the Turkish war machine as he could while the Sultan was distracted with more pressing threats to Ottoman authority in Asia.

Inevitably, Dracula's progress across Turkish territory was a murderous affair. It was meant to be. If Vlad was to inflict serious damage to the Ottoman capacity to wage war across the Danube, he needed not only to destroy buildings and butcher livestock, but also to devastate the local population. His fierce pack of Wallachian horsemen did just that, sowing fire and despair across the landscape. The success of the Impaler's assault may be measured by reports of frightened Turks evacuating the Ottoman capital at Constantinople, far from the frontline. Dracula boasted of his exploits in letters to King Matthias – accompanied by gruesome hauls of the severed heads of his victims, adding, 'I have killed men and women, old and young... 23,884 Turks and Bulgars without counting those whom we burned in homes or whose heads were not cut off by our soldiers... Thus Your Highness must know that I have broken the peace with the Sultan.' Was that final comment an example of Vlad's elusive sick humour, the strange villainous laughter one sometimes suspects followed the strangest of his atrocities? Did the young Hungarian King appreciate the 'joke'?

Yet Vlad and Matthias were very different men, and the basic intent of the Voivode's message to Corvinus was deadly serious. Should the Hungarian monarch be in any doubt, the gift of two sacks overflowing with severed heads, noses and ears which Dracula helpfully included as a gift to accompany his missive emphasised the gravity of the situation. Did Dracula hope to impress Matthias? Raise a lust for blood in Hunyadi's heir? Perhaps even intimidate the young King? Whatever the Voivode's intent, he had misread his proposed ally, and, as his campaign ground to a halt, Dracula still stood largely alone. In the eyes of some patriotic Romanian historians, the Voivode was taking on the status of a lone crusader, the only leader who had heeded the Papal call-to-arms, a Wallachian Winston Churchill, who, like Britain's bulldog Prime Minister in 1940, stood defiant against withering odds. Many European contemporaries saw him in such a light. Church bells rang in support of his campaign across Christendom, feasts were held in his honour, and the Pope began to take a keen interest in the exploits of this daring Vlach warlord. He didn't, however, venture to dub Dracula an Athlete of Christ, evidence perhaps of misgivings at the Vatican over growing reports of the Voivode's excessive methods.

We should not automatically assume that Vlad's indiscriminate campaign of slaughter across Ottoman territory would have stigmatised him in many medieval eyes. His disinterest in the distinction between Turkish Muslim troops and Bulgarian Christian civilians on his orgy of carnage may have raised a few eyebrows, but the idea of murdering the peasantry as a legitimate form of economic warfare was well established in medieval custom. Co-ordinated raiding was a standard Ottoman strategy for weakening potential conquests. In Europe, the practice became known as *chevauchée*, and was a signature strategy of the English in the Hundred Years War, vital in keeping their more powerful French foe on the back foot. According to the historian Kelly DeVries, classic *chevauchée* tactics involved 'a quick cavalry raid through the countryside with the intention of pillaging unfortified villages and towns, destroying crops and houses, stealing livestock, and generally disrupting and terrorizing rural society. Most of the troops used in a *chevauchée* during the Hundred Years War were made up of light horse or hobelars. The mercenary groups known as the "Free companies" were also prominent in using the chevauchée.' This combination of nimble, well-trained cavalry and mercenaries mirrored the force Dracula led across the Danube in the winter of 1461.

Speed was the key to success for his limited objectives. The rapidity of Vlad's advance makes it highly unlikely that the Wallachian force featured any artillery, and was thus ill-equipped to capture any well-defended Ottoman stronghold that could not be taken by surprise. While accounts of pitched battles dominate our image of medieval warfare, most wars were actually resolved by siege. The English may have won celebrated battles like Agincourt and Crécy, but their failure to capitalise on such victories by capturing enemy strongholds rendered such triumphs largely irrelevant to the ultimate outcome of the Hundred Years War. John Hunyadi lost at least as many engagements as he won against the Ottomans in the field, but his true effectiveness as a general lay in his ability to recover from defeat and secure territory, denying the Turks the strategic stronghold at Belgrade and making a fitting climax to his distinguished career. The damage Dracula had inflicted upon Mehmet's western provinces was impressive, but he knew that it was just the first act of a forthcoming war, the bold opening shot in a conflict which would decide the fate of both the Voivode and his realm, as he had left his Ottoman opponent with no choice but to respond.

As the snows began to melt in the spring of 1462, the Wallachians retreated back west, while the vengeful Ottoman Sultan began to amass an army to crush the presumptuous Voivode who had dared to defile his lands and insult his person. If Dracula had intended to provoke a response, he had succeeded. The Sultan mustered a force of Janissary infantry, Sipahi cavalry, Azab skirmishers and Ghazi fanatics, supported by his famed artillery train; it was an army second only in size to the host he had used to humble mighty Byzantium nine years before. As news of the assembling army filtered westward, Vlad's letters to potential allies, particularly Hunyadi's son King Matthias, became increasingly emphatic in their pleas for assistance. If Wallachia fell, warned the Voivode, then the rest of Eastern Europe would inevitably be next on the Ottoman agenda. The Impaler had deliberately coaxed the Islamic genie out of the bottle, most likely in the hope that it would compel Christian leaders to join a Crusade that would shatter Ottoman power. It was a huge gamble, which looked increasingly unlikely to pay off. Papal support had raised funds, but little action, while the response from Buda remained decidedly lukewarm. Most distressingly, perhaps, one of Dracula's few personal allies was contemplating the coming storm with a view not to support his friend but to take advantage of Wallachia's weakness…

***

Historian Sean McGlynn begins *By Sword and Fire*, his book on 'cruelty and atrocity in medieval warfare', on a contemporary slant. He describes how watching the televised scenes of carnage from the Yugoslavian Wars of the 1990s seemed disturbingly reminiscent of the historical period he had been studying. 'I was witnessing scenes of warfare that had been described in the pages of the medieval chronicles: sieges, as at Sarajevo, where Serbian troops used donkeys to supply their troops in the hills around the invested city, from which heights the besiegers lobbed missiles onto a predominantly non-combatant population; the ravaging of the countryside, with troops burning, killing, stealing and raping their way across the land, the columns of smoke from razed villages punctuating the process of driving generations of families from their homes in a deliberate policy of ethnic cleansing; and the massacres, most notably at Srebrenica, where Muslim men and boys were murdered in their thousands. The parallels were striking; it seemed that in warfare there was nothing new under a blood-red sun.'

While McGlynn's book is primarily focused on Western Europe in the Middle Ages, his observations of shocking parallels between medieval warfare and the brutal conflict that engulfed the Balkans in recent history are even more pronounced when examining the wars waged by Vlad the Impaler in the 1400s. Many of the seeds of ethnic and religious tension that bore such vile, bloody fruit in the recent Balkan wars were first sown in Dracula's era, the atrocities and heroic defeats that provided fresh battle cries among anguished patriots and power-hungry warmongers still echoing with shrill insistence six centuries on. The shocking outbreak of violence on Europe's eastern fringes encouraged Western commentators to look at the turbulent history of the Balkans for the first time in a generation, as the spectres of long-forgotten massacres rose from the grave, footnotes of medieval history that were dry tinder for a bitter ethnic conflict that took the world by surprise as it quickly began to burn out of control.

In the late 1980s, prior to the domino collapse of communism throughout the Eastern Bloc, a formerly undistinguished party apparatchik stepped up to become the president of a gradually splintering Yugoslavia. After the 1980 death of General Tito, the anti-Soviet communist who maintained peace in the region via a mix of diplomacy and the threat of force, the ethnic and religious differences that permeated the conjoined regions began to come to a head once more. (A similar dynamic can be seen at work with the removal of the tyrant Saddam Hussein from power in Turkey's neighbouring country Iraq, by the Americans in 2003. The festering resentment among the Shiite minority against the dominant Sunni Muslims would explode into what was, to all intents and purposes, civil war. As we see in the history of the Impaler, tyranny may sometimes be the glue that binds a society together.)

The new nationalism of the times encouraged the different groups to see themselves not as part of one nation ('the former Yugoslavia', as it would soon become known), but as citizens of the Balkan states of Serbia, Bosnia-Herzegovina, or Croatia, or even to agitate to become part of an enlarged Albania. Arguments centred on the legitimacy of national borders established both before and after the Ottoman invasions, when, as folklore has it, Bosnia – a neighbouring Balkan region to the west of Wallachia – 'fell quietly' to the Turks. So it was that Yugoslavia's Muslim population of Bosniaks and ethnic Albanians became the target of rabble-rousing speeches by the apparently unassuming law student and career politician Slobodan Milosevic, elected President of the Federal Republic of Yugoslavia in 1987. No Hitler or Codreanu, perhaps, he still managed to harness a xenophobic spirit among Serbian nationalists with his talk of 'the events of 600 years ago' which, he claimed by inference, were somehow still ongoing. The landmark address by this new Serbian firebrand became known as the Gazimestan speech, delivered at Kosovo in 1989. The date and location were significant. It was a commemoration of the Serbian defeat by the Ottoman Empire six centuries before – the Battle of Kosovo had long held a mythic status in Serb history as the point at which the Serb people lost both their pride and their national identity – and nationalist sentiments were reaching boiling point.

'None should be surprised that Serbia raised its head because of Kosovo this summer,' declared Milosevic at Gazimestan to a passionate crowd of at least a million Serbs. 'Kosovo is the pure centre of its history, culture and memory. Every nation has one love that warms its heart. For Serbia it is Kosovo.' Many Serbs had travelled hundreds, even thousands of miles to attend the event commemorating the heroic end of Serbian independence at the hands of the Muslim Ottoman

Sultans, being held on the very field where it had happened. Ominously, perhaps, that field was in the district known as Kosovo, an area where Muslim ethnic Albanians were in the majority over Serbs, who represented the majority in most of the Yugoslavian Republic. Nationalistic and religious tensions had been building steadily since Tito's death seven years before, tensions some accused Milosevic of exploiting or even inspiring in his quest for political power.

'Six centuries ago, Serbia heroically defended itself in the field of Kosovo, but it also defended Europe,' the Serbian President told his rapt audience at Gazimestan. 'Serbia was at that time the bastion that defended the European culture, religion, and European society in general.' The sense of betrayal implicit in Milosevic's rhetoric, of a nation abandoned to hold the line alone against Islamic aggression while the rest of Europe stood idle, echoes in patriotic Romanian accounts of the career of Vlad Dracula. Articles published in 1976, inspired by the 500th anniversary of Vlad's death, emphasised the Voivode's role as a lone Crusader resisting Ottoman aggression. His leadership helped turn Wallachia into 'a wall that the enemy could occasionally penetrate or leap over, but could never pull down to allow the borders of the tri-continental empire to sprawl north of the Danube, and install pashas or muezzins in Tîrgovişte, Bucharest, Suceava, or Iasi'. One embittered Romanian historian insisted that, in the days of Dracula, 'in line with an already established tradition, Christendom relied on the Carpathian countries in the struggle without ever really helping, for its aid never reached Moldavia or Wallachia in time...'.

The historical accuracy of the Serbian myth Milosevic invoked at his Gazimestan address has been widely contested. 'Today, it is difficult to say what is the historical truth about the Battle of Kosovo and what is legend,' confessed the Serb President himself in his speech. 'Today this is no longer important.' The Serb defeat by the Turks at Kosovo was just one act in the complex drama of the loss of Serbian independence, a chaotic process that defies the easy framework of 'good versus evil' favoured by nationalist demagogues, and one that continued long after 1389. In the battle that truly established Ottoman power on European soil at Nicopolis, just seven years later, it was a charge by Serbian cavalry, allied with the Turkish Sultan, which ultimately doomed the Christian army. In a classic example of the black ironies of history, during the 1400s it was arguably the Albanians, under the legendary Athlete of Christ, Skanderbeg, who represented the greatest threat to Islamic dominance of the Balkans. Indeed,

Skanderbeg is regarded as an inspirational hero by Yugoslavia's Muslim minority, even though he had made his name by slaughtering Muslims. As the Serbs were quick to point out, there was even a Waffen SS Division named in his honour, recruited by the Germans from Yugoslavia's Albanian Muslims, who were vigorous in persecuting the region's Serbian population in the 1940s. It is estimated that over 500,000 people were murdered and 250,000 displaced in Yugoslavia during World War 2, the overwhelming majority Eastern Orthodox Serbs, largely the victims of Catholic Croats and Muslim Bosniaks, who were both enthusiastic allies with Nazi Germany.

Perhaps the defining document of the spectres of hate that haunt the Balkans is the 1945 novel *The Bridge on the Drina* by the Croat author Ivo Andrić, which was awarded the Pulitzer Prize for Literature in 1961. Unsurprisingly, it details the lengthy construction of a bridge over the River Drina in Bosnia, though the titular structure represents a metaphor for the comradeship and conflicts between the different peoples of the region. The book opens in the 1500s, with a young Serbian boy conscripted into the Ottoman Empire by the Devşirme, and concludes as World War 1 erupts in 1914. Interestingly, from our perspective, the novel's most infamous scene depicts the execution, at the order of the Turkish authorities, of a young Serb nationalist who attempts to sabotage the bridge. The victim is impaled upon the bridge, to serve as an example to any future rebels. This graphic scene has been cited on numerous occasions as one of the most harrowing in modern literature. The episode is also referenced in a scientific paper issued in 2009 by medics from the University of Kansas Hospital, concerning a 45-year-old man who came for treatment after a broomstick was thrust through his body, reportedly as a consequence of an accident in his bathtub.

The paper, entitled 'Survival Following Rectal Impalement through the Pelvic, Abdominal, and Thoracic Cavities: A Case Report', cites the scene from *The Bridge on the Drina* as perhaps the most famous example of such an injury in fiction. 'In his book, Andrić describes an executioner hammering an oak stake through a man's rectum, precisely guiding it "in the right direction", consciously careful not to harm "any of the more important internal organs", until it finally exited superiorly "close to the right shoulder muscle, level with the right ear," and "had not seriously damaged the intestines, the heart, or the lungs". Proper placement of the stake was intended to prolong suffering by lengthening the victim's post-impalement survival time. Although this type of impalement did take place throughout the Middle Ages, the particular execution Andrić describes is entirely fictitious from a historical standpoint. Nonetheless, his description of the impaled object coursing super laterally to the right through the pelvic, abdominal, and thoracic cavities, as well as his depiction of the injuries the victim sustained, is likely accurate as evidenced by the survival of the patient presented in our report.'

While the Kansas doctors are happy to dismiss impalement as an anachronistic relic of medieval barbarity, others are not so sure. In the 1980s a building volume of rumours began to circulate in Yugoslavia blaming Albanians and Bosniaks for a series of lurid crimes committed against Serbs, portrayed as victims of prejudice and intimidation in their own land. The bullish Serbian tabloid press picked up on one bizarre story in particular, with curious echoes of the days of Dracula. In May of 1985, a Serbian peasant named Djordje Martinovic was admitted to hospital with a bottle stuck up his arse. The bottle's neck had broken, further aggravating the patient's pain and damage. Martinovic insisted to doctors that two unidentified Albanians had forced the bottle up his back passage in a motiveless assault. However dubious such claims might sound to a cynic, the story captured the imagination of Serb nationalists, who began to portray the victim as some kind of surreal martyr.

In his book *Infidels*, Andrew Wheatcroft writes that 'in time the facts became less important than the symbolism. Newspapers began to call it "impalement" and linked it to atrocities committed "in the time of the Turks". This was widely taken as a reference to Andrić's description of such an incident in *The Bridge on the Drina*. The Serbian Academy of Sciences issued a long memorandum that referred to the Martinovic case, and said it was "reminiscent of the darkest days of Turkish impalement". A writer who had researched the case put it bluntly: "Here we are dealing with the remnants of the Ottoman empire... [Albanians] stuck him to a stake, this time just wrapped in a bottle. In the time of the Turks, Serbians were being impaled too, though even the Turks were not the ones who did it, but rather their servants – Arnauts [the old term for Albanians]."'

It's striking evidence both for the enduring power of impalement as the most notorious form of execution and the indelible link between the practice and the Turks – and by inference all Muslims – in many eyes in Eastern Europe. If, as some contend, it was Dracula who inspired the Ottoman Sultans to adopt this appalling technique, then it left a mark upon hostile foreign views of the Turks for centuries thereafter. If it was the other way around, and Vlad became the Impaler after witnessing Ottoman atrocities, it's easy to see why he might adopt the technique as the form of death most likely to make an impact upon witnesses. 'Albanians in general were implicated in a crime that was at best uncertain,' adds Wheatcroft. 'In the end the evidence came down to the fact that this is how the Turks had behaved, and the Albanians were their surrogates. Ten years after the event, Julie Mertus observed that "the power of the Martinovic case lay in its ability to invoke the primary imagery of Serbian oppression: the Turkish barbarity of impaling".'

Episodes like the Martinovic case contributed to a stifling climate of ethnic tension in Yugoslavia. After over four decades of apparent harmony under Marshal Tito, generations of bitter rivalry and cherished memories of ancient atrocities most had believed dormant began to rise from the grave, to tear Yugoslavia limb from bloody limb. An uneven triangle of conflicting nationalist factions emerged, of Serb, Croat and Bosniak warlords all eager to stake their claim to as much of the disintegrating Republic as they could. In the early 1990s, inspired by Croat provocation, the Serbs, who controlled most of the modern military equipment inherited from the defunct Yugoslav Army, would begin to take control of increasing amounts of territory with the aim of creating a 'Greater Serbia', redrawing the map to fit a mythic history. The spectres of centuries of appalling savagery, stretching back to the Middle Ages, were unleashed upon the Balkans. In *By Sword and Fire*, Sean McGlynn notes that, when President Milosevic was charged with war crimes at The Hague in 2002, the chief prosecutor explicitly accused the Serbs of acts of 'medieval savagery'.

In the mid-1990s, a Bosniak propaganda video entitled *The War in Bosnia* was first seen by this writer when it was handed out free by campaigners in Hyde Park. Containing footage from Bosnian TV and, more so, from within the hastily formed and under-equipped Republic of Bosnia and Herzegovina (RBiH) armies and militias, it gives a nightmarishly authentic (if undeniably partisan) account of a small pluralist society under attack – where, as the pre-war footage underlines, the Islamic crescent once hung alongside the Star of David.

In the early days of the war, Serbian forces are seen shelling civilian housing in the Sarajevo district (where the assassination of Archduke Ferdinand had precipitated World War 1). An old woman lies facedown in a pool of blood in the street. In a small Skoda-type car, a dead toddler slumps decapitated. 'Until the invasion of Bosnia and Herzegovina,' runs the solemn voiceover, 'history had never recorded that an army had included within its targets maternity hospitals,

hospitals, schools, orphanages, mosques, churches – even cemeteries. Nowhere before had any army targeted men, women and children waiting in line for food and medicine. Nowhere before had anyone hired professional killers to kill anything that moves in a city under siege.' Such propagandist rhetoric aside, hindsight (and captured video imagery) makes it clear that the Serbs were subjecting the citizens of RBiH to a policy of total war. Despite the video's triumphalist tone that hailed the preservation of Bosniak society by their courageous ragtag army as of May 1995, the worst was yet to come.

On 11 July 1995, the Serbian army entered a United Nations-endorsed 'safe zone' to begin the worst wartime massacre of European civilians since World War 2. As the Cetniks – to give the Serbian soldiers their historical title – besieged the town from the surrounding mountainside, the only defence of the barely-armed Muslims lay with their strongman Naser Orić, a modern warlord. 'We did what we had to do,' Orić guardedly admitted when later interviewed on camcorder, claiming, 'We respected the Geneva Convention – and sometimes we didn't respect it. But the Serbs had the logistics and technology – we had only our lives.' While Serb apologists speak of 'Muslim atrocities' which most surely occurred, this time – unlike in World War 2 – the Serbs had the upper hand, and they wielded it with unfettered brutality.

In a powerful BBC documentary film on the ensuing events, a tourist information video from the immediate post-Tito era uses updated East European folk music to promote 'Srebrenica, a beautiful spa and resort [...] that dates from Roman times'. This was before the town became the target of Serbian nationalist troops led by General Ratko Mladić. Mladić spoke directly to a Serb cameraman recording his military incursion: 'Here we are today, on July 11 1995, in Serbian Srebrenica, just before a great Serb holy day. We give this town to the Serb nation. Remembering the uprising against the Turks, the time has come to take revenge on the Muslims.' It was a grimly reverse mirror image of the situation in Vlad III's time: now a belligerent invasion force that made much of its Orthodox Christianity would unleash itself upon an assimilated Muslim population.

None seemed to remember, but Srebrenica itself had also endured a visit from Dracula in his final campaigns of 1476, the town having been captured by the Ottomans 26 years before. While Vlad's artillery bombarded the walls, a contingent of his troops disguised as Turks gained entry into the gates by deception. The ruse worked beautifully, and the town soon fell. Vlad treated survivors with his customary brutality. 'He tore the limbs off Turkish prisoners and placed their parts on stakes,' the Papal legate reported to his master in the Vatican, 'and displayed the private parts of his victims so that when the Turks see these, they will run away in fear.' They didn't run for long, and the town was soon back in Turkish hands, blossoming into a centre for the region's Bosniak Muslim population in the intervening centuries.

This was not a situation the Serb nationalists were willing to tolerate, and in the summer of 1995, Srebrenica would once again witness the wholesale butchery of Muslims in a massacre of Bosniak males that would last for three days. At a fenced-off enclosure which was once the Potočari refugee camp, a crumpled laser-printed note was pasted; when translated into English, it read: 'ON 13 JULY 1995, UNPROFOR [UN Protection Force] TROOPS HANDED OVER 3,000 MEN AND BOYS TO THE HANDS OF THEIR EXECUTIONERS.' This simply-stated accusation relates how an ineffectual Dutch UN peacekeeping force (with a remit to keep the peace but not to enforce it) allowed the Serbian troops to disperse the inhabitants of the camp, with all males from the ages of 12-77 sexually segregated and removed from their families.

On Friday 14 July, the killings moved into industrial mode. Hundreds had already been murdered in a packed warehouse by gun and grenade fire; hundreds more were moved to Bratunac, a Serbian village five miles outside Srebrenica, where they were crammed into a schoolhouse, blindfolded and shot; others were removed to further villages, farmhouses and warehouses, where they were also killed. Up to a total of about 4,000 had died by Sunday 16 July.

Many Bosnian Muslims had taken to the hills to survive. As the first of them were rounded up, a malnourished man named Ramo Osmanovic was filmed by a Serbian video cameraman calling out from an enclosure in a field, 'Come to Ramo!'

'Fuck Ramo!' interjects an observer's voice. 'Say, "Come to the Serbs!"'

'Come to the Serbs, they will not hurt you!' hollers Ramo, compliant at gunpoint. He also calls out the name of his son, Nermin. The video footage is the last trace of him before forensic archaeologists dug up the mud-shrouded skeletal remains of the town's Muslims. He and Nermin number among the 7,414 missing and murdered Muslim males of Srebrenica.

After this 'ethnic cleansing' (the euphemism of Milosevic's government being widely adopted), Srebrenica became a purely Serbian town. Understandably, even the surviving families of the massacre's victims had no wish to live alongside the families of their executioners.

VLAD THE IMPALER

Before the Bosnian war that began in 1992, three-quarters of the town's population had been Muslim; remarkably, over the last decade up to a million Bosnian Muslim refugees have opted to return to the homes they were driven from.

Mladić is still believed to be at liberty in the Bosnian region today, though in possible ill health. His contemporary Milosevic died of cardiac arrest whilst continually disrupting his trial for war crimes in The Hague, in March 2006. At the time of writing, Bosnian Serb leader Radovan Karadzic is on trial for his part in the conflict after thirteen years on the run – a conflict which he describes as 'just and holy', and lays squarely at the door of Bosnian Muslims.

'The story of Srebrenica may seem to be a throwback to medieval savagery,' opined the voiceover of the BBC documentary *A Cry from the Grave*, 'but it's essentially a story of our times, a catastrophe recorded by camcorder.' That same phrase – 'medieval savagery' – echoed throughout coverage of the brutal, messy wars that dismembered the former Republic of Yugoslavia, and the post mortems – literal and figurative – that followed. Yet the motives for the atrocities appear to be timeless. Factionalism, tribalism, nationalism, religion – the long memories of the peoples of a battle-scarred region – factors that lie at the heart of the bitterest conflicts throughout history. The international community's reaction to the crisis in the former Yugoslavia remains controversial. From some perspectives, the UN acted too slowly, facilitating the massacres that shocked the world. Others, not least many Serbs, saw things differently. NATO's intervention was nothing less than US-led imperialism, thwarting Serbia's legitimate efforts to reclaim territory that had been stolen from them by Croat, Bosniak and ethnic Albanians in previous generations of ruthless ethnic cleansing, not least the Serb spiritual heartland of Kosovo. Regarded with particular suspicion was the US Senator Joe Biden, identified as the driving force behind the controversial NATO bombing campaigns that finally compelled the warring Balkan factions to come to the negotiating table. In some Serb eyes, it was Biden, not Milosevic, who was the war criminal.

Biden had no doubts about the success of US-led action in the Balkans, and used it as a success story to promote a similar policy in post-war Iraq in his bid to become the Democratic candidate for the American Presidency in 2008. 'Look, we've had 20,000 Western troops in a place where there's more sectarian violence – from Vlad the Impaler to Milosevic – than in 5,000 years of history in Iraq,' he argued in a televised debate between the candidates. 'And what did we do? We separated the parties. There's not one single troop has been killed, not one, in the last 10 years. There is peace. There is a circumstance where the genocide is ended. They're becoming part of Europe.' He may well have plucked Vlad the Impaler from the air as the most colourful icon of brutality from Europe's eastern fringes (if so he did so more than once, using the analogy in at least one other interview). It's an analogy unlikely to endear the Senator to either Serbian or Romanian patriots. The Serbs are hardly likely to warm to the idea of having one of medieval history's most infamous tyrants roped in with their history for dramatic effect. Similarly, the Romanians are unlikely to appreciate a figure they see as a national hero flagged as an exemplar of sectarian violence, or indeed, if the Romanian academic Carmen Andras is anything to go by, to agree with Romania being metaphorically 'pushed towards the "Balkan" area with its inherently negative connotations'.

Such patriotic pride (and arguable chauvinism) aside, was Dracula a propagator of ethnic and religious violence that makes him akin to modern war criminals like Slobodan Milosevic? We've already witnessed Vlad's savage raids on the Transylvanian territories like Braşov, where the Saxon merchants are often regarded as his chief victims. Yet, while some Dracula apologists identify traitorous Vlach dissidents and rivals as his true targets, and others have even emphasised the bourgeois status of his victims to portray the Impaler as a medieval class warrior, not even the Saxon propagandists who broadcast the Voivode's crimes in order to blacken his name accuse him of racism. There were certainly grounds for Vlad to grow up with a racial chip on his shoulder as one of the Vlachs, the people routinely oppressed by the Saxon and Magyar populations of Eastern Europe. Yet even Dracula's fiercest critics must concede that he appears at least to have been an even-handed butcher, dealing out death with the same enthusiasm without any apparent prejudice or favouritism – the only exception being the Turks, who he appears to have hated with a special ferocity, though this was probably personal, political and religious rather than racial (remember that many 'Turkish' soldiers who he impaled with such enthusiasm would have been ethnic Europeans, willing converts, or products of the Ottoman Devşirme).

If racial politics have intruded into the story of Vlad the Impaler, they appear to have done so in the 20th century. The past hundred years have seen racism rise to the head of the list of secular sins, propelled in no small part by the horrors of World War 2, which obliged a reluctant world to recognise the potential that radical nationalism and racial prejudice had to breed unspeakable atrocities.

VLAD THE IMPALER

The disgust many outsiders felt at the massacres of the Yugoslav Wars was amplified by the ethnic motive behind much of the brutality, leading many to brand the conflict medieval in its savagery. Yet to have nationalist violence you need to have nations, and as we've already noted, the history of national identity is highly controversial. Certainly ethnic differences, underlined by language, were enough to establish the medieval system of apartheid that subjugated Transylvania's Vlach population. But it wasn't until the 1800s, with the troubled birth of a unified Romania, that Vlad the Impaler was drafted into service as a nationalist icon. Previous to that, interpretations of the Impaler as a national hero are speculative, even romantic notions. There is evidence that Dracula envisioned a unified Christian front against Ottoman expansion, and that he may have cast an acquisitive eye over the neighbouring principality of Transylvania, but little to support enduring depictions of the Voivode as a pioneering visionary of Romanian national identity.

Bram Stoker's 1897 novel *Dracula* seeded many of the nationalist controversies that have since embroiled Vlad. Critics who minimise connections between Stoker's fictional Count and his historical namesake point out that the novelist misidentifies the Vlach Voivode as a Székely, Transylvania's anomalous Hungarian-speaking warrior class who still represent a large ethnic minority in Romania today. (The origins and ethnic identity of the Székely are still debated today – Bram Stoker gives a particularly fanciful version of their ancestry in *Dracula*, identifying them as the descendants of Scythian witches and the warrior hordes of Attila the Hun.) As more Romanians became aware of Stoker's popular novel, a theory gained ground that identified the book as a deliberate attempt to slander a national hero, as masterminded by Romania's historical rivals in Hungary. While dismissed by outsiders as an absurd conspiracy theory, there is no denying the passion behind many such accusations.

In *History of the Romanians*, Dogaru and Zaharaide put the case forcefully (if ungrammatically), explaining that 'the vampire tyrant has thrown an undeserved blame directly on the image of the hero prince and indirectly on the Romanian people that gave birth to such a monster. Is it indeed a pure happening [co incidence?] that, in the full swing of racist upsurge, of magyarising the Romanians and the Slavs by force in the dying Austrian-Hungarian empire, the "information" was delivered to him by a Hungarian, the professor Vámbéry from the University of Budapest? Did maybe Vámbéry and the Hungarian historians not know the truth?' Ármin Vámbéry was a distinguished

Hungarian scholar and acquaintance of Bram Stoker, whom some have suggested was the model for the character of the vampire hunter Van Helsing. Inevitably, in the contentious realms of *Dracula* scholarship, Vámbéry's role in the horror novel's conception remains hotly contested. Florescu and McNally suggest that the Hungarian provided Stoker with invaluable historical background for his novel, while Elizabeth Miller maintains that there is no evidence they ever discussed the Gothic chiller which the Anglo-Irish author was researching. Most Western scholars, however, dismiss the Romanian idea that Vámbéry deliberately fed Stoker poisonous misinformation about Dracula in order to denigrate a national hero as patriotic paranoia. Of course, Stoker's novel didn't really take off until it was adapted by Hollywood in 1931. Romanian conspiracy theorists were given further grist to their mill when a Hungarian actor named Bela Lugosi was cast in the title role…

We've already met the modern Romanian politician most vigorous in stoking ethnic friction between Romania and Hungary, Gheorghe Funar, the 'Mad Mayor' of Cluj, who attracted national headlines with his policies designed to marginalise and drive out the region's Magyar-speaking minority. Happily, Funar was no Milosevic, and his brand of patriotic politics fell on increasingly stony ground in 21st-century Romania. He was expelled from the Romanian National Unity Party in 1997, and voted out of office in Cluj in 2004. While still an MP for the quasi-fascist Greater Romania Party, most now prefer to regard Funar as an outdated aberration. However, his flamboyant rabble-rousing antics as Mayor of Cluj were enough to keep him in office for 12 years, so he clearly struck a chord in post-communist Romania. What might Dracula have made of this populist radical? It's likely Cluj's Mad Mayor might have enjoyed a stake in 15th-century Transylvania for tampering with the monuments to Matthias Corvinus in the Hungarian King's birthplace. For, far from fomenting trouble for King Matthias, Dracula was fervently courting the support of his Hungarian neighbour, even proposing a marriage alliance – which implied a willingness to convert to Catholicism – in his eagerness to secure an alliance. With the full fury of the Ottoman Empire bearing down upon his border, Vlad badly needed allies, and nationalism be damned…

***

Mehmet's Ottoman army was finally assembled and ready to advance upon Wallachia by late spring in 1462. Riding at the Sultan's right hand was his sometime lover – also Dracula's brother and rival for the throne – Radu the Handsome. As a scenario with such undertones of unresolved filial conflict and aberrant sexual relationships, the campaign has all the components of a particularly bizarre Greek tragedy. On a more pragmatic level, as ever in medieval military history, accurate troop numbers are hard to come by, and most contemporary figures are likely to be exaggerations. Some sources insist that the Sultan had mustered an army of 400,000 men, while the most conservative estimate puts his force at just under 100,000. Whatever the true figure, we can be confident that the Ottoman force comprehensively outnumbered and outgunned Dracula's army. Vlad was also at a substantial disadvantage in terms of training and military technology. While Mehmet was at the helm of a state-of-the-art military machine – complete with skilled military engineers and artillery support – the majority of the Wallachian force consisted of volunteers, many of them doubtless conscripted because they were more afraid of Dracula than the approaching Turks.

The Voivode could traditionally call upon two different forces the Small Host and the Great Host. The Small Host consisted of the Voivode's personal retainers, his loyal boyars and any mercenary forces he could afford to maintain. It was the army fielded, according to local law and tradition, for foreign adventures, invading neighbours or supporting allies. A mobile, well-armed and well-trained cavalry force, it was the Small Host that Vlad had led over the Danube in the winter of 1461. The Great Host added to that force the free peasantry and citizens of the realm, commanded by local leaders, and consisting of a greater proportion of infantry, often lightly armed and poorly trained. The Great Host could only be convened at times of national crisis, most notably invasion, such as the situation that faced Wallachia in the spring of 1462.

If those military historians who believe that Dracula was trying to create a 'war-orientated economy' – where a patriotic people's army replaced the fickle boyars he had purged – are correct, it's possible that this is why Vlad forced Mehmet's hand, compelling the Sultan to initiate an invasion. A war on Wallachian soil allowed the Voivode to field the largest army possible, which would test the brutal domestic policies designed to forge his population into a society of dedicated warriors. 'A fighting pattern that we nowadays call a people's war was born out of the will to defend the freedom of his people and the military skill of his leaders in that great struggle that set the Romanians against one of the strongest empires of the time,' in the words of the

Romanian military historian Lieutenant Colonel Constantin Cazanisteanu in a 1976 article on the Impaler, betraying the Communist dogma of the day. It is also of course equally possible that Dracula simply lashed out at the Ottoman Empire in 1461 – as some say he simply lashed out blindly at his own population – and that he simply dealt with the consequences of his actions as they arose. In 1896, the Romanian historian Ion Bogdan dismissed Vlad's campaign as 'a battle lost through flight'.

Whatever the truth about Vlad's strategy (or lack of it), the fact remained that by the summer of 1462, Wallachia faced a devastating invasion force upon its eastern borders. The first line of defence was the River Danube. While Dracula's small cavalry force had slipped over the frozen waterway easily the previous winter, it presented a more formidable obstacle to Mehmet's large, cumbersome army, one no doubt made more troublesome by the damage Vlad had previously inflicted on Turkish infrastructure surrounding the Danube. The Wallachians shadowed the Ottoman force on the opposite bank, ready to inflict maximum losses on the Turks when they were at their most vulnerable trying to secure a crossing. After one abortive attempt, driven back by showers of Wallachian arrows, Mehmet resolved to make his move under cover of darkness in the first week of June. A Serbian known as Constantin of Ostrovitza, drafted as a child into the Janissary corps as part of the Devşirme, later recorded his experiences of the campaign, leaving a notably balanced account of the war from the Ottoman side. He recorded the battle for the Danube as follows...

'When night began to fall, we climbed into our boats and floated down the Danube and crossed over to the other side several miles below the place where the Impaler's army was stationed. There we dug ourselves trenches, so that cavalry could not harm us. After that we crossed back over to the other side and transported other Janissaries over the Danube, and when the entire infantry had crossed over, then we prepared and set out gradually against the Impaler's army, together with the artillery and other equipment that we had brought with us. Having halted, we set up the cannon, but not in time to stop three hundred Janissaries from being killed ... Seeing that our side was greatly weakening, we defended ourselves with the 120 guns which we had brought over and fired so often that we repelled the Prince's army and greatly strengthened our position ... The Impaler, seeing that he could not prevent the crossing, withdrew. After that the emperor crossed the Danube with his entire army and gave us 30,000 coins to be distributed among us.'

VLAD THE IMPALER

Once the Janissaries were safely on the western bank of the river, it was time for Vlad's forces to fall back. He had no intention of fighting a pitched battle with the Sultan's vastly superior army, but instead resolved to fight the kind of guerrilla war that Skanderbeg had previously employed against the Ottomans to such devastating effect. While the Turks had far more men who were better trained and better equipped than Dracula's Wallachian army, he had home advantage. The local knowledge of his scouts and skirmishers would allow him to fully exploit the terrain, to make the very land fight for him. It was classic asymmetric war – the term coined by Andrew J. R. Mack in the influential 1975 article 'Why Big Nations Lose Small Wars'. In asymmetric war the two combatants are radically mismatched in terms of power or resources, leading to outcomes that confound the expectations of conventional strategists. The term is often employed to explain how a 'superpower' like the USA could be humbled by an apparently weaker foe in conflicts like the Vietnam War, though equally, the Indian Wars of the 1800s were a protracted asymmetric conflict where the US confirmed conventional views on military strength. As we shall see, both wars have parallels in Dracula's showdown with Mehmet.

Even Dracula's most determined detractors concede that Vlad's resistance against the Ottoman war machine in the summer of 1462 represented his 'finest hour', however inappropriate such Churchillian rhetoric may sound for a man capable of such cruelty. A merciless Machiavellian perhaps, very likely a sadistic psychopath, his defence of Wallachia is evidence of a man who led from the front, who never gave up in the face of hideous odds. Vlad had easy options – quiet retirement on a pension, appeasement, simple flight – and many of his Balkan contemporaries took such paths, silently disappearing into the footnotes of Eastern European history. It never even occurred to Dracula to contemplate such a route. Perhaps part of the mystery of why such a vile, barbarous creature can still command such respect among the good folk of Romania today is resolved here. We live in an age where the comfortable leaders who pull our collective strings and send young men to war are all the while sheltered in distant bomb-proof bunkers or behind air-conditioned, anonymous desks, where the bloodshed manifests as computer spreadsheets. However little Bram Stoker may have known of the historical Dracula, in his horror novel he allows his monster Count a heroic past. As eager as the Voivode was to inflict pain and horror on others, he never flinched from the prospect that he would most likely meet a similar fate. Nobility is too strong a word for such valour, though it is easy to see why some might find such a character charismatic, even inspiring.

In the summer of 1462, Vlad the Impaler's leadership skills would be tested to the limit. The eyes of Europe were upon him, though still no Christian prince saw fit to send anything more substantial than prayers to bolster his desperate position. Not only were there no allies on the horizon, but his messengers brought back shattering news. Vlad's cousin, his brother-in-arms from Suceava, the man he had helped place on the throne of Moldavia, had made an alliance with the Ottomans. Dracula's reaction to his betrayal by Stefan the Great of Moldavia is not recorded, though we do know his response. With Stefan marching on the Wallachian fortress of Cilia, Vlad was obliged to split his forces, dispatching a contingent he couldn't spare to intercept this unexpected threat on a second front. Things looked grim. One account leaves us with a snatch of Dracula's address to his assembled troops: 'It would be better that those who think of death should not follow me...'

CHAPTER XI

Into the Forest of the Impaled

Vlad's defence against the advancing Turkish horde was a classic scorched earth policy. Just as he had left the Ottoman territories bordering the Danube a smouldering wasteland in the winter of 1461, Dracula despoiled his own land, leaving nothing on which the Ottomans could live. Crops were burnt, villages razed, wells poisoned, and any livestock that could not be herded away was butchered and spoilt. Dispossessed Vlach peasants either joined the exodus westward, or fled to hiding places in the forests or mountains. While medieval armies conventionally relied upon pillage and forage for supplies, a professional force like the Ottoman army could sustain itself under such conditions, but the morale and health of the ponderous Turkish forces were seriously tested. Dracula enjoyed an unexpected ally in the shape of the weather, as the region experienced a punishingly hot summer.

If the Turks wanted to take Wallachia, Dracula planned to make them march through Hell. The heat and desolation soon began to take their toll. Turkish sources report that even the best of Mehmet's Azabs could find no clean water. 'The intensity of the heat caused by the scorching sun was so great that the armour of the Janissaries melted like wax,' reported another veteran of the campaign, in hyperbole that reflects the infernal conditions the army faced. 'In this parched plain, the lips of the fighters for Islam dried up. Even the Africans and Asians, used to desert conditions, used their shields to roast meat.' In one of several indications of Vlad's energetic and innovative strategies, those water courses he couldn't staunch or poison, He diverted to form swamps to further slow the Ottoman advance. Deliberately, or otherwise, the Voivode was creating not only the most difficult terrain possible for his opponent, but also the unhealthiest, creating the patches of stagnant water which wise army commanders throughout the ages have avoided as breeding grounds for fever and malaise.

One of the more interesting aspects of Dracula's defensive

campaign, frequently overlooked or even dismissed as fanciful, was the Voivode's pioneering use of biological warfare. M. J. Trow pretty much dismisses the idea as implausible in his *Vlad the Impaler*, though others are willing to entertain the possibility. There are accounts which suggest that Vlad summoned those of his people afflicted by the plague, instructed them to dress as Turks and to infiltrate the Ottoman army in the hope of infecting as many enemy soldiers as possible. Any of these human biological weapons who successfully led to the death of a Turk, need only bring his victim's turban back as evidence in order to be given a reward. Certainly, the second part of this story does seem absurd – would Vlad really want infectious plague victims clutching turbans visiting his camp in search of bounty? But the substance of the idea bears further scrutiny.

While tales of battle dominate accounts of warfare, the truth is that disease claims many more lives than are usually recorded in such records of armed conflict. The ambition of losing fewer troops to disease than to enemy action is one that eluded generals until well into the 20th century. Discussing Early Modern warfare in his classic 1934 study *Rats, Lice and History*, Hans Zinsser dismisses the famed battles of the era as 'only the terminal operations engaged in by those remnants of the armies which have survived the camp epidemics'. Fortune favoured not the brave, so much as the healthy. Even if medieval chronicles favour detailing valorous feats of arms, there's no reason to suppose that disease didn't play just as substantial a role in the campaigns of the Middle Ages. Many Hungarian knights cited an outbreak of the plague as their reason for refusing to join John Hunyadi's final battle against the Ottomans at Belgrade in 1456. Hunyadi's death of disease shortly afterwards suggests such excuses had some substance.

Some historians believe that the first use of biological warfare – deliberately infecting an opponent's forces with disease – occurred at the Black Sea port of Caffa in 1347 (now the city of Feodosiya in the Ukraine). After a protracted siege of several months, a Mongol army began to succumb to disease in their camp surrounding the city, defended by a Genoese garrison. 'The Tartars, fatigued by such a plague and pestiferous disease, stupefied and amazed, observing themselves dying without hope of health, ordered cadavers placed on their hurling machines, and thrown into the city of Caffa, so that by means of these intolerable passengers the defenders died widely,' recorded one eyewitness. 'Thus there were projected mountains of dead, nor could the Christians hide or flee, or be freed from such disaster.'

The Mongols failed to take the city, but in *Six-Legged Soldiers*,

VLAD THE IMPALER

Jeffrey A. Lockwood describes the attack as the 'most devastating act of biological warfare in human history', one which 'would take 200 times more lives than the atomic bomb dropped on Hiroshima six centuries later'. Such a calculation is controversial, as it assumes the theory that the outbreak of plague in Caffa was the doorway through which the Black Death entered Europe, finally accounting for something as much as half of the continent's population in the years following the siege. Some experts have challenged the effectiveness of the Mongols' grisly farewell present to the people of Caffa; others doubt that the city was the main avenue by which the disease spread westward. Yet the fact remains that the practice of hurling corpses and other unsanitary matter at the enemy figured in numerous bitter sieges thereafter. At the siege of Karlštejn Castle in 1422, Emperor Sigismund's garrison was pelted with dead bodies and 2000 carriage-loads of shit, resulting in an outbreak of disease.

Even today, biological agents are recognised as capricious and difficult weapons, inclined to backfire or simply dissipate in unsuitable conditions. Many deadly bacteria are surprisingly fragile outside of their natural life cycles. Previous to our modern scientific understanding of epidemiology this would have been truer still. Yet, our ancestors certainly knew about the basic principles of contagion, even if they didn't understand the biological science behind it, and some military leaders attempted to use it to their advantage. We can't be certain that Vlad Dracula dispatched plague victims to mingle among the enemy army, or indeed – if he did – that this had any effect on the Ottoman force. But it's an intriguing possibility, one that fits well with the developing picture of Dracula as an ingenious and energetic tactician, willing to entertain and exploit any strategy in order to achieve his ends.

On a more conventional level, Vlad's army – by now perhaps better fed and no doubt better motivated than the invaders – kept the pressure on Mehmet's unhappy horde. His nimble cavalry exploited their familiarity with the landscape to mount constant hit-and-run raids on the Ottoman flanks before disappearing into Wallachia's impenetrable forests and precipitous rough ground. Turkish stragglers were picked off mercilessly, foraging parties ambushed. Pits were dug, lined with stakes, to trap the unwary. It's reminiscent of the guerrilla warfare the North Vietnamese employed when fighting US forces in the 20th century, and it had a similar effect, sapping not just manpower but morale at an alarming rate. While the environment may have been different – the humid jungles of Southeast Asia contrasting with the arid plains of Southeast Europe – the thoughts going through the minds of embattled American Marines and fatigued Ottoman Janissaries must have been very similar. 'Although the Romanian prince had a small army, we always advanced with great caution and fear and spent nights sleeping in ditches. But even in this manner we were not safe,' recalled the Janissary Constantin of Ostrovitza.

However, with no sign of support from Europe, the badly-outnumbered Voivode was running out of options. Even if he could get the better of Mehmet in a war of attrition, the Turks could still afford to take the losses, while Dracula's resources were already stretched to the limit. Much of his army was also his nation's workforce, and had they left any harvest to collect, it looked increasingly unlikely there would be anyone to collect it. The scorched earth strategy was, in effect, subjecting your own lands to *chevauchée*. It echoes the anonymous American officer who during the Vietnam War in 1968, made the immortal observation that 'it became necessary to destroy the town to save it,' in reference to the decision to shell and bomb a provincial Vietnamese capital regardless of the consequences to the inhabitants. While Dracula – like the US Major – may have felt any sacrifice was justified in order to defeat the enemy, the local populace may not have felt the same cast-iron conviction.

The fact that, despite the constant harassment by Vlad's troops and the destruction of Wallachian lands, the Ottoman war machine kept steadily rolling forward, must have sown seeds of doubt in all but the most dedicated of Dracula's followers. Supplies must now also have begun running low in the Wallachian camp, further dampening morale. His unique style of leadership no doubt helped keep the troops in line. The Russian account describes how the Voivode undertook an unorthodox form of troop inspection after clashes with the enemy. 'Those who were wounded from the front received great honour and were made knights, but those who had been wounded from the back were impaled on a stake through their back passage with Dracula saying thus: "You are not a man but a woman."'

Crucially, the Turkish forces were now approaching the Wallachian capital of Tîrgoviște. The loss of the capital would have delivered a shattering blow to Dracula's cause, and his army could not keep retreating forever. The artillery which had done so much to slow the Ottoman progress would surely prove their worth in either a pitched battle or a set-piece siege, and Vlad could not realistically entertain either possibility. Skanderbeg had successfully humiliated Mehmet's father Murad in 1450, when he bogged down the Turkish invasion force besieging his stronghold at Krujë while his Albanian guerrillas harassed the Turkish army, finally obliging the Sultan to lift the siege and beat a retreat in the face of unsustainable losses. Yet Tîrgovişte was not as formidable as Krujë, and unlike Skanderbeg, Vlad could not count on his Wallachian forces either to defend the city or maintain a protracted resistance without his direct command. Perhaps the limits of rule by fear were beginning to show…

With his back against the wall, the Voivode did what he did best, and lashed out. The engagement south of Tîrgovişte, on the stifling night of 16/17 June 1462, is difficult to qualify as a battle. It is often referred to simply as the Night Attack – a reflection that in many ways it simply represented a massive escalation of the constant harassment of the Ottoman army by Vlad's troops. It's sometimes referred to as the Night of Terror, in recognition that it also represented a climax of the psychological warfare Dracula had been waging on the advancing Turks. When Romanian nationalists attempted to claim the Impaler as a patriotic hero in the 1800s, the conflict was dignified with suitably romantic titles such as the Battle of the Torches, chosen by the artist Theodor Aman for his stirring depiction of the event.

The significance of the night in contemporary eyes is suggested by the wildly differing accounts of events we have from different sources. Dracula's strategy appears to have been simple. Two Wallachian forces would approach the Ottoman encampment under cover of darkness to conduct a surprise attack. The goal of the raid was audacious – penetrating the heart of the Turkish base in order to slay the Sultan himself. It was an insanely risky plan – particularly as Dracula planned, as ever, to lead from the front (some accounts even suggest that he personally scouted the Turkish camp beforehand in disguise). But like all the best crazy plans, it just might work. The death of the Sultan practically guaranteed the retreat of an Ottoman force, as commanders rushed back to the capital to ingratiate themselves with the new regime. Dracula's days at the Ottoman court meant he was probably familiar with the layout of a classic Turkish camp. They were like miniature travelling cities, while the tents were helpfully colour-coded. The huge red tent at the centre of the camp, surrounded by a wooden palisade formed by a circle of wagons, would contain their target.

That image – of circled wagons – is also resonant of another military conflict with odd echoes of the Wallachian war of 1462. It's possible to see parallels between the mobile warfare between Vlad's guerrilla army and Mehmet's Ottoman troops and the engagements between the 7th Cavalry and Native Americans depicted in classic Hollywood Westerns. Like the 'Red Indians' of cinematic cliché, Vlad's best warriors were predominantly longhaired horsemen, harassing their foes with bows and lances, while like the 'palefaces' Mehmet's best troops were uniformed and fought back with firearms. (The name of one of Vlad's elite classes of cavalry – the Viteji – even translates roughly as 'braves'.) The Ottoman advance across hostile Wallachia has something akin to the stereotypical scenes where the wary heroes of countless Westerns enter Indian territory, shadowed by the natives, who subject them to constant hit-and-run raids and sneak attacks by night, employing the terrain to their own advantage. Wallachia was the Ottoman Empire's 'wild west', and just as European immigrants thought that the doctrine of 'Manifest Destiny' entitled and compelled them to drive ever westward to civilise and exploit America's native population in the 1800s, so the Turks had believed the will of Allah bestowed upon them a similar mandate to introduce Islamic civilisation to the populace of Eastern Europe four centuries earlier.

To stretch our analogy a little further, on the night of 16 June, 1462, Vlad planned an audacious attack with parallels to the battle plans of the Sioux Chief Sitting Bull of 25 June, 1876. In the Battle of the Little Big Horn, the underestimated Native American forces surrounded and destroyed General George Custer's complacent troops in a battle that became immortalised in US mythology as Custer's Last Stand, just as Vlad's desperate gambit four centuries before became the stuff of legend in Romanian national myth as the Night Attack. Here, perhaps, the parallels end. Sitting Bull enjoyed a superiority of numbers, allowing him the luxury of a daylight attack, while Dracula's men were still both substantially outgunned and outnumbered by the professional force they faced. The Voivode may have hoped to take his opponent's metaphorical scalp, but he faced a tougher challenge than the Sioux Chief. One of the fullest accounts of Dracula's famous Night Attack was recorded by a Papal legate of the day, probably dictated to him by a Wallachian veteran of the battle (though some believe the words came indirectly from the Voivode himself)…

'The sultan besieged him [Dracula] and discovered him in a certain mountain where the Wallachian was supported by the natural strength of the place. There Dracula had hidden himself along with 24,000 of his men who had willingly followed him. When Dracula realised that he would either perish from hunger or fall into the hands of the very cruel enemy, and considering both eventualities unworthy of brave men, he dared commit an act worthy of being remembered: calling his men together and explaining the situation to them, he easily persuaded them to enter the enemy camp. He divided the men so that either they should die bravely in battle with glory and honour or else, should destiny prove favourable to them, they should avenge themselves against the enemy in an exceptional manner. So, making use of some Turkish prisoners, who had been caught at twilight when they were wandering about imprudently, at nightfall Dracula penetrated into the Turkish camp with part of his troops, all the way up to the fortifications. And during the entire night he sped like lightning in every direction and caused great slaughter, so much so that, had the other commander to whom he had entrusted his remaining forces been equally brave, or had the Turks not fully obeyed the repeated orders from the sultan not to abandon their garrisons, the Wallachian undoubtedly would have gained the greatest and most brilliant victory. But the other commander (a boyar named Gale) did not dare attack the camp from the other side as had been agreed upon…Dracula carried out an incredible massacre without losing many men in such a major encounter, though many were wounded. He abandoned the enemy camp before daybreak and returned to the same mountain from which he had come. No one dared pursue him, since he had caused such terror and turmoil. I learned by questioning those who had participated in this battle that the sultan lost all confidence in the situation. During that night the sultan abandoned the camp and fled in a shameful manner. And he would have continued this way, had he not been reprimanded by his friends and brought back, almost against his will.'

The account, of course, throws a very positive light on the Impaler's mission as a qualified success, one that failed only because of the cowardice of his second-in-command. Other sources saw the action very differently. The Turkish chronicler Tursun Bey portrays the Wallachian attack as a comedy of errors, where Vlad's confused men couldn't flee fast enough. 'Their defeat was so great that even ten-year-old children who were apprentices and servants in the army killed many Infidels twice as powerful as themselves,' he boasts in his sycophantic account. In reality, Vlad may well have come tantalisingly close to achieving his goal, fighting his way through the chaos to the tents where he thought his quarry lay. He got the wrong tents, finding two of Mehmet's advisors instead, and as the Janissary corps rallied around the Sultan, Dracula was obliged to signal a retreat.

As a hard-headed Janissary, a professional soldier rather than a propagandist, Constantin of Ostrovitza probably gives the least partisan assessment of the night's confusing events: 'They massacred horses, camels and several thousand Turks. When the Turks had retreated in the face of the enemy, we repelled the enemy and killed them. But the Sultan had incurred great losses.' Great losses, perhaps, but not enough to halt the Ottoman advance towards Tîrgovişte. Dracula may have unnerved, even shocked the Sultan and his men with his audacious surprise attack, but he had his own problems. If Gale had let the Voivode down, it was an indication of a building crisis of confidence in Vlad's army. His bold plan to assassinate Mehmet had failed, he had taken yet more casualties he couldn't afford in the process, and now nothing stood between the Ottomans and Tîrgovişte.

That isn't strictly true, however. Something did stand in the path of Mehmet's advance, but it was a far from conventional force, not least because the men manning their posts were all dead. The sight that met the eyes of the Ottoman scouts as they approached Tîrgovişte did not enter the annals of military history, but was a landmark in the realms of historical horror. It established Vlad as *Kaziglu Bey* – Impaler Prince – in Turkish lore thereafter. If it was the Turks who inspired Dracula to experiment with the horrors of impalement, on that day he demonstrated that he was the master of that infernal art, the Ottomans mere fumbling novices. On the road to Tîrgovişte the Turks encountered an unspeakable garden of horror – which thenceforth became known as the Forest of the Impaled – barring their progress to the Wallachian capital. Sources speak of mind-boggling numbers of transfixed bodies in this surreal monument to sadism. Few deny that Dracula erected this demonic display, even if his apologists prefer to pass over it quickly. Questions, however, remain. How many human beings were pinioned on sharpened poles in Vlad's unholy Forest? Is the oft-quoted figure of 20,000 plausible? Who were they and how long had they been there? Turkish prisoners-of-war from recent skirmishes, hideous human trophies from the campaign of the previous winter, or, as some even suggested, Vlad's own people, obliged to make the ultimate sacrifice as soul-blasting testimony to Dracula's limitless savagery?…

***

In *True Horror*, there is an effectively gothic staged evocation of the 'Forest of the Impaled', which has the look of a vintage late 60s/early 70s Brit horror movie about the witch craze. Most contentiously perhaps, from a historical point of view, the scenario accepts the version of the story that has Vlad impaling his own subjects on the hills outside Tîrgovişte as a deterrent to the Ottoman invaders.

Perhaps most realistically, the budgetary limitations of the TV doc restricted the figures of the impaled to maybe two dozen extras at most. It's the scenario which seems to ring most true: if Vlad was prepared to torture, impale or crucify the inhabitants of his own principality, then it seems somehow conceivable that the unfortunates would be a random selection – rather than, as has been suggested, the population of an entire suburb, numbering anything up to 20,000 victims.

As intoxicatingly horrible as the folk tales are, one has to ask how feasible are the numbers given for Vlad's massacres of his own populace. If we consider that such provocatively inhumane acts were committed to preserve a kingdom with an estimated population of 470,000, then the wild statistics suggest Vlad would have at least decimated his own subjects.

As psychological warfare, however, it's a tactic that's second to none. The Ottoman Turks, while a formidable fighting force, also had a reputation for ruthlessness and extreme cruelty, as we have seen. In order to repel them, or sway them from their purpose, such a tableau of physical agony and the disintegrating human form would need to be *in extremis*; for all the historical contradictions, there's every suggestion that Vlad achieved this somehow. Once again, the affrighted conscience asks itself: *If he can do this to his own people, what the hell is he going to do to us?*

In the earlier days of 'Dracula studies', however, historians Florescu and McNally, authors of *In Search of Dracula*, presented a radically different take on the same scenario. In the early 1970s documentary film based on their study, Christopher Lee moonlights from portraying Vlad the Impaler to deliver the following voiceover: 'History records only that Vlad sensed treachery and captured the entire Turkish force. He impaled them on a forest of stakes outside the walls of his capital, Tîrgoviște, placing the envoys on two stakes higher than the rest, in deference to their rank.' The screen shows a monochrome diagram of impaled bodies, similar in its almost cubist style to a painting by the artist War Arrow (*The Dance*) commissioned for this book.

'He then launched his famous campaign along the Danube River. With a force of between ten and twenty thousand men, consisting mainly of rapid-moving cavalry and peasant conscripts, Vlad pushed all the way to the Black Sea.' This section of narrative is accompanied by sepia-tinted footage from an unidentified feature film, depicting an Eastern European army battling the Turks.

'At first, Vlad met with great success. After his capture of the fortress of Giurgiu, he wrote to King Matthias of Hungary that 23,809 men had been slain and impaled. Vlad was certain of the figure, because their heads had been carefully counted – apart from 884 who had been burnt in their houses, and whose heads of course could not be connected.

'During the famous "Night of Terror" he boldly attacked the Sultan's camp. However, his bodyguard emerged and Vlad was forced to retreat.

The road to Tîrgovişte now lay open, but the Turks were greeted by the grisly remains of the Sultan's troops and envoys impaled by Vlad the previous year, blackened by the sun and half-eaten by birds. The Sultan was moved to tears and said, "What can we do with a man like this?"'

The quaint spectacle of reducing a man as ruthless as Mehmet the Conqueror to tears aside, this version of the story does at least make some sense of the logistics. If the Turkish soldiers were killed and then impaled post-mortem, it eliminates the conundrum of how exactly one subdues more than 20,000 soldiers of the most feared army on earth and makes them wait in line to be stuck onto a wooden spike. Otherwise, whither the restraining mechanism? How many Wallachian soldiers or *armas* would be required to subdue and execute that many Turks? Given the difficult logistics, might up to 60,000 executioners be required for a third as many Turks? Where would they be held while they awaited execution, in a Europe that had yet to develop a prison system in lieu of inflicting death or extreme corporal punishment on the condemned? And under such conditions, would not a large contingent of Turkish prisoners be compelled to defy and slaughter a great number of their captors, given their fearsome fighting prowess?

The Florescu and McNally version does at least take a logical way around this point, given the suggestion that the impalement victims were long dead before their peers set eyes on them. Indeed, it's less likely that they'd be 'blackened by the sun' than turn quickly black as they began to decompose in the open air.

'Impaling is a very public, very noisy, very smelly method of killing people,' acknowledges *Anno Dracula* author Kim Newman in *True Horror*. 'While the victims were being impaled they made a lot of noise, they discharged a lot of body fluids, and anyone within a whiff – let alone earshot – would have realised that something very unpleasant was going on and would have been frankly willing to do anything to avoid that fate.'

However, given the much more protracted timeframe of Florescu and McNally's Tîrgovişte impalements, is it not also likely that over 20,000 corpses rotting in the open would have exposed the city of Tîrgovişte to a great danger of diphtheria or cholera? Perhaps even the plague, once the region's rats got a sniff of the spoiled rich pickings on offer?

Whatever the true statistics (or specific ethnicity) of the victims at that time, history still suggests that Vlad committed a grandly theatrical atrocity at that time which gave his enemy pause for thought. Numbers aside, the traumatic impact of the grim spectacle he unleashed seems to have been felt throughout Europe. In Mei Trow's study of the Impaler, he posits that a remark made by Richard III of England to the Silesian knight Nicolas von Popplau may have referred to Vlad: 'I wish that my kingdom lay upon the confines of Turkey,' mused Richard, apparently longing for the national hero status that written history (and Shakespeare's dramatic propaganda) would deny him. 'With my own people alone and without the help of other princes, I should like to drive away not only the Turks, but all my foes.'

Von Popplau's diary quotes Richard as saying this in May 1484, over two decades after Vlad's historic routing of the Turks in 1462. In the Netherlands, the Dutch artist and grotesque visionary known as Hieronymus Bosch lived out an obscure parochial life which overlaps with the several reigns of Vlad III. While relatively little is known of Bosch's life, it's believed that his intricately detailed triptychs of Heaven and Hell, which still fascinate with their proto-surrealist imagination, were authentic representations of his Christian beliefs.

Torture became phantasmagoria in one of his admonitory depictions of Hell, *The Last Judgement* of 1505. Amongst the many damned souls tormented by a variety of demons, anthropomorphic animals and mismatched human body parts is a man impaled on a thin wooden pike from head to toe, with an arrow entering his navel and exiting his back as in the martyrdom of St Sebastian. Three luckless individuals are impaled on the branches of the shortest and spiniest of trees, at varying angles; one helmeted figure, who remains vertically aloft, has one of the branches passing through his genital region and thigh.

Once again, it cannot be known how familiar Bosch was with the stories of Vlad the Impaler – though the Germanic pamphlets written about him were certainly circulating in Europe at this time (see next chapter). All we know for certain is that the Wallachian warlord and the Dutch devotional painter (who created most of his works in the decades immediately following Vlad's death) were both singular products of their Christian faith, and it's certainly within the boundaries of possibility that the mass atrocities at Tîrgovişte and other locations filtered their way into the mythology of Northern European religious art.

***

The aftermath of the Forest of the Impaled episode offers a number of puzzles beyond the numbers and identity of the cadavers who were the horrific scene's Vlad's contribution to improving military however, for he is also the man who invented psychological warfare. In his 1977 essay, 'Vlad the Impaler – Current Parallels with a Medieval Romanian Prince', George Cioranescu quotes the Romanian soldier Lieutenant

Colonel Constantin Cazanisteanu, who observes that '"in addition to traditional tactics, Vlad was also capable of perfectly handling the methods of psychological warfare," demoralizing the enemy who, in the vicinity of the city of Tîrgovişte, ran into a whole forest of Turks impaled at the order of the Wallachian prince. As a result, the Turks lost their military confrontations with the Romanians. "The Sublime Porte [Ottoman Empire] was obliged to show respect for a country that had proved it could, at any time, produce a man of Vlad the Impaler's stature; it was compelled to revise its claims upon a prince who was determined to make no concessions."' Cioranescu's second quote is from Cezar Avram's 1976 article, 'A Brilliant Personality of Our National History', which suggests the Communist state-sponsored nationalistic slant of such a conclusion.

For all that, less-biased versions of the progress of the Ottoman invasion of Wallachia in 1462 largely agree that, in the wake of discovering the Forest of the Impaled, Mehmet turned his horse around and headed back east. Most are willing to accept the explanation that the Sultan was so horrified by what he saw that he lost all stomach for the fight with his ruthless opponent. It's an anomaly that doesn't bear much scrutiny. For one thing, Mehmet was no stranger to bloodshed and torture – indeed, in common with many Ottoman leaders he had been responsible for more than his share. For another, even if the Sultan abandoned Tîrgovişte in the company of much of his army, a substantial force remained in Wallachia under the command of Radu the Handsome. Dracula's ghoulish masterstroke of psychological warfare was not the turning point conventional accounts often suggest. It was actually the prelude to Vlad's downfall, one of his last acts as Voivode before he was obliged to make a desperate flight westward, leaving his hated brother Radu in command of the capital with nothing to stop him claiming the Wallachian throne. One intriguing possibility is that previous histories haven't fully understood the thinking behind the Forest of the Impaled.

Why didn't Dracula simply fall back to Tîrgovişte and man the defences, in imitation of Skanderbeg's successful strategy at Krujë in 1450? As we've already suggested, this may have reflected weaker defences in the Wallachian capital and weaker loyalties among his officers. The military historian and wargamer John Bianchi reflects such a view in his own assessment of why Dracula concluded his showdown with Mehmet with a humiliating retreat to Transylvania accompanied only by a skeleton force of supporters. 'I think Vlad's campaign was essentially doomed because he never had the chance to establish loyalties in his own country that would guarantee his forces would hold together. Wallachia was always an Ottoman vassal through this period and also always a Hungarian vassal – meaning that Wallachian princes never knew how firm a footing they were on. Skanderbeg didn't face quite the same situation. Even his family's enemies, the Thopias, found themselves against the Ottomans more often than with them. Had Vlad been in power even a few more years before 1462, he could have weathered the last attack and chased the Ottomans all the way back beyond the Danube.'

This still leaves us with the question of the Forest of the Impaled – sufficient apparently to frighten off Mehmet the Conqueror, a seasoned campaigner with plentiful blood on his own hands, but not enough to scare away an untried, comparative innocent like Radu the Handsome. Pestilence and famine followed campaigning armies as surely as night followed day, and, as we've already suggested, claimed many more victims than swords or arrows. Tantalising records suggest that plague had shadowed the Ottoman army in Wallachia, apparently actively encouraged by Dracula by infiltrating the afflicted into the Turkish army, and perhaps even creating the unhealthiest landscape he could for the advancing invaders. (Swamps, of course, spread other diseases than the plague, but it's unlikely Vlad would have made the distinction.) Might the Forest of the Impaled have been another aspect of the Voivode's innovative experiments in biological warfare? (From a purely pop culture perspective, it's an intriguing if tenuous link, considering the enduring links between vampirism and contagion in both traditional vampire lore and modern media manifestations.)

Classic medieval germ warfare consisted of hurling infected cadavers at the enemy, but this was a tactic only appropriate in attack for a force equipped with siege weaponry. What might be the equivalent defensive tactic? Placing numerous rotting corpses in the direct path of enemy advance, secured by poles perhaps? Might the Forest of the Impaled have been composed, at least in part, of plague victims? This is largely speculation, but offers a more plausible explanation for the effect Dracula's infamous display had on Mehmet the Conqueror. Nothing would motivate the Sultan to abandon the sun-baked plains of Wallachia faster than the prospect of plague, an indiscriminate assassin that claimed kings and commoners alike. If this does help explain some of the more puzzling aspects of this incident, it is only one piece of the puzzle, even if it's an important one. It's impossible to ignore the propensity for impalement Dracula had already established, and even today biological warfare remains an inexact, unreliable weapon. Yet the idea that the fleeing Impaler's last desperate parting shot was in part a bacterial threat explains why it frightened the Sultan so effectively, and indeed – if plague was breaking out – why Dracula's own forces melted away so rapidly.

There were other explanations for why Vlad may have suddenly found his support ebbing at such a rapid rate, reasons that test our now familiar question of whether it is better to be feared than loved. Dracula's efforts to defend Wallachia against an invasion he had himself provoked had left the realm a basket case. The Hungarian alliance which the Voivode had made a central pillar of his strategy – itself an unpopular political move among many Vlachs – had conspicuously failed to materialise. When Vlad had stood up as a Crusader against the Turks, the rest of Europe had offered nothing more than supportive words. Whatever modern Romanian strategists like Lieutenant Colonel Constantin Cazanisteanu may say, Vlad Dracula's campaign against the Turks had proven a costly, if valiant, failure. One which concluded with the defeated Voivode racing towards his castle at Poenari, his stronghold on the Transylvanian border, rebuilt, according to popular lore, by the enslaved boyars who had survived his infamous purge of Wallachia's aristocracy in the Easter of 1457.

A truly Machiavellian cynic might conclude that his savage purge had not been brutal enough. Dracula desperately tried to muster the meagre forces that remained to him from his mountain refuge, his only option now clearly to attempt to regroup and make yet more pleas for assistance from the Hungarian King. Meanwhile, Radu the Handsome was presenting his case to the aristocracy of Wallachia. Finally proving himself more than a pretty face, Dracula's brother approached the boyars with an outstretched hand, in contrast to Vlad's mailed fist. Wallachia had been an Ottoman vassal for many years – was alliance with the Turks really such an imposition? Radu offered peace and cosmopolitan values in contrast to his brother's draconian justice and fevered hatred of Islam. In many respects, Radu's words were sweet reason, the sort of sensible diplomatic argument that should prevail in order to avoid the kind of brutal strife which swallowed Yugoslavia in the 1990s. From a more hostile perspective, this is the kind of self-serving collaboration and appeasement that facilitated the rise of the Third Reich. In Wallachia in 1462, Radu's candidature was welcomed, from both a war-weary population and an aristocracy sick of living under a pall of fear and paranoia. Wallachia had a new Voivode, and Vlad Dracula was once more a fugitive, his enemies hot on his heels...

CHAPTER XII

Rogue's Galleries and Chambers of Horror

As we have seen, Vlad Dracula had the dubious pleasure of living in – and contributing to – what the oft-quoted Chinese curse of questionable provenance describe as 'interesting times'. (Somewhat appropriately, the fate is third in a triad of unfortunate circumstances preceded by 'May you come to the attention of those in authority' and 'May you find what you are looking for'.) His era represented the period where gunpowder transformed warfare. Previously something of a wild card on the battlefield – unreliable status symbols most effective at damaging enemy morale – it was in the 15th century that firearms and cannons established themselves as indispensable components of a well-equipped army. More directly relevant to Dracula's story, at numerous levels, were burgeoning innovations in printing technology. The pen may or may not be mightier than the sword, but astute leaders soon learned that printing presses could do as much damage to their enemies as the latest innovations from the smoky depths of the artillerist's workshops. Black ink did at least as much to precipitate Dracula's downfall as black gunpowder.

Whether from bad luck, bad judgement or sheer bloody-mindedness, Vlad successfully alienated some of Europe's most energetic print innovators during his early years as Voivode. The Germans were leading the field in revolutionising print technology in the mid-1400s, facilitating the mass production of books and documents, so when Dracula lashed out at Transylvania's Germanic population with his early atrocities, he unwittingly triggered a wave of bad press that swept westward across Europe. His principal Saxon victims were also from those sectors of society most likely to be literate, and to have strong links to networks of support that transcended national borders. Some might argue that his brutal treatment of Transylvania's Saxon merchant class was justified – at least by the standards of the age – as a legitimate response to the economic repression of the native Vlach population. Some might even suggest that Vlad's murderous hostility to the German monks in his Eastern Orthodox realm was an understandable – if extreme – reaction to generations of Catholic evangelism, where the clergy routinely operated as spies and agents of sedition against Orthodox governments. It's certainly true, however, that in Dracula's decision to subject the region's influential German-speaking population to the horrific 'justice' that became his trademark, Vlad inadvertently gave voice to his many victims. The early printing presses of Europe would immortalise Dracula; the pages that came off the presses in Vienna, Nuremberg, Bamberg and Leipzig some 500 years ago would ensure the Impaler an afterlife in ink, not least in books such as the one you now hold in your hands.

Most modern manifestations of the 15th-century Voivode come via his cloaked, undead namesake, as conjured by the Victorian author Bram Stoker in his 1897 Gothic novel *Dracula*. As already suggested, the extent of any relationship between the historical figure and the fictional vampire is hotly contested. Many Romanian patriots, however, are in little doubt that it was Stoker's chiller that triggered the avalanche of Western media which rebranded a Wallachian hero as the Prince of Darkness, and turned his Transylvanian birthplace into the archetypal home of supernatural evil. Yet Stoker's novel was far from Vlad's first appearance in the realms of horror literature. We must step a little carefully here, for the term 'horror' to describe a genre wasn't coined until the 1930s, in response to the success of a new style of Hollywood thriller, not least *Dracula*, starring the Hungarian actor Bela Lugosi. (It was the 1931 film, and not Stoker's source novel, which actually made Dracula into a household name.)

Yet the Dracula pamphlets of the 1400s were unquestionably sold on their capacity to horrify the reader, even if the concept of a dedicated horror genre was still centuries away. They were also works of political propaganda, the later versions perhaps documents of lurid historical record, but the chief selling point was a promise of ghoulish chills. These were advertised most obviously via the woodcut illustrations that decorated some of their covers. They did not depict Vlad the warrior battling the Turks (and pamphlets detailing the atrocities of the Turks were popular), or the Voivode governing his subjects, but Dracula the monster, surrounded by the transfixed and butchered remains of his victims. If there had been horror movie posters in the Middle Ages, they'd have looked a little like these grim little woodcuts. (As an aside then, it is perhaps curious that some take such offence at the confusion between Stoker's vampire Count and the 15th-century warlord. Compared to the Voivode's career of wholesale brutality, the Count's designs on the necks of a few demure Victorian virgins seem positively benevolent. If anyone were in a position to sue for defamation of character over the confusion, it should surely be the fictional Count!)

We don't know whether Bram Stoker ever saw any of these lurid pamphlets. He certainly had access to one at the British Library, and Florescu and McNally suggest it's quite possible that the author looked at the pamphlet and its morbid cover illustration, though the ever-sceptical Elizabeth Miller points out that there is no evidence for it. Perhaps more intriguing is whether Vlad had ever seen, or was at least aware of, the macabre printed accounts of his misdeeds. If so, what did he think? Was he insulted? Pleased that his psychological warfare had proven so successful? We don't know, though Dracula wasn't shy of boasting of the butchery during his campaign against the Turks in 1461, sending not just accounts of his massacres, but those grisly souvenirs to the King of Hungary. Vlad would no doubt have been less than impressed to find his portrait hanging in the galleries of Ferdinand, Archduke of Austria, at the Archduke's castle of Ambras in the 1500s. For Vlad's likeness wasn't housed in Ferdinand's impressive gallery of portraits, or among his collection of fine militaria, but in the Archduke's cabinet of curiosities.

There, Vlad's picture was kept company by paintings of those who had become extraordinary by virtue of genetic conditions or accidents – men who had survived with lances through their heads or had been born with withered limbs – 'freaks', in the bigoted lexicon of the carnival barker. There is, however, nothing to suggest anything abnormal about the subject in this, the best known of the portraits of Vlad the Impaler. (It seems likely to be a copy of an original which the Voivode actually sat for, and which many believe was the inspiration for the appearance of Dracula in many of the early German pamphlets.) Rather, the portrait belonged in Ferdinand's collection of bizarre and macabre curios because its subject was a moral aberration. The fact that Ferdinand, a noble who also fought against the Turks, considered him in this light might just have offended Vlad. Dracula was quite clearly being almost literally demonised long before Bram Stoker began looking for a suitable name for the villain in his new supernatural shocker.

Ultimately, however, did it matter? Was Vlad's almost mythic reputation for cruelty beyond his own borders justified? Part of the answer to the first question rests quite heavily on how much importance you attach to your own legacy. While Vlad came down to us through history as 'the Impaler', his cousin Stefan, Voivode of Moldavia, enjoys a far more flattering reputation in the history books. This is despite apparently allying with the Turks in the summer of 1462 and attacking the very man who put him on the throne, his friend Vlad, when Dracula was at his most vulnerable. It's an unedifying incident that most Romanian historians prefer to gloss over. Stefan's long rule and future successes against the Ottomans have earned him an unassailable place in Romanian history which leaves little room for such uncomfortable suggestions of duplicity and opportunism. Yet, had Vlad defeated Mehmet in 1462 and successfully struck back at his ungrateful Moldavian neighbour, might we now be referring to Vlad the Great and Stefan the Impaler?

Dr Constantin Rezachevici's article, 'Punishments with Vlad Tepeş' suggests just such a possibility. The Romanian historian attempts to defend Dracula's legacy, both by suggesting his reputation for cruelty has been overstated, and attempting to show many other contemporary rulers were at least as bad. Among those he chooses for points of comparison is Stefan (anglicised as Stephen in this version of the essay): 'Stephen the Great, voivode of Moldova (1457-1504), whom seventeenth-century chroniclers named "the Good" and who was ordained in 1993 as "The Rightful Voivode Stephen the Great and Saint," was no less cruel than Vlad Tepeş. After the victory in the battle near Vaslui, on 10 January 1475, he impaled almost all the Turkish prisoners, except the prominent ones: then he burned the corpses, leaving heaps of bones, according to Polish chronicler Jan Dlugosz. The same chronicler informed that during the battle at Lipnic, with the Tartars, Stephen the Great made the son of the Han (ruler) of Crimea his prisoner. The Han sent 100 envoys who demanded the release of his son – in a threatening, cheeky tone. Stephen ordered that the son be quartered, in the presence of the envoys, who were then impaled, except one – whose nose was cut, then sent to the Han to tell him what he had seen. It is difficult to believe that Tepeş could have acted any more roughly.'

There's more. Rezachevici relates how on 27 February 1470, Stephen attacked the Danubian port of Braila, in Valahia, where 'he shed much blood and burnt the town to the ground, and left no-one alive, not even the children in the womb of their mothers'. Then again, after the victory of 28 November 1473, against 13,000 Turks and 6,000 Valahians, 'whoever fell alive in his hands he impaled – through the

243

navels, one on top of the other – some 2300 of them. And he stood there in their midst for two days.' This is a nightmarish scene, worthy of Vlad Țepeș, described matter-of-factly by someone who was undoubtedly an eyewitness. So how does Rezachevici account for the disparity in the reputations between the sainted Voivode of Moldavia and his monstrous cousin? It wasn't because Stefan's excesses went unrecorded – Rezachevici states that the Moldavian even sent a copy of one such account to Nuremberg himself in 1502. The difference was twofold. One was that a co-ordinated campaign of black propaganda against Dracula suited the purposes of the Hungarian King, who some accuse of helping to finance it. The other was that, as we have already noted, Vlad's Saxon victims were uniquely well-placed to disseminate such material courtesy of the state-of-the-art printing technology available to their compatriots in Germany.

***

'These stories were preserved in pamphlets that seem to have had quite a wide readership across Europe,' acknowledges Kim Newman in his interview for the 2009 *True Horror*: 'Dracula' documentary. 'They were full of all the lurid details of the terrible things he'd done. There's a very tabloid edge to this sort of literature. It's sensational literature; the real reason it's a best-seller is that it's very gruesome stuff.' Indeed, the original Germanic Dracula stories – the so-called Saxon pamphlets – may have been among the only non-religious bestsellers of 15th-century Europe. In the TV doc's presentation of their origins, it also managed to add another thin layer of the mythologisation that's been underway ever since the first thousand pamphlets rolled off the early post-Gutenberg presses.

'Our key sources for Dracula are the experiences of three religious men,' narrates regular TV and radio historian Tessa Dunlop. 'Brother Jacob, Brother Hans, Brother Michael – and the youngest, and historically the most important, was Jacob.' In one of the TV show's key (and least bloody) dramatic reconstructions, fresh-faced Jacob (barely out of adolescence), nervous Michael and stoic fatalist Hans await their fates in the Voivode's dungeon. They are German Catholic monks of the Benedictine order, and have been arrested (the original pamphlets, rather than the film, suggest) in 1462, in the wake of Vlad's persecution of the Saxon merchants and a tyrant's paranoid belief that the social or ethnic groups he has wronged are conspiring against him.

In an interesting unintentional twist, the programme's makers, in seeking to illuminate the 'true story', have woven elusive fragments of fact ever more closely into the elements of myth. There can be little doubt of Brother Jacob's existence – he provided the first accounts of Vlad for the minnesinger (court minstrel or troubadour) Michel Beheim, which in turn formed the basis of his epic ballad on Vlad Dracula's excesses. Beheim was a popular performer, and his 'Dracula' became his greatest hit, particularly with his most powerful patron, Emperor Ladislaus V, and may well have provided the model for the popular German pamphlets which followed. *True Horror*'s chief historical authority on Vlad, author M. J. Trow, has however opined in his own study that Brothers Michael and Hans may have been fictional constructs, righteous victims created to throw into sharp relief how fortunate Jacob was to survive the Voivode's court.

'The three monks waiting in their cell knew that they were going to have this day of reckoning when they were going to be summoned,' narrates Ms Dunlop the media historian, with no hint that the narrative may be apocryphal. 'But they didn't know when they were going to be summoned, what they were going to be asked. There was no surety when it came to Vlad, you *did not know* what the outcome would be. He *enjoyed* having that power over people, he clearly enjoyed watching them squirm.'

It's dramatic stuff, irrespective of the fact that the despot described with such certainty is one of the more shadowy and unknowable figures of late medieval history. In the tradition of low-budget horror movies, the drama-doc's budgetary restrictions lend it a claustrophobic intensity that works in its favour. Outside the monks' cell door, we see a sharpened pike that carries obvious implications. 'You have a stake placed outside a cell and you see that all the time through the only window you've got,' narrates Mei Trow somewhat fancifully. 'It was placed there deliberately, under Vlad's orders, for maximum psychological pressure.' The detail of the stakes outside the cell appears to come from another episode in the Vlad legend: in Trow's own book he describes this psychological terror tactic as applied to 'emissaries sent by Matthias Corvinus, king of Hungary'. (In fairness to Mei Trow, he may have been subject to the classic TV doc editing techniques whereby interviewees appear to support hypotheses of which they are quite unaware.) Any attempt to strip away the myth of Vlad the Impaler and arrive at some ultimate 'truth' is, it seems, fated only to add further layers of mythology.

'We certainly know that Vlad liked to play his mind games, and he would lay traps for people,' seconds Laura Richards, a forensic psychologist noted for her contributions to TV docs on Jack the Ripper and the Moors Murders. 'He's incredibly narcissistic; people are there for his own enjoyment.' It seems a sound enough judgement, if one bears in mind that Ms Richards is relying on 15th-century pamphlets and folk tales rather than an interview with the subject at Broadmoor psychiatric hospital. 'There was no real way of getting around Vlad and his twisted mind,' continues Tessa Dunlop with her own narrative. 'This man was volatile, inconsistent, totally arbitrary in the way that he took or made decisions. So the monks waiting in their cell, knowing they were going to have this day of reckoning, a time when they were summoned to account for themselves in front of Vlad, would not have known how to play their cards.' The 'Day of Reckoning' scene, as a piece of dramatised folklore, makes its point effectively.

***

'A Gregorian monastery so poor it can't provide shoes?' Vlad asks mockingly of the barefoot monks.

'We are of the Benedictine order, my lord,' replies earnest Hans. 'We dress humbly to seek our place in Heaven.'

'How quickly do you want to get there?' retorts the Impaler, and the guards laugh.

'As quickly as our Lord demands.'

'And who is your Lord?'

Hans hesitates a moment. 'The same as yours, my lord.'

Vlad addresses the youthful and clearly terrified Jacob. 'You, come closer. Tell me, where do you think I will go when I die?' Jacob is naturally hesitant. 'ANSWER ME! Tell me, before I kill you. Slowly.'

'Let me answer you, my lord', Brother Michael suddenly implores.

'Now Michael faced an agonising choice,' interjects Trow as narrator. 'As a Christian he must have known that Vlad's soul was going to burn forever in hellfire.'

Instead, the monk indulges in a classic piece of theological sophistry: 'I know that you will attain salvation, because your appointment is by God. God in Heaven knows the good you have done. Who else could defend a modest country like Wallachia against Islam? Men have misunderstood you on Earth, but in Heaven you will be vindicated.'

'In that split second in which he had to make up his mind,' comments Trow, 'he lied. Vlad Dracula was no fool. He knew exactly what Michael was doing; he was lying to try to save his skin.'

'Goodbye,' Vlad calmly announces, and Michael is impaled on the spot.

'So, little one, come,' the Impaler says as he calmly resumes terrorising Jacob. 'Would you lie to me too? No. No, you are still pure. Still so pure. Tell me, little one,' he intones threateningly, 'where will I go when I die?'

'Prepare a stake for me!' howls Hans, full of indignation. 'You kill in the name of God but you will never, ever meet Him. It's possible even the Devil himself will not bother with you! But if he does, you will be discarded to the darkest corner of Hell. Yours will be an eternity of isolation, and insignificance. Alone, weak.'

Vlad explodes, demanding to perform the impalement himself. But amidst his fatal pain and suffering, Hans retains a sense of irony: 'Thank you, my lord,' he gasps. 'You are bringing me closer to my true Lord, the true power, and the glory, the one who rules in Heaven and Earth, and in this pitiful country you claim to rule! Bastard!'

Vlad cuts him short by plunging a dagger into his chest. Hans pushes the dagger down to speed the process, and dies with his hand clutching Vlad's face.

***

'Hans knew he was going to die, so he stood up to Vlad,' comments Mei Trow. 'I'd like to think that Hans regarded it as a triumph, in the split second before he died. I think he would have regarded it as victory.' It's a dramatically satisfying moment, with the historian's comments underlining the defiant self-destruction one finds in a blood-and-thunder historical epic movie like *Spartacus* or *The Vikings*. The only caveat is that the scene – as Trow himself acknowledges in his book – may be entirely fictional. But to deride it purely on this basis would be to overlook the resonance of myth and legend. The above dramatisation is based on how the story is told in the original Beheim epic poem, entitled *The Story of a Bloodthirsty Madman Called Dracula of Wallachia*. In the Russian version of the Dracula stories brought back to the court of Ivan III by Fedor Kuritsyn, the situation is reversed. Here there are only two monks (Hungarian this time) who are being held prisoner and asked about the welfare of Vlad's immortal soul.

'You have done badly,' answers the first, fearlessly pious monk in the manner of the Saxon version's Hans. 'You punish without mercy.' The second gives an altogether more obsequious response: 'God gave you, monarch, your powers to punish wrong-doers and reward those doing good. Certainly they have done evil and have received what they deserved,' he flatters, apparently self-servingly. But the result is different this time. The flattering monk is given a payment in gold coin and safe passage to the Hungarian border; the monk who dares to condemn piously is 'impaled from the bottom up'.

The different outcomes of the two versions fulfilled different needs: in the Saxon version, Vlad's mercilessness and impiety demonise him as a persecutor of humanity; in the tsarist Russian version, we are given a blunt lesson in the divine right of the autocrat to rule as he pleases, in the cause of holding a volatile society together. In the 21st-century television version of the story, the real punchline is held till the end. 'Now you,' Vlad demands yet again of the youthful Brother Jacob, 'tell me where I will go when I die.'

'It's a very, very difficult question to answer,' underlines M. J. Trow. 'What on earth could Jacob say which would mean that he survived? We don't know what answer Jacob gave, it's not recorded. But whatever he said, he did survive.' Indeed, we don't know if Jacob was compelled to answer the question at all, as we don't know whether the scenario ever really took place. But it serves its purpose in delineating the origin of the Dracula legends. 'The Dracula story gets out with Brother Jacob,' notes Kim Newman, 'who gets away alive. That's why the name "Dracula" is kind of carved in blood across the archive.' 'Brother Jacob's stories of Dracula were retold in pamphlets and spread across Europe,' read the documentary's closing subtitles. 'Dracula's bloody legacy, fact and fiction, began with the release of Brother Jacob.'

The film neglects to go further into Vlad's fearsome reputation as a warrior against the Ottomans, his controversial status in Romania's national mythology, or even to touch upon the circumstances of his death, again probably due to budgetary limitations. But it does at least acknowledge (if only implicitly) how what we do know of Vlad's atrocious deeds is largely dependent on propaganda pamphlets from the 15th and 16th centuries.

The stories that originated in Michel Beheim's epic ballad eventually fragmented into a number of oft-repeated tales told in Germanic dialect. M. J. Trow numbers these at 32 stories in total (while also suggesting that some may have received a sensational rewrite in the court of Corvinus, to further blacken Vlad's reputation). The pamphlets began to be distributed – mostly via the monasteries of Mitteleuropa at first – as early as 1463, well within the Impaler's lifetime. As we know, his grisly reputation would long outlive him, and the stories about him seem to have posthumously gained in popularity.

By 1499, one of the German pamphlets contained the now famous woodcut of Vlad enjoying his feast among the impaled dead and dying of Braşov. The text begins ominously, if rather quaintly: 'Here begins a very cruel frightening story about a wild bloodthirsty man, Dracula the *voivod*. How he impaled people and roasted them and hacked them into pieces like a head of cabbage.' It's a peculiar image that recurs many times. 'There is lurid description page after page of just how awful it was,' says Mei Trow in the TV doc. 'Of how people were impaled and they were hacked to pieces, their heads removed like cabbages, the images are absolutely horrific! And this is the important thing: some of it was based on fact.'

Exactly how much of this is factually correct remains a moot point, of course. But the vegetable imagery seems to suggest the bland staple diet of much of Europe at the time – that is, boiled cabbage leaves mostly leavened with black bread or potatoes, perhaps with a little meat, should the diners be affluent enough to have access to slaughtered cattle, swine or poultry. That the metaphor recurs so often ('he had men hacked up like cabbage') also seems to suggest a flaying of the flesh, a peeling away of the top layers of skin that can only find its simile in the light flowering leaves of the cabbage plant. ('And then he ordered that some of his people be buried naked to the navel … He also had many roasted and the skin peeled off others.') It reaches its bizarre apotheosis in the following description: 'In the year 1460, on St Bartholomew's Day in the morning, Dracula crossed the forest with his servants and looked for the Saxons, of both sexes, around the village of Amlas and all those that he could gather together he ordered to be thrown, one on top of the other, like a hill and to slaughter them like cabbage, with swords and knives [...] And then, he ordered that more of his boyars be decapitated and he took their heads and he used them to grow cabbage. After this, he invited their friends to his house and he gave them the cabbage to eat. And he said to them: "Now you eat the heads of your friends." After this he ordered that all of them be impaled.'

Vlad III in the Germanic pamphlets is undoubtedly a monster. 'He had a big family uprooted,' reads one of the descriptions of his attacks on Braşov and its satellite towns in the late 1450s, 'from the smallest to the largest, children, friends, brothers, and he had them all impaled.' This was reputedly the family of Albert the Great, defector to the Danesti, the demise of whose proclaimed heir to the throne, Dan III, is also described: '[Vlad] had them make a grave according to the custom of the Christians and he had [Dan's] body slaughtered by the grave.'

Many of the atrocities already described or imagined in this book are recounted, again in the folkloric language of the fairytale. Others stand alone as one-off atrocities: 400 'young boys and others from many lands' who have come to Wallachia as students to learn the language are slaughtered all together, on suspicion of being spies: 'He had a great pot made with [...] a great fire made underneath it and had water poured into the pot and had men boiled in this way.' A gypsy tribe are made to cook and eat one of their own number when he is caught stealing – and in a variation on the same theme, 300 gypsies are compelled to 'eat the others until there are none left'. We also hear that 'he had mothers impaled and nursing children, and he had one- and two-year-old children impaled'.

As one of the Saxon pamphlets claimed, 'All the bloodthirsty persecutors of Christendom, such as Herod, Nero, Diocletian and other pagans, had never thought up or made such martyrs as did this bloodthirsty berserker.' (All in the supposed defence of Christendom, of course, though Vlad's wrath knows no bounds: '[the victims] were pagans, Jews, Christians, heretics and Wallachians'.) There may be kernels of truth in all of the above – even perhaps a smidgeon in the old wives' tale about growing cabbages from severed heads – but it's clear that the Saxon Vlad was growing into a mythic monster and a gothic archetype: the 'real Dracula' indeed.

***

The legend of Billy the Kid, the young cattlehand-turned-outlaw killed at age 21, has spawned dozens of books and scores of films. Throughout most of the 120-year period since his death, the 'official' history has been that recounted in the book ostensibly written by Sheriff Pat Garrett, who shot dead the Kid: *The Authentic Life of Billy the Kid, the Noted Desperado of the Southwest, Whose Deeds of Daring and Blood Made His Name a Terror in New Mexico, Arizona and Northern Mexico.*

But in fact Garrett's memoir was ghost-written by a man named Ash Upson, an alcoholic ex-newspaperman. Suspiciously, where it's stated that the Kid was born in New York City on 23 November 1859, this was the date (though not the year) of Upson's own birthday. Around the turn of the third millennium, the century-old legend was further undermined by research suggesting the Kid was really a second-generation Irish immigrant christened Henry McCarty – not William H. Bonney, as legend has it, though this seems to have been an alias. Such is the mystery surrounding him; it's no longer even certain whether the classic photo of Billy the Kid – showing a surly-looking, squat young man leaning on a rifle – is definitely McCarty/Bonney.

In fact, few of the details of the Kid's popular biography stand up to scrutiny. His infamy rests on the belief that, according to Ash Upson, 'Billy killed 21 men, one for each year of his life!' Legend has it that he committed his first murder aged 12, while protecting his mother from bullies in Silver City, New Mexico – but the recent historical research suggests his family were living in Kansas at the time. It is, however, a fact that his first arrest was in 1875, aged 16, for stealing clothes from a Chinese laundry, after which he escaped jail the same day. Billy was next heard of in New Mexico three years later, able to speak fluent Spanish and riding with an outlaw gang known as the Regulators – fiercely loyal to cattle rancher J. H. Tunstall, who would be murdered during the Lincoln County Cattle Wars. Despite the litany of murders attributed to him, the Kid's first substantiated killing would occur when he shot a blacksmith named Frank Cahill in Camp Grant, Arizona.

It's said that Billy killed him because of an insult, but research by New Mexico's Billy the Kid Outlaw Gang (a Wild West historical group) suggests that, after an argument over a card game, Cahill wrestled Billy to the ground, whereupon Billy grabbed Cahill's own gun and shot him. The Kid was found guilty of murder and sentenced to hang, but was helped to escape – during which, still wearing shackles, he gunned down two deputies named Bell and Ollinger. Despite the Regulators executing several men believed responsible for the murder of Tunstall, only one of those killings can be directly attributed to the Kid: that of a bounty hunter named Joe Grant, which, once again, can be defined as self-defence in a sum total of four historically verifiable killings.

***

In 1991, an action movie was produced for the family audience by India's vast film industry, in the Tamil language. *Captain Prabhakaran* pitted the heroic forest ranger of the title against a fearsome jungle bandit (or *dacoit*) with a bushy moustache, named Veerappan. The character was so fierce that it seemed perfectly in keeping for him to cut off the head of one of the eponymous hero's colleagues and display it to taunt the police. What seems more remarkable is that the villain was based on a genuine dacoit gang leader, then at large, and that for much of the Southern Indian Tamil audience he already held the status of a folk hero.

Koose Muniswamy Veerappan had first taken to the forests of the Karnataka region aged 18, to join a gang of poachers. Coming to the ascendant as a gang leader, his status as India's foremost ivory poacher (his number of elephant kills is estimated at up to 2000, though a sympathetic journalist dropped one of the zeros in his interview with the fugitive) and smuggler of sandalwood paints him as a one-man environmentalist's nightmare. But in rural regions, where the industrious poor would give anything to join the environmentally rapacious global economy, he became known as 'India's Robin Hood'.

Exactly how heroic Veerappan was seems to be determined by which ethnic subgroup his defenders or detractors belong to. There is little disputing his ruthlessness: in 1987, he kidnapped a government forestry officer and hacked him to death; he also abducted and murdered five members of another gang of poachers. Over the next several years, the killings of local police officials culminated in the shooting and decapitation of the region's deputy conservator of forests, by the name of Srinivas. It was this event that was alluded to in the *Captain Prabhakaran* movie – though Srinivas's decomposed head was only found, displayed on a rock in a Vlad-style tactic to terrorise Veerappan's enemies, two years after the film's release.

It was the kind of behaviour that made him a menace to the authorities and an outlaw hero to the rural poor – those poor who also lionised dacoits like Phoolan Devi (the 'Bandit Queen'). In 1991, the same year as the Tamil action movie, a highly popular Kannada language action film simply called *Veerappan* starred Indian movie hero Devaraj in the title role. At the film's fictional climax, when Veerappan is apparently placed under arrest by a special taskforce of forest rangers, he is revealed to be a decoy who leaves the real dacoit leader at liberty.

The authentic Veerappan – formerly a shadowy, semi-mythical figure, before the Indian movie industry put a spotlight on him – was powerful enough to adopt paramilitary tactics against the special taskforce assigned to capture him, killing several dozen in audacious raids with firearms and grenades. It was acts like the 1993 mining of a bus that killed 43 passengers – civilians as well as police – that provided a different perception of him outside his ethnic group and caste, and in the Bollywood movie industry. By the time he was represented in a mainstream Hindi film, 1999's *Sarfarosh*, the fierce character 'Veeran' (Veerappan is actually Tamil for 'brave') was depicted as a Tamil terrorist.

***

The Russian storytellers and folklorists who engaged their people with their own variations on *Povesty o Mutyanskom Voyevode Drakule* were rather more forgiving of Vlad's excesses. Following in the footsteps of monk and chronicler Elfrosin the Sinner, they acclaim him 'as cruelly clever as his name' (meaning 'devil' here, rather than 'dragon'). He was also portrayed as a staunch moralist. 'Dracula so hated evil in his land that if someone committed a misdeed such as theft, robbery, lying or some injustice, he had no chance of staying alive,' notes one tale approvingly. 'Whether he was a nobleman or a monk or a priest or a common man, or even if he had great wealth, he could not escape death.' The narrator goes on to tell the folk tale about how the Impaler provided a fountain for thirsty travellers, whereat they could drink from a gold cup. Of course, the cup is never stolen for fear of an ignominious death.

This is reinforced by the famous tale of the robbed Hungarian merchant. When 160 ducats are stolen from the merchant's coach, the Voivode explodes and demands that the thief be apprehended or else. He also reimburses the merchant, but with a total of 161 ducats. When the Hungarian double-checks the amount, he makes a return visit to Prince Vlad to give back the extra coin. 'Go in peace,' commands Vlad sanguinely. 'If you had not told me about the additional coin, I was ready to impale you, together with the thief.' Again, this is recounted as a moral parable; the probability that Dracula imposed barbaric penalties mainly to assuage his own bloodlust remains unspoken.

Remaining popular during the reign of Ivan the Terrible (see Chapter Six), the Russian stories are infected with a simplistic self-righteousness that reveres the autocracy of the ruler above all else. Their variation on the nailing of the Turkish emissaries' turbans stresses that any ambassador who presented himself to the Voivode improperly dressed was playing dice with his own life. Sentencing one foreign diplomat to the stake, Vlad tells him, 'I am not guilty of your death, but your own sovereign.'

But the most bizarre moral piety is exhibited in the retelling of the Hungarian emissary's arrival at Braşov, where Vlad feasts heartily amidst the dead and the dying impaled. This time, the ambassadorial visitor exhibits neither displeasure nor disgust when instructed to join the Impaler's table. 'Monarch!' he exclaims. 'Should I have done anything that earned me the death sentence, do with me what you will. For you are a just and true judge.' It's a rather unconvincing take on a twice-told tale, taking the idea of the villain-as-hero – and indeed the willing victim – to the unlikeliest level.

VLAD THE IMPALER

***

Billy the Kid's downfall came about because, instead of crossing the Mexican border to safety, he rode for the home of the love of his life, Paulita Maxwell. It was there that her wealthy rancher brother alerted Sheriff Garrett to the Kid's presence. When outlaw-turned-lawman Garrett shot the young man through the chest, Billy never drew his gun – possibly because he never had the chance, or didn't believe his old acquaintance Garrett would kill him in cold blood (though some Wild West buffs theorise that Billy was unarmed). He lies buried in the military cemetery at Fort Sumner, New Mexico, where his grave and those of two of the Regulators are surrounded by iron bars to keep out souvenir hunters.

The recently unearthed testimony of his schoolteachers paints the young Henry McCarty as an intelligent and sensitive boy, with girlish features and a talent for singing and dancing that won him a lead part in a minstrel revue at the Silver City Music Theater. It was only at the age of 14, after his mother died of TB and he was placed in the care of a saloon keeper's family, that he drifted into the petty theft that resulted in him becoming a full-fledged outlaw. Ultimately, the Kid's sociopathic reputation may have been a result of scapegoating by the 'Santa Fe Ring', the cattle owners who had local politicians and law enforcers in their pockets. One journalist described him as a 'desperate cuss' who led a gang of rustlers, bandits, killers and rapists – by the time McCarty reached his 21st birthday, 'Billy the Kid' had become a byword for banditry, reputedly affording him much amusement.

Many myths originated in the popular *Billy the Kid* dime novels that followed. And further confusion is added by an outlaw who operated in the infamous town of Tombstone, William 'Billy the Kid' Claiborne, and anecdotal rumours that Texas outlaw 'Brushy Bill' Roberts – later a performer in Buffalo Bill Cody's Wild West Parade – was really the Kid, and escaped Garrett to live out his life in Mexico. Since the advent of the motion picture, the myth of Billy the Kid has vacillated between unbridled savagery and outlaw heroism. Waspish liberal littérateur Gore Vidal embraced the more savage legend in his screenplay for *The Left-Handed Gun* (1958), starring Paul Newman as a kind of Wild West James Dean. As one reviewer stated, 'Newman plays Billy as a mental defective who becomes enmeshed in a myth-making vice that is both his immortality and his destruction' – though in truth the Kid was well-educated and sent several erudite letters to New Mexico Governor Lew Wallace (author of *Ben-Hur*), to ask him for a pardon from his murder conviction. By the time of the 1989 Turner Network Television production, *Gore Vidal's Billy the Kid*, Vidal revised his view to depict a young man whose witnessing the murder of his friend/mentor/employer Tunstall sets him on a merciless but noble trail of revenge. In the most popular recent treatment of the legend, the two *Young Guns* films (1988/90) with Emilio Estevez as the Kid, the Regulators are a kind of Hollywood Brat Pack, whereas in reality Billy was the baby of the bunch. Later, in 2000, American historian Frederick Nolan published his edited and annotated version of *Pat F. Garrett's The Authentic Life of Billy the Kid*, illustrating how the legend of the Kid as a mass-murdering equivalent of the modern urban 'gang-banger' was a result of Garrett's self-justification.

***

In the late 1990s, victims of the Veerappan gang's ruthlessness included at least a further 19 police officers and nine government officials from Southern India's Karnataka Forest region. Tellingly perhaps, Veerappan himself was reputed to the executioner of his own son, familiarly known as 'Baby Veerappan'.

It was this ruthlessness that was reflected in the Hindi action movie *Jungle* (2000). 'Where beasts feared to tread, he made it his home. Where the scorching sun could not reach, he shined in the cold bloodedness. Where the police never managed to catch him, he always killed them,' ran the (possibly imperfectly translated) publicity tagline. There was little doubt where the inspiration for the character Durga Narayan Chaudhary (Bollywood character actor Sushant Singh) comes from – no heroic figure here, he holds a busload of passengers hostage for ransom, executing several of them.

It was contemporary to this film's release that the real Veerappan had his closest flirtation yet with the Bollywood film industry. On 30 July 2000 he kidnapped veteran Indian movie star Rajkumar and held him captive in the forest. It was a total of 109 days before Dr Rajkumar (as he was respectfully known by his Indian audience) was released, denying rumours of a large ransom payment to the dacoit, and of his own ill treatment. Indeed, some reports suggested that the actor had put on weight during his time in captivity, and that the usually murderous bandit may have been a little starstruck.

In 2001, Malayalam comic actor Mamukkoya was featured in the title role of *Korappan the Great*, as a leader of a gang of jungle dacoits sought by bounty hunters. In 2002, the kidnapping and gunshot execution of former Karnataka politician H. Nagappa did not seem to compromise the real Veerappan's heroic status among the rural Tamils who often sheltered him – knowing full well they risked retribution from the dacoit leader if they refused, and violence from the forestry police if they aided him. But it strengthened the resolve of the authorities to bring him to ground.

On 18 October 2004, Veerappan and four of his gang members left the forest to seek urgent eye surgery for the dacoit leader. An ambush, apparently by the pursuing Tamil Nadu Special Task Force, left the legendary jungle man and three others dead. Rumours that Veerappan had been drawn into a 'false encounter' – that is, set up for assassination – drew a sanguine response from a Karnataka government spokesman, who merely stated, 'You have every liberty to come to any conclusion.'

The hospital that held the bandit king's body was besieged by public mourners and sightseers. The regional government issued mortuary photos of Veerappan with one empty eye socket and a neat bullet-hole through his forehead. One further layer of legend was added by those who insisted that his trademark huge handlebar moustache had been drastically trimmed, and that therefore he may not have been the real Veerappan at all.

His grieving widow felt no such ambiguity. When it was suggested to her by producers from regional Makkal TV that they should dramatise her husband's life, she granted them a series of interviews apparently unaware that she was being recorded. When some of the detail found its way into the hit 2007 Indian series *Santhanakaadu* ('Sandal Wood'), which ran to 125 episodes, she naïvely believed that her widow status would allow her to block transmission. The broadcasts went ahead, and added their own layer of myth by suggesting the bullet-ridden dacoit had actually died by poisoning.

***

It wasn't until the 16th century that the popular stories of Vlad the Impaler began to turn up on his home territory, in the nascent Romania. As perhaps is unsurprising, some of these oft-old tales acquired a nationalistic spin. In the story of the visiting merchant, the missing money is measured at 100 lei (Romanian national currency), but the denouement is rather different: 'Master merchant, at my court people do not know what a lie is,' the Voivode proudly announces. For his supposed mendaciousness in pursuing an honest Romanian peasant for allegedly stolen money, it is the merchant who finds himself impaled on a stake.

Given that the vast majority of Romanians were of the peasant class and the Romanian language wasn't written down till the 1500s, the limited literacy of the era means that only a handful of Vlad stories (eight, according to M. J. Trow) were recorded in print by his native countrymen. This Dracula may still be a cruel despot, but in every other sense he's a moral exemplar: 'This prince was very severe, but also just. He would not tolerate thieves, liars and lazy people.' He's also ruthlessly single-minded in his pursuit of what's best for his Wallachian subjects. Even the mass impalement of 500 boyars and their families is recounted in mildly approving tones, the suggestion being that tough times in the land of the Vlach call for tough actions. In prescribing Vlad's punitive sadism as a panacea for the social ills of the time, the tone foreshadows the more sophisticated satire of the nationalist poet Eminescu (see Chapter Nine), who called for the resurrected Impaler to 'set fire to the prison and the lunatic asylum' – after first ensuring government officials were entombed therein. (The Romanian stories, while they predictably ascribe noble motive to Vlad's burning of the beggars, do at least undermine the eugenic ideal of eliminating the poor by wiping out one generation: 'Beggars will cease to exist only with the end of the world.')

And so the popular mid-European folklore of Vlad the Impaler passes from black propaganda to cautionary tales to hero-worshipping apologias for his deeds. In their fairytale-like accounts of his life, we can perhaps briefly glimpse some of the facets of this contradictory and near-inscrutable historical figure. But it is in popular culture that all such opposing aspects are finally synthesised and reconciled. By the time of Francis Ford Coppola's 1992 production of the rather presumptuously titled *Bram Stoker's Dracula*, the vampire count and the impaler prince are one – the latter seen to commit his atrocities only against the Turks, the marauding enemies of his country, thereby becoming a more morally acceptable monster for the audience.

The penny-dreadful approach to the biographies of contemporary rogues and villains throws up numerous alternative archetypes. After almost a century of legend and myth-making, the latter title character found his classic screen depiction in Sam Peckinpah's *Pat Garrett and Billy the Kid* (1973). It takes Garrett's characterisation of the Kid at his word – a long, lean, 30-year-old Kris Kristofferson plays the diminutive 21-year-old as a volatile, womanising, renegade figure, while the real Billy, as the recent research indicates, was raised by his late mother as a good Christian, a non-smoker who rarely drank, disdained profane language, never associated with prostitutes and was faithful to his one girlfriend. But Peckinpah's Billy is the violent rebel archetype that appealed to the *Wild Bunch* director – Bob Dylan's soundtrack songs urge Billy to hang onto his woman if he's got one, 'Remember once in El Paso you shot one' – a monstrous fictional act unrepresentative of young Henry McCarty.

At the time of Veerappan's shooting in 2004, Bollywood producer Ram Gopal Varma had a film in development entitled *Let's Catch Veerappan*. The course of events dictated a title change to *Let's Kill Veerappan*; at the time of writing this book, it has gone back into development (now just called *Veerappan*), one of two mooted Indian rival biopics. In an extremely rare interview with a sympathetic Tamil newspaper editor in 1996, the dacoit leader lamented the various cinematic depictions of himself. 'I have seen *The Godfather* a hundred times. That is the kind of film our filmmakers should make about me,' he insisted. In the interview, besides blithely admitting to somewhere over a hundred killings, it was revealed that Veerappan's great unfulfilled ambition was to achieve symbiosis with Bollywood and produce his own biopic of himself.

The three disparate figures of Vlad the Impaler, Billy the Kid and Veerappan are ultimately subject to the famous maxim coined in the Kid's natural idiom, the Western: 'When the legend becomes fact,' the newspaper editor in John Ford's *The Man Who Shot Liberty Valance* famously instructs, 'print the legend.'

***

We last left Vlad Dracula fleeing westward towards his lofty stronghold at Poenari in the dying days of the summer of 1462, with his brother Radu and a contingent of Turkish soldiers breathing hard down his neck. The events of the next few weeks have a storybook quality that almost begs fictional treatment, and indeed they have inspired episodes in recent films that have endeavoured to bridge the gap between the fictional vampire Count and his 15th-century historical namesake. Once installed at Poenari, Vlad knew that time was not on his side. The castle was, however, in a reassuringly precipitous location close to the Transylvanian border, where he anticipated a rendezvous with the young Hungarian king, Matthias Corvinus, to discuss plans to help him retake the Wallachian throne. Yet King Matthias was taking an agonisingly long time to reach their appointed meeting place at Braşov, and Dracula's pursuers were now approaching his mountain refuge.

Ominously, Radu's men had been delayed because they were manhandling a contingent of the fearsome Ottoman artillery to Poenari.

The Hungarian King's leisurely progress was no accident. Whilst we have hailed Dracula as a prototype Machiavellian prince, perhaps the mantle fits Matthias rather better. He was in no hurry to keep his appointment with the Voivode. Indeed, while greeting Dracula's pleas for assistance with a friendly face, behind the scenes the King was carefully preparing a character assassination of the controversial Wallachian crusader. Every inch the Renaissance Prince – Matthias assembled the most impressive library in Europe by many estimations – the Hungarian King appreciated the building power of the written word as a political weapon. There are two suggestions as to why Matthias planned to double-cross Dracula. Some suggest that he had effectively embezzled revenues raised in the name of launching a crusade against the Turks and spent them on securing his own position in Hungary. An authentic crusader against the Ottomans like Vlad not only made the cautious Hungarian look bad, but provided a viable scapegoat for his own failure to take the offensive. The other motivation was tied up in international politics. Threatened on his borders by rival Christian monarchs, the last thing Matthias needed was renewed conflict with the Ottomans. Dracula, whose overriding instinct was to attack, was a liability. A loose cannon like Vlad on his southern borders was a far bigger threat to his long-term plans than allowing an Ottoman puppet to take charge of Wallachia. Dracula was about to fall victim to a pincer movement by those two newest weapons on the battlefield: printed propaganda and gunpowder.

So the story goes, Dracula first became aware of an imminent assault upon his refuge at Poenari courtesy of a traitor in Radu's camp, still loyal to Vlad, who fired a message attached to an arrow through a castle window. The arrow extinguished a candle, before the archer saw Vlad's bride reading the message, warning the castle's defenders to flee as the walls would be no match for the Ottoman guns. As a result, Vlad's bride hurled herself into the river below rather than encounter the attacking Ottomans. (The episode is recreated in the prologue to the 1992 blockbuster *Bram Stoker's Dracula* to explain Vlad's enduring bitterness at the world, though the script takes substantial liberties with the original account to create a more romantic interpretation.) Dracula, however, fled, taking a secret passage out of the castle in order to avoid detection – in the ensuing pursuit, it is said he lost his infant son. (This detail features in the low-budget 2003 film *Vlad*, in another attempt to humanise the clichéd monster of modern mythology.)

Vlad now crossed the border into Transylvania, Hungarian territory, once more a fugitive with only his reputation, bravery and a few loyal troops to protect him. The wait must have seemed endless, but finally, as the last leaves began falling from the trees, news arrived that King Matthias had reached Braşov in November of 1462. While Vlad was anxious to begin his counter strike on his brother Radu as soon as humanly possible, Matthias prevaricated for a further five long weeks. Eventually, he agreed that Dracula should lead an expeditionary force back into Wallachia as the vanguard of a full-scale invasion by the Hungarians. It was a ruse. Once Dracula was safely outside of Hungarian jurisdiction, Matthias's men separated Vlad from his loyal troops, then arrested him and brought him back to Braşov as a prisoner.

The fact that Matthias went to such careful lengths to capture Vlad on neutral territory, after such a long delay, suggests a number of things. For one it illustrates the difference in style between a true Machiavellian like Matthias and a more impetuous character like Vlad, who was more inclined to act upon impulse or rage. For another, it shows that the Hungarian King was nervous of simply taking Dracula prisoner, even though he was effectively at his mercy. It wasn't so long, after all, since bells had been rung and feasts held in Dracula's honour in the capitals of Europe, celebrating the Voivode's victories over the Turks. Matthias produced a dossier of letters, purporting to be from Vlad to Mehmet and other leaders, offering to betray the Christian cause. Many European leaders of the day smelled a rat, and most modern historians dismiss the letters as forgeries, concocted by Matthias himself. It was here that the Hungarian King's more subtle propaganda campaign came into play. The idea of Dracula as a traitor to the Christian cause seemed doubtful to many. But Vlad's building reputation, fed by the popular German pamphlets, as 'the Impaler'– a dangerous maniac driven by sadism – was probably adequate to silence most public resistance to his arbitrary arrest.

While patriotic Romanian historians have blamed Bram Stoker's 1897 novel for stigmatising a national hero, in truth, Dracula had already been entrapped by horror stories during his own lifetime. The elephant in the room remains how accurate these medieval horror stories were: pure fiction, exaggeration, or authentic accounts of what might happen when a psychopath is allowed to wield unfettered power? Was Matthias Corvinus simply a Machiavellian shelving an inconvenient piece in the diplomatic game, or an enlightened ruler muzzling a mad dog? The answer to these questions is perhaps to be found in the inner workings of the Impaler himself. A private, even justifiably paranoiac figure, Dracula's soul remains a closed book, but his psychological profile offers a fertile field for informed speculation. The fascination with deviant behaviour that made the German pamphlets bestsellers 500 years ago certainly hasn't diminished. In the years following the printing revolution that began in Germany during Vlad's era, we have accumulated an increasing body of knowledge on what might motivate a man like Dracula…

CHAPTER XIII

Philosophy in the Abattoir

Desire subverted can turn sexual lust into a lust for violent conquest. On the wilder shores of pleasure, the furthest extremes of pain may wash up alongside all the other various psychic detritus. The joy in destruction shared by tyrants such as Vlad the Impaler or Ivan the Terrible can be seen as a distortion of the sexual drive found in all healthy human beings. Such are the explanations for the psychosexual condition we call sadism – to which we will soon return at length.

In the classic Freudian reading of sexuality, the idea that sex and death may be intertwined is encapsulated in the image of Eros and Thanatos; that is, the sex drive exists in part to counteract the death instinct, a perverse compulsion for extinction, and pathological conditions arise if the two conjoin rather than merely co exist. It's a fascinating but ultimately unprov able concept – like so much of Freud's early psychoanalytical theory, he was feeling his way toward an explanation of the human condition expressed in mythic archetypes. As with his assertion that the libido, or sex drive, was the wellspring of all human activity (as opposed to just one of a number of primal expressions of human energy or creativity), it's hard to reject the idea but at the same time impossible to measure how far it might genuinely describe the human predicament.

The now old-fashioned theorising of Freud did at least offer the first sketchy charts to begin mapping out the regions of human sexuality. Of his more prominent early students, it was the Austrian Wilhelm Reich who would most instantly agree with the statement that opens this chapter. He saw the flowering of Nazi ideology in the German homeland where he spent most of his life, and later attributed *The Mass Psychology of Fascism* (as in his 1933 study of the same name) in part to a subversion of the human organism's need for orgasmic ecstasy. Torchlight marches, book-burning, the iconography of the swastika and the fetishism of the uniform, indeed the whole Nazi pageant, were, as seen through the eyes of Reich's later theorising, created from the skilful subversion of life-affirming sexual energy by men such as Hitler and Goebbels. (Reich's theorising found tacit agreement after the war in George Orwell's classic dystopian satire *1984* – among the few features of Orwell's totalitarian state based on Nazi Germany rather than Stalinist Russia or grey post-war England were the Anti-Sex League, a repressively orgasmic 'Two Minutes' Hate', and scientists working to eradicate the orgasm in favour of a future epitomised by the image of 'a boot stamping on a human face – forever'.)

The Freudian/Reichian concept of sexuality as a potent physical force – which, if harnessed malevolently, may become destructive – takes many forms. One self-styled philosopher who (as yet unnamed) has already cast a shadow over this book, wrote of 'an electric fluid that circulates through the hollows of the nerves … the carrier of pain and delight …'. These phrases were used in a piece of Utopian fantasy much at odds with the works he is infamous for. 'The sexual passion is to the others what the nervous fluid is to life itself,' he also wrote, pre-dating Freud and Reich by well over a century, 'it sustains them all and gives force to them all.' But here, in a very different literary context, he places the words in the mouth of a sexually violent aristocratic libertine, the type of character with whom his creator, the Marquis de Sade, would become synonymous.

***

In the shadow of the great stone cathedral, the sinner makes his earthly atonement. Whatever pious utterances spill forth from his worried lips, his suffering shall be his only redemption now. Bound and strung up in the shape of a pinion, his wrists and ankles fastened by rope at sharp angles to his trunk and lower body, the transgressor meets the eyes of the baying crowd but seeks not the mercy of his sovereign who watches from afar. The sentence is passed, the die is cast. All that remains is for him to implore unto the Heaven which, his condemners remind him now, he has mortally offended.

'For the offence of taking the life of one of His Majesty's men …'

They say that the captain of the guard died at the condemned man's hand. Found in a back alley with his throat slit, he might have fallen prey to any one of a number of vagabonds and rascals. But, no. With accusation flowing in only one direction, from his fellow denizens of the streets, it is enough to secure the inescapable end which a merciless God has bequeathed him.

VLAD THE IMPALER

A scream – a beast's shrill whinny – is forced from the flayed chest of a man. As the chief executioner's blade makes its incision, the leather-gloved hand strips away the covering of skin over flesh and musculature. Those in the crowd who do not flinch and turn away are entranced by the grim spectacle. A few laugh, but this is as likely the fearful gibbering of the simple-minded as the amusement of the cruel at heart.

And all the time the monarch watches from a distance, aloof and imperious.

'... and for the unnatural coupling which has made him profane in the eyes of the Lord our God ...' The herald reads aloud from his scroll, prefacing the further torments which will reduce the miscreant to a mass of twitching, convulsing nerve ends.

The executioner makes a shallow cut beneath the small fabric pouch which preserves the condemned's modesty. The pain is sharp, but still merely another lick of fire to a body aflame with the severing of skin from bone. It is only as the gloved hand reaches within the pierced scrotum that the condemned man starts to feel his very essence being turned inside out. The manly organs which, according to the arresting guards' lies, had offended their maker by being placed unnaturally within she with whom he was apprehended, are plucked from their fleshly hiding place and held aloft to warn the watching crowd.

Such pain has never found words to express it. As the condemned's human form is carved asunder, the howling of the wounded beast that he hears seems to come from somewhere outside of himself. In his unending agony, he no longer knows if the fact that she who shared his bed will share a similar fate is an extension of his torment or a comfort to it.

And there upon his suffering, all the time, is the inscrutable gaze of his liege. But does not the handful of royal courtiers surrounding the monarch hear in his frozen stillness a quickening of the breath? Do their worldly sensibilities detect perhaps an invisible warmth within the loins?

'... and shall thereupon, to the point of death ...'

No sooner than the ultimate sentence is announced, it is executed. The final incisions are made to the condemned man's lower trunk. His muddy, glistening bowels are excised and put on show. The mob respond in all their various manners: there are gasps; vomiting; laughter. But yet, still, the condemned, his eyes widened in pain for perhaps the last time, continues gulping down air.

And the monarch's gaze is fixed upon him with a satisfied smile, struck by the aesthetic beauty that recalls the sacred torments of the saints.

***

The merciless king imagined above is not Vlad the Impaler, but one of his European contemporaries. In his essay 'Punishments with Vlad Tepeş' (see Chapter Seven), Professor Constantin Rezachevici cites Louis XI of France, who ruled from 1461-83, as a monarch whose administration routinely inflicted cruel punishments and was reputed to 'delight in the cries of his victims'. However, as Professor Rezachevici points out, the French king does not share Vlad Dracula's reputation for sadism; his cruelty was merely of a tone with the late Middle Ages and, more specifically, the 15th century. Although the Romanian academic does indulge in special pleading for a national hero, the suggestion that Vlad was not a particularly monstrous ruler given his times (as also asserted in the 1987 TV documentary *Dracula: The Great Undead*, in the dark velvet tones of Vincent Price) is clear enough.

Neither was the motivation for such extreme punishments said to be cruelty in itself. Another more infamous near-contemporary of Vlad's, Father Tomas Torquemada, Grand Inquisitor of Spain from 1483-1496, was driven in his pursuit of heretics against the teachings of the Catholic Church (principally the unfortunate Jews, whose religion had provided the bedrock of Christianity) by a similar moral conviction that he inflicted pain by divine right, that God was sitting on his shoulder and nodding assent to the suffering.

In his study *Torture*, Edward Peters describes the basic techniques whereby Torquemada would have wrung confessions from his victims, in the prelude to their execution: 'The techniques of torture used chiefly in early European history principally assaulted the musculoskeletal system, heat sensory receptors, and highly innervated tissue. The strappado – suspension by ropes – and the rack greatly distended and often dislocated muscles and joints. In the case of strappado by traumatically extending the muscles of the arms and the brachial plexus and by depriving the muscles of an adequate blood supply (muscle ischaemia) through constriction of the arteries, and by dislocating joints at hand and shoulder, intense pain was generated. In the case of the pressure-type legsplints and thumbscrews, the pain thresholds of innervating fibres were lowered by mechanical pressure. In that of the rack, tendons, tendon sheaths and joint capsules were assaulted. In addition to these pains, early European torture techniques may also have involved referred pain: pain in areas other than those directly stimulated, caused by the activity of 'trigger points', extremely sensitive areas of the upper chest and back … In the somewhat later techniques of the legsplint and thumbscrew, the skeletal and vascular systems and their surrounding highly innervated tissue are assaulted by mechanical pressure.'

Regarded via modern hindsight, we find one of the blueprints for historical sadism in the Holy Roman Catholic Inquisition that blighted medieval Europe and manifested for hundreds of years – particularly in the longstanding Spanish Inquisition. Its instruments of torture against heretics – like the strappado, the rack and the grotesque auto-da-fé , rituals of penance followed by mass burnings at the stake – now seem the perfect expression of a sadistic sexuality which seeks to deny sex itself, and to mortify the flesh. One of the Holy Inquisition's alternative modes of execution was sawing and quartering, a gruesome process which started at the groin. In this sense, Torquemada and his successors as Grand Inquisitor may be seen as sadistic figures, although they would not have recognised it in themselves – and neither would his near-contemporary Vlad the Impaler, a pious Christian despot who inflicted mutilations of the human form in apparent opposition to carnal licentiousness, as well as against every other moral transgression great or small.

'It's easy to issue an order that somebody else carries out', observes Mei Trow in *True Horror*: 'Dracula,' 'but Vlad is a hands-on killer and that makes him a very different kind of man indeed.' 'He's a sadist in the sense that he likes to be hands-on,' concurs forensic psychologist Laura Richards, who we can safely assume has met some of Vlad's modern-day counterparts out in the field. 'He's doing it rather than ordering people to do it. Or even when he orders people to do it it's still a form of control, but he wants to be upfront and personal to it. It wasn't just about controlling things for the purposes of maintaining his empire, it was about the personal gratification that he got from it himself.'

Such cast-iron certainty may seem incongruous, given that what we know about Vlad's activities outside the Ottoman Wars originates from folkloric propaganda pamphlets. But then, given that the nature (if not the number) of his trademark punishments seems incontrovertible, we have to ask: what is the likelihood of ordering or committing such mutilations *without* receiving some form of gratification from it? (This question may be extended beyond Vlad perhaps – to all the merciless despots and holy terrors of his day and beyond.)

'He continued effecting the worst and most heinous way of torturing people and seemed to get a real sense of enjoyment from doing it,' continues Richards in the TV doc. This introduces a scene of Vlad ramming it home to a blonde wench over the dining table, accompanied by the screams of an impaled priest outside. The contention is clear: there was no greater stimulant to his sexual desire (or indeed his epicurean appetite) than cruelty, and sometimes the two elements may have combined.

There are probably few historical figures whose careers are more open to psychosexual analysis than that of Vlad. To understand him better, perhaps we should turn our attention for a moment to the very different figure whose name lends us the term 'sadism'.

***

Donatien Alphonse François de Sade, son of a French aristocrat whose mismanagement began a steady decline in the family fortunes, was born in Provence in June 1740. Heir to the title of marquis, he attended College Louis le Grand in Paris from age nine, where he was schooled in the traditions of pederasty and buggery by the Jesuit Brotherhood. It began a lifelong hunger for sodomy on both the giving and receiving ends that marks Sade as both a literal sadist (a term coined after him and which he never heard in his own lifetime) and masochist (after the flagellant Leopold von Sacher-Masoch). By his twenties, the young libertine had developed a fetish for sacrilegious sexual acts that included forcing a young prostitute to insert a communion wafer in her vagina and masturbating on a crucifix. It was the kind of impious prank that would have earned certain death two or three hundred years previously, and it granted him the unwanted attention of the Paris vice squad. It also began a career that saw him swerving continually between extreme acts and attitudes, and mealy-mouthed contrition in order to save his skin: 'I deserve the wrath of God. All I do is lament over my misdeeds and hate my errors,' swore Sade during his first prison sentence at the fortress of Vincennes, and it can be argued that Sade got off lightly in a Europe where the Holy Roman Inquisition was still at work.

But there was no real inclination to change his ways. At Easter 1768, Sade was arrested for the maltreatment of a 36-year-old beggar-woman named Rose Keller. It's a pertinent reminder to the more liberal-minded members of the Sade cult – that is, those readers who regard his works as those of an unjustly persecuted social commentator or satirist – that he was also a rather vicious sex criminal. Keller was flogged with a whip to a degree that left deep weals, before she managed to escape out of a window. She claimed to have been begging alms but not selling her body; Sade begged to differ, and later complained in his writings about a judge 'moved to pity for the thrashed arse of a street-walker', as if her abjection excused his violence; polite society was outraged, not for the victim but for the incident's occurrence on a Christian holiday.

(Rose Keller also claimed that the Marquis had threatened to bury her if she didn't co-operate. It's redolent of early 1970s England and the last victim known to have been set free by sex-murder partners Fred and Rose West – except that, as far as we can tell, Sade never killed anyone. Little known, however, is an incident whereby human bones were discovered in the grounds of Sade's chateau at La Coste, after a servant girl had left the premises. Sade later explained this in a letter to his wife from prison as a prank by one of the other girls. 'I'm a libertine, but I'm neither *a criminal* nor *a murderer*,' protested Sade. But his divided and extreme nature remains in evidence, his activities curtailed by an unfeasibly long period of imprisonment for much lesser offences.)

With the connivance of his social climbing mother-in-law, Madame de Montreuil (whose family lend their name to the Paris Metro station), he received a temporary period of banishment from Paris. But after he conducted his meekly faithful young wife, Renée Pélagie, and her sister, Anne Prospère, away to a provincial chateau which provided the venue for orgies, his matronly saviour became his nemesis. After a scandalous incident in Marseilles in which Sade and his valet, Latour, engaged in a several-way bisexual bout of bondage and buggery with four teenage girl prostitutes, the girls all fell violently ill with some form of poisoning. They recovered and withdrew all charges, as the poison turned out to be the ineffective aphrodisiac Spanish Fly, but by then the fugitive Sade and Latour had been variously beheaded and hanged in effigy; for sodomy was, even then, seen in France as an affront to God and carried a potential death sentence. With Sade still at liberty, the orgies continued in a country house at Lacoste. While there is no conclusive account of her daughters taking part, de Montreuil was incensed.

And so, in 1777, began the longest period of Sade's imprisonment, facilitated by a *lettre de cachet* his mother-in-law obtained from Louis XVI. In his relatively luxurious prison at Vincennes, Sade read Enlightenment authors and philosophers Voltaire and Rousseau; he turned his own hand to light drama in the style of Molière and, more resonantly, to writings which increasingly reflected his own atheistic and extreme libertarian views. He practised sodomy on himself with wooden dildos supplied by his wife and, when moved to the Bastille, wrote an epic (and temporarily lost) work entitled *The 120 Days of Sodom* – which, in its ever more extreme accumulation of sadistic (and repetitive) masturbatory fantasies, reflects his statement that 'when one's prick is aloft it is horror, villainy, the appalling that pleases'. When, after 12 years of imprisonment, Sade was moved from the Bastille when it was stormed by a revolutionary mob during the early upheavals of July 1789, the manuscript was left behind. It would eventually surface in the early 20th century, having lost little of its power to shock and to nauseate (and sometimes, over the course of its many hundreds of pages, to bore.)

Sade was eventually freed by the French Revolution in 1790, regarded by some revolutionaries as a victim of the *ancien régime* – and suspected by others of being the haughty old aristocrat that, at heart, he was. For in his most infamous writings as a free man, he would describe contemporary French society as composed of 'two classes ... one the rich slaves of their pleasures, the others the miserable victims of fate'. While some implicit sympathy for the poor and wretched can be detected in their abject treatment in his novels, it should be remembered that the younger Sade took every opportunity to sexually exploit the poor and desperate, and there can be little realistic doubt that his depictions of hypocritical aristocrats and authority figures who abuse their power in pursuit of perverted gratification were born of his personal fantasies. His basic philosophy – which, while he sought to publicly deny it, would resurface again and again in his writings – is best summed up in a phrase from his infamous novel *Justine*: 'Abandon your stupid restrictions and give all beings the same right to avenge themselves for any wrong done to them: you will no longer need any written laws.' Great news for the self-indulging libertine; cold comfort even for those with the wherewithal to avenge their violated loved ones; tough luck for the powerless and exploited. But then perhaps Sade's attitude is perhaps more concisely summed up in *Philosophy in the Boudoir*: 'He's no sort of man who doesn't want to be a despot when he has a hard on.'

On release, Sade continued his fated attempt at a career as a man of letters, writing rejected works for the stage and, more relevant to our purposes, those infamous books to which he dare not put his name and adamantly denied authorship: *Justine, or The Misfortunes of Virtue*, its companion piece *Juliette, or The Prosperity of Vice* and *Philosophy in the Boudoir*. 'I have made it fit to stink out the devil,' he admitted to an associate of *Justine*, reflecting its gruesomely entertaining hybrid of his own philosophy of amorality and a hefty gothic concoction designed to raise some cash. 'Even the most debauched heart, the most degenerate intelligence, the most bizarrely obscene imagination could create nothing so outrageous of reason, decency and humanity,' condemned republican newspaper *The Friend of the Laws*. A final lost work, *The Days of Florbelle, or Nature Unveiled*, was seized by the police, who noted, 'De Sade wanted to go beyond the horrors of *Justine* and of *Juliette*,' before they destroyed the manuscript.

In his imprisonment, Sade had fantasised about revenge on his mother-in-law: 'I watched her skinned alive, dragged over spikes and then thrown into a vat of vinegar.' In the actuality, as 'Citizen Sade', one of the Revolution's unlikeliest active members, he found the subsequent Terror, the guillotining and 'the horror of the massacres carried out [to be] unparalleled'. As such, he was personally responsible for placing the Montreuils on a list which saved them from the revolutionary blade, claiming that having Madame in his power and showing her mercy was his best revenge. But it seems likely that the overheated and vengeful imagination which produced *The 120 Days* in prison was at last able to take a deep breath and cool itself.

In any case, Citizen Sade's freedom proved short-lived. The revolutionaries who had suspected him of being an old aristo and 'a most immoral man, profoundly suspect and unworthy of society' had their way. He was incarcerated for most of the rest of his life in the lunatic asylum at Charenton, where for a while he could at least stage plays with the inmates. Even then his infamy preceded him – but it was in the late 20th century that he finally became a modern figure, when his works could be openly published and he could provoke all over again with his unevenly scurrilous writings and equally contradictory philosophy.

But it is for the pathological side of his nature that we most readily remember him. By the 1890s, the psychosexual/criminological term coined by Richard von Krafft-Ebing in his *Psychopathia Sexualis* was derived from the Marquis's name: sadism. It saved Sade from the kind of historical obscurity faced by Prince Vlad before Stoker gradually brought him back into view. For in his final days, the iconoclast his posthumous admirers dubbed 'the Divine Marquis' had felt so divided and defeated that he requested an unmarked burial, so that 'the traces of my grave shall vanish from the surface of the Earth as, I hope, remembrance of me shall fade from the minds of men'. His son disobeyed this request, laying his radical atheist father to rest in the parish church at Charenton with a simple cross for a marker.

***

While the grand old gothic church of Notre Dame had briefly become the Cathedral of Reason during the Revolution that Sade hoped would disperse God once and for all (indicating how mankind will always need to worship at some kind of altar), Catholicism's grip was reinstated by Maximilien Robespierre, the great zealot of the Terror. Robespierre had briefly targeted Sade for the guillotine, before his own neck went under it. But in his pious mass murderousness, Robespierre is perhaps closer to Vlad Dracula than the debauched and inconsistent Marquis could ever have been.

For Vlad could never have recognised any virtue in a man like Sade – his decadent lifestyle and rejection of the Christian tradition would only have ended him in one place in the Wallachia of the Middle Ages, a veritable universe away even from the murderous Terror of revolutionary France. And yet, can we not detect the shade of Vlad in the sadistic authority figures of Sade's most infamous writings, whose pious actions are a mere pretext for their cruelty and debauchery?

In the *True Horror*: 'Dracula' documentary, the Benedictine monk Brother Hans apocryphally testifies, 'I know of a time he impaled a whole family of Saxons, and as they slowly died the filthy bastard brought his throne and watched.' This is followed by an ultraviolent horror tableau of three members of a family impaled together as if at their personal Golgotha – with a screaming young woman hoisted into central position. All that creates a cushion between the viewer and the sheer physical horror is the baggy shapelessness of their period garb.

'And as he watched, the smell of the blood aroused his appetite,' continues Hans. 'He had a table laid, a feast served, right there. And as he dined he watched them on the stakes, dancing and twitching like frogs. And they say Dracula declared how graceful they looked.'

This is the TV programme's reduction of the epicurean massacre at Braşov to a more manageable three bit-part players. But it also hints strongly at a little-spoken truth in the Vlad Dracula story: if he did not draw direct sexual arousal from his extreme punitive code, then aesthetic pleasure must at least have been present. In a brief interview, the ever-provocative pop-artist Boyd Rice opines that he doesn't believe Vlad was a sadist, but was acting in a purely Machiavellian manner to preserve his throne and the independence of Wallachia as an Orthodox Christian principality. It's a rational view, but perhaps the irrationality of the human condition provides the best answer. For Rice, who long delighted in challenging the self-aggrandising pieties of liberal consensus, has been candid enough to admit in an interview that he himself has 'always felt like a sadist' – but in an aesthetic rather than crudely sexual sense, in that he found that the sufferings of much of humanity's great herd provided him with a pleasurable *Schadenfreude*.

So it may have been with Vlad Țepeș. In fact, given the legendary events at Brașov, it's hard to maintain that a man who found his appetite stimulated by blood, screams and bodily mutilation wasn't electrified by the spectacle of great cruelty. But there are elements of these legendary punishments that may slit open an even darker, more literally Sadeian vein.

Later in the *True Horror* programme, there is a scene of a crying cherub at the foot of the bloody stake where his mother is impaled, twitching. A sinister cutaway reveals an intemperate Vlad motioning to his *armas* to raise the toddler onto a stake, between mouthfuls of meat and wine. 'I think the idea of Vlad impaling children is one of the most difficult because to us it is the most horrendous,' acknowledges interviewee M. J. Trow, 'but we have to remember that children were a commodity, children will grow up to become possible enemies. They're cute today, but tomorrow they are the guy who will kill you.' In this sense, Trow is implicitly acknowledging Heinrich Himmler's rationale for murdering the children of the Jews during the Holocaust – that he couldn't 'allow a generation of avengers to grow up'. 'And sick though it might sound, you've got the whole logistical problem: what do you do with the small child whose mother and father you've just impaled? You kill them as well.'

So was the purpose of Vlad's most extreme actions merely pragmatic and were his punishments inflicted merely to maintain fear, in effect to help him become the Machiavellian Prince made flesh? Or did this pious puritan have more in common with the gross libertines of Sade's *The 120 Days of Sodom* – respectively the Bishop, the Banker, the Duke and the Judge – whose every moralistic machination is an excuse to stimulate their jaded senses?

In an infamous 1991 London theatrical adaptation of *The 120 Days*, director Nick Hedges (the prankster later responsible for a hoax video which convinced the tabloid press they'd seen Princess Diana frolicking with her lover Major Hewitt) distils the essence of the scenario when he has a veteran procuress telling the libertines the following story:

A Police Chief – a notorious bugger – kidnapped a father

and daughter on the highway and imprisoned them in a dark dungeon. There, with a pistol held to the man's head, he forced the father to fuck his own daughter, after which he roped the two victims together and sodomised both. Next he informs the father that the girl must die, but offers him the choice of killing her himself, which will be quick and cause little pain; or, if he prefers not to kill his own child, then he, the Police Chief, will do the work, but the father shall have to witness it all, and the girl's agonies will be atrocious. Rather than see her undergo frightful tortures, the father decides to kill his daughter with a noose of black silk, but while he is preparing to dispatch her, he is seized, bound, and before his eyes his child is flayed alive and thrown into a bonfire. The father is strangled. This, says the libertine, is to teach him a lesson not to be so eager to choke the life out of his children, for 'tis barbaric.

'By fuck, the whore's story has got me stiff!' acclaims the Judge. As extrapolated from Sade's own excitement by abusive power dynamics, the meaning is obvious: the emotional charge or sexual lubricity provided by playing God and denying a victim's right to live is made all the more delicious by making them observe the destruction of their children.

(Hedges denied this: 'When you read [Sade's] books as a whole, it's quite clear that the behaviour is being attacked, not advocated,' he told this writer. While *The 120 Days* remained lost until long after Sade's death, the markings on the Marquis's MS indicated that he intended it for publication, despite its obsessive repetition of perverse detail seemingly for his own masturbatory benefit. The ever-ambiguous Sade himself wrote in his correspondence of fellow libertine authors whose 'only purpose when they publish their vile books is that their crimes shall outlive themselves...their damnable works will bring others to commit yet more crimes, and this knowledge consoles them as unavoidable death ends their lives'. It seems largely a matter of his mood at the given moment as to what side of this particular line he was on.)

So can Vlad the Impaler's ruthless destruction of whole families, if not entire village communities, be interpreted as a grand scheme to allow him sadistic fulfilment? Given the complex nature of the man and his historical situation, it seems as much of an oversimplification as to say that Hitler and Himmler designed the Nazi Holocaust as an outlet for their own sexual gratification (though one of the most extreme post-Sadeian writers, Peter Sotos, has only part-seriously made that suggestion).

But then what of the methodology itself? Given the almost unspeakably extreme nature of the injuries, compounded by gross humiliation, there's no punitive measure that could better fit the modern international legalese definition of 'cruel and unusual punishment' – or indeed of the term 'sadistic'.

On *True Horror*, Mei Trow seemed unequivocal (far more so than in his book) as to the basic cause-and-effect Freudian origin of Vlad's cruelty. 'I don't think it's too far a reach to say the whole obsession with impalement comes from the anal intercourse that Vlad would have gone through,' he remarked of the suggestion that the young Dracula may have been raped – or seduced – in the Ottoman court. 'In many ways, the impalement that characterises him is "payback".'

But then, as we have seen, anal impalement as a punishment was not created by Vlad, and may have had its origins anywhere from the Ottoman Empire, to the Saxon punitive code, to the earliest Roman crucifixions. However, the scene that accompanies Trow's words is rather more intriguing in its attempt to trace the origins of his behaviour. It shows the child Vlad anally impaling a little grey mouse which he had captured in his spacious cell on a stick, at the end of a wordless visit from a gentleman of the Ottoman court. Again, the implications are obvious: the boy has been sexually abused by a Turkish nobleman whose power lends him legitimacy; in seeking to displace his pain and humiliation, in the Freudian sense, he transfers it onto a helpless creature. The pattern throughout his life will recreate this displacement on a progressively larger scale, Vlad's desire for expiation never fully satiated, but increasingly finding pleasure in the pain and humiliation of others.

It's an interesting hypothesis, though once again the film's makers are bending the original source material to make it fit; in the original Dracula stories, it is the adult Vlad who tortures the hapless rodent when living as an esteemed captive of Matthias Corvinus. But this in itself is interesting, as it's suggestive of the sadistic fetish (or paraphilia) now christened by forensic psychologists as picquerism – the sexual excitement caused by puncturing or intruding on the human body with a sharp weapon. It also evokes one of the modern criminals most readily associated with the term 'sadist'.

In the mid-20th century, Scottish juvenile delinquent Ian Brady was torturing other people's pets to achieve some emotional charge. By his own admission, one such hapless creature was a cat buried alive in a graveyard. Brady was the illegitimate child of a Glasgow waitress who would be placed with foster parents at the behest of the local authority. He has recounted to correspondents such as Colin Wilson that his childhood was basically happy, his foster carers were kind people and that he never suffered any kind of traumatic abuse. But he would serve a stretch for housebreaking in the British borstal (juvenile prison) system which left him raging at the world like Carl Panzram (see Chapter Four) – albeit sans the sexual abuse and the worst physical violence that characterised Panzram's (anti-)socialisation. (When this writer opined to criminologist and author Carol Anne Davis that Brady may have been one of those rare individuals 'born bad', she countered with the opinion that lying in his cot as a baby all day, alone in his own filth as his hard-pressed mother scratched a living, had negated any ability to empathise with others' suffering at the most formative stage of his development.)

Criminal history would determine that Brady became the serial killer readily spoken of in the same breath as the Marquis de Sade. 'I guess it's unfortunate that *Justine* was found among Ian Brady's possessions,' *120 Days* adapter Nick Hedges told this writer, 'but I don't think he stood up in court and said, "This is why," did he?' Indeed, Brady said very little, stonewalling all the way in his trial for three of the five murders of children and teenagers committed by him and his lover, compliant fellow 'Moors Murderer' Myra Hindley. But there is no doubt that he'd swallowed the elusive Marquis's philosophy of amoralism whole, and used it to justify his actions towards Myra and another potential 'disciple'. But Sade's philosophy was used in adulthood by Brady to reinforce how he already felt and thought. As his early victimisation of animals shows, Ian Brady would have been a 'sadist' even if he hadn't had the intelligence to pursue the term to its etymological source; he would behaved sadistically even if Sade had never been born and the term did not therefore exist. For Sade may have given us 'sadism', but only in the defining word and concept. The actions seem to have been ever-present.

So where does this leave one of history's most extreme reputed sadists – a man who would have impaled child murderers and atheists alike (Brady shared Sade's rage at a God he claimed he didn't believe in), while remaining capable of the utmost cruelty himself?

Vlad the Impaler may perhaps have found some affinity with the serial sex murderer: if the story of his torture of the poor mouse while under house arrest in Hungary holds true, then it suggests a compulsive obsession that would manifest cruelty toward non-human victims if greater outlets were denied him. The transplantation of this scenario back to his youth evokes the sliding gradient whereby serial killers often begin by torturing animals years before they are able to victimise a human being.

But did our holy defender of Christianity subvert his sexual drive in the Reichian sense – suppressing carnal desire until it was expressed in the sadistic impulses of the morally righteous man, much as Torquemada and even Louis XI may have done? It's possible that Vlad's religious faith may actually have contributed to his sadism, manifesting in the brutal moral conviction of the religious psychopath. For all his defence of Christianity, however, whichever faith Vlad swore allegiance to at the time seems to have been a flag of convenience. His conversion to his captors' Roman Catholicism while forced to live under the auspices of Corvinus seems to have caused him no great problems, possibly because he'd already shown such flexibility as a prisoner of the Muslims in his youth. However, the Russian monks who otherwise tended to lionise Vlad in their *Povesty o … Drakule* lamented it as a betrayal of the Orthodox religion: 'Dracula loved the sweetness of life temporal, rather than life endless and eternal, left his [Russian Orthodox] faith, and in giving up the Truth he lost the light and took on darkness.'

In other words, Dracula was an earthly sensualist rather than a spiritual personality, and religious dogma held very little actual sway with him. He associated Christendom with his ancestral territory which provided his eastern frontiers, and therefore with his own hard-won temporal power. As has been suggested in this book, God is Will to a man like Vlad Tepeş. As such, he may be closer than his religion might suggest to the Sadeian libertine, who sees himself as acting with the same authority as a dethroned (and indeed nonexistent) God.

In the TV drama-doc, Brother Hans decries Vlad's atrocities to his fellow monks, as they nervously await their fate: 'He killed babies that never had so much as a wicked thought in their lives. Killed their mothers, cut off their breasts. Cut off the heads of the infants and …' Hans is cut short by the appalled protests of his brother in Christ, but to complete this nightmarish scene we turn to the Saxon Dracula pamphlets: 'He also had the mothers' breasts cut out and the children's heads pushed through the holes in their mother's bodies and then he impaled them.' And then further: 'He also roasted the children of mothers and they had to eat their children themselves.' And further still: 'He cut the breasts off women and forced their husbands to eat them; after that he had them impaled.'

If we accept that Vlad's actions were born of a uniform brutal pragmatism, then what purpose is served by the protracted psychological suffering of the already condemned parents, who are forced to witness the atrocities committed quite arbitrarily against their innocent children? The almost cartoonish extremity of this infernal scenario takes us back to the epicurean massacre scene of *Titus Andronicus*, and to Sade: in the extravagantly sado-gothic companion volumes *Justine* and *Juliette*, ever more extreme orgies are described in which new levels of atrocity are piled one on top of the other. As previously seen in *The 120 Days*, children are flayed and roasted alive; pregnant women are disembowelled. In one of the climactic passages of *Juliette*, the eponymous female libertine has only recently been reunited with her lost young daughter when an elder male debauchee urges her to participate in his violation of the child: incredibly, she does, allowing him to rape the little girl and then pitch her helpless body onto a burning brazier. 'Your treacherous influence sweeps her away,' pants Juliette in orgasmic rapture, 'it stifles in me all other feeling but that of crime and outrage.' Except the anti-heroine clearly feels more excited than outraged, as she ensures her daughter stays trapped within the fire and burns to death.

The ultimate transgression of cannibalism in the Saxon Dracula pamphlets (at least in its enforced second-hand variation, the Voivode seemingly never partakes of human flesh himself) is also echoed in *Justine* and *Juliette*, in a cannibalistic orgy where roasted human breasts and buttocks are consumed. In this literary sense, Sade's brutal *philosophie*, taken out of *le boudoir*, may perhaps better describe Vlad than any subtle Machiavellianism: 'His acts of oppression, violence, cruelty, tyranny, injustice – all these diverse expressions of the character engraved in him by the hand of the power which placed him in the world are therefore quite as simple and pure as the hand which drew them. And when he uses all his rights to oppress the weak … he is therefore doing the most natural thing in the world.'

All our evidence, of course, is drawn here from the ever more outrageous atrocities recounted in the pamphlets, and from Sade's warped fictional imaginings. While it's true that cannibalism is regarded by forensic psychologists as the ultimate sexually sadistic transgression, its urge to dominate and possess going beyond even the murder and necrophiliac rape of a victim, there are few documented cases of the sadist forcing others to consume human flesh. (This seems largely the domain of fiction, from Shakespeare's first Roman tragedy to Thomas Harris's later Hannibal Lecter novels.) But, if we're looking for evidence of Vlad as a clinical (rather than fictional) sadist, the evidence is still there.

The Russian Dracula pamphlets also describe some of the most horrendous acts, but this time with a patina of moralistic approval. Deflowered and unmarried virgins, adulterous wives and sexually active widows all have 'their sinful parts cut out' before being bound naked and mutilated on a stake in the marketplace. The barbaric sexual moralism is obvious, but so is the recurring suggestion that if Vlad did not experience gratification from these sexual mutilations, then he simply could *not* have behaved in this way. For all our caveats about his living in desperate, violent times, there is such a thing as human revulsion at the most extreme abuses of the human form and this is expressed in the pamphlets that were roughly contemporary to his era.

The isolation of the 'sinful parts' is rather redolent of Ed Gein, the repressed (and celebrated, in pop culture) Wisconsin necrophile of the 1950s who cut the vulvas from recently buried women and two murder victims in order to dress in their skin and organs, and effect a magical transformation in his own mind. But then Gein was not a sadist. When he killed, he did so quickly with one shot to the head. The suffering of the victims was not the object; he merely needed their bodies to indulge his necrophiliac compulsion and the erotomania that gained its biggest kick from his wearing a woman's skin.

However, the coexistence of moral puritanism and the sadistic desire to undress, invade and ultimately possess the body of the sexually attractive young woman whose desirability enrages and excites is a mainstay of sadistic sex killers. In the 1993 prison writing anthology *Knockin' on Joe*, published by one of your co-authors, compiler Sondra London breaks from recounting the crimes of her former boyfriend, *Killer Fiction* author G. J. Schaefer, to sympathise with the rage which desirable women made him feel. Schaefer, a Florida deputy sheriff, was convicted of hanging two teenage girls in local swampland, a sadistic terror-and-death scenario that he sometimes boasted (and often denied) he may have replicated up to 30 times. One of his co-inmates at Florida State Prison, Ted Bundy, is recognised as one of the USA's most prolific sex killers, likely responsible for many more crimes than the handful for which he went to the electric chair. In the countdown to his 1989 execution, he took the moral high ground in a number of interviews by railing against the pornographic magazines he claimed had corrupted him; however, his onetime next-door neighbour on

Death Row claimed that Bundy was never seen with a skin mag, but got his kicks poring over the cover shots of terrorised women in bondage on the covers of true detective magazines. In conversations recounted in true crime study *The Riverman*, Bundy begrudgingly admitted to being turned on by possessing a victim's rotting head as a trophy, to the sight of which he reputedly masturbated in the privacy of his room.

In terms of their crimes, the one anecdote that may connect Vlad Dracula with a Bundy or a Schaefer is also possibly apocryphal, though better documented than the wilder tales of enforced cannibalism. In the documentary film based on Florescu and McNally's *In Search of Dracula*, Christopher Lee narrates over footage of himself as Vlad the Impaler: 'Dracula had a peasant mistress who lived in a poor outlying part of Tîrgovişte. He visited her often, but his interest was purely physical. The woman, on the other hand, fell in love with Dracula and grew afraid of losing him. One night she told him that she was going to have his child. Dracula became angry, and said that this would *not* be. He then cut her open from her loins to her breast, and said, "Let the world see where I have been and where my fruit lay!"' This accompanies an implicitly sadistic but non-graphic image of Lee drawing his sword to disembowel a grimacing, long-haired brunette. The story is retold in a differing version in the Russian pamphlets, with their customary moralistic slant. 'He had a girl, a mistress,' recounts Brothers Hans in *True Horror*: 'Dracula'. 'She came to him with good news [pregnancy]. But Vlad didn't take her word for it. He had her examined to ensure she was really pregnant.'

There follows a scene of an old midwife crossing herself, and Vlad kissing his mistress (a Scandinavian-looking blonde this time) before opening her belly with his sword. 'He cut her open so that the whole world could see she had no baby inside,' describes Hans. The Russian emphasis is on the Voivode's supposedly righteous rage at his mistress's lying, but in both dramatisations the relish that the actor displays is that of the serial sex killer.

In his dismissal of the Sade cult in his typically quirky *The Misfits: A Study of Sexual Outsiders*, Colin Wilson describes the Marquis de Sade as wanting 'to be Genghis Khan, Vlad the Impaler and Ivan the Terrible all rolled into one'. That may well be the sum of Sade's basest instincts, but it's equally true to say that occasional parallels are thrown up between Vlad and archetypically fictional or clinically authentic cases of sadism. In *Juliette*, the libertine Noirceuil proselytises to his potential victim, 'I must have my pleasure, and I could not have it without torturing you and without seeing your tears flow ... when

279

torturing you, tearing you into pieces, I am enacting no more than the one deed that can move me, as that lover, dolefully taking his mistress's cunt, carries out the one deed that pleases him ...'

It could almost be the premonitory speech by Prince Vlad before the sadistic murder of his unnamed mistress; his most infamous deeds are written in blood and also likely stained with his semen.

CHAPTER XIV

Exit the Dragon

Vlad Dracula must have wondered what lay in store for him as he headed towards Hungary, as the prisoner of King Matthias Corvinus, in the winter of 1462. The reason given for his arrest – an alleged plot to conspire with the Ottomans – did not bode well for the captive Wallachian's future. Vlad himself had firm ideas on how to deal with traitors – many of his worst atrocities were committed against those he considered guilty of treason – and the idea that the worst penalties were reserved for turncoats, rebels and collaborators was widely accepted in medieval law. But Matthias was a self-conscious product of the Renaissance, and a very different man to the humbled Voivode whose name was now synonymous with medieval savagery. Corvinus was also a very different man to his father, the legendary warlord John Hunyadi. Hunyadi was above all a soldier who shared Vlad's fierce dedication to fighting the Turks. While he appreciated the power of the sword, Matthias also aspired to the role of statesman; the Machiavellian Prince as a more pragmatic, enlightened leader, prepared to advance his cause through diplomacy or, as Vlad had discovered, cunning.

For, at the same time Matthias was accusing Dracula of conspiring with the Ottomans, he was engaged in pretty much that very activity himself, signing an armistice with Mehmet the Conqueror. He is widely believed to have spent the money he had received to launch a crusade on buying the sacred royal crown of Hungary. It had fallen into the hands of his rival, the Holy Roman Emperor Frederick III, and cost the King a cool 60,000 ducats. But its purchase allowed Matthias to finally be officially crowned King of Hungary, adding further legitimacy to his somewhat precarious claim to the throne. The deal he struck with the Sultan included recognising Vlad's brother, Radu the Handsome, as Voivode of Wallachia, a price worth paying as far as the Hungarian King was concerned. He needed time to consolidate his rule, as neighbouring Christian princes eyed his territory hungrily and ambitious rebels and lawless mercenary bands still threatened stability within his own borders. A cessation in hostilities also gave Mehmet welcome breathing space to deal with problems he was experiencing on his Asiatic frontiers. Both rulers appreciated that any ceasefire could only be temporary, but it served a purpose.

Before he entertained any rash thoughts of crusades, Matthias knew he needed either to harness or at least muzzle Hungary's ambitious aristocracy. His father had been obliged to ride out against the Ottomans all but alone on his final campaign of 1456. Matthias had no intention of finding himself in the same position, and raised his famed Black Army, their substantial numbers drawn primarily from Hussite heretics and soldiers from the surrounding realms, all clad in the menacing midnight hue that gave the force its name. The Black Army is frequently referred to as a mercenary force, though professional army is a more appropriate description – Matthias had raised one of Europe's first regular standing armies, in imitation perhaps of the Janissaries whose professionalism gave the Ottoman Empire an edge against the ad hoc forces of its foes. The Hungarian King's progressive approach soon bore fruit, as his new professional army in their ominous black uniforms proved themselves upon the field, while the canny King consistently outmanoeuvred his opponents at the negotiating table.

So where was Dracula during all of this? We do know that his worst fears about what awaited him when he reached Hungary proved unfounded. How unfounded is a more complicated question. Records do not show Vlad's name among the lists of political prisoners held by the Hungarian King, and we may safely assume that the exiled Voivode was under house arrest rather than chained to a damp dungeon wall. Russian accounts suggest he was imprisoned, where 'he learnt how to sew and thus he kept himself alive in the prison', but even this version concedes that Vlad had access to the local market, an unusual privilege for a conventional prisoner. It seems likely that the Wallachian enjoyed increasingly comfortable confinement, initially in Buda, then at Corvinus's summer residence at Visegrád, some 20 miles north of the Hungarian capital. Visegrád was a showpiece for the King's credentials as a Renaissance prince, a palace replete with works of art and his internationally famous library. After a lengthy confinement (perhaps four years, though some believe longer), Dracula was moved again – presumably for 'good behaviour' – to a town house in Pest (the city across the river from Buda, now combined as the Hungarian capital of Budapest). While there, the Voivode appears to have married and fathered two sons. Accounts even suggest that the lucky bride was a relative of Matthias (perhaps even his sister), implying not only that Vlad was living the life of exiled royalty, but also that – despite arresting Dracula in 1462 – the wily Matthias had not wholly forgotten his vague previous promises to the Wallachian, and was at the very least eager to dangle the prospect of possible redemption in front of his infamous prisoner.

Brutality for its own sake didn't interest King Matthias. While Dracula became known for the excruciating executions that almost invariably followed his rough justice, hence widely dubbed 'Vlad the Impaler', Corvinus was revered for the quality of his judgements, earning the epithet of 'Matthias the Just'. Even if politics had demanded the removal of Vlad from the political stage in the 1460s, removing him from the action entirely would have represented the wanton waste of a potentially valuable future asset. Just as in his youth, when Dracula had found himself held hostage at the court of the Ottoman Sultan, Vlad was now maintained at the court of King Matthias, a royal beast in a gilded cage ready to be unleashed when his royal captor thought the fierce Wallachian's unique talents might best serve his Machiavellian schemes. There are even accounts of Matthias deliberately having Dracula in attendance whenever envoys from the Sultan were visiting, the implicit threat that he could release *Kaziglu Bey* – 'the Impaler Prince', now held in almost supernatural dread in Constantinople – enough to lend an intimidating edge to the Hungarian position.

John Bianchi makes some interesting observations relating to Dracula's period of incarceration. 'I underestimated Vlad from my initial reading of the region and period, and it's easy to do that when you see he had short reigns that always ended in military revolt,' confesses the military historian and wargamer. 'You conclude he couldn't have been that good, but you start to see some strengths that made him a formidable opponent and which also allow you to see why Matthias kept him at Visegrád. Yes – as a prisoner, but also as a potent chained threat that he threatened to unleash on the Turks for many years. Vlad's measure of success, in a way, is that he helped Matthias establish a very peaceful rule in close proximity to a Turkish empire that needed to expand to survive. It's a very great measure of the Turks' fear of him that they never mounted a major campaign against Hungary while Vlad was a guest at Visegrád.'

Vlad was also the source of morbid curiosity among Matthias's many Christian guests, a century before the Impaler's portrait took pride of place among Archduke Frederick's famous cabinet of curiosities at Scholl Ambras. Indeed, that portrait – which shows Dracula as a placid, perhaps handsome figure in opulent Eastern European dress – was very probably copied from a portrait painted from life at Visegrád or Pest. Those curiosity seekers who came looking for the monster described in the German horror pamphlets circulating throughout Europe may have been disappointed. Though perhaps not, if the Russian sources are to be believed: 'They say that when he was in prison he didn't forget his evil habits, but he caught mice and bought birds in the market and then he executed them, some by impaling them on stakes, others by beheading, and from some others he took the feathers off before letting them go.' It's a story easy to file under 'too good to be true', if it wasn't confirmed in communications written by a horrified Papal representative at the Hungarian Court.

The only other story we have from Dracula's Hungarian incarceration which hints at a spark of the old Impaler is also detailed in the Russian narrative, explaining how 'a certain evildoer came to his house and hid and those who were looking for him came and started to look for him and found him. And Dracula rose and took up his sword, jumped off his bed and cut off the head of the guard who held the evildoer and let the evildoer go. And the others ran away and they came to the chief and told him what happened and the chief with his officials went to the King complaining about Dracula. And the King sent to him asking: "Why did you do this evil?" and he responded thus: "I didn't do any evil, he killed himself. Anyone who attacks in a house of a great ruler will die thus. If you had come to me and found the evildoer in my house I would have either given him to you or would have asked for him to be reprieved." When the King was told this he started to laugh and was amazed at Dracula's heart.' The story has a certain ring of truth about it, consistent with Vlad's previous record of brutal egotism and his draconian sense of hands-on justice. In the case of King Matthias, the episode is indicative of a building level of indulgence towards his reluctant guest – evidence perhaps of Dracula's growing status at the Hungarian Court, even that Matthias was contemplating unleashing his bloodthirsty new in-law.

Sometime around 1474, Dracula's captivity was officially over, after some dozen years as a reluctant guest of the Hungarians. Much had happened in this intervening period, helping to explain why the astute Matthias finally decided to inflict the Impaler upon a trembling Eastern Europe once again. He had established Hungary as the powerhouse of Eastern Europe by a combination of deft diplomacy and efficient military action. One European leader who had proven his match was Vlad's cousin, Stefan the Great of Moldavia, who met the Hungarians in the field at the Battle of Baia. It was a duel between the Hungarian King's new army of professionals and the traditional Great Host of Moldavia, Stefan having proven a master at mustering and motivating his people. Matthias had invaded in force in response to the Moldavian's capture of Cilia, the strategic strongpoint that had inspired Stefan's betrayal of Dracula in 1462. (Vlad's men had successfully defended it, but it fell to the Moldavians three years later.) Against the odds, Stefan prevailed in a famous victory at Baia, Matthias fleeing the battlefield with no fewer than three wounds. (Stefan was himself wounded in the leg during the first Moldavian assault on Cilia, limping thereafter, interpreted by some as a judgement for his betrayal of his cousin Dracula.)

Friction between Stefan and Matthias had been aggravated by political and personal factors. The Hungarian King had given shelter to Stefan's uncle Petru Aron, who was not just Stefan's rival for the Moldavian throne, but the man who murdered his father in 1451. Stefan took an active interest in Wallachian politics. He gave active support to Basarab, the quiet, scholarly Danesti pretender who had long laid claim to the voivodeship of Wallachia. With Stefan's formidable support, Basarab seized the throne from Vlad's brother, Radu the Handsome, in 1473, then twice more in 1474. The pendulum swing of power between the rival Voivodes was brought to a decisive halt in 1475, when Radu died. Tradition declares him the victim of venereal disease, though this may well be more of a comment upon the handsome Voivode's supposedly dissipated character than any medical evidence. Stefan's forceful support for Radu's enemy was motivated by his desire to place a strong and reliably anti-Ottoman ruler on the Wallachian throne. Basarab, however, was swiftly proving to be neither.

By this time, tension between Stefan the Great and Matthias Corvinus was easing. Both were reasonable, intelligent men who recognised that unified action was required if they were to face the Ottoman threat that was once more intensifying (the death of Petru Aron, captured and killed after the Battle of Baia, also helped heal old wounds). Basarab's increasing tendency to appease, or even collaborate with the Turks, worried them both. They agreed that the time was ripe to unleash Wallachia's secret weapon, and in the summer of 1475, Vlad Dracula rode south once more at the head of a Hungarian army, alongside his new ally Matthias Corvinus.

The Impaler also appeared willing to forgive his cousin Stefan – a decision no doubt sugared by the prospect of reclaiming the Wallachian throne – and they renewed their vows of mutual support. A multinational Christian force of Hungarians, Moldavians, Serbs and dissident Wallachians countered Ottoman forays into Moldavia and struck hard into Turkish-held territory in Bosnia. (It was during these engagements that the Impaler committed his atrocities in Srebrenica that we have previously described.) The heavy defeats delivered to Mehmet's forces by Stefan earned him the title of 'Athlete of Christ' in 1475.

Dracula's crucial support of Stefan's forces when the tide appeared to be turning, in the summer of 1476, earned him both the gratitude of Moldavia and what he had craved during his many years of Hungarian exile. In late November of 1476, Vlad Dracula was officially declared Voivode of Wallachia for the third time. This, his final reign, would last little more than two months. Before the end of the year, Dracula was dead, slain in battle somewhere north of Bucharest, the city he had recently adopted as his new capital.

Describing Vlad the Impaler's legacy as ambivalent is something of an understatement. There were numerous question marks left hanging over his mangled corpse in December of 1476. Who mourned him as a hero or conversely celebrated the death of a monster? More immediately, who killed the Impaler? It's something like the military history equivalent of a traditional murder mystery, with no shortage of suspects. There was surely a sense of regret in many European capitals when the news made its slow progress westward, if for no other reason but that Vlad's demise robbed Christendom of an indomitable fighter – just as there were certainly Ottoman celebrations at the death of a man who had taken on an almost demonic aura in Islamic eyes, a bogeyman mothers used to frighten naughty children in Constantinople. Five centuries later, in Dracula's homeland, by then part of the Socialist Republic of Romania, Dracula's death was unambivalently commemorated as the martyrdom of a national hero. Yet even here, a strong air of uncertainty, of the truth swallowed by a miasma of propaganda and myth, prevails …

***

"He's running checks on his mother's womb, he's gonna be reborn real soon."
'– Blues for Ceauşescu', written by Cathal Coughlan, performed by the Fatima Mansions, 1991.

Marxism-Leninism and the more traditional despotism of Prince

Vlad III may make strange bedfellows, but, as we've seen, they are not entirely incompatible. In the beginnings of the fall of communist Europe – when Eastern European states began to reverse the 'domino effect' that US conservatives feared would take place in Southeast Asia, then throughout the entire Third World – the non-Soviet powers were the first to go. At the close of the 1980s, the vacuum created by the demise of Tito's benign dictatorship was beginning to dissolve Yugoslavia, as its component states started to declare independence and to eye each other with belligerent suspicion.

As Milosevic and his comrades solemnly announced their intent to continue the Ottoman Wars of five and six centuries previous, one of their eastern neighbours had been stubbornly ignoring how the ground was moving beneath his feet.

Nicolae Ceauşescu was in many ways a more archetypal 20th-century Communist leader. Surviving propaganda and home-movie footage shows a jaunty, rather bumptious man with a thinning bouffant, his beaky features as angular as those of his backcombed wife, the ubiquitous Elena. As Romania's head of state for almost 25 years, he may have seemed to some an unlikely figure to sit at the centre of a personality cult. Not so for many Westerners, including President Nixon, who preceded his historic visit to Mao's China in 1972 by three years in travelling to a much smaller communist nation, and Elizabeth II of England, who invited the Romanian Conducător (leader) to Buckingham Palace to be made an honorary knight (GCB – Grand Cross of the order of the Bath). Despite the Cold War-era paranoia that manifested in having his food tasted by his aides and checking their room for bugs, this commie was the kind of anti-Russian autocrat that the West could do business with. In the 1970s, he would also place himself on a prominent edge of the historical personality cult that has created this book.

As a virtual lifelong communist, Ceauşescu had his political baptism of fire in the turbulent 1930s. After a series of arrests for distributing 'communist and anti-fascist propaganda' (this was the era when much of Europe was divided into demagogues urging street battles over the two opposed totalitarian ideologies), he received his first prison sentence as an agitator in 1936, aged 18. As secretary of the Communist Youth Organisation, his intermittent returns to jail would insulate him from the social upheavals that led to the death of Codreanu (the communists' political opposite number – see Chapter Nine) and indeed protect him from persecution by the Iron Guard.

The young Ceauşescu spent much of the World War 2 years

incarcerated. It was only when the tide of the war had definitively turned in 1944, and Stalin's Red Army invaded Romania, that the faithful party apparatchik stepped up to fulfil what he would later describe as his historic destiny. When the Romanian Communist Party seized power in 1948, he became a fixture in the Politburo of party leader Gheorghe Gheorghiu-Dej. On the death of the leader in 1965, Ceauşescu's fellow communists would elect him to the head of the party by virtue of his stance of independence from the Soviet Union. Nicolae Ceauşescu would consolidate this with his condemnation of the Soviet invasion of Prague in 1968, and his reception by the West as the kind of moderniser and neo-liberal with which they could hold a dialogue. It's largely with hindsight that he came to be regarded as a rather tawdry political bully who established an arbitrary political dynasty from among his own family – particularly the uneducated Elena, whose bizarre accumulation of honorary university degrees led to her official title of Comrade Academician Doctor Engineer.

In 1976, Ceauşescu's government also presided over the historic anniversary commemorations of a most controversial national figure, then thrown into a posthumous spotlight by the success of Florescu and McNally's *In Search of Dracula*. In the December of that year, Romanian state cultural life marked 500 years since the death of Vlad the Impaler – depicted not as the blueprint for a Western bogeyman (Dracula movies were banned under Ceauşescu as anti-Romanian propaganda), but as one of the fathers of Romanian nationalism – the title once accorded to Codreanu by Hitler.

Most startlingly, perhaps, Vlad was held up as a model for the government of a struggling independent nation. While there certainly don't seem to have been any interesting 'Impalement Day' parades in the street, the intellectual life of Romania (as directed by the state) marked the several reigns of the Impaler Prince with memorial paintings and statues, a biographical play and, in the bureaucratic everyday, a Posta Romana stamp featuring the best known portrait of Vlad Tepeş.

There was also a spate of articles commissioned in the Romanian academic press. Historians and theoreticians praised the Impaler for 'the modern style in which he conducted himself as head of state' (Dan Zamfirescu, 'A Modern Prince'), while elevating him to the status of other, less controversially celebrated (though perhaps almost as bloodthirsty) Romanian Voivode heroes, such as Michael the Brave or Vlad's own cousin, Stefan the Great. In his 1976 magazine article, 'Vlad the Impaler – Current Parallels with a Medieval Romanian Prince', written to coincide with the commemorative events, historian George Cioranescu sought perhaps the most pertinent parallel between the 15th century's fearsome and fearless despot and the Romanians' contemporary leader. At that time, the decade-old estrangement between Romania and the Soviet Union was undergoing a periodic thaw; nonetheless, Cioranescu was able to strike an analogy between Vlad the Impaler and Ceauşescu, a leader guiding the nation through relatively much gentler times: 'The historical articles published on the Impaler's anniversary sometimes do contain cryptic and allusive wording of a sort that could be understood by a reader "in the know" to imply an anti-Soviet stand, if references to the Ottoman Empire were read to mean the Soviet Union, and Western Christendom to stand for the democratic West.' (A reflection of the skewed perception that Ceauşescu's foreign policy made him the maverick leader who stood between the two belligerents of the Cold War.)

The inspirational leader of a plucky independent principality, standing courageously against the two bullying monolithic empires that surround it. Perhaps this is what Ceauşescu meant by his grandiose remark that, 'A man like me comes along every 500 years.' ('He's gonna be reborn real soon.') In the eventuality, the commemorations would certainly cement into legend the idea that, in Vlad the Impaler, Romania's mini-scale Stalin had found his own personal Ivan the Terrible. In the state-sponsored press, many of Vlad's most infamous (and historically verifiable) acts, from the persecution of the Saxon merchants (standing up to the capitalist exploiters) to the burning of the beggars and cripples (eradicating social parasitism and dishonesty) were justified because 'he had a clear-cut political goal in mind that justified his actions, not simply one that served as cover for the gratification of his cruel instincts,' wrote Romanian political historian Nicolae Stoicescu. All blood was shed for the common good.

So, just how much did Ceauşescu have in common with his notorious medieval forebear? Not much on the surface, though it is possible to draw some parallels between their personalities. 'Nicolae Ceauşescu was very demanding, tough, severe and precise,' recalls Stefan Andrei, who worked under the Romanian leader for over 20 years in high-ranking positions, including foreign minister. 'He got angry very quickly. He was hard-working, punctual and naturally intelligent ... He had been influenced by the fact that he went to prison at a very young age, before he was 18.' Might this also be an accurate description of the enigmatic character of Vlad Dracula? Ion Mihai Pacepa, a high-ranking general and minister in the Romanian government who later defected to the USA under an assumed name, also offers an intriguing insight in to his old boss's personality. Pacepa recalls a bizarre meeting with Ceaușescu in the summer of 1978, on a boat near the President's summer residence, the leader favouring private meetings on the lake for particularly sensitive matters.

'Ceaușescu had long been fascinated by the structured society of the white pelicans in the Danube delta,' said Pacepa. 'The old birds – the grandparents – always lay up on the front part of the beach, close to the water and food supply. Their respectful children lined up behind them in orderly rows, while the grandchildren spent their hours horsing around in the background. I had often heard Ceaușescu say he wished Romania had the same rigid social structure. "Put an Uzi in the hydrofoil too," he said – the small Israeli sub-machine gun was his favourite. Ceaușescu was as passionate a hunter as he was a bird watcher, and, after happily observing a pelican colony for a while, he would always reach for his Uzi.' During this meeting, Ceaușescu revealed that he wanted Pacepa to assassinate the director of Romania's Radio Free Europe and blow up its headquarters in Munich. 'The end of Ceaușescu's sentence was masked by the methodical rat-a-tat of his Uzi. He aimed with ritual precision, first at the front line of pelicans, then at the middle distance, and finally at the grandchildren in the back,' recalls Pacepa, who fled to the West the following day.

The story recalls a joke contemporary in Romania under communist rule, which went roughly as follows: Ceaușescu is at an international conference, being held on an ocean-going yacht, alongside the American President and the leader of the Soviet Union. While gesturing, the American President's gold wristwatch comes loose and drops over the side. Without pausing to think, one of his CIA bodyguards takes off his shades to dive into the sea, climbing back on board with the watch in his teeth to a round of applause. Not to be outdone, the Soviet President takes off his own watch and deliberately throws it over the side, gesturing to one of his own KGB bodyguards. Attracted by the commotion, sharks are now approaching the ship, but the KGB man dives after the timepiece without hesitation, returning with his superior's watch to a similar round of admiring applause for his bravery. With this, Ceaușescu unclips his watch and casts it over the side into the water, now thick with shark fins. Nobody does anything, so the Romanian President turns to a member of his Securitate secret police and orders him, 'Retrieve my watch!' 'No,' responds the agent, at which point one of the other Securitate police turns to his neighbour and observes, 'Now, there is a truly brave man!' It's easy to imagine the citizens of 15th-century Wallachia making similar jokes about the terrifying reputation of their own infamous leader.

Ceauşescu's political goals became ever more central state-directed in the 1970s. Despite his posturing against Stalinism, his Securitate were becoming ever more directly involved in the running of the country. While no large-scale massacres are known to have occurred in modern Romania, the Securitate wielded an iron fist that could punish anti-Ceauşescu dissent by destroying an individual's work prospects, or removing them from society to endure Soviet-style psychiatric treatment or state torture in prison. Within their own borders, they became as feared as the despised Stasi of East German communist leader Erich Honecker (an ally of Ceauşescu's, for all the latter's quibbles with the Warsaw Pact).

In 1971, while he was starting to be feted by the West, Ceauşescu had made his own state visits to China and North Korea, where he was impressed by state planning on a large scale. Since his rise to power in the 1960s, he had already restricted divorce to a level of near-impossibility and criminalised all forms of abortion in order to expand the Romanian population (then growing into tens of millions, reflecting the expansion of territory and assimilation of peoples since Vlad's medieval reign). It was a virtual inversion of the Maoist policy that decreed one child per family to produce the optimum number of people for a vastly populated China, but it would have a similarly profound impact.

***

The black-browed babe-in-arms bawls pitifully. Howling alone in his crib, in the communal paediatric ward where similarly afflicted children are housed (or warehoused), the child has torn the drip feed from his arm and howls alone, as none heed the call to heal his punctured little arm, or to replace his starving body's nutrients.

If we let our eyes train along this scene in the orphanage's hospital ward, then we can see that our baby boy is merely one of dozens of such children left to cry alone in their pain and malnourishment, with an insufficient number of staff to attend to them. They mirror each other side by side in their iron cots, howling alone in the darkness. Listen to them – children of the night, what music they make …

But they are not alone now. Breaking into the shadows of the hospital ward, one diminutive male figure steps forward and places a patriarchal talon upon the child. The baby is alarmed at first, making a shrill intake of breath, but then soothed slightly by this father figure's repetitive stroking motion.

'You have soothed the little boy's pain, Nicolae.' The woman's crackling, aged tone rises above the crying of the babies. 'Let us alleviate his suffering altogether.'

Ceauşescu, the immortal undead, looks upon the witch-like features of his bride, Elena. In his dignity, the father of the nation does not respond to such flattery. Instead, he sharply restores the drip tube to the child's arm, raising a crescendo of wailing from the baby. Then, carefully and lovingly, he disconnects the feeding end of the tube from the empty syringe, and inserts it gently between his wife's lips. She begins to draw on the infected baby's lifeblood. Ceauşescu and his bride will feed well tonight ...

***

This kind of satirical conflation of Ceauşescu and Dracula – not the Wallachian warlord, but the vampire of Western popular culture – was a common metaphor in Eastern Europe during the dictator's final years. A Gothic urban myth no doubt, but one that didn't quite seem so implausible in the case of Ceauşescu, as more accurate rumours of the beloved leader's galloping hypochondria and paranoia began to circulate. Safety agency staff disinfected every location before he visited, a chemist accompanying him on foreign visits, whose duties included destroying his excrement to deny foreign agents the opportunity to inspect it. According to Ion Mihai Pacepa, Ceauşescu wore every suit of clothes only once, each outfit destroyed after use, to be replaced by a fresh suit, taken from a sealed transparent bag from a climate-controlled warehouse. 'The rule was to keep a year's supply in stock: 365 suits, 365 pairs of shoes, and so forth,' said Pacepa. The Romanian President's obsession with his own health and safety was not reflected by any concern for his own population.

His disastrous policy of forbidding abortion and restricting birth control – aimed at building Romania's workforce – had led to a large-scale problem of child abandonment among those unable or unwilling to accept parenthood. (There are distant echoes here of Vlad's ruthless attempts at strengthening his populace, regardless of the consequences.) Compounding this, the wilful blindness that disregarded the AIDS explosion of the 1980s, perceiving it merely as a problem of decadent Western homosexuals and drug addicts, had led to the pitiful spectacle of children's orphanages becoming Darwinian dustbins, filled with babies and toddlers whose immune deficiency systems had given up on them and left them to die – much like their adult carers in the Romanian state Utopia.

As the wide spread of AIDS became an inescapable fact, so its imagery began to permeate horror genre fiction. Blood, infection, dissipation – its grim components led to an ironic overhaul of the vampire in fantastic fiction. It was these same factors that fed into the satirical image of Ceauşescu and Elena as vampires – compounded, perhaps, by the state leader's perceived affection for the reign of Vlad the Impaler, and certainly not helped by the building of his luxurious villa at Snagov, close to the monastery where Vlad's headless skeleton was believed to have been interred (of which more anon).

It would only take a couple more years for Western genre authors to inherit the Ceauşescu vampire archetype from Central European political satire, accelerated by a sudden chain of historic events. As horror author Dan Simmons says in the opening of his vampire novel, *Children of the Night*, 'We flew to Bucharest almost as soon as the shooting had stopped, landing at Otopeni Airport just after midnight on December 29, 1989 ...'

***

The father of the nation was slow to react to the changes which fell upon him so rapidly. Re-elected leader of the Communist Party in November 1989, this latest act of hubris pre-dated the fall of Ceauşescu by a few weeks, if not days. When the chips were finally down, Nicolae and Elena tried to escape to Snagov by helicopter. They never made it, instead making a diversion by helicopter for Tîrgovişte before finally being captured at Christmas 1989. Tîrgovişte seems an even more irrational destination – offering no escape route and no hiding place; the fact that it is the former capital of Wallachia and houses the imperial residence of Prince Vlad led some to romantically suggest Ceauşescu wanted to make a last stand at the home of his hero.

The Ceauşescus were tried at a shabby old government building on Christmas Day, on the novel charge of 'genocide by starvation, by lack of heating and lighting'. When it was clear that the game was at a dead end, Elena defiantly ordered the turncoat guards to 'kill us together if you want to kill us'. She was less haughty as they were immediately bound up with rope and told by the leader of their firing squad, 'No one can help you now,' in the age-old language of the vanquisher and the vanquished. The first lady's words when it became clear their fate was sealed were less dignified: 'Go back up your mother's cunt!' The bloody end of the Ceauşescus, riddled with bullets, is immortalised in easily accessible news footage. It would be celebrated by those they had persecuted and mourned by those to whom the communist era had granted an affordable standard of living.

It remains much disputed among historians as to whether Ceauşescu genuinely saw Vlad the Impaler as a role model. What can be known is that, after his execution, the state ban upon Western gothic fiction was rescinded. In the years of tortuous transformation to a capitalist economy, a theme park was planned to exploit Romania's main figure of folklore and legend: Draculaland, a combination of Disneyesque riffs on Stoker and historical sadism for all the family, built in the Impaler's birthplace of Sighisoara. (At the time of writing, the theme park plans happily seem to have stalled indefinitely.)

As modern historians pick the bones out of the Ceauşescu era, it has been argued that the communist leader granted no greater historical importance to Vlad than to Stefan the Great or Michael the Brave, and that there are fewer streets named after the Voivode in Bucharest (the city he established as his new capital in the final days of his reign) than there are commemorating his cousin. This seems to be missing the point, however, that in merely being placed alongside Romania's other great nationalist warriors, the Impaler still maintains his status as a hero of the people. While for many, Vlad Dracula's violent death in 1476 represented the overdue end for a bloodthirsty psychopath, for many Romanians it was the tragic climax to the career of a champion of the Romanian people.

***

Curiously enough, at least for many outsiders who saw in the execution of the Ceauşescus only the justified extinction of two tyrants at the hands of their long-suffering populace, a similar ambivalence lurks over the death of Communist Romania's first couple in 1989. Ten years after the event, *The Independent* newspaper interviewed Dorin-Marian Cirlan, one of the three elite paratroopers who made up the firing squad. 'You have to picture how it was then,' Cirlan explained. 'Rumours were swirling – there was panic everywhere on the radio, on television, even on the army radio frequencies. It was like the coming of the Apocalypse.' Among the rumours was wild talk of an imminent Russian invasion or a US-backed coup, both reasons given for the trial's undue haste and lack of proper procedure. 'I could hear everything through the door,' Cirlan recalled, 'and I knew then that there was something wrong with the trial. Elena was complaining, refusing to recognise the court. The so-called defence lawyers were acting like prosecutors. But I was a soldier obeying orders. It was only later that I realised what a mockery it all was.' In the trial's Kafkaesque conclusion, the judge allowed the couple the statutory ten days of appeal allowed by Romanian law, before ordering that the sentence be carried out immediately.

While few would deny that the Ceaușescus had much to answer for, there has been a building unease among Romanians about what had happened in Romania in 1989, that the popular revolution on the streets concealed a calculated coup, the fruit of a conspiracy hatched behind closed doors. It's a suspicion now shared by Dorin-Marian Cirlan: 'It wasn't a trial, it was a political assassination in the middle of a revolution,' he says of the execution he was a party to. Romania was the only Eastern Bloc country whose government fell violently. When the new democratic Romania emerged from the chaos, many of its citizens were depressed to discover that many of the country's new elite were familiar faces from the Communist era. Some political commentators have subsequently identified the execution as the definitive example of the ultimate sanction required when a tenacious leader refuses to give up office despite being in a hopeless situation. While the Communist governments of her Eastern Bloc neighbours all folded peacefully, only Romania's regime clung onto power at the risk of sending the nation spiralling into the kind of civil war which was soon to traumatise Yugoslavia to the west. Ceaușescu's death may have been a state-sanctioned assassination, rather than the punishment of a people's court as it was widely portrayed in the media, but if it was what was necessary to stabilise Romania, few foreign commentators were likely to raise any objections.

Was Vlad the Impaler the victim of the 'Ceaușescu option' in the winter of 1476 – felled not by his enemies, but at the hands of allies who now regarded him as a dangerous liability? The nebulous facts surrounding the death of Dracula give plenty of meat for the medieval conspiracy theorist to get their teeth into, a 15th-century Romanian equivalent of the assassination of John F. Kennedy. As with the JFK controversy, there is a grassy knoll, though in Dracula's case it is generally described as a hill, and was the location of both the assassin and his victim. The fullest account we have of Vlad's final hours comes from the Russian source, which records how the 'Turks came to his land and started to seize it and he attacked them and the Turks fled and the armies of Dracula started to kill them without mercy and chased them out. And Dracula was so happy he rushed to the top of the hill to see how the Turks were being punished, and he got separated from his army and those who were near him thought that he was a Turk and one of them hit him with a spear. When he saw that he was being killed by his own people, he killed five of his killers with his sword and was killed with many spears and thus he died.'

It's not a very convincing story. Friendly fire occurs in every war, but is far more likely with modern weaponry than at the distance of the length of a spear. Would Vlad's men really not have recognised their own leader, who was scarcely a quiet retiring figure by any measure? It's been argued that Dracula might have been disguised as a Turk, though this too seems a somewhat weak explanation for Vlad to have been accidentally killed, particularly if he took five of his assailants with him. The Christian army that invaded Wallachia in 1476 was a multi national force, so might Dracula have found himself among foreign allies who didn't recognise him or even understand his language? Yet the vast bulk of the allied forces had headed home some time before, the Hungarians riding back north and the Moldavians east, leaving Dracula to mop up Basarab's rebels on his own. This was perhaps a mistake, as Basarab still enjoyed the support of a number of Turkish forces on the Wallachian border, and appears to have crossed the Danube and surprised Vlad somewhere outside Bucharest, outnumbering the Voivode's army by two to one.

How much could Dracula trust his own men? The aura of fear he had relied upon in his glory days had been much diminished during his long years of Hungarian captivity. His armies had deserted him in 1462, preferring peace under an Ottoman puppet to war and terror under Dracula, and there's every reason to suppose they might do so again. Indeed, when Vlad resumed his rule of Wallachia he did so among an unprecedented number of foes, friends and relatives of the countless victims of his last brutal reign, at least some of whom must surely have found their way into Dracula's army. Any one of these men might plausibly hatch a plot to 'accidentally' kill their commander. Stefan had left 200 of his best men as personal bodyguards for the Impaler before he returned home to Moldavia, suggesting that the astute Moldavian Voivode doubted the loyalty of Vlad's native troops. Records report that only ten of Dracula's Moldavian guards survived the attack upon their charge, something which again doesn't fit with the idea of Vlad being slain by accident by his own men, but rather suggests a fierce last stand against a determined foe. It's quite possible that the Russian source simply reflected a certain national bias. They appear to have believed that part of Vlad's pact with Matthias Corvinus involved converting to Catholicism: 'Alas, he couldn't bear the temporary troubles of the prison and instead prepared himself for eternal punishment by leaving our Orthodox faith and adopting the Latin falsehood.' The Russian account takes a notably more critical attitude to Dracula after his supposed apostasy, and their version, with the Voivode victim to mistaken identity, might have been an embroidery designed to deny an apostate the dignity of a glorious last stand.

'The captain named by King Matthias, Dracula, together with 4000 men, was butchered by the Turks,' according to the pragmatic report that reached the ears of the Holy Roman Emperor Frederick III. Other reports circulating in the months following Dracula's demise, however, continued to refer to it as an assassination, rather than a simple death in battle. If we accept, for a second, that Vlad wasn't simply overrun by Basarab's Turkish troops on the battlefield, and was the victim of a plot, then the next question is, who was behind it? The list here quickly runs into a roll call of pretty much everyone who crossed paths with the Impaler during his violent life. As well as his own people, and the Saxons of Transylvania, Vlad had inflicted vile, humiliating punishments on many other factions, from the gypsies to the local Catholic clergy, all of whom would have a strong motive to ensure Dracula didn't have the chance to inflict his inimitable style of rule upon Wallachia once again. Even his purported friends can't be ruled out as suspects. Both Matthias of Hungary and Stefan of Moldavia had betrayed Vlad before, and might have felt it time to cut short the rule of a volatile ally who represented the definitive loose cannon on their respective borders. They might equally have been wary of being seen as directly responsible for a man who, while regarded as a monster in many quarters, was still also seen as an effective crusader by many who were insulated from his methods.

This is, of course, pure speculation – history as JFK-style conspiracy theory – but it is easy to slip into the habit of assuming that behind every death is a sinister secret when studying the history of the period, where Machiavellian machinations appear to lurk behind many of the pivotal episodes. An Austrian chronicler of the day named Jacob Unrest offers a version of the Impaler's death that combines the obvious conclusion that Dracula was slain by his Ottoman opponents with an element of intrigue: 'Dracula was killed with great cunning, because the Turks wished to avenge the enmity which he had borne against them for so long and also the great damages inflicted upon them. They hired a Turk [to pose] as one of his servants with the mission of killing him while he served him. The Turk was apparently instructed to attack

Dracula from the back. He was then to cut off his head and bring it back on horseback to the sultan.' Other accounts suggest that Dracula's head did indeed make its way to Constantinople, where it was displayed on a pike to reassure the populace that *Kaziglu Bey* was finally dead. However, it's difficult – though not impossible – to imagine a Turkish spy murdering and then smuggling the severed head of the enemy leader from the enemy camp undetected. The balance of probability must still rest on Vlad Dracula simply falling in battle with Basarab and his Turkish allies. If he was betrayed, the likeliest scenario is that his army dissolved around him, unwilling to fight for a ruler they now hated as much as they feared, leaving the Voivode to make a last stand supported only by his Moldavian guard.

The story of a figure as dark and powerful as Dracula somehow demands a more remarkable, even romantic end than falling in a meaningless skirmish to a lucky rival. In the specific case of Vlad the Impaler, this also applies to the fate of his headless corpse, which appears to have wandered posthumously in a way likely to satisfy the Gothic appetites of modern horror fans, at least in a fashion. In their classic pioneering works on the Voivode, *In Search of Dracula* and *Dracula: Prince of Many Faces*, Florescu and McNally include chapters on the fate of Dracula's cadaver – 'Snagov: The Mystery of the Empty Grave' and 'The Mystery of the Grave' respectively. The two eminent Dracula scholars track Vlad's mortal remains (sans head of course) to the monastery of Snagov, situated on an island on Lake Snagov, some 20 miles north of Bucharest. So the story goes, Vlad built the monastery, and in gratitude for his patronage, the monks retrieved the Impaler's body and interred it in the chapel there. Then the mystery begins…

Much of Florescu and McNally's research rests upon an excavation of the chapel at Snagov carried out by Romanian archaeologists at the site in 1930s (coincidentally, just after Hollywood made Dracula a household name with its black-and-white horror movie). The team were particularly interested in a large flagstone in front of the altar, which monastic tradition suggested was actually Vlad the Impaler's tomb. Its unusual location reflected the disdain the Greek Orthodox monks felt for the monastery's former patron, constantly walked over by sandalled feet, while the generations of services held over the Impaler's mortal remains might finally purge his black soul. To the disappointment of the archaeological team, there was nothing beneath the slab but a pit containing animal bones and sundry detritus, apparently pre-dating Dracula by many centuries. Attention then shifted to a second potential tomb to one side of the chapel entrance. This proved more promising, containing a coffin, within which were the skeletal remains of a headless corpse, with vestiges of the corpse's attire lying on the bones. Might this be the last resting place of Dracula himself?

The Romanian archaeologists believed so, and transported their finds to the City of Bucharest History Museum. The next twist in the tail is worthy of an Indiana Jones flick, or the first reel of a sequel to the *Hellboy* supernatural action franchise. When the German army approached Bucharest during World War 2, diligent Romanian curators packaged up the nation's treasures to be sent for safe keeping in the mountains, under the protection of Nicolae Iorga, Romania's most eminent historian. Among them were the finds from Snagov. In a hokey horror film, the convoy would have been intercepted by a secret Nazi special operations squad, tasked with securing the remains of Dracula in order to try and harness their occult power. In reality, they simply disappeared. The fact that the overstretched Romanian authorities were obliged to conscript convicts to conduct such missions makes it likely that the artefacts were pilfered or dumped. We don't know, but the reports of the team from the original Snagov excavation contained enough detail for informed speculation on the remains found in the alleged tomb of Dracula, even if the items uncovered are lost to us.

Florescu and McNally caught the contagious excitement of the archaeologists who had opened the tomb in the 1930s. The contents could indeed be from the 15th century. The fragment of cloth found on the corpse matched the colour of the ceremonial cloak worn by members of the Order of the Dragon. A ring and a buckle recovered from the coffin 'were typical of the kind of gift a noble woman of high standing might make to her favourite knight, victorious in a tourney', observe the American scholars in *Dracula: Prince of Many Faces*. 'Indeed, this precious trophy from an unidentified lady was undoubtedly the one acquired by Dracula's father on the night of his successful tournament following his investiture in the Dragon Order at Nuremberg on November 8, 1431. Dracul later bequeathed the trophies, together with his cherished Toledo sword, to his oldest surviving son, Dracula, at the time an exile in Turkey. The precious relics in the tomb represented the sole surviving legacy from the murdered father to his son.'

Florescu and McNally's enthusiasm is equally contagious, but at this point their exemplary scholarship is eclipsed by the magnetic romanticism of the Dracula myth. Had Dracul's Toledo sword been discovered in the tomb, that would be one thing. But a ring and a buckle are slim evidence upon which to hang such conclusions, not least when they link to a supposed tryst between the future Wallachian Voivode and a mysterious lady in Nuremberg, which is romantic speculation at best. The fragment of cloth proves nothing. Indeed, there is no evidence to suggest that Dracula was a member of the Order of the Dragon, even if we accept that a scrap of 500-year-old fabric might be identified as a Draconist robe. A withering torrent of cold water was poured upon the Florescu McNally theories concerning the burial of Dracula by the Romanian academic Dr Constantin Rezachevici in his paper 'The Tomb of Vlad Ţepeş: The most probable hypothesis', delivered at a Romanian symposium on the Voivode in 2002.

Dr Rezachevici demonstrates that, while much of Florescu and McNally's research has a firm grounding in Romanian historical scholarship, that scholarship is built on a series of flawed assumptions. For example, while it has often been stated that Dracula built, or at least substantially expanded, the monastery at Snagov, Vlad the Impaler is one of the few Wallachian Voivodes who doesn't appear to have had anything to do with the institution. His father Vlad and grandfather Mircea made donations to Snagov, as did his Danesti rival Vladislaus and even his apostate brother Radu. So, indeed, did subsequent Voivodes. But, even though he made donations to other religious institutions, there is nothing to connect Dracula with Snagov. Rezachevici suggests that many of the 'traditions' linking the monastery with the Impaler were invented by bored monks in the 1800s, such as the story that there was once 'in the southern buildings, a torture room in which the culprit – after subjection to fire and iron – was thrown into the lake by catapult or pulley. With the demolition of the old houses, the torture room and the pulley disappeared.' He similarly dismisses tales in which references are made to Dracula's name and image being deliberately erased from the monastery by hostile monks as 'a fantastic absurdity', invented to amuse, and perhaps attract, visitors.

'Even today, in 2002, various parish priests try to find all kinds of princely tombs in their churches, and if they cannot find them, some are ready, unfortunately, to invent them, then demand approval to carve tombstones for them,' observes Rezachevici. 'One such priest in Harlau upholds that prince Petru Rares (son of Stephen the Great) was buried in his church, although contemporary documents placed the tomb in his own church, the monastery Pobrata Noua.' Why would Greek Orthodox monks wish to deride or expunge the reputation of a ruler who had done them no harm, who indeed had given generously to Orthodox institutions, such as Mount Athos? Even if they did, placing his final resting place to one side of the chapel entrance seems an odd way of doing it. The Doctor convincingly suggests that the inventions of fanciful monks in the 1800s, keen to add romantic interest to their monastery, combined with the enthusiasm of the archaeological team of the 1930s to make an exciting discovery, created a myth. A myth that gained critical mass in the 1970s with the renewed interest in Vlad, spurred by the 500th anniversary of his death and the publication of *In Search of Dracula*. Most damningly, Rezachevici observes that the current chapel post-dates Dracula by a century, which makes it highly unlikely that the mysterious grave is truly from the 15th century.

So how did Snagov become so inextricably associated with Dracula? Rezachevici concedes that, as far back as the 16th century, the monastery was mistakenly linked to the Impaler, something he attributes to the institution's unusually grim history, which made it a natural fit with the region's most bloodthirsty figure in folk memory. It was the resting place of many of the aristocrats executed in the 16th and 17th centuries, earning itself the title of 'the cemetery of the politically beheaded'. He lists an impressive catalogue of horrors witnessed within the walls of Snagov, as it transformed from a place of worship into a prison for political prisoners. 'As a result of so many executions of boyars, of tortures and long prison-terms, well into the eighteenth century, no wonder that Snagov got a bloody reputation – an ideal placement for the tomb of Vlad! Besides, in 1840, Snagov was the first monastery officially turned into a place of confinement for revolutionaries of the 1848 movement. In 1853 or 1854, the ferry overloaded with chained detainees went down, drowning all – which increased its notoriety.' The island became thick with ghoulish folklore, of lost spirits, treasure concealed in the lake (Dracula's hoard, the only witnesses impaled), and churches claimed by the water, whose bells still rang in a storm. The perfect environment to house the spectre of Romania's most infamous icon, perhaps, but not a plausible location for his grave in historical terms.

So where is Dracula buried? To solve this enigma, Dr Rezachevici goes back to Vlad the Impaler's final hours. He suggests that Dracula was killed in battle, not north of Bucharest as is commonly assumed, but to the south of the Romanian capital. The location of the Impaler's last stand has been misidentified by previous historians because of the familiar confusion between Dracula, and his father Dracul, who did die near Snagov. It is far more likely that the Impaler might have been surprised south of Bucharest, closer to the border. Here the 'grassy knoll' comes into play in Rezachevici's theory, as he observes that, while the Russian account insists that Dracula was slain on a hill, the territory north of Bucharest is uniformly flat. So, if Dracula was slain, as Rezachevici insists, on the road south of Bucharest, what became of his headless corpse? Nobles were commonly buried in a chapel associated with them close to their place of death, so he suggests that Dracula was interred at Comana, a monastery south of Bucharest in Giurgiu County that the Impaler is known to have established. There is a village in Giurgiu County named Vlad Tepeş, though any hope of finding Dracula's tomb at the nearby monastery is slim indeed, as the institution Vlad founded there 500 years ago has been built over numerous times.

Dr Rezachevici concludes his fascinating paper on a sceptical note. 'Most legends dissipate under a closer scrutiny,' he concludes. 'In 1933, a talented reporter, F. Brunea-Fox, dived in Snagov to find the so-called fallen wooden church (the small church built by Vladislaus II, demolished prior to 1844). He found nothing. In his words: "Void. Because this is the fate of legends, dear readers – when you investigate them."' Admirable words for a scholar, perhaps, but a sentiment confounded by the story of Dracula. It is highly doubtful that Dr Rezachevici would have dedicated his expertise to the subject of 'The Tomb of Vlad Tepeş' were it not for the legend surrounding his subject. While there is no way that he could have predicted his bizarre fictional afterlife, the real Dracula deliberately made himself a dark living legend in order to further his ambitions, a figure of fear more than equal to anything printed on any page or projected on any screen. That legend, in turn, was instrumental in his downfall. It facilitated his arrest in the 1400s, and ensured the afterlife that vexes his apologists today.

In conjunction with his collaborators Dan Minculescu and Steve Schifani, John Bianchi set out to recreate Vlad's era on the tabletop through wargaming, and in the process produced one of the best concise military histories of Eastern Europe in this vitally important, unjustly neglected field. One that is unlikely to have been published without the saleable title of *Vlad the Impaler* and the Dracula legend. Attempting to faithfully recreate the challenges and dilemmas faced by Dracula and his allies and foes, employing the best scholarship on the topic, offered Bianchi an intriguing angle on matters, seldom evident from a more traditional approach. 'While he was not a successful ruler, he established himself as someone that the Turk didn't want to face if they could avoid him,' observes Bianchi. 'John Keegan, in *The Mask of Command*, talks about the different types of commanders and how certain types are theatrically aware and use theatre and artifice as military tools. That's Vlad. One campaign was all it took for him to instil fear in the Turks, and you can see from the stories that were told and which continue to be told that he took pains to cultivate the mask of a cruel and ruthless enemy. Even if only one of those stories is true, and who can say which are and which are not, then you'd be a fool to go near his realm except as a friend.'

Devil or Dragon, monster or martyr, sadist or saint, that mask stares at us still…

EPILOGUE

Un-Dead

What is immortality? It's the elusive prize that's been offered by most of the world's successful religions in exchange for the unquestioning obedience of their devotees. Ironically, religion has in turn been responsible for more than its fair share of lives cut short, of wars fuelled by faith, savagery and sacrifice motivated by the conviction that life everlasting awaits the devout believer beyond the gates of death. Yet grand funereal monuments from almost every culture pay testament to sneaking doubts among even the pious that the immortality promised by priests may be no more than a comforting illusion, or even a theological confidence trick. In the absence of spiritual survival, living on in the memory of future generations represents the pragmatist's key to a form of immortality. Ensuring your earthly remains are interred in a spectacular edifice is an obvious method of keeping your memory alive, but stone edifices last only as long as the respect for the memorials survive, and yesterday's sacred monument easily becomes nothing more than a convenient source of materials for tomorrow's disrespectful builders, or an outdated impediment to be built over or demolished by those unmoved by the legacies of the long-dead.

A more ambitious approach to such secular immortality is to live a memorable life – become the author of great (or terrible) deeds that will assure you a place in the collective identity of your culture or nation. This can overlap with religious ideas on immortality, as establishing yourself as a spiritual exemplar can win you a place in the theological records of your people, becoming a thread in the creed priests employ to weave into the dogma that guides the daily lives of the faithful. An obvious example is Catholic saints, though the Norse gods worshipped in pre-Christian Scandinavia and Germany are widely believed to have originally been tribal chieftains, their powers and exploits magnified to supernatural extremes by generations of retelling, until they evolved into deities. As priesthoods tended to try and become

304

not just the moral arbiters but also the scribes or at least bards of their society, a friendly relationship with the religious authorities was vital if you wished to create a positive posthumous presence for yourself in posterity. It is no accident that offending Saxon monks was pivotal in establishing Dracula's villainous reputation in print and verse, while the more positive, heroic image he enjoyed among Romania's Vlach peasantry survived only via folktales handed down through the fragile medium of the oral tradition.

For centuries, such folktales went largely unheard beyond the firesides of the backwaters of the medieval principality of Wallachia, while the Saxon pamphlets gathered dust in libraries and private archives, grisly echoes of a time many would rather forget. It was the stirring of Romanian nationalism in the 1800s that inspired eager eyes and ears to seek out these stories once again. As the Vlachs struggled to unite as a nation and to shake off the shackles of both the Ottoman and Austro-Hungarian Empires, they needed heroes, icons their ideologues and balladeers could hold up as legendary forebears to stir the blood of a new generation of Romanian freedom fighters. Some fit the bill more easily than others. Stefan the Great was an obvious candidate, as was Michael the Brave, who led the fight against the Turks in the 16th century. Others were more problematic. John Hunyadi was certainly hero material, but his role as a Hungarian general made him an ambivalent figure in the Romanian canon. Vlad Dracula's legendary brutality on the surface makes him an equally awkward candidate, but desperate times call for extreme measures, and the Voivode's merciless brutality made him even more attractive for those looking for a leader who would clearly stop at nothing to achieve his ends.

It was no coincidence that Europe's Age of Revolution, when many traditional empires crumbled under pressure from nationalist movements, coincided with the emergence of the Romantic Movement in literature and art in the early 1800s. Patriotism and passion were leading themes among the Romantics, who reacted against the cult of reason propagated during the Enlightenment of the 1700s by emphasising emotion over rationalism, the violent emotions of revenge and fervour as well as less volatile feelings such as compassion and sentimentality. Thus the Romantics have been seen as propagandists for both modern individualism and prophets of the darker extremes of nationalism that coalesced as Fascism in the 20th century. Romanian Romantics, consciously creating a national mythology, invoked Vlad as the iron soul of the Vlach people, a fearless warlord during terrible times. Dracula was depicted in heroic canvases, most notably by the 19th-century Romanian artist who painted vivid versions of the famous Night Attack and the episode where the Turkish envoys had their turbans nailed to their heads (reproduced in this book). Romania's foremost Romantic poet Mihai Eminescu eulogised Dracula in his 1881 poem 'The Third Letter' (quoted in Chapter Nine); the Voivode features in a similar light in Ion Budai-Deleanu's epic 1875 verse *Tiganiada*, and appears as a patriotic war hero in Dimitrie Bolintineanu's 19th-century epic 'Battles of the Romanians'...

> The assembly of soldiers
> Shout with people:
> 'Long live the Impaler!'
> The terrified boyars jump through the window
> While Dracula drives spikes into the Turkish
> envoys' heads.

'But another picture was also emerging', according to Dracula expert Elizabeth Miller. 'In 1874, Romanian poet Vasile Alecsandri wrote a narrative entitled "Vlad Tepes and the Oaktree" which reprimands the harshness of Vlad, particularly with respect to the impalements at Tîrgovişte. However, the chief challenge to the "Vlad as hero" concept came from renowned historian Ion Bodgan, whose treatise *Vlad Tepes* (1896) questioned the traditional image of Vlad by presenting him as a bloodthirsty tyrant whose cruelty could only be accounted for in terms of mental aberration, a sick man who killed and tortured out of sadistic pleasure. Bogdan even went so far as to depict Vlad as a politically weak leader. Needless to say, the publication sparked a vigorous debate.' Of course, a year after Bodgan's study was published, another book appeared in English, a work of fiction that would ensure Vlad's immortality far beyond the Romanian-speaking world, Bram Stoker's Gothic chiller *Dracula*...

While a steady stream of sympathetic treatments of the Impaler continued to be published in Romanian (Miller lists 'the poem "Vlad Tepes" by Tudor Arghezi (1940), the short story "Soimul" by Radu Theodoru (1967) and Georgina Viorica Rogoz's novel *Vlad, fiul Dracului* (1970)') two events combined to open the international floodgates on fictional and historical treatments of Vlad in the 1970s. The publication of Radu Florescu and Raymond McNally's *In Search of Dracula* in the USA in 1972 popularised the connection between Stoker's familiar vampire Count and his obscure historical namesake in the English-speaking world. It wasn't news to everyone. Specialists familiar with Eastern European history must have noticed the coincidence long before. There was a lively correspondence on the subject in the pages of *The Times Literary Supplement* in September of 1971, followed in December by an article by Gabriel Ronay in *The Times* itself, outlining the links between Vlad the Impaler and Dracula, and drawing upon research from the sixth congress of onomastic sciences (the study of names) at Munich in 1958.

The article was no doubt pre-publicity for Ronay's book on the topic *The Dracula Myth*, first published in 1972 (and hence pre-dating Florescu and McNally's *In Search of Dracula* by a year). As a native Transylvanian (he left the region as a refugee in 1956) Ronay doubtless had a head start on local lore over many of his Western colleagues while, as an ethnic Hungarian, his scholarship was condemned by some Romanians as part of the Hungarian conspiracy to blacken Vlad's reputation. ('Four years after the formal disbanding of Ceausescu's communist thought police, Mihai Ungheanu, a Dracula apologist, devoted an entire book, tellingly entitled *The Falsification of Dracula*, to put me in the dock,' he later observed.) In a negative review of the Florescu McNally study, the academic Bacil Kirtley claims to have first drawn public attention to the link in a 1956 article for *Midwest Folklore* entitled '*Dracula*: the Monastic Chronicles and Slavic Folklore'. Regardless of who was actually first, however, it was *In Search of Dracula* that first captured the popular imagination in the US, making an impact on depictions of Dracula in Hollywood productions which would ultimately introduce Vlad the Impaler to pop culture, though this was not a development universally welcomed.

In the 1970s, Nicolae Ceauşescu's unorthodox policy of blending international socialism with Romanian nationalism was in full force just as the 500th anniversary of Dracula's death was coming up. As the actor Christopher Lee discovered when he went to Romania in 1971 to film the documentary version of *In Search of Dracula*, the locals were not particularly sympathetic to comparisons between Vlad the Impaler and Count Dracula. In 1973, the Dracula Society formed in England; 28 members made a Transylvanian Expedition 'which covered one thousand miles of Romania in under twelve days,' according to Society founder Bernard Davies. He describes the visit as a 'historic tour – the first ever to visit the settings of Stoker's *Dracula* as well as the sites associated with Vlad the Impaler,' and the trip solicited some coverage from the British press. Davies praises the 'awe-inspiring' hospitality of the locals and the 'friendliness and generosity of the ordinary

Romanian villagers,' though confesses most of the natives didn't appear to have 'the faintest idea' why his group was visiting Romania. This may explain why the Transylvanian Expedition didn't encounter the suspicion Christopher Lee and his crew experienced two years earlier, as Lee could scarcely deny the reason for their visit after he had visited some of Vlad's old haunts dressed in the Impaler's distinctive regalia.

Tension over the conflicting views of Dracula between foreign visitors and Romanian patriots reached a crescendo in 1976, when Communist state-sponsored celebrations of Vlad as a hero of the people came into a collision course with the Capitalist entertainment industry that was beginning to treat the Voivode and the vampire as the same entity, with a growing income of much-needed tourist dollars at stake. The noted Romanian writer and Communist loyalist Adrian Paunescu expressed the official party line in 1986 when he dismissed *Dracula* as 'political pornography directed against us by our neighbours' (again reflecting the cultural conspiracy theory that blamed Hungary for inspiring Stoker to name his evil character after a Romanian hero), adding that the confusion between the Impaler and the Count was part of a concerted campaign 'by reactionaries of every colour to slander the very idea of being Rumanian as well as the eternal idea of Rumania'. (Paunescu is still involved in Romanian politics, currently an active member of the Social Democratic Party of Romania, though his reputation as 'Ceauşescu's court poet' has tainted his image among those voters not nostalgic for the nation's years as a socialist republic.)

While outraged Romanian patriots would eventually receive support from Western academics led by Elizabeth Miller, keen to emphasise the distinctions between Stoker's character and the medieval Voivode for scholarly reasons, they were cultural Canutes standing against a tide of media. At the very least, Florescu and McNally's study had finally given the Count a Christian name, Vlad, which was employed thenceforth in most fictional depictions of Dracula. Many adaptations took it further, employing the controversial new back-story the Count had acquired to create a new incarnation of the world's most famous vampire, who after decades of depictions in Western popular culture was becoming a little long in the tooth. If Stoker's Dracula had wholly reinvented the 15th-century Voivode (beyond all rational recognition by many assessments), the big screen had transformed the character into something the Victorian novelist would hardly have recognised (much to cinema's most famous Count, Christopher Lee's dismay). The curious re-unification of Dracula with his historical namesake in the

1970s inspired a whole new spin on the cloaked bloodsucker beloved of horror fans, which had as little in common with previous cinematic Counts as he did with the Wallachian warlord.

***

The first Hollywood film to take Florescu and McNally's research on board was a TV movie, directed by Dan Curtis (television's foremost horror specialist) and starring Jack Palance. As a character actor of Ukrainian ancestry, best known for playing craggily intimidating villains in Hollywood action flicks, Palance might seem the ideal choice to play the Count as an Eastern European warlord. Yet this 1973 production of *Dracula* doesn't emphasise the character's past as a Balkan warrior, but rather employs the Count's previous history to reinvent him as arguably the screen's first romantic vampire prince. 'We learn in flashbacks that Vlad's adored queen was brutally murdered by the Turkish army,' writes Nina Auerbach in *Our Vampires Ourselves*. 'Van Helsing repeats this traumatic butchery when he slaughters the transformed Lucy [Dracula's first English 'bride']. Palance flings open the coffin, embraces her mutilated corpse, and weeps – an uncharacteristic vampire activity up to the 1970s, but one in which Jack Palance indulges copiously.' Against all expectations, Palance's Dracula is the heroic lover, as Richard Matheson's script co-opts elements of history in a somewhat cavalier fashion to create a lost love for his tormented lead. This not only goes against Stoker's versions of the Count, who is a species of single-minded supernatural sex-criminal, but also the historical Dracula, who from what we know subjected his unlucky consorts to savage acts of casual sadism.

'Stoker's vampire was too self-imprisoned to reflect in a mirror, but Palance's Dracula is grand enough to project himself into an epic image: the large portrait of Vlad Tepes that dominates his study,' writes Auerbach of the final sequence, where the Count is pinioned with a spear in front of a heroic painting of Vlad the Impaler, the camera panning to the picture against a soundtrack of martial music and cheering soldiers. 'A scroll over the final titles, gives us some vague historical information, but our first sight of the portrait shows us only a vigorous warrior on horseback with a lovely little queen standing by him. The queen's face is that of Jonathan's fiancée, Lucy. Though the queen is painted on a diminutive and subordinate scale proper for the wife of a great man, her reincarnation as Lucy is Dracula's sole concern.' Despite Auerbach's enthusiasm, the Curtis *Dracula* wasn't a hit, though the idea of the Count being ennobled by giving him a romantic motive for his bloodthirsty designs proved influential, and Dracula's quest for a lost love reincarnated in a modern victim would become a standard plot device in numerous future versions.

Versions such as the 1979 *Dracula*, adapted from a hit Broadway play by director John Badham, with a big budget evident in lavish Gothic sets, and a classy cast headed by the heartthrob Frank Langella in the title role. It was the most romantic version of the tale thus far filmed, with Langella's character closer to a saturnine escapee from a Mills & Boon novel than any bloodthirsty Voivode (some unkind critics have referenced the film's psychedelic special effects and the lead's snazzy 70s threads and dubbed this incarnation 'disco Dracula'). Nevertheless, the publicity department did exploit the historical angle, most notably in a poster that featured 'thirteen facts' you needed to know before you experienced the film. Such as the three following…

'Dracula is actually Vlad Dracul, a Transylvanian count born in Wallachia in 1431, known as Vlad the Impaler, he was a ferocious warrior who impaled his enemies on oiled, rounded stakes, then watched with pleasure as they died in agony.' (Which is broadly accurate aside from the familiar confusion between Dracula and his father.) 'Dracula, in the 15th century, had several mistresses who took erotic delight in his cruelty, even when it was directed at them. During the last three years of his life he became convinced that drinking the blood of young maidens would give him tremendous strength.' (Here we are clearly departing from any kind of historical record into the realms of sadomasochistic fantasy.) 'Dracula's actual castle fell into smouldering ruins after Vlad's mysterious death in 1476. A search of the castle's dungeon produced a strange surprise: a coffin, covered by a rotted purple shroud, containing a signet ring, the remains of a royal tunic, and fresh black earth.' (This is interesting in that it appears to reference the items described in Florescu and McNally's investigation into the Snagov mystery, though the crumbling castle and fresh black earth are clearly pure classic Hollywood horror hokum.)

The Badham *Dracula* was also a box-office flop, though in many respects it prefigured arguably the most successful, and certainly the most expensive adaptation of Stoker's novel to date. The famous director Francis Ford Coppola elected to title his 1992 version *Bram Stoker's Dracula* to highlight his adaptation's fidelity to the Victorian source material. Critics were quick to point out that the Coppola version was no more faithful to the novel than many previous *Dracula* movies. The discrepancies start at the beginning, where the film opens with a prologue in 1462, with Dracula returning from victory over the Turks, only to discover that his bride has killed herself after receiving a false report that he has died in battle. Distraught, Vlad curses God, condemning himself to unholy immortality. This is clearly drawn from Florescu and McNally not Stoker, the suicide of his bride at Castle Poenari in 1462 adapted to allow a more romantic interpretation of the tragedy. That interpretation is extended to make *Bram Stoker's Dracula* the story of the forlorn Count's desire to find the reincarnation of his lost bride, though again this owes something to John Badham and Dan Curtis, and nothing to Bram Stoker.

Bram Stoker's Dracula is just as sentimental as Badham's version, Gary Oldman playing the Count as a doomed romantic cursed by his condition, itself the result of a broken heart. He does, however, look like Vlad the Impaler – complete with long hair and moustache – at least after the consumption of fresh blood in London makes him younger (the Count gradually getting younger is a feature of the Stoker novel seldom featured in previous versions of the story). 'Francis gave everybody little tasks to get to their character,' said Oldman of the director's unorthodox preparation for *Bram Stoker's Dracula*. 'He'd send them off to do balloon bonding, or Keanu [Reeves – the film's wooden hero] would go and ride horses. I said, "What do I do? I'm 400 years old and I'm dead!" So I stole from the historical figure.' It's debatable how seriously we should take Oldman's claims to method acting. Not least because, while the script and special effects allow his Count at times to become literally monstrous, it is impossible to see the sadist behind Oldman's star-crossed lover. The historical Vlad who sexually disembowelled his consorts on a whim is wholly absent from Oldman's tortured but tender interpretation of the role.

However far Francis Ford Coppola had taken us from the medieval Voivode and the Victorian fictional original, the success of his *Dracula* encouraged a wave of cash-ins and spin-offs, some of which focused on the historical background he explored in his prologue. In 2000, a TV movie entitled *The Dark Prince: The True Story of Dracula* was released, an action-packed historical war picture with the German actor Rudolf Martin in the title role (Martin also played the fictional Dracula in the TV series *Buffy the Vampire Slayer*). Also cast was Roger Daltrey (better known as lead singer with The Who) playing the Hungarian King Janos, a conflation of John Hunyadi and Matthias Corvinus. That historical fudge is typical of a film that doesn't play fast and loose with the facts, so much as prioritise Hollywood storytelling over historical fidelity. It is, for example, at least as accurate in historical terms as

VLAD THE IMPALER

Braveheart, for what that's worth (and *Braveheart* was employed as a promotional opportunity by the Scottish National Party). *Dark Prince's* biggest liberties with the facts come in the film's conclusion, which has Vlad murdered by his brother Radu, before the script suggests Dracula is then destined to walk the earth, presumably as the vampire of pop fiction fame.

Another film that dipped into Romanian history for its plot was the 2003 chiller *Vlad*. The plot uses large sections of – broadly accurate – medieval flashbacks to set the scene, whereby a sacred necklace belonging to the Dracula family goes missing in modern Romania. The artefact has mystic powers, and a trio of students (two Americans, a Romanian and an Englishman) get caught between rival factions, including the supernaturally resurrected Impaler himself, who are all fighting to take possession of the necklace. The film has a low budget that is often painfully apparent, with some pretty woeful acting from the young leads and feeble continuity, but the authentic Romanian settings, strong score and sheer audacity of the story, which weaves elements of history with modern horror motifs, make for a commendably bold stab at an original Dracula picture.

Dracula is of course now an international phenomenon, and the film industries of numerous different nations have given their own spin on the story. The first *Dracula* film was long thought to be *Nosferatu*, an unofficial 1922 German version, where the studio changed the characters' names – and hence dropped any possible Impaler connections – to avoid copyright issues. (Their efforts failed, and Stoker's widow successfully sued, the court ordering all prints destroyed, though happily some survived.) Recent research, however, suggests that the first Dracula film was a Hungarian production entitled *Drakula halal* (*The Death of Dracula*) that pre-dated the German movie by at least a year. The film is now believed lost, but it appears this Drakula wasn't a Wallachian warlord or a vampire, but an evil hypnotist. Regardless, it seems likely that the Hungarians would have remembered who the original historical Dracula was, making him, rather than Stoker's Count, the probable inspiration for the lead villain's moniker.

If the Hungarians were likely to remember the original Dracula long before Florescu and McNally broadcast the connection, then that counts double for the Turks, where *Kaziglu Bey* had survived as a bogeyman long before Stoker put pen to paper. Beginning in the 1950s, Turkey supported a vibrant, if threadbare film industry. In 1952, the producer Turgut Demirag decided to make a domestic version of the

Dracula saga, entitled *Drakula Istanbul'da* (*Dracula in Istanbul*), based upon the novel *Kazikili Voyvoda* (another Turkish name for the Impaler, though the book itself is a loose adaptation of Stoker's novel). Production values can be inferred from this member of the crew, who recalled in an interview with authors Pete Tombs and Giovanni Scognamillo for the book on weird world cinema *Mondo Macabro* how they achieved the effect of a low mist over a graveyard. 'We didn't have the necessary equipment,' recalled the art director. 'We had to have a backlit cloud of smoke lying on the ground. How did we create this cloud? In a very simple way. The 30 or 40 members of the crew, each with three or four cigarettes in their mouths, puffing away relentlessly, lying on the ground just out of shot!'

Despite such less-than-special effects, *Drakula Istanbul'da* proved a big hit in Turkey upon release. The connections between the moustachioed Impaler and the bald, dinner-jacketed fiend featured in the film were nominal, though it's notable that this was perhaps the first film to make the connection. It's likely that it never occurred to most of those on the Turkish production that anybody wouldn't be aware of the – to them – obvious link between the Stoker character and the 15th-century tyrant. In the 1960s, there was a vogue for historical action thrillers in Turkey, which opened the gates for Dracula to strut his bloodthirsty stuff on Turkish sets, with a persona more obviously indebted to the infamous Wallachian Voivode. Many of these films were adapted from popular Turkish action comics, whose heroes were drawn from the heyday of the Ottoman Empire, swashbucklers who wielded their scimitars for the glory of the Sultan – Malkoçoglu was one such daring swordsman who defeated the fiendish Impaler in a series of Turkish medieval action flicks, another was Kara Murat. The films are notable for including sequences recreating several of the most notorious episodes from the life of Vlad the Impaler. Dracula's swansong on the Turkish screen appears to have been in *Kara Boga* (*The Black Bull*) a 1974 film in which the inimitable Impaler is finally dispatched for good.

Of course there are two sides to every story, and in 1979 – in perhaps a late addition to state-sponsored Communist commemorations of the 500th anniversary of Dracula's death – the Romanian director Doru Nastase released the film *Vlad Tepes*. A straight historical retelling of the life and times (but not crimes) of Vlad the Impaler complete with epic battle scenes, it's bracing stuff. It's also difficult to track down except as a streaming video over the internet, and while there is rumoured to be a subtitled version in circulation, this also proved elusive. Viewed under these less than ideal conditions, it's still fascinating to see the Romanian case for the defence, in history's indictment of one of their national heroes, rendered in celluloid. Is it convincing? Perhaps not, for while it would be unfair to dismiss Nastase's film as propaganda (any one of a thousand Hollywood movies are far more naked in their crass cheerleading for the 'American way') it's still difficult to swallow whole the notion of a leader whom the film's title expressly admits was known as 'the Impaler', as a noble soul ambushed by events. In many respects, *Vlad Tepes* the film, like its historical subject, faced an almost insurmountable foe. While Dracula faced the might of the Ottoman Empire in the 1400s, in the 1970s Nastase's plucky film was up against an equally formidable foe, in the shape of the international entertainment industry.

***

Florescu and McNally's contribution to Dracula lore had a lasting impact on one of pop culture's most popular icons. Crucially, *In Search of Dracula* was published just as familiarity was in danger of breeding affection for a character originally established as an archetype of evil. In 1971, a *Count Chocula* breakfast cereal was launched, aimed at younger consumers, while the following year the Count debuted, a *Sesame Street* character designed to teach basic maths to kids. If Dracula was to retain any kind of menace, he clearly needed to develop an edge, and Florescu and McNally's study offered the ideal solution by giving the over-familiar cliché in his cloak and dinner jacket a definitively disreputable past, courtesy of an exotic and unimaginably horrific historical legacy. While the cinema of the era was definitely getting more visceral, with films like *The Texas Chainsaw Massacre* pushing back boundaries at the drive-in in 1974, most folk still weren't ready to contemplate the kind of gut-churning sadism at the root of the Dracula legend over their popcorn. Or indeed, on the written page outside of dry historical accounts, yet the germs of the story were beginning to work themselves into the pulp horror of the era.

Despite the growing infantilisation of the character in Western culture, there was an explosion of adult vampire fiction in the 1970s. The sheer volume of material that emerged precludes any workable survey of the titles from this formidable bloody tide of pulp that embrace the Impaler legend. (Elizabeth Miller name-checks authors such as Gail Kimberley, Peter Tremayne and Fred Saberhagen, though this only touches the tip of the Impaler iceberg.) Florescu and

McNally's work also caught the imagination of writers working in the definitive pulp medium of comics. They did so at a point that comics were slowly, painfully coming of age. In 1954, a psychiatrist named Dr Fredric Wertham published a book entitled *The Seduction of the Innocent*, blaming juvenile delinquency on comic books. It inspired a moral panic which led directly to the Comics Code Authority (CCA), a censorship body which forbade anything but the most innocuous material, effectively stunting the growth of the medium in the US and outlawing horror in any shape or form in mainstream titles. By the 1970s, however, some of the major American publishers began to test the boundaries, eager to introduce more challenging and mature themes.

By coincidence, perhaps, the market leader (alongside rival DC) Marvel decided to test the waters with a horror title the same year that *In Search of Dracula* was published. The new title was *The Tomb of Dracula*, the artist Gene Colan basing his Count on Jack Palance (though there is also something of Clark Gable about this Count). 'His bone structure is perfect,' said Colan of Palance (who of course actually played the part the following year). 'Serpentine. It's worked out well.' Dracula soon became the most popular of Marvel's new horror characters, and in 1973 he was given another comic – technically a magazine with comic strips to avoid CCA censorship – entitled *Dracula Lives!* In the second issue, Dracula's origin is retold in a story entitled 'That Dracula May Live Again!' which clearly owes much to Florescu and McNally. Set in 1459, Dracula is originally Vlad the Impaler, valiantly fighting the Turks, here led by a villainous bald warlord named Turac. When Vlad is mortally wounded on the battlefield, Turac decides a warrior as fearsome as Dracula would make a valuable ally, and takes him to a gypsy woman to be revived by magical means. Turac kidnaps Vlad's wife and child to ensure Dracula's loyalty, but when Vlad discovers that Turac has raped his wife, Dracula, now a vampire thanks to the gypsy magic, wreaks bloody revenge on the Turks.

Subsequent issues detailed more of this comic book incarnation of Vlad the Impaler's exploits in medieval Eastern Europe, involving more details lifted (often somewhat haphazardly from Florescu and McNally). The character remained sufficiently popular to continue to reappear in other Marvel titles even after *Dracula Lives* was cancelled in 1975 and *The Tomb of Dracula* ceased publication four years later, and Dracula found himself crossing swords with the publisher's stable of superheroes. His foes have included popular characters like the

VLAD THE IMPALER

Silver Surfer, Thor and the X-Men, most recently featuring in a 2006 four-issue mini-series *Apocalypse vs Dracula*, which opens with a prologue set in Romania in 1459, reinforcing again the links between Marvel's Lord of the Undead and the historical Vlad. It's an intriguing journey that has led an obscure Eastern European medieval warlord to become a fixture in the lurid, pulp world of American superheroes, a bizarre culture clash in many respects, though there is some tenuous continuity in that some trace the roots of the modern comic book to the early illustrated pamphlets of the 15th century, which would of course include the Saxon horror stories that first spread the Impaler's infamy.

Other comic book writers and artists have interpreted the historical Dracula, such as Roy Thomas and Esteban Maroto, who in 1993 penned the three-issue mini-series *Vlad the Impaler*. The first two issues are a relatively straight retelling of Vlad's career – rendered with the colourful bombast typical of classic comic books – though they can't resist concocting a climax whereby Dracula becomes undead in the finale. Among the more inventive and acclaimed recent interpretations of the historical Dracula is the 2008 title *Impaler* by writer Daniel Harms and artist William Timson. In this, Dracula is a vampire hunter not a vampire, battling a particularly vicious species of the undead in this gritty, downbeat horror saga. Having combated them in his own era in 15th-century Wallachia, the Voivode travels through time to confront the undead in contemporary America. 'He's a pretty fascinating character, so I tried to pull in as much historical reference as I could to help flesh him out as a character,' says Harms of his brutal anti-hero. While powerful, well-written titles like *Impaler* were offering evidence of how far the comics medium has come over the past couple of decades, with graphic novels (the approved term for 'more mature' comics) now enjoying some respect as literature, the historical Dracula was making a surprise manifestation in more conventional fiction…

***

'There is evidence that Dracula's father gave Dracula over to the Turks when he was a boy in a political bargain, and that Dracula acquired some of his taste for cruelty from observing Ottoman torture methods … At the end of the 19th century, a disturbed and melodramatic author – Abraham Stoker – gets hold of the name *Dracula*, and fastens it on a creature of his own invention, a vampire. Vlad Tepes was horrifyingly cruel, but he wasn't a vampire, of course. And you won't find any mention of Vlad in Stoker's book, although his version of Dracula talks about his family's great past as Turk-fighters.'

Our opening quote is from an American university history professor character in Elizabeth Kostova's aptly titled 2005 bestseller, *The Historian*. Prior to this successful (and heavily promoted) feminine historical-lit take on the legacy and spectre of Vlad, the Wallachian Voivode was already undergoing a process of rehabilitation in the modern popular novel.

In 1995, a history and political science graduate named Michael Augustyn had published a novel entitled *Vlad Dracula: The Dragon Prince* with a small press, Vasso Books. Reprinted in 2004, the new edition was a better work than its vanity press imprint (iUniverse) might suggest. To some extent stripping away the Stoker-isms from the name of Dracula, its generic tone was exemplified by the heading 'A Historical Novel'. Its sympathies can also be gauged from part of the cover blurb: 'His principality of Wallachia was caught between two voracious predators: the kingdom of Hungary and the Ottoman empire. They tried to break Dracula with overwhelming force and *terror*. But Dracula turned their own tactics against them, and against criminals and factions in his own land ...'

To some extent, the short spate of Vlad novels seems to have been inspired by Gary Oldman's winningly melodramatic conflation of the Voivode with the vampire in *Bram Stoker's Dracula* (1992). But to Augustyn, there also seemed to be something of the man's-gotta-do-what-a-man's-gotta-do western hero in Vlad. His cruelty is the characteristic ruthlessness of the 15th century, but rationalised with a longing for law and order: 'It is my God-given duty to bring order to this land,' he tells a thief he has just sentenced to be torn apart by two horses. 'How many years have thieves plagued us? Thieves and murderers and rapists? Don't they know me yet?' This Voivode epitomises the term harsh-but-fair: in one tender moment with his bride, she tells him that she hears the laughing voices of the perished wives and children of the enslaved boyars who died building Poenari Castle. Dracula feels a small twinge of conscience which communicates his divided humanity to the reader (while inviting incredulity at how so sensitive a man might have wiped out the boyars' families in the first place). His trademark acts of cruelty are also attributed – as your authors are inclined to concur – with the savagery of the times: 'And before he sent me to Tirgoviste the sultan tried to give me a private lesson,' Vlad tells his cousin, Stefan the Great, 'the fate of those who betray him – Impalement ... That is the Turk's best weapon. *Terror*.'

VLAD THE IMPALER

Vlad is depicted as purely a product, if not an outright victim, of his time and place.

'While much is claimed as fact regarding his life,' claims Augustyn in his foreword, 'one of his biographers explained it to me best: *East Europe, Fifteenth Century* … Few records survived the turmoil of the region.' For all that, the author makes a pretty good fist of communicating the tensions of Vlad's life, times and predicament – he wears the research and the regional vernacular lightly, although in the central text of the 2004 edition the terms *jihad* and *Allahu Akbar* are oft utilised to emphasise the clash between Christian and Muslim civilisations. This grasping for a contemporary realism is finally undermined post-Vlad's death, when a spectre appears in the final pages: 'In a black shroud-like cape. With Dracula's visage. And green eyes.' Jettisoning the 'Historical Novel', the ghostly figure is identified, after all, as a vampire.

No such supernatural conceit infects *Vlad: The Last Confession*, the 2009 work by historical novelist C. C. Humphreys. The author of numerous pop-historical novels – including the Jack Absolute series, which uses the dastardly figure of a British agent in the American war of Independence in much the same way that George Macdonald Fraser appropriated Flashman from *Tom Brown's Schooldays* – Humphreys did his homework every bit as much as Augustyn. On a narrative level, what chiefly concerns him are Vlad's conflicting drives and motives: 'tyrant and lawgiver, crusader and mass slaughterer, torturer and hero, lover and murderer' runs the blurb, and the author makes a fair stab o encapsulating these supposedly contradictory impulses in his main character (along with a rather elastic interpretation of the philosophy behind Machiavelli's *The Prince* which is shared by this book).

The question of religious motivation is not sublimated here, but (as the title suggests) emphasised to explore how a mass killer and self-professed Christian might, in death, expect to enter his Father's house justified. The bloodiness of religious iconography is up-played: 'A month before, in a village near Targoviste [sic], a statue of the Virgin had blossomed stigmata. The wounds of Christ the Son appearing on Mary the Mother, on each of her palms, at her ankles, weeping blood.' The pain of the suffering Christ and the saints is commingled with that of Vlad's victims. Even a wild boar's head baked for Vlad's wedding feast stands 'at the crossway of the crucifix, mounted upon a stake'. But his tutors in inflicting pain, as history would suggest, were not the Holy Inquisition but the Ottoman Muslims:

'When his eyes had adjusted, he looked around, saw that he was in a windowless vault, large enough so that the ceiling was lost to shadow … though not what dangled from it: pulleys, chains, nooses. More things were piled against walls – metal rods, tongs, a rack of knives … "Welcome, princeling. Welcome to Tokat."' Amongst the techniques that the young Dracula is instructed in is the traditional foot torture of the bastinado. His more extreme punishments may be his own innovation, but there's little doubt as to how extreme cruelty has been inculcated in his psyche.

Well researched and heavily fictionalised, *Vlad: The Last Confession* concludes with a narrative twist which has Vlad meeting his contemporary, Mehmet the Conqueror, in the days after he has supposedly been beheaded. The book found a readership and has passed through several editions, but in terms of popularity it was eclipsed by Elizabeth Kostova's debut novel, *The Historian*, which took the mystery of Vlad's burial place as its central plot to become an international bestseller. It owes much of its success to avoiding categorisation as a 'horror' novel, though the author both has her cake and eats it by conflating the concept of Bram Stoker's *Dracula* with Vlad III.

A work of fictionalised scholarship by an author with an academic background, *The Historian* begins with an ersatz 'Note to the Reader' (pre-dated 2008 – three years after publication) that observes, 'the glimpses of territorial conflict between an Islamic East and a Judeo-Christian West will be painfully familiar to a modern reader'. In fact, its panoramic historic scale will be familiar to anyone who has made their way through this book – albeit Ms Kostova's framework is very sedately and gradually filled in, unlike the violent collision between arcane and modern history that is the wont of your authors.

The Historian is a more fluidly-written take on the genre of scholarly detective fiction popularised (though not originated) by Dan Brown in *The DaVinci Code*. As the historian heroine traces the historical lineage of Vlad III – via a manuscript apparently inscribed with the Seal of the Dragon, first passed to her similarly academic father, and his own murdered mentor – we travel on a route of scholarship from Istanbul, via a mythical lost Shakespearean play entitled *The King of Tashkani* (supposedly based on Mehmet II) and an apocryphal testimony called *The Tale of Stefan of Snagov, Faithfully Transcribed by Zacharias the Sinner*, briefly passing through the Romanias of Codreanu and Ceaușescu. That it ultimately climaxes after a rather anaemically described vampire killing is, at least, an acknowledgement that the historical and generic figures have merged together in the imagination: the Impaler is the Vampire/the Vampire is the Impaler.

***

Dracula has a long-standing association with music. The epic verse, composed in 1463 by the popular German poet Michel Beheim which is one of our primary sources on Vlad, was designed to be sung accompanied by an *Osterweise* ('Easter-song') melody. In more recent years, the Impaler has found many of his most enthusiastic musical interpreters in the electric realms of heavy metal. With its lyrical fascination with the Gothic and ghoulish, and aesthetic attachment to blood and thunder medievalism, metal would seem a pop cultural realm ripe for conquest by Vlad the Impaler. Yet, despite metal being born around 1970, it wasn't until the 1980s that the historical Dracula first began making his presence felt in the genre. It was then that heavy metal began to splinter into an increasingly bewildering array of subgenres, with each new development typically darker, faster and more aggressive than the last. Thrash metal, which first emerged in the 80s, led to the gore-obsessed, guttural frenzy of death metal of the 90s, which in turn led to the spiky, demonic sonic blizzard of black metal which now dominates the jagged, cutting-edge of cult metal. A relevant evolution running alongside these styles is gothic or doom metal, played by bands that did the unthinkable and actually slowed the tempo (sometimes to funereal sluggishness) in the pursuit of ominous atmospherics and an evocative, even darkly romantic sound.

Early Impaler references in the 80s tended to be tenuous, jokey, or both. In 1984 an influential Canadian extreme metal band formed named Voivod, whose experimentalism has subsequently seen them being dubbed progressive metal. The title of their 1986 debut album *War and Pain* gives a good idea of their lyrical themes, and while it seems likely they borrowed their moniker from Vlad, their material has never strayed to the battlefields of Wallachia. The Minnesota band Impaler also no doubt borrowed their name from Vlad, while their 1986 debut album *If We Had Brains We'd be Dangerous* equally gives a good idea of their approach, though the offal and blood they throw about at shows might have made Dracula feel at home. The definitive American shock rock band GWAR formed in 1984. As much a theatrical performance as a musical entity, members come on stage dressed as ghoulish aliens, gorily dismembering foam-rubber effigies of famous people while playing gleefully offensive songs. Their second album *Scumdogs of the Universe* (1990) featured an ode to 'Vlad the Impaler', featuring one of the more unorthodox retellings of the Dracula story ('When he was a boy, they sent him to the Turks, But you know they didn't like him because all the Turks were jerks...')

Perhaps the most successful band to embrace the Impaler is Cradle of Filth. A British band formed in 1991, they began as early exponents of the black metal style, before a combination of success (anathema to black metal's self-styled elitists), increasingly polished delivery and ominously erotic imagery led many pundits to challenge their cult credentials and re-brand Cradle as Gothic metal. Cradle of Filth named their enthusiastic fan club the Order of the Dragon in tribute to Vlad the Impaler, adopting the Order's seal as a band emblem. (Though, as they're scarcely choirboys, Cradle adapted the original, removing the Crusading Order's cross and replacing it with a nocturnal lunar symbol.) The past couple of decades have seen an explosion of metal bands internationally, fuelled by the easy access to recording and promotional opportunities offered by the internet, though such new technology hasn't made it any easier to make a living as a musician.

As a rule, death metal bands are drawn to the blood and gore implicit in the Impaler story, while Gothic metal bands explore the fictional Dracula connection. Black metal bands were originally inspired by the occult overtones some have attached to the story, but increasingly an interest in nationalistic, rightwing politics has coloured the interpretation of the Impaler among many such bands. Among the countless metal bands who have recorded Vlad-inspired material are the Swedish black metal stalwarts Marduk who dedicate the second half of their 1998 album *Nightwing* to the Impaler. Founded in 1992, the French cult black metal act Vlad Tepes named themselves after Dracula's Romanian name, the Polish black metal band Graveland's 1994 debut *Carpathian Wolves* includes the track 'Impaler of Wallachia', while the Italian death metal band Necrodeath recorded an entire album dedicated to Vlad entitled *Draculea* in 2008. A bewildering list of other metal bands have recorded songs entitled 'Vlad the Impaler', including Italy's Wotan (in 2007), Germany's Witching Hour (2009) and the USA's Locusta (2010), all focusing on the medieval horror of the story.

By way of contrast, the video for British indie group Kasabian's 'Vlad the Impaler' features dandyish comedian Noel Fielding wandering the countryside in unconvincing medieval tyrant drag. One of history's most feared figures has finally been reduced to camp status. Though, with its rock 'n' roll cliché lyrics and typically vague metaphors, it's hard to know exactly what the 2009 song is actually about. The nearest it comes to the mythical or historical significance of Vlad is in the obscure, 'We need to raise the dead, we need to raise the people,' which is its least cryptic line.

In its recorded form, the main point of the song seems to be the promotional video filmed in the lurid tones of a 1970s horror/exploitation movie, directly based on the intermission and trailer sequence of *Grindhouse*, filmmakers Tarantino and Rodriguez's tribute to the low-budget double bills of the era. Announced as a 'Ricardo Elfio film', to invoke the Italian exploitation cinema of the 70s, Fielding is closer to an old drive-in movie vampire or zombie (which is presumably the point). His use of the wooden stake he carries along with him as a weapon has a more crudely Freudian interpretation than any of the theories in this book – his mock-splatter movie killing of a young woman on a tennis court, in particular, brings an obvious penile element to the term 'Impaler'. Fielding presumably got the role of Vlad in part due to his own mild androgyny, and also because of his portrayal of a parody goth in a UK TV sitcom. His sitcom character, Richmond, is a stereotypically mopey and morbid character fan of those metallic Draconists, Cradle of Filth. In spite of whatever reasons Kasabian may have for taking Vlad as their (non-)subject, the contention is clear: the pop-culture concept of Vlad the Impaler is pure camp, so bring on the gothic clowns for a bit of mummery.

Kasabian take their name from the eponymous Linda, the Manson Family member who turned state's evidence against Charlie and his acid-assassins, which seems a cute way to evoke the supposed cutting edge while staying on the side of the angels. However, two decades back (an infinity, in terms of pop culture), the pioneer of industrial music and electro-noise Non – Boyd Rice to his select but dedicated bands of devotees and detractors, and to his former friend Charlie Manson – was hailing Vlad as one of 'history's men of steel – may their spirits live forever'.

The dedication ran on the 1991 Non compilation album, *Easy Listening for Iron Youth*. With other dedicatees including Hasan-i-Sabah, Jack the Ripper and Anton Szandor LaVey, the liner notes might almost be said to have set an agenda for your authors' *Devil's Histories* series; with the famous woodcarving of Vlad at the 'epicurean massacre' on the cover, it was certainly wearing its flinty heart on its sleeve. We asked Boyd Rice if he still regarded Vlad as one of history's men of steel.

'Definitely,' he replied in affable tones. 'You have to remember that at the time of that album I was living in San Francisco, which has to be about the most ultra-liberal place on the planet, and I was reacting against that. I was getting so much flak from every direction because of some of my views, so Vlad seemed an appropriate icon. I wasn't being ironic at the time. I believed that there wasn't enough discipline, that we needed a harsher system to balance things and Vlad represented that. To me it seemed eminently reasonable then, though,' he reflects on differences in his attitude back when he was in his early thirties, 'perhaps not in hindsight.' As Rice gently suggests, however, 'People do respond to extreme things, and I think people remember Vlad because he took everything one step further than everyone else. I'm willing to bet that in 500 years nobody will remember Mother Theresa.'

Besides his sonic experimentation and extolling of lost pop-culture artefacts, Rice was once known as the cultural provocateur behind the Abraxas Foundation – the 'social Darwinist think tank' that extolled Machiavelli, Nietzsche and historical figures like Vlad and Cesare Borgia. In a celebrated 1991 interview with the infamous underground magazine *ANSWER Me!*, entitled 'Rice Ain't Nice', he defined 'peace' as 'a rare state which has only existed when a despot has been fearsome or strong enough to impose it. The image of your head on the end of a stick is a strong incentive toward "visualising world peace".' It's easy to imagine who Rice might have had in mind. So, does the Wallachian warlord still fulfil his anti-ideal of social Darwinist leadership?

'Absolutely,' Rice concurs, 'Vlad did everything for a reason, even if he inevitably indulged in a little overkill. He thought the merchants were bleeding his country dry, so he massacred them. He was draconian, but in his own mind at least, fair. He was a man of his era, and in that day and age cruelty was the norm. I don't think he was a sadist – everything he did was Machiavellian. It was routine then to burn people alive, to boil them in oil, to disembowel them. If Vlad wanted to make any kind of impact, he had to up the ante. If barbarity is the norm, then you have to take things to extremes if you hope to employ fear as a weapon to wage psychological warfare.'

It's a long way from the camp dressing-up box aesthetic of the Kasabian video – or even indeed the theatrical posturing and growling of black metal. 'I think overexposure can ruin pretty much anything,' reflects Rice on Vlad's threatened appropriation as a piece of cultural kitsch. 'Ten years back, you'd see all of these teenagers in Charles Manson t-shirts. He used to be this visceral figure whose acts had all of these dark undertones. Now he's become a little camp. Maybe Vlad is the only figure who can't be re-evaluated or reinvented that way.

VLAD THE IMPALER

Historians have even re-evaluated Genghis Khan, the tyrant who left huge pillars of human skulls in his wake. Now there are books about Genghis Khan as this enlightened figure, as a skilled horseman, as a brilliant tactician. Outside of Romania, I think maybe Vlad the Impaler is one figure they'll never really re-evaluate because his acts were so extreme. When I was looking at Vlad in the eighties I wasn't trying to re-evaluate him, to find his better side – I was actively embracing the aspects of Vlad people hated, his draconian side, his cruelty. I was looking at him from a romantic, even idealistic viewpoint – there was no realism in my exploration of the character,' Rice rather disarmingly admits.

His exploration of history's man of steel was manifest in the most incongruously effective manner. On his classic 1989 album *Music, Martinis & Misanthropy* (credited to Boyd Rice & Friends), the repetitive noise and tape loops of Non were discarded in favour of sweet la-la-ing cocktail music, and a spoken-word-against-acoustic-backing style inspired by the albums of 1960s poet Rod McKuen and TV comedy show host Jackie Gleason. To this disparate mix add a huge dollop of the hatred of humankind inherent in the title, as in the album's key track, 'People'. On 'People', Rice reasonably and intolerantly reflects aloud on what he'd like to do to society's stupidest and pettiest everyday irritants: 'Something cruel. Something mean. Something just.' By the end of his misanthropic cocktail rant, Boyd has really picked up a head of steam: 'We need a gardener. A brutal gardener. An iron gardener. Whatever happened to Vlad the Impaler?' We believe he's passed on, Boyd, but still, Vlad is at the head of a ruthless roll call of honour that also invokes Genghis Khan, Ayatollah Khomeini, Hitler, Mussolini, Nero and the Emperor Diocletian. Small wonder, perhaps, that in the Boyd Rice of the 1980s and 90s, the morally pious found the man they love to hate – the man who would be Impaler, if not outright Führer.

'In the world we live in today, everything seems to have become an abstraction,' Rice reflects on his reasons for indulging in tyrant chic. 'Can you even conceive of seeing 20,000 people impaled? Even 500 would be totally mind-numbing. People don't seem to feel things these days, and I think that's sick in a way. When I was writing about Vlad I was far younger and more immature, and for me the subject was a total abstraction. We see people being shot on the TV all the time and it just seems abstract. It's particularly easy when you're young to talk about violence in that blasé way – saying you're going to kill someone – and it doesn't mean anything. We're just so cushioned. If you live on a farm and you want to eat chicken, you're going to have to kill the bird, pluck it, prepare it – for most of us it just comes in a packet now. It's easy to forget that we're living in a very unique period in history. In most eras, slavery, torture and all of these awful things were the norm. We may have terrorism today, but despite that we live in uniquely comfortable times, surrounded by this cushion.'

For the thoughtful and provocative Rice, Vlad is no camp gothic image but an emblem of the violent undercurrents that have shaped our world. But Boyd Rice is a man who likes his creature comforts, and his aloof, detached worldview doesn't preclude a little kitsch gastronomy. 'There's a Romanian Vlad the Impaler Restaurant in Chicago,' he appraises. 'It has this incredible Vlad stained glass window. I was reluctant at first, because I'd heard Romanian food was terrible, but it was actually very good.' If the eatery gained anything at all from the ethos of its long-dead patron, it might not be a comfortable place to take a vegetarian. That will be one joint where they have no trouble recognising what's on the end of the stake.

***

If anything is likely to ruin the Impaler with over-exposure, to subject Dracula to the kind of re-evaluation that makes Boyd Rice despair, it is a high profile script, in development at time of writing. Entitled *Vlad* and written by Charlie Hunnam, the actor best known for his role in the acclaimed biker drama series *The Sons of Anarchy*, it's been picked up by Summit Entertainment, the studio responsible for the twee teen vampire film franchise *Twilight*. 'As the script stands now, we don't touch on vampirism,' insists Hunnam. 'That was my one non-negotiable area when we were developing it, and thankfully, nobody suggested that we should delve into it at the end. But you can clearly see the things that Bram Stoker took [as inspiration]…' If that sounds ominous to those keen to finally sever the link between the historical Voivode and Stoker's fictional Count, Hunnam has at least clearly done his homework.

'It's a very big and sweeping story,' he explained to entertainment correspondent Mandi Bierly. 'The majority of time focuses on him [Vlad] as a young man assuming his rule as a prince, but we actually go all the way through his life. Basically what happened was, the Ottoman Empire was expanding at an exponentially fast rate with a father-son duo of sultans, who increased the size of their territory tenfold within 50 years. They got over the Danube into Wallachia, which is the southern part of modern-day Romania. Romania used to be three separate principalities: Wallachia, Transylvania, and Moldavia... [After being captured] Radu was treated like a prince by the Ottomans, and Vlad was trapped like a slave, like a prisoner. About eight years after they got taken by the Ottoman, his father was murdered, and Vlad decided he was going to escape, avenge his father's murder, take his throne back and oppose the Ottoman.'

Questioned over who he saw in the title role, Hunnam suggested either Colin Farrell or Christian Bale, two Hollywood heartthrobs who would surely change the Impaler's popular image forever, if they are cast, or indeed if *Vlad* actually gets made in the unpredictable realms of Hollywood. 'Vlad was such a brutal man, and the trick is to make him sympathetic,' says Hunnam. 'That was the challenge, and if we've succeeded in any way in this script, I truly believe that it's genuinely making him sympathetic.' This begs the question of how explicit Vlad's sickening atrocities will be in a film that surely cannot simply overlook them. Perhaps for the first time a major Hollywood production could feasibly put something that horrible explicitly up on the screen.

The watershed was the 2005 film *Hostel* which raised the bar on how much harrowing gore, naked sadism and suffering was permissible in a mainstream horror picture, leading to the coinage of the derisive term 'torture porn' among disgusted critics. We've already touched upon the theme of culture shock in Eli Roth's hit movie, but the director has also talked about some of the influences that inspired *Hostel*, the cultural changes that made such a film not only feasible but popular. 'I think that we're in this weird, post-9/11 world where, if you think about it – y'know, I'm 35 – but there are kids that were 10, 11, 12 years old when that happened that are now 16, 17, 18,' Roth said in an interview with the Groucho site to promote the sequel *Hostel 2*, when asked about the appeal of such visceral films. 'They're growing up with "You're going to get blown up. Terror Alert Orange. Don't travel overseas. Every time you fly, X-ray your shoes, or someone will blow up the plane." That is what they're infused with. Plus the images coming back from the Iraq War, a never-ending war that – guess who's next on the firing line? That war is not over. There's no end in sight.'

Rue Morgue journalist Aaron von Lupton describes parallels between *Hostel* and real world events as 'obvious. While the first film was bringing in $47 million at the box office, news stories were breaking about American soldiers torturing prisoners who had gone on a hunger strike at Guantanamo Bay by strapping them into restraint chairs and force-feeding them. Restraint chairs became the key torture device (used by the fictional company called Elite Hunting that caters to the sadistic whims of the rich and depraved) in the *Hostel* films. While Roth's original intent was seemingly to feed a desire to see cocky American frat boys punished for their arrogance, the movie ultimately fed off a disturbing new image in the public consciousness... Film critic David Edelstein would appropriately dub films such as *Hostel* and *Saw* 'torture porn' in a now-famous 2006 *New York Magazine* article. In it, he suggested that audiences' new obsession with torture came from a political atmosphere in which we'd all approve of torture if it's being done for the 'right' reasons. A bold claim perhaps, but one that might explain film censors' acceptance of this violent imagery.

While it seems unlikely that a film starring Colin Farrell or Christian Bale will be torture porn (at least if their agents have anything to say about it), it's difficult to imagine how else you could make an honest film about Vlad the Impaler. In one throwaway remark, Charlie Hunnam mentions the 'Christian vs. Muslim' subtext in his script for *Vlad*. 'He was doing what he thought was right,' says Hunnam of what makes the Impaler sympathetic. 'He was the one who was being invaded and whose religious beliefs were being stripped away.' Those same sentiments echo in today's trouble spots. For many of the most dedicated warlords in the conflict President George W. Bush dubbed the 'War on Terror', hostilities did not begin in 2001, but stretch back over a millennium. The attacks on the World Trade Center and the Pentagon on 11 September were just the latest atrocities in a campaign that stretches way back, to the Middle Ages, to the Fall of Jerusalem in 1099, the sack of Constantinople in 1453, the Forest of the Impaled in 1462... In a 2004 article for *The Spectator* on 'Extremism in the Defence of Liberty', Paul Robinson argues that there is 'a seriously psychopathic tendency on the loose' in the West, particularly the US, which advocates matching Islamist terrorism with a terror-based response. ('Whoever fights monsters should see to it that in the process he does not become a monster,' observed Friedrich Nietzsche.) 'Frances Kamm, a professor of philosophy at Harvard University, has been doing the lecture circuit in America and England, promoting the view that it may be legitimate to target non-combatants directly,' writes Robinson. 'She argues that if an attack planned against a military target is likely to kill, say, 50 innocent people in collateral damage, you might as well just kill 40 of them directly. What's more, if it will help to terrorise others, you should kill them "in a particularly horrible way". You can then congratulate yourself on having saved ten lives! Better yet, you are only allowed to "terror-kill", as she calls it, as many innocent people as you could have killed anyway.' Parallels with Dracula and such a proposed 'terror-kill' philosophy scarcely require comment. If Vlad the Impaler's violent life poses any questions to us today they are about when the end justifies the means. At what point does our ruthless dedication to a cause – security, patriotism, piety, honour – endanger our humanity? The answer to that question determines whether we should see Dracula as a hero of his people or the son of the Devil...

Select Bibliography

Auerbach, Nina – *Our Vampires, Ourselves* (University of Chicago, 1995)

Augustyn, Michael – *Vlad Dracula: The Dragon Prince* (iUniverse, 2004)

Barber, Noel – *Lords of the Golden Horn* (Arrow, 1988)

Bianchi, John with Dan Minculescu and Steve Schifani – *Vlad the Impaler* (BL Publishing, 2006)

Blandford, Neil and Bruce Jones – *The World's Most Evil Men* (Octopus, 1985)

Cioranescu, George – 'Vlad the Impaler – Current Parallels with a Medieval Romanian Prince' (Radio Free Europe, 1977)

Codreanu, Corneliu Zelea – *For My Legionaries: The Iron Guard* (Liberty Bell, 2003)

Del Quiaro, Robert – *The Marquis De Sade: A Biography and a Note of Hope* (Messidor, 1994)

De Sade, The Marquis – *The 120 Days of Sodom* (Arrow, 1989)

De Sade, The Marquis – *Juliette* (Arrow, 1991)

De Sade, The Marquis – Three Complete Novels: *Justine/Philosophy in the Bedroom/Eugenie de Franval* (Arrow 1991)

Dogaru, Mircea and Mihail Zahariade – *History of the Romanians* (Amco, 1996)

Edwardes, Allen – *The Jewel in the Lotus* (Julian, 1959)

Embleton, Gerry and John Howe – *The Medieval Soldier* (Windrow & Greene, 1994)

Eminescu, Mihai – 'Scrisoarea a III-a' (c.1883)

Fine Jr., John V. A. – *The Late Medieval Balkans* (University of Michigan, 1994)

Florescu, Radu R. and Raymond T. McNally – *Dracula: Prince of Many Faces* (Little, Brown, 1989)

Florescu, Radu R. and Raymond T. McNally – *In Search of Dracula* (Robson, 1997)

Foss, Clive – *The Tyrants* (Quercus, 2006)

Fregosi, Paul – *Jihad in the West* (Prometheus, 1998)

Gaddis, Thomas E. and James O. Long – *Killer: A Journal of Murder* (Macmillan, 1977)

Gallonio, Rev. Father Antonio – *Tortures and Torments of the Christian Martyrs* (Feral House, 2004)

Garrett, Pat F. – *The Authentic Life of Billy The Kid*, with notes and commentary by Frederick Nolan, (University of Oklahoma, 2000)

Gerolymatos, André – *The Balkan Wars* (Spellmount, 2004)

Haining, Peter (ed.) – *The Dracula Scrapbook* (New English Library, 1976)

Haining, Peter (ed.) – *The Dracula Scrapbook* (revised edition) (Chancellor, 1987)

Hearst, Patricia Campbell, with Alvin Moscow – *Patty Hearst* (Corgi/Avon, 1988)

Hedges, Nick – *The 120 Days of Sodom: A Play* (adapted from the Marquis De Sade) (Delectation, 1991)

Hitler, Adolf – *Mein Kampf* (Pimlico, 1992)

Holmes, Richard and Martin Marix Evans – *Oxford Guide to Battles* (Oxford University, 2009)

Huizinga, J. – *The Waning of the Middle Ages* (Pelican, 1972)

Humphreys, C. C. – *Vlad: The Last Confession* (Orion, 2009)

Inalcik, Halil – *The Ottoman Empire* (Phoenix, 2000)

Judah, Tim – *Kosovo: War and Revenge* (Yale University Press, 2000)

Kaplan, Robert D. – *Balkan Ghosts* (Vintage Books, 1996)

Kemp, Peter – *H. G. Wells and the Culminating Ape* (Macmillan, 1996)

Kinross, Baron J. P. D. B. – *The Ottoman Centuries* (Harper Collins, 1977)

Kostova, Elizabeth – *The Historian* (Time Warner, 2006)

Larkin, David (ed.) – *Fantastic Art* (Pan, 1973)

Lawrence, T. E. – *The Seven Pillars of Wisdom* (Penguin, 1990)

Leggett, George – *The Cheka: Lenin's Secret Police* (Oxford University, 1986)

Light, Duncan – 'The Status of Vlad the Impaler in Communist Romania: A Reassessment' (*Journal of Dracula Studies* #9, 2007)

Lockwood, Jeffrey A. – *Six-Legged Soldiers* (Oxford University, 2009)

Love, Brenda – *The Encyclopaedia of Unusual Sexual Practices* (Abacus, 1995)

Machiavelli, Niccolo – *The Prince*, translated with notes by George Bull (Penguin Classics, 2003)

McGlynn, Sean – *By Sword and Fire* (Weidenfeld & Nicolson, 2008)

Melton, J. Gordon – *The Vampire Book* (Visible Ink, 1999)

Milgram, Stanley – *Obedience to Authority* (Pinter & Martin, 2010)

Miller, Elizabeth – *A Dracula Handbook* (Xlibris, 2005)

Miller, Elizabeth – *Dracula: Sense and Nonsense* (Desert Island Books, 2000)

Molloy, Peter – *The Lost World of Communism* (BBC, 2009)

Newark, Tim – *Medieval Warlords* (Blandford, 1987)

Nicolle, David – *Armies of the Ottoman Turks* (Osprey, 1983)

Nicolle, David – *Hungary and the Fall of Eastern Europe* (Osprey, 2008)

Nietzsche, Friedrich – *Beyond Good and Evil*, translated by R. J. Hollingdale (Penguin, 1973)

Nietzsche, Friedrich – *Human, All Too Human*, translated by R. J. Hollingdale (Cambridge University, 1996)

Nietzsche, Friedrich – *On the Genealogy of Morals*, translated by Francis Golffing (Doubleday, 1956)

Nietzsche, Friedrich – *Thus Spoke Zarathustra*, translated by R. J. Hollingdale (Penguin, 1961)

Nietzsche, Friedrich – *Twilight of the Idols*, translated by R. J. Hollingdale (Penguin, 1969)

Peters, Edward – *Torture* (Basil Blackwell, 1985)

Rezachevici, Constantin – 'Punishments with Vlad Tepeş – Punishments in Europe: Common and Differentiating Traits' (*Journal of Dracula Studies* #8, 2006)

Rice, Boyd – *Standing in Two Circles: The Collected Works of Boyd Rice* (edited by Brian M. Clark), (Creation, 2008)

Rigby, Jonathan – *Christopher Lee the Authorised Screen History* (Reynolds and Hearn, 2001)

Rogerson, Barnaby – *The Last Crusaders* (Little, Brown, 2009)

Ronay, Gabriel – *The Dracula Myth* (Pan, 1972)

Shakespeare, William – *Complete Works* (Collins, 1974)

Simmons, Dan – *Children of the Night* (Headline, 1993)

Stoker, Bram – *Dracula* (Jarrolds, 1966)

Tombs, Pete – *Mondo Macabro* (Titan, 1997)

Trow, M. J. – *Vlad the Impaler* (Sutton, 2004)

Tuchman, Barbara W. – *A Distant Mirror* (Penguin, 1984)

Welsh, Frank – *The Battle for Christendom* (Constable & Robinson, 2008)

Wheatcroft, Andrew – *Infidels* (Viking, 2003)

Wilkinson, William – *An Account of the Principalities of Wallachia and Moldavia* (Arno, 1971)

Wilson, Colin – *A Criminal History of Mankind* (Grafton, 1985)

Wilson, Colin – *The Misfits: A Study of Sexual Outsiders* (Grafton, 1988)

Wilson, Colin – *The Outsider* (Phoenix, 2001)

Index